Jorma Larimo
Editor

Contemporary Euromarketing: Entry and Operational Decision Making

Contemporary Euromarketing: Entry and Operational Decision Making has been co-published simultaneously as *Journal of Euromarketing*, Volume 16, Numbers 1/2 2006.

Pre-publication
REVIEWS,
COMMENTARIES,
EVALUATIONS . . .

"A N IMPORTANT CONTRIBUTION TO MARKETING IN THE EUROPEAN CONTEXT. . . . It consists of two important areas that are on the cutting edge of research, market entry, and operational decision making. . . . Particularly important for European scholars because European markets are rapidly expanding and require a much deeper understanding from both academics and practitioners which this publication provides. The market entry part of the publication OFFERS NOT ONLY SIGNIFICANT INSIGHT INTO THE PROCESS BUT IT ALSO PROVIDES A SOUND THEORETICAL FOUNDATION consisting of previous studies that enhance the understanding how markets ought to be effectively and efficiently entered. The part dealing with operational decision making should ESPECIALLY BE USEFUL TO RESEARCHERS who are seeking fundamental comparisons between markets that are operationally and fundamentally different."

George Tesar, PhD
Professor of Marketing and International Business Emeritus
Umeå School of Business
Umeå University, Sweden

Professor of Marketing Emeritus
University of Wisconsin-Whitewater

Contemporary Euromarketing: Entry and Operational Decision Making

Contemporary Euromarketing: Entry and Operational Decision Making has been co-published simultaneously as *Journal of Euromarketing*, Volume 16, Numbers 1/2 2006.

Contemporary Euromarketing: Entry and Operational Decision Making, edited by Jorma Larimo, DSc (Vol. 16, No. 1/2, 2006). *Examines the strategies of small and medium-sized firms that sell their products and services in European markets.*

European Perspectives in Marketing, edited by Erdener Kaynak, PhD, DSc (Vol. 13, No. 2/3, 2004). *"ESSENTIAL READING for businesspeople, policy makers, marketers, academics, and postgraduate business students. . . . A MUST-READ for all who do business in Europe or plan to do so." (Marin Marinov, PhD, Professor of Marketing and International Business, Gloucestershire University)*

Euromarketing and the Future, edited by Lynn R. Kahle, PhD (Vol. 12, No. 3/4, 2003). *Expert analysis of likely consumer and marketing developments in the European markets.*

Internet Applications in Euromarketing, edited by Lynn R. Kahle, PhD (Vol. 11, No. 2, 2001). *Examines cutting-edge theory and practice in internet marketing from North American and European perspectives.*

Foreign Direct Investment and Strategic Alliances in Europe, edited by Hong Liu, PhD (Vol. 10, No. 1, 2001). *Foreign direct investment (FDI) and strategic alliances are among the most popular modes of international market entry and expansion in major markets by multinationals. This book integrates FDI issues with those of strategic alliances to deliver insights into both areas and provides up-close perspectives on specific segments of the European market. It uses case studies, a wide-ranging survey, and the expertise of authorities in the field to shed light on the when, why, and how of investing and forming alliances in the volatile environment of the European market.*

Global Marketing Co-Operation and Networks, edited by Leo Paul Dana, BA, MBA, PhD (Vol. 9, No. 2, 2000). *"Excellent. . . . well-referenced. . . . very useful. I for one have found it to be current, effective, and useful for developing my own research and teaching materials." (Claudio Vignali, BA, MPhil, DipM, Senior Lecturer, Manchester Metropolitan University, United Kingdom)*

Cross-National Consumer Psychographics, edited by Lynn R. Kahle (Vol. 8, No. 1/2, 1999). Cross-National Consumer Psychographics *provides marketing professionals and students with data from several applications around the world of the list of values (LOV), so you can consider the implications for understanding consumers cross-culturally. Through this unique book you will find how different countries and different individual consumers may be segmented based on their social values so you can develop the best marketing strategies for your products.*

Newer Insights into Marketing: Cross-Cultural and Cross-National Perspectives, edited by Camille P. Schuster, PhD, and Phil Harris, BA (Hons) (Vol. 7, No. 2, 1999). *This new book analyzes and investigates international marketing strategies to determine effective marketing practices of businesses in the global arena.*

Green Marketing in a Unified Europe, edited by Alma T. Mintu-Wimsatt, PhD, and Héctor R. Lozada, PhD (Vol. 5, No. 3, 1996). *"Takes a well-researched and heartfelt approach to the 3 P's of environmental marketing–preservation, protection, and proactive product development." (Debbie Thorne, PhD, Director, Center for Ethics, The University of Tampa)*

International Joint Ventures in East Asia, edited by Roger Baran, PhD, Yigang Pan, PhD, and Erdener Kaynak, PhD, DSc (Vol. 4, No. 3/4, 1996). *"A valuable resource for anyone interested in joint ventures anywhere in the world." (Sunder Narayanan, PhD, Assistant Professor, School of Business, Columbia University)*

Ethical Issues in International Marketing, edited by Nejdet Delener, PhD (Vol. 4, No. 2, 1995). *"Provides an invaluable education to the reader and encourages the reader to think about important issues that increasingly confront businesspeople in their dealings within a global marketplace." (George V. Priovolos, PhD, CPA, Assistant Professor, Marketing Department, Hagan School of Business, Iona College)*

The Impact of Innovation and Technology in the Global Marketplace, edited by Shaker A. Zahra, PhD, and Abbas J. Ali, PhD (Vol. 3, No. 3/4, 1994). *"The editors have captured the excitement of the present day technological innovations with a wise selection of scholarly articles. Grab this book and read it before it's too late!" (Raymond A. K. Cox, PhD, Professor of Finance, Central Michigan University)*

Contemporary Euromarketing: Entry and Operational Decision Making

Jorma Larimo, DSc
Editor

Contemporary Euromarketing: Entry and Operational Decision Making has been co-published simultaneously as *Journal of Euromarketing*, Volume 16, Numbers 1/2 2006.

International Business Press®
An Imprint of The Haworth Press, Inc.

New York • London • Victoria (AU)
www.HaworthPress.com

Published by

International Business Press®, 10 Alice Street, Binghamton, NY 13904-1580 USA

International Business Press® is an imprint of The Haworth Press, Inc., 10 Alice Street, Binghamton, NY 13904-1580 USA.

Contemporary Euromarketing: Entry and Operational Decision Making has been co-published simultaneously as *Journal of Euromarketing*, Volume 16, Numbers 1/2 2006.

The development, preparation, and publication of this work has been undertaken with great care. However, the publisher, employees, editors, and agents of The Haworth Press and all imprints of The Haworth Press, Inc., including The Haworth Medical Press® and Pharmaceutical Products Press®, are not responsible for any errors contained herein or for consequences that may ensue from use of materials or information contained in this work. With regard to case studies, identities and circumstances of individuals discussed herein have been changed to protect confidentiality. Any resemblance to actual persons, living or dead, is entirely coincidental.

The Haworth Press is committed to the dissemination of ideas and information according to the highest standards of intellectual freedom and the free exchange of ideas. Statements made and opinions expressed in this publication do not necessarily reflect the views of the Publisher, Directors, management, or staff of The Haworth Press, Inc., or an endorsement by them.

Library of Congress Cataloging-in-Publication Data

Contemporary Euromarketing : entry and operational decision making/Jorma Larimo, editor.
    p. cm.
    "Contemporary Euromarketing: Entry and Operational Decision Making has been co-published simultaneously as Journal of Euromarketing, Volume 16, Numbers 1/2 2006."
    Includes bibliographical references and index.
    ISBN 13: 978-0-7890-3540-0 (soft cover : alk. paper)
    ISBN 10: 0-7890-3540-5 (soft cover : alk. paper)
1. International business enterprises–Europe. 2. International trade–Europe. 3. Marketing–Europe. I. Larimo, Jorma.

HD62.4.C654 2007
658′.049–dc22
                                                   2006028752

The HAWORTH PRESS Inc
Abstracting, Indexing & Outward Linking
PRINT and ELECTRONIC BOOKS & JOURNALS

This section provides you with a list of major indexing & abstracting services and other tools for bibliographic access. That is to say, each service began covering this periodical during the year noted in the right column. Most Websites which are listed below have indicated that they will either post, disseminate, compile, archive, cite, or alert their own Website users with research-based content from this work. (This list is as current as the copyright date of this publication.)

(continued)

- *Ovid Linksolver (OpenURL link resolver via CrossRef targeted DOI links) <http://www.linksolver.com>* 2005
- *Postharvest News and Information (CAB ABSTRACTS, CABI) <http://www.cabi.org>* . . . . *
- *ProQuest 5000 International <http://www.proquest.com>* 1991
- *ProQuest European Business <http://www.proquest.com>* 2006
- *Rural Development Abstracts (CAB ABSTRACTS, CABI) <http://www.cabi.org>* 2006
- *Scopus (See instead Elsevier Scopus) <http://www.info.scopus.com>* 2005
- *SwetsWise <http://www.swets.com>* 2001
- *TOC Premier (EBSCO)* 2007
- *World Agricultural Economics & Rural Sociology Abstracts (CAB ABSTRACTS, CABI) <http://www.cabi.org>* . . . . *
- *zetoc (The British Library) <http://www.bl.uk>* 2004

*Exact start date to come.

Bibliographic Access

- *MediaFinder <http://www.mediafinder.com/>*

- *Ulrich's Periodicals Directory: The Global Source for Periodicals Information Since 1932 <http://www.bowkerlink.com>*

Special Bibliographic Notes related to special journal issues [separates] and indexing/abstracting:

- indexing/abstracting services in this list will also cover material in any "separate" that is co-published simultaneously with Haworth's special thematic journal issue or DocuSerial. Indexing/abstracting usually covers material at the article/chapter level.
- monographic co-editions are intended for either non-subscribers or libraries which intend to purchase a second copy for their circulating collections.
- monographic co-editions are reported to all jobbers/wholesalers/approval plans. The source journal is listed as the "series" to assist the prevention of duplicate purchasing in the same manner utilized for books-in-series.
- to facilitate user/access services all indexing/abstracting services are encouraged to utilize the co-indexing entry note indicated at the bottom of the first page of each article/chapter/contribution.
- this is intended to assist a library user of any reference tool [whether print, electronic, online, or CD-ROM] to locate the monographic version if the library has purchased this version but not a subscription to the source journal.
- individual articles/chapters in any Haworth publication are also available through The Haworth Document Delivery Service [HDDS].

As part of Haworth's continuing committment to better serve our library patrons, we are proud to be working with the following electronic services:

AGGREGATOR SERVICES

EBSCOhost

Ingenta

J-Gate

Minerva

OCLC FirstSearch

Oxmill

SwetsWise

LINK RESOLVER SERVICES

1Cate (Openly Informatics)

CrossRef

Gold Rush (Coalliance)

LinkOut (PubMed)

LINKplus (Atypon)

LinkSolver (Ovid)

LinkSource with A-to-Z (EBSCO)

Resource Linker (Ulrich)

SerialsSolutions (ProQuest)

SFX (Ex Libris)

Sirsi Resolver (SirsiDynix)

Tour (TDnet)

Vlink (Extensity, *formerly Geac*)

WebBridge (Innovative Interfaces)

Contemporary Euromarketing: Entry and Operational Decision Making

CONTENTS

ABOUT THE EDITOR

Jorma Larimo, DSc, is currently Professor of International Marketing at the University of Vaasa in Vaasa, Finland. He is also the Responsible Director of the Graduate School in International Business (FIGSIB) in Finland and has the position of a Docent at the Turku School of Economics in Finland. He has received his doctoral degree in Marketing at the University of Vaasa. In addition to several visiting lecturer and doctoral degree evaluation committee membership roles in Finland, he has acted in respective roles also, e.g., in Sweden, Denmark, the Netherlands, Estonia, Russia, and Australia. Furthermore, he has been a member of evaluation committees for Professorships both in Finland and in the USA. He is the Finnish representative on the board of the European International Business Academy (EIBA) and a member of the editorial board of Management International Review (MIR).

His studies have been published in several international journals like *Journal of Business Research*, *Journal of International Business Studies*, *Management International Review*, *Journal of Euromarketing*, *Journal of East-West Business*, *Journal for East European Management Studies*, *European Business Review*, and *Asian Business & Management*. His research focuses on the export and internationalization behavior, strategies, and performance of small and medium-sized companies; foreign direct investment and divestment behavior and strategies; international joint venture strategies and performance; and on entry and marketing strategies in Central Eastern and Eastern Europe.

Preface

The paper by Kuivalainen et al. presents a conceptual growth model with typical starting points, pathways and outcomes of international growth. We illustrate the model with five case studies from the domain of the software industry in Finland. The model comprises three categories of components: First, the three archetypes of *starting points* presented are a start-up, a small firm and an established firm. These different starting situations are analyzed by using a set of dimensions important for the subsequent internationalization of the firm. Second, three *typical pathways* through which a firm's internationalization process proceeds are suggested. These are born global, collaborative, and organic pathways. The three main distinguishing dimensions used to define the pathways are (1) speed, (2) risk level, and (3) degree of independence. Third, three *possible outcomes* are depicted, largely in terms of strategic or competitive postures that firms reach after successful initial internationalization. These include niche, market specialist (focus) and global generalist positions. This kind of typology, even if simplified, helps managers to map their paths and positions and to look for alternatives, challenges and opportunities with regard to internationalization. They may want to ask, for example: "Which pathway should we choose?" or "What should we do to shift to another (faster) pathway?"

The five cases present firms starting from different situations, adopting diverse pathways, and ending up, for now, as market or global niche players. Two of the case firms are classified as following the born global pathway, one as following the collaborative pathway and two as following the organic pathway. It is only natural that the outcomes do not include global generalist or large multinational firms, especially as we are dealing with small, rather young Finnish firms.

It is evident that industry characteristics create a need for firms to grow and internationalize rapidly, even if to date real international Finnish software success stories are limited. However, the Finnish software cluster has ambitious vision and objectives. By the year 2015, the cluster should have a turnover of over €15 billion, and employ 60,000 persons, both domestically and internationally. At least 40 companies should have grown into global leaders and among the top three in their market. This growth objective is a challenge for public policy makers in charge of supporting the development of the software industry. The reason for not "making it big" might relate to the fact that most Finnish software firms do not possess enough financial resources and market-specific knowledge for a full-scale "attack"; therefore often their destiny is to "linger on," "fade away," or to be taken over by a large multinational firm. What is more, finance-related problems which typically build up with increased international exposure often pose the greatest difficulties for exporters.

The Finnish public and industry support system for SMEs covers all the traditional support areas, such as financial aid, training, as well as motivation and information. However, it is still somewhat diffuse and fragmented, and the support does not always reach those it aims to support. Currently, the professed objective is to find and support firms with high growth potential. It is important to remember that antecedent conditions for high growth include the existence of high-growth markets, the ability to choose proper path and strategy for growth, an international outlook, as well as more traditional ones such as fi-

[Haworth co-indexing entry note]: "Preface." Kaynak, Erdener. Co-published simultaneously in *Journal of Euromarketing* (International Business Press, an imprint of The Haworth Press, Inc.) Vol. 16, No. 1/2, 2006, pp. xxi-xxviii; and: *Contemporary Euromarketing: Entry and Operational Decision Making* (ed: Jorma Larimo) International Business Press, an imprint of The Haworth Press, Inc., 2006, pp. xiii-xx. Single or multiple copies of this article are available for a fee from The Haworth Document Delivery Service [1-800-HAWORTH, 9:00 a.m. - 5:00 p.m. (EST). E-mail address: docdelivery@haworthpress.com].

nancing and an entrepreneurial mindset. Accordingly, it is reasonable to argue that better targeted internationalization assistance programs should be developed for internationalizing software firms. We suggest that the targeting could be improved by taking the experience of the managers as the supplementary basis for segmenting the services. The managers of internationally growing software firms very often have prior international experience and this should be accounted for when developing new programs.

The objective of the study by Nummela and Pukkinen was to find out whether partner commitment to export co-operation leads to a higher degree of success. A distinction was made between commitment to internationalisation, to co-operation, and to the group, and the role of these factors in successful co-operation was examined. A Finnish promotion programme–export circles–was selected as the focus of the study. All of the participant firms from the years 1998-2002 were contacted in autumn 2003, and the majority of them agreed to take part: the response rate was 75 percent. The findings indicate that the different types of commitment are related to success in export co-operation, particularly in terms of the achievement of financial objectives and the impact on the internationalisation process.

Although governments invest considerably in various types of export promotion, our knowledge of the effectiveness of the export-promotion efforts is yet limited. This study highlights the fact that even if export co-operation seems to be a rewarding and commonly used form of assistance in several countries, its successful implementation includes considerable challenges. The public bodies involved in the process need not only carefully pick the companies for the programme but also continuously monitor the development of their attitudes and behaviour. Particularly the partners' commitment to internationalisation, to co-operation and to the group in question are issues which should be observed and in case of negative development an intervention might be necessary in order to turn the export co-operation back into a positive development track.

The study by Hallbäck and Larimo was focused on young, small firms that initiate international operations soon after establishment, hereafter referred to as International New Ventures (INVs). Previous studies have shown an increasing amount of these types of firms in different parts of the world, especially in the last fifteen years. Earlier research on INVs has taken different approaches, from which the most general have been either to explore and explain the rationale behind domestic versus international new ventures or to research the INVs in relation to traditional, gradually internationalizing firms (often larger firms). More research was needed to analyze the different types of INVs rather than to treat these as a homogenous group different only from the domestic or gradually internationalizing firms. Consequently, this paper was focused on exploring two research questions: (1) Are INVs different from one another in terms of their international development of operations? and (2) If they are, how and why are the differences manifested in these firms?

The results based on the analysis of eight INVs from different industries showed that both initial and subsequent development of the INVs varied with regard to geographical breadth and type of operations abroad. The case firms were all focused on serving special niche markets that were narrowly spread across countries. While the operations were often based on one core product and/or technology idea, the range of offerings was widened through different modifications and adaptations of the core offering (for an example through software). The results highlight the importance of the founding conditions, the internationalization motives and the international experience of the founding managers on the INV's development in the early phase. The growth of turnover and financial performance (such as annual net profit) varied considerably in the case firms. While this study revealed no single success formula for the market or operation modes, some important notes may be highlighted when looking at the highest performing ventures. Entry into new countries is in these firms based on earlier contacts of the firm managers (especially in the first entries) as well as on strategic issues rather than "psychic proximity." Along with sales potential, also the R&D and marketing co-operation prospects in the markets play an important role in the entry decisions. The so called lead markets such as USA, Japan and Germany are of strategic importance to many knowledge-intensive INVs. In the case of a new venture having limited resources, the entry into these markets and realization of their potential (in terms of sales and product development) might be best executed using various parallel sales channels and partners such as local distributors and OEM- and Brand Label-customers that have a strong presence at the market. Regarding the policy implications, the subsidies received for export operations seem less relevant triggers for internationalization of new ventures. Furthermore, the variety of international entry and expansion operations calls for the need for a more versatile assistance by the government.

Internationalization is often seen as a critical ingredient in the strategy of firms to achieve growth and superior performance, but this issue has not yet been extensively studied in academia. As Kuivalainen and Sundqvist believe that managers of exporting firms could benefit from better understanding of the performance implications of export intensity, this study focused on examining what is the role of rapid internationalization for the firm performance.

Based on the analysis of 783 Finnish exporting firms we found that the size of the firm made a difference in the effect of rapid internationalization on firm performance. The authors studied export intensity with a three-dimensional measure consisting of number of regions and countries a firm exported to, and export turnover relative to the firm's experience with international operations, namely exporting. Following the recommendations of Cavusgil and Zou (1993), and Matthyssens and Pauwels (1996) among others, we measured the aspects of the firm's performance studying separately export sales, export profits and export efficiency.

Based on the analyses, it seems that smaller and larger firms enjoyed the better performance in relation to the internationalization intensity than the firms which were "stuck in the middle." Analyses revealed also that small and large firm differed from each other. For small firms higher internationalization inten-

sity means better sales performance, better profit performance and indirectly also better efficiency performance, whereas for large firms higher internationalization intensity reflects only better profit performance.

For small firms it can be said that the higher the extent of internationalization, the better the performance. As our results imply that smaller export intensive firms enjoyed all performance effects (i.e., sales, profit and indirectly efficiency) it seems that more geographically wide market spread may be beneficial for these firms. This kind of result has been found also elsewhere, e.g., Madsen (1989) found that it would actually be better for very small firms to spread their efforts over several markets, as they may not have the resources to follow a market concentration strategy successfully.

Our results indicate that for large firms high internationalization intensity leads towards better profit performance. Rapid internationalization affects also indirectly the sales performance, as the path from profit performance to sales performance was significant.

In general both practicing managers and researchers alike should focus more on performance implications of rapid internationalization among small exporting firms and study in a more in-depth manner all the factors and key issues which may reap the performance benefits.

The present study by Rialp and Rialp has shown that the level of intangible resources (whether of a human, organizational, technological or relational character) may affect the born-global character of an exporting firm. More concretely, according to our results, the Spanish exporting firms that can be considered as being born globals seem to differ in terms of their level of export capability due to a rather heterogeneous distribution of intangible resource endowments among firms (mostly in terms of human capital and organizational resources), apart from other considerations regarding firm size and the class of product/sector in which they compete.

In their opinion, our results shed light on issues relevant to policy-makers, practitioners, and export researchers. Hence, the evidence generated in this research could be useful for public policy-makers and export promotion agencies, which are generally very interested in improving a country's exports; mainly in terms of better estimating and developing the export potential of those firms according to their differences in terms of size and/or resources including, of course, intangible ones. The efficiency of these institutions could be enriched by means, for instance, of concentrating differently their efforts on firms showing distinct patterns and prospects towards exporting according to their specific resource endowments.

Regarding the associated managerial implications of this study, since it has confirmed the importance of intangible resource management for developing export behavior, first, and perhaps the most important thing, we think that just by giving strategic priority to the continuous creation and development of this type of knowledge-based resources, exporting can become a more contributing activity for the firm. Second, it appears that certain intangible resources of an organizational and human dimension, such as employees training practices, managerial attitudes, and more effective organizational arrangements for exporting, also impact on a firm's more rapid development of export capabilities.

Finally, for academics and researchers interested in the area of export behavior, we have shown the relevance that the theoretical framework known as the resource-based view of the firm, and the issue of intangible resource analysis in particular, may have also for increasing our knowledge about key determinants of export behavior. In particular, the application of RBV has demonstrated to be extremely insightful for making future research both more theoretically and empirically rigorous.

The stages through which firms go during the process of international expansion is fraught with risks and challenges that often lead to dissatisfaction with foreign operations and even to outright failure of the international venture. At the same time, internationalization is important to both individual companies as well as to their countries' governments, which have a vested interest in promoting exports and other forms of international engagement. Therefore, research in international marketing and business has dealt extensively and for a long time with the two themes that are addressed in this article: the stages of interna-

tionalization, and their link to the firm's performance. However, past studies do not capture recent developments in the international environment, such as the evolution of networks of firms and/or mergers and acquisitions that reduce the strategic autonomy of the acquired firm.

The present study by Martín and Papadopoulos is based on a survey of 200 Spanish companies and used cluster and other forms of analysis to identify the stages of international expansion and their potential link to performance. The results show four initial phases in internationalization that are similar to those found in earlier research, but also a new stage at the end of the process, "Globalization," which has not been reported before. A link between internationalization and international aspects of firm performance was found, but the relationship with the firm's overall performance (including domestic operations) was less clear and requires additional research. The data also show a non-monotonic "valleys and peaks" relationship of performance across the five stages, suggesting that firms face critical challenges at key points during their international expansion.

The traditional "stages" model, confirmed and expanded in this study, points to the potential rewards from international activity for firms that survive the process and suggests that support programs by governments, and efforts by management, for launching and sustaining international operations will be well placed. In particular, the study reaffirms earlier findings concerning the value of experience in, and commitment to, international operations, in increasing the chances of international success. The identification of discrete stages of internationalization, and the distinctive profiles of firms in each cluster, makes it easier for public institutions to target programs to the different needs that prevail in each stage. At the same time, managers can use the findings to identify critical points that can endanger further international progress, or can be used as a launch pad for ensuring it, by examining the data for the critical turning points that seem to be playing a determining role in the success of internationalization. Similarly, examination of the findings for each cluster can be used to highlight the kinds of strategies that may help firms in earlier stages to accelerate their expansion and take steps to increase their chances of success (for example, firms experienced in international operations use a much wider range of entry modes and are far more likely to have articulated specific international objectives than their counterparts at earlier stages of development).

The paper by Servais et al. focuses on international sourcing as an entrepreneurial act and aims at demonstrating that it is actually at the core of internationalisation processes of small firms, both established and international new ventures. Another issue of this paper is to understand how these firms, characterized typically by scarce financial and managerial resources, can engage in managing international value chains and not only being the passive agent of subcontracting agreements. The breadth of international sourcing activities and the nature of the ties established under these agreements is investigated through an empirical survey on 150 Italian SMEs, comparing early with late internationalising ones.

Small firms–both late and early international ones–appear widely involved in international sourcing activity. The predominant model of international SMEs is actually the one of a firm which contemporarily imports and exports goods and services. Their sourcing activity is diversified in terms of assets exchanged, with early international firms relatively more prone to purchase goods characterised by higher assets specificity and complexity. The kind of ties established reveal two interesting phenomena: SMEs prefer relationships with similar firms (i.e., small and medium sized) and maintain them over the long term. This outcome is even stronger in the case of early international firms, where a relatively higher degree of formalisation in relationships is coupled with higher percentages of long term ties and of supplying relationships with small firms.

The managerial and policy implication of this contribution are relevant:

- from a managerial point of view, we call for attention on the issue of international sourcing, because most firms are involved in this activity but they are not always well aware of the impact it may have on the overall competitiveness and in opening new export markets as well;
- secondly the international business planning both for new ventures and for existing firms should take into deeper consideration the core issues related to international sourcing, notably the "*where, who, what, why, how, how much, how long*" contractual issues, instead of focusing primarily on the foreign selling estimates, which depend heavily on the former;
- thirdly, this contribution calls for the adoption of a portfolio view of sourcing contracts where domestic and foreign agreements are mapped and monitored according to their importance and complexity;
- from a policy point of view, this contribution highlights that export supporting programs are frequently characterized by a partial perspective in pursuing the competitiveness of domestic firms and should take into account the co-existence and mutual impact of foreign selling and sourcing.

The formation of international joint ventures (IJVs) and other types of alliances has increased markedly during the last twenty years for several reasons (see, e.g., Contractor & Lorange, 1988). Although the importance of partner selection with regard to any type of cooperation has generally been agreed on, the amount of research focusing on the relationship between partner selection and the performance of international joint ventures (IJVs) in more detail has so far been surprisingly limited. According to a recent review on IJV articles in selected major journals on the field, Reus and Ritchie (2004) conclude that there is limited empirical research on the role and impact of partner selection criteria especially on IJV outcomes such as performance.

The goal of the paper by Larimo and Rumpunen is to analyze the influence of various foreign partner specific, IJV location specific and investment-specific variables on the relative importance of task- and partner-related selection criteria. Furthermore, the study analyzes the relationship between IJV performance and the relative importance of the selection criteria. The empirical part of the study is based on a sample of 60 IJVs established by Finnish companies in various foreign countries during the 1990s.

The study provides new knowledge on the distinctive features of the criteria used in IJV partner selection between those firms who are engaged in high-performing ventures and those whose performance does not meet expectations. The study shows that the firms who were satisfied with the performance of the IJV placed a high value on such selection criteria as trust between partners, commitment and top management compatibility. Also, the criteria of cultural similarity and prior relationship, despite of low overall mean values, were significantly more important for the companies who were satisfied with the performance of the IJV.

According to the results of the study, trust and commitment are, on average, the most important criteria when partners for an IJV are selected. However, the results indicate that trust and commitment alone do not guarantee a successful future for the IJV without a strategic fit between the partners, enhancing the resource base and competitiveness of the foreign (and local) partner.

Furthermore, the paper includes an examination of the impact of the IJV context on partner selection, providing insight on how the characteristics of (a) the foreign partner, (b) the IJV location, and (c) the investment influence the way the selection criteria are weighed when a partner for the venture is selected. Several significantly influencing variables are presented, stressing the importance of the IJV context when a partner for a venture is selected. Thus, the study provides essential information on how to approach the selection of an IJV partner by taking into account numerous features of the IJV context.

The objective of the paper by Dianoux et al. is based on the research trend which aims at better understanding of the politics of the advertisers' printed communication in Central and Western European countries: the Czech Republic and France. The paper also attempts to respond to the questions posed by Whitelock and Chung (1989): "Which approach is adopted by practitioners is, however, still a matter for some speculation, since the

writers have confined themselves to giving only anecdotal examples in support of their arguments." This approach is useful for advertisers who wish to improve the standardisation of their advertisements. Indeed, as shown by Solberg (2002), the level of standardisation is significantly affected by the level of market knowledge. According to the authors, the more a firm knows the local markets the more it can locate the similarities between them, and the more it can standardize its advertisements. It has to be noted that sometimes another resistance to standardization comes from the local executive staff because of their desire to be in control. For instance, Toshiba France had refused to use the slogan "In touch with Tomorrow" because the French consumers would not have accepted it, and the Philips Company already had a slogan with the same idea. Eventually, Toshiba Headquarters requested a survey which showed that there was no problem. Since then the slogan has been used in France and has been a success. This indicates that if the headquarters had known the local market well beforehand, it would have been easier for them to argue their case.

Literature indicates that there are numerous marked differences between the Czech and French consumers. Despite the tendency towards standardized multinational communication, it seemed probable that the advertisers, voluntarily or not, had a natural inclination to adapt their communications to the local circumstances in the two countries. We therefore had to find this tendency in the contents of the advertisements in the Czech Republic and France. The following hypothesis had to be demonstrated:

> Hypothesis 1: the Czech advertisements differ substantially in their contents, their forms, and their discourse from the French advertisements.

In order to record the contents of the ads in the two respective countries, an observation pattern had to be created. This was established after the principal elements of the difference were identified and listed on the basis of literature review. At the same time, the research criteria had to be limited to a reasonable number so as not to complicate the task of the observers, nor to multiply the risk of error. We divided them according to the three headings held by Okazaki (2004):

- the type and amount of information
- the creative strategy used
- the cultural values reflected by the message

The sample of the compiled ads was based on the 5 most important categories of magazines (managers, men, seniors, teenagers and women) in the two countries. For each of the 5 categories of magazines, the 2 most distributed ones were selected in an area of the Czech Republic and in an area in France. All the ads have been checked in respect of their format in each magazine. Overall, 577 different ads were used in the evaluation, which represents an average of nearly 29 ads per magazine.

The results from the product categories show that the most significant differences occurred in the categories of computers, automobiles and books, while in the other categories there was no difference between the Czech and French reviews being studied.

The principal differences between the Czech and French ads are as follows: the size of French ads is twice larger than the Czech ads, which are more frequently produced in black and white and without the elderly and children. The number of the product features and the indication of prices are other noticeable divergences found in the basic structure and content of advertising.

On the other hand, some convergences appear as well, such as the human presence, or the use of testimonials and celebrities. Based on the above results we can recommend that smaller formats, produced in black and white, and with more detailed technical descriptions as well as the mention of the prices, be published in the Czech Republic. This apparently suits the Czechs better than the French people. However, the assertion by Taylor (2002) that "what is practiced is what is effective" might not always be true, and future research will, hopefully, find out if the differences that we had found between the two countries are relevant to better effectiveness of the ads.

The research by Prugsamatz et al. investigates the effect of provocative imagery, on Norwegian and Thai consumers' attitudes to-

ward products. This study focuses on cross-cultural advertising using a nested experiment designed to investigate the impact of the provocative contents of a print advertisement on the two different cultural groups. Current studies suggests that the use of provocative appeals such as sexual content in advertisements increases the amount of interest and attention of audiences (Bello et al., 1983) and it can also be assumed that emotional and political appeals could elicit a similar degree of interest and attention especially in terms of the shock value across national and cultural boundaries (Vezina and Paul, 1997). This study agrees with Vezina and Paul's (1997) theory; however, it is argued that perhaps there is a difference in the level of transference of shock values to different cultures. In other words what may be a very "shocking" advertisement for Norwegians may not necessarily elicit the same amount of shock from Thais.

The implementation of emotional advertisement messages by advertisers specially designed to "shock the emotions and make the brain itch" (Moore, 1989) is a widely utilized advertising strategy. Such advertising strategies are aimed at stimulating both positive emotions and negative emotions by usually employing high impact, sensually evocative appeals (e.g., several cosmetic companies' use of highly attractive models and romantic backdrops in perfume advertisements) or graphic and extreme negative emotional advertising appeals (e.g., government sponsored anti-smoking ads, road safety campaigns, anti-alcohol abuse campaigns, etc.).

An understanding of consumers' attitudes toward different products when exposed to provocative imagery is crucial for marketers in terms of understanding whether such imagery would influence their product rating and to what extent does it do so. The findings in this study are therefore of importance to marketers and advertisers, as they can contribute in forming certain guidelines on where and how to place advertisements for consumer goods. Additionally the managerial implications of this study provide that perhaps differences in cultural values elicit different shock values and perhaps certain images used in some cultures may not be as shocking for them as it is in others.

For this study, 100 adult subjects per culture were asked to rate two different products (Walkman and chocolate). For each culture, an experiment group (group A) and a control group (group B) was established. Significant differences in product ratings and attitudes were found between the groups for each culture. Norwegian respondents' attitudes were on average more negative than Thai respondent's attitudes when exposed to the provocative imagery. The findings suggest the need for advertisers to consider the impact of such provocative material in these cultures. On the basis of the findings of this study, it is suggested that a provocative image with an emotional appeal has an impact on attitudes toward products. The findings in this study are therefore of importance to marketers and advertisers, as they can contribute in forming a better understanding of how to design print advertisement especially when the advertisement is targeted at a cross-cultural audience. Furthermore it establishes that the power of provocative imagery is significant but the level of transference (across national boundaries) may not be consistent. Therefore it is important for advertisers and marketers to measure the level of transference prior to launching of such types of ad campaigns. Finally, this study also provides an understanding of the impact of provocative stimuli on Norwegian and Thai consumers' attitudes.

International counterfeiting is a worldwide phenomenon with a negative impact on host economies and firms doing business internationally. The total number of seizures at the external borders of the European Union (EU) increased in all Member States, between 2000 and 2004. The products confiscated by customs officials were mainly clothing and accessories, media (CDs and DVDs), watches and jewellery. The most counterfeited brands range from Nokia cellular phones to Nintendo games. The most important source countries of counterfeit goods to the EU were located in Asia (China, Thailand and Hong Kong), but some developed countries were also very common origins. Despite increasing international concerns (EU, World Trade Organisation), few systematic studies have been carried out to provide empirical evidence.

The paper by Santos and Ribeiro sheds some light on the impact of political (corruption and economic freedom) and economic (economic development and trade) factors on the attraction of international counterfeiting to EU member countries. Our empirical tests show that countries' attractiveness to international counterfeiters is quite closely linked to corruption. The more corrupt a country's policies and institutions are, the more attractive it is to international counterfeiters. Another finding is that economic development (measured by GDP per capita) is inversely associated with international counterfeiting. The lower a country's standard of living is, the easier it becomes for international counterfeiters to enter the market. The hypothesized linkage between lower economic freedom and counterfeiting, on the one hand, and between the former variable and imports on the other, do not appear to be significant in explaining the attraction of counterfeit goods to the external border of the EU.

International counterfeiting must be seen as a public policy issue that affects society as a whole and one that needs intervention from both nation-states and international authorities. Another key partner in the fight against counterfeiting is international companies. Brand owners need to have their own intellectual property protection in place and develop anti-counterfeiting tactics to prevent or reduce trademark counterfeiting. Global mutual cooperation between international companies is also important to lobby governments and politicians in general to ensure more effective enforcement of IPR (Intellectual Property Rights) laws and alert users and consumers about fakes.

Any realistic strategy to deal with this complex phenomenon must start with an explicit recognition that there are those who supply counterfeit goods, but there are also consumers willing to pay for them. This suggests the need for sustained improvements in education, employment, and income, as well as for social and economic policies that favor law enforcement.

Erdener Kaynak

Introduction

Jorma Larimo

Small and medium-sized firms (SMEs) are increasingly operating in foreign markets. Furthermore, the amount of firms which undertake to sell, sometimes even a substantial share, of their product/service offerings in international markets at or near their founding has increased, especially since the 1990s (see, e.g., Dana, 2004; Moen & Servais, 2002; Knight, Madsen & Servais, 2004). These types of firms are often called international new ventures (INVs) or born globals (BGs), and they have received increasing attention in the international business research recently. Therefore also in this volume the first six articles will focus on the internationalization of SMEs, especially on the behavior and strategies of these INV/BG type of firms as well as on their success in foreign markets. Because the foreign operations of several companies include both outward and inward types of operations and the successful operation in foreign markets demands increasingly cooperation with foreign partners, the analysis of the foreign operations included in this collection is extended to cover also foreign sourcing and partner selection for international joint ventures.

The rest of the publication is devoted to two additionally important issues in international operations–to the impact of culture on advertising related issues and to international counterfeiting. The expansion of the European Union to include several Central Eastern and Eastern European countries from May 2004 on has increased the importance of analyzing the similarities and differences in advertising between the old and new member states. Furthermore, the new forms of advertising are used increasingly raising the question of effect of, e.g., provocative imagery on consumers' attitudes. Finally, the role of international counterfeiting has increased clearly recently. However, more detailed knowledge of the role of international counterfeiting, e.g., inside European Union, is very limited.

Internationalization cannot be seen as an isolated activity within growth-oriented SMEs. Indeed, internationalization and growth are very often intertwined, especially in knowledge-intensive industries such as software. The aims of the paper by Olli Kuivalainen, Jani Lindqvist, Sami Saarenketo, and Toivo Äijö are the following: First, to present a conceptual growth model with typical starting points, pathways and outcomes of international growth; and second, to try to demonstrate its validity with short case examples from the domain of the software industry in Finland. Because of the special context, also the characteristics of the industry and the specific challenges software firms are facing are presented.

The authors suggest that the real-life multitude of paths to growth and internationalization can be grouped into three distinct and more or less typical pathways which can be labeled as: organic, collaborative, and born global pathway. The authors present five case studies of Finnish software firms. The illustrative cases represent firms starting from different situations adopting diverse pathways and ending up initially as market niche players.

[Haworth co-indexing entry note]: "Introduction." Larimo, Jorma. Co-published simultaneously in *Journal of Euromarketing* (International Business Press, an imprint of The Haworth Press, Inc.) Vol. 16, No. 1/2, 2006, pp. 1-6; and: *Contemporary Euromarketing: Entry and Operational Decision Making* (ed: Jorma Larimo) International Business Press, an imprint of The Haworth Press, Inc., 2006, pp. 1-6. Single or multiple copies of this article are available for a fee from The Haworth Document Delivery Service [1-800-HAWORTH, 9:00 a.m. - 5:00 p.m. (EST). E-mail address: docdelivery@haworthpress.com].

Available online at http://jem.haworthpress.com
doi:10.1300/J037v16n01_01

Two of the cases were classified as following the born global pathway, one as following the collaborative pathway and two as following the organic pathway. The case firms supported the views on holistic growth strategies or "episodic" internationalization as they moved between pathways rather than systematically chose and stuck to one. Based on the results the authors present public policy implications and areas for future research.

The objective of the study by Niina Nummela and Tommi Pukkinen was to find out whether partner commitment to export co-operation leads to a higher degree of success. A distinction was made between commitment to internationalisation, to co-operation, and to the group, and the role of these factors in successful co-operation was examined.

Co-operation in exports offers partners several advantages, such as the possibility of combining and sharing information, resources and knowledge as well as of spreading the costs and risks related to internationalization. From the policy perspective, too, co-operation and network formation are attractive as they offer economies of both scale and scope when the export assistance is targeted on a group of firms instead of individual companies.

A Finnish promotion programme–export circles–was selected as the focus of the study. All of identified and still existing 300 participant firms from the years 1998-2002 were contacted in autumn 2003, and 75 per cent of them participated in the structured telephone interviews.

The findings indicate that the most committed companies had achieved the goals set for export co-operation better than those with lower levels of commitment. Companies that were committed to both internationalization and to co-operation achieved the best results. On the other hand, those that were committed to one or the other did not succeed any better than those with weak commitment. The findings also indicated that, in terms of success, companies' own commitment to the export circle is more significant than their perception of the commitment of others. Nevertheless, the most successful cases were the ones with the highest commitment of all types. Based on the results the authors present several avenues for further research related export co-operation includ-ing, e.g., the use of better measures for export performance and a more dynamic research design.

Different from the earlier research with its tendency towards a rather homogenous view on International New Ventures (INVs), the contribution of the study by Johanna Hallbäck and Jorma Larimo is the identification and understanding of the possible variety among INVs. The authors aim in their study at exploring the following: (1) Are INVs different from one another in terms of their international development? and (2) If they are, how and why are the differences manifested in these firms? The pioneering INV-framework by Oviatt and McDougall (1994) is applied. Despite that their work is one of the pioneering and most cited ones in the INV and international entrepreneurship literature, it has rarely been applied to an empirical analysis. The Oviatt and McDougall framework is accompanied in the article by a long-term perspective on their development and inclusion of several factors as possible agents of the differences.

Based on the analysis of eight INVs, the results highlight the importance of the founding conditions, the internationalization motives and the international experience of the founding managers on the INV's development in their early phase. Both initial and subsequent development of the INVs varied with regard to geographical breadth and type of operations abroad, and the results call for a framework that goes beyond typological categorization and includes various situational factors, e.g., more emphasis and tools to analyze the source of foreign location advantage and unique resources that need to be developed.

The case firms were all focused on serving special niche markets that were narrowly spread across countries. While the operations were often based on a core product and/or technology idea, the range of offerings was widened through different modifications and adaptations of the core package. One key feature of the best performing INV case companies in the study was that they used parallel sales channels and partners such as local distributors and OEM- and Brand Label-customers which had a strong presence in the target markets.

Internationalization is seen as a critical ingredient in the strategy of firms to achieve growth and superior performance. Although this has been a subject of intensive research during the last few decades, there is still a scarcity of empirical research to determine when rapid, accelerated internationalization, in other words, increase in export intensity is profitable. The study by Olli Kuivalainen and Sanna Sundqvist focuses on the three issues: (1) Are the commonly used export performance measures useful? (2) Is rapid internationalization (increase in export intensity) profitable? and (3) Does the relationship between internationalization intensity and a firm's export performance differ across firms with different resources (i.e., the effect of the size of the firm)?

Based on a sample of 783 Finnish exporting firms the authors explore the relationship between export intensity and different types of performance by structural equation modeling (SEM) analysis. Their base model does not show any significant relationships between these two constructs. However, when studying small and large firms separately, the results differ. For small firms higher internationalization intensity means better sales performance, better profit performance and indirectly also better efficiency performance, whereas for large firms higher internationalization intensity reflects only better profit performance. Furthermore, the results indicated also differences in the results from various market areas, and adjustment to geographic/cultural proximity could develop more sophisticated measures of multinationality.

In spite of the increasing amount of research being currently conducted on international new ventures (INVs) and/or born globals, a more accurate assessment of the strategically valuable resources and capabilities managed and/or controlled by a firm, as a key antecent for it to become a successful born global firm is still needed.

The study by Alex Rialp and Josep Rialp is aimed at investigating a firm's export adaptation and performance by adopting, as an increasingly accepted theoretical framework, the resource-based view of the firm (RBV). In particular, the relevance of different resources, mainly intangible ones, in the development of specific capabilities to conduct earlier export activities becomes their main research interest.

The authors test whether several intangible resources may have influenced the fact that a firm started its export activity almost from inception, and also whether the results achieved from this activity (as measured through the export intensity ratio) are indeed better than those obtained by other firms that were not exporting from inception.

The authors test their model with a sample of 1,102 Spanish manufacturing firms. Results of the study show that the level of intangible resources (whether of a human, organizational, technological, or relational character) may partly affect the born-global character of an exporting firm. More concretely, the Spanish exporters that can be considered as being born globals seem to differ in terms of their level of export capability due to an heterogeneous distribution of intangible resource endowments among firms (mostly in terms of human capital and organizational resources), apart from other issues regarding firm size and the class of product/sector in which they compete. The authors state that perhaps the important thing, just by giving strategic priority to the continuous creation and development of intangible knowledge-based resources, exporting can become a more contributing activity for the firm. Furthermore, it appears that certain intangible resources of an organizational and human dimensions, such as employees training practices, managerial attitudes, and more effective organizational arrangements for exporting, also impact on a firm's more rapid development of export capabilities.

Overall it appears that current empirical research has not kept pace with potential changes to the traditional stage-based internationalization theory of the firm, which may have changed over time, let alone with its link to export performance. In light of this, the paper by Oscar Martín Martín and Nicolas Papadopoulos has two main objectives: (1) to explore and describe the stages of a specific internationalization model based on a contemporary sample of Spanish firms; and (2) to analyze the firms' performance in relation to their stage in their internationalization process.

The empirical part of the study is based on cluster analysis of data from 200 interviews with Spanish companies. The results show four initial phases in internationalization that are similar to those found in earlier research, but also a new stage at the end of the process, "Globalization," which has not been reported before. Firm performance in relation to the stages of internationalization is analyzed using eight indicators, which yield somewhat different results for distinct measures of international versus overall performance. The data also show a non-monotonic "valleys and peaks" relationship of performance across the five stages, suggesting that firms face critical challenges at key points during their international expansion. The study concludes with three main management and public policy implications based on the results, and suggestions for several potential future directions for new research in the area.

Exporting internationally represents in the international business literature the predominant foreign activity of small firms. Mainstream literature is, however, challenged by markets globalization which represents not only a wider set of selling opportunities, but also of sourcing opportunities. This is true also for small firms, which aim at maintaining/improving/creating their international competitive advantage, tapping knowledge wherever located and establishing new systems of ties.

The paper by Per Servais, Antonella Zucchella, Giada Palamara focuses on international sourcing as an entrepreneurial act and aims at demonstrating that it is actually at the core of internationalisation processes of small firms, both established and international new ventures. Another main goal of the paper is to understand how these firms, characterized typically by scarce financial and managerial resources, can engage in managing international value chains and not only being the passive agent of subcontracting agreements.

The breadth of internationals sourcing activities and the nature of the ties established under these agreements is investigated through an empirical survey on 150 Italian SMEs, comparing early with late internationalising ones. The developed research propositions find adequate support. Small firms–both late and early international ones–appear to be widely involved in international sourcing activity. The predominant model of international Italian SMEs is actually the one of a firm which contemporarily imports and exports goods and services. Their sourcing activity is diversified in terms of assets exchanged, with early international firms relatively more prone to purchase goods characterized by higher assets specificity and complexity. This kind of ties established revealed two interesting issues: SMEs prefer relationships with similar firms (i.e., small and medium-sized) and maintain them over the long term. This finding was even stronger in the case of early international firms, where a relatively higher degree of formalization in relationships was coupled with higher percentages of long-term ties and of supplying relationships with small firms.

The formation of international joint ventures (IJVs) and other types of alliances has increased markedly during the last twenty years for several reasons. Although the importance of partner selection with regard to any type of cooperation has generally been agreed on, the amount of research analyzing the relationship between partner selection and (IJV) performance in more detail has so far been surprisingly limited. The goal of the paper by Jorma Larimo and Sami Rumpunen is to analyze the influence of various foreign partner specific, IJV location specific and investment-specific variables on the relative importance of task- and partner-related selection criteria. Furthermore, the study analyzes the relationship between IJV performance and the relative importance of the selection criteria.

The empirical part of the study is based on a sample of 60 IJVs established by Finnish companies in various foreign countries mainly during the 1990s. The results indicated that of the 29 task- and partner-related selection criteria the three most important ones were: trust in the partner, strong commitment to the venture, and trust between partners.

IJV location specific and investment-specific variables had influenced the relative importance of the partner selection criteria used by the Finnish companies, while foreign partner specific variables had a much more limited influence. The influence of contextual variables in general was seen to be stronger on task-related criteria. Finally, the results indicated clear differences in the relative importance of the selection criteria between better and poorly performing IJVs.

From the management point of view the results indicate that partner-related selection criteria have been the most important selection criteria. Furthermore, differences in the relative weights of selection criteria between well and medium-to-low performing IJVs were noteworthy. An additional interesting finding was that all of the eight companies which were extremely satisfied with the IJV performance stated that the most important selection criteria was a task-related selection criteria. Thus, as also may be expected, trust and commitment alone do not guarantee a successful future for the IJV–there has to exist, for example, enough strategic fit between the partners in order to enhance the resource base and competitiveness of the foreign (and local) partner.

The largest number of studies exploring the cross-cultural differences between advertisements have concentrated on just a few countries: USA, the Western European countries (France, Sweden, the UK, etc.), and the leading countries in Asia (Japan and Korea). Countries such as those from the former Soviet block have had very few studies despite their increased economical importance and the integration of several of these countries into the European Union in May 2004. The aim of the research by Christian Dianoux, Jana Kettnerová, and Zdeněk Linhart is to determine the main features in which the Czech and French advertisements are similar and in which they differ.

The study concerns the content analysis of 577 printed advertisements published in the 10 most representative magazines in the Czech Republic and France. The five largest categories of magazines in terms of their focus are represented as follows: women, men, businesses, seniors and juniors. The results show some noticeable divergences in the basic structure and content of advertising, such as the size, the presence of children or elderly people, the number of product features and the indication of prices. Thus, the hypothesis that the Czech ads differ substantially in their content and their form, from the French ads, is largely supported by the data collected. Concerning cultural values the authors found

strong tendency towards the French marks being higher in whatever the items were. Furthermore, some convergences appeared as well, such as the human presence, the use of testimonies and/or celebrities and the mention of the brand only. The results give both for the Czech and French managers hints for the planning and realization of print advertising. Furthermore, the study opens up new possibilities for future research in order to verify the key factors, which advertisers could standardize or adapt for their advertising campaigns.

A number of past studies have made valuable contributions to the understanding of the differences among cultures in terms of informational and emotional contents in advertisements as well as use of humor, comparative cues, and sex role portrayal. These studies examining cultural differences in advertising expressions can be grouped into two broad categories: the first category of studies has examined advertising expressions across cultures, and the other category has analyzed advertising expressions in countries that have less obvious cultural differences. Despite growing interest and research in cross-cultural advertising, little has been done to address the influence of provocation on consumers' attitudes.

The study by Sunita Prugsamatz, Lars Ofstad, and Michael Allen investigates the effect of provocative imagery on Norwegian and Thai consumers' attitudes toward products. The study focuses on cross-cultural advertising using a nested experiment designed to investigate the impact of the provocative contents of a print advertisement on the two different cultural groups. A total of 100 responses were collected in both countries. The respondents were asked to rate two different products (Walkman and chocolate). For each culture, an experiment group (group A) and a control group (group B) was established. Significant differences in product ratings and attitudes were found between the groups for each culture.

Results indicated that the advertisement had a more negative influence on the Norwegian respondents' attitudes toward the products and their subsequent product ratings than it did on Thai respondents. Additionally, Norwegian respondents' attitudes toward the chocolate and Walkman were significantly different (less favorable) when the image was present than when it was not present. The Thai respondents' attitudes toward the products were neutral (no significant difference) even when the provocative image was present. This finding could be attributed to the differences between the two cultures (high versus low context cultures). Additionally, it could be that Thais may have more exposure to provocative and typically chocking imagery (i.e., poverty, etc.) than Norwegians. The findings suggest the need for advertisers to consider the impact of such provocative material in these cultures.

In the last two decades counterfeiting and piracy have grown to a point where they have now become a widespread phenomenon with a global impact. It has fed on the steady growth of the information society and international trade, on the internationalization of the economy, on the expansion of communication infrastructures and on the emergence of modern, sophisticated technologies that are easy to use for the purpose of copying products. Also, new, highly active markets for the production and consumption of counterfeit and pirated goods have sprung up in Central and Eastern Europe, and in Asia (particularly in China).

The paper by J. Freitas Santos and J. Cadima Ribeiro adopts a host country approach to empirically test the factors that attract international counterfeiting to the European Union. The authors collected data from the 15 countries of the EU in the years 2000, 2001, and 2002, and analyze the data using ordinary least squares (OLS) regression method. The most counterfeiter host country inside the EU has been Germany, followed by the United Kingdom and France. The clearly most counterfeited products inside the EU have been clothing and accessories, followed by CDs (audio, software, etc.) and DVDs.

The empirical tests of the study show that countries' attractiveness to international counterfeiters is closely linked to corruption. Another finding is that economic development (measured by GDP *per capita*) is inversely associated with international counterfeiting. Therefore, counterfeiting must be seen as a public policy issue that affects society as a whole and that needs intervention from both nation-states and international authorities. Other key partners are brand owners, who need to have their own intellectual property protection in place and develop anti-counterfeiting tactics to prevent or reduce trademark counterfeiting. Global mutual cooperation between international companies is also important to lobby governments and politicians in general to ensure more effective enforcement of IPR (Intellectual Property Rights) laws and alert users and consumers about fakes.

REFERENCES

Dana, L. P. (ed.)(2004). Handbook of Research on International Entrepreneurship. Cheltenham, UK: Edward Elgar.

Knight Madsen & Servais (2004). An inquiry into born-global firms in Europe and the USA. *International Marketing Review* 21:6, 645-665.

Moen, O. & P. Servais (2002). Born global or gradual global? Examining the export behavior of small and medium-sized enterprises. *Journal of International Marketing* 10:3, 49-72.

Oviatt, B. & P. McDougall (1994). Towards a theory of international new ventures. *Journal of International Business Studies* 25:1, 45-64.

doi:10.1300/J037v16n01_01

International Growth of Finnish Software Firms: Starting Points, Pathways and Outcomes

Olli Kuivalainen
Jani Lindqvist
Sami Saarenketo
Toivo Äijö

SUMMARY. Internationalization cannot be seen as an isolated activity within growth-oriented SMEs. Indeed, internationalization and growth are very often intertwined, especially in knowledge-intensive industries such as software. Consequently, the aims of this paper are the following: First, to present a conceptual growth model with typical starting points, pathways and outcomes of international growth; and second, to try to demonstrate its validity with short case examples from the domain of software industry in Finland. Because of the special context, also the characteristics of the industry and the specific challenges software firms are facing are presented. Suggestions for future research directions are also given. doi:10.1300/J037v16n01_02 *[Article copies available for a fee from The Haworth Document Delivery Service: 1-800-HAWORTH. E-mail address: <docdelivery@ haworthpress.com> Website: <http://www.HaworthPress.com> © 2006 by The Haworth Press, Inc. All rights reserved.]*

KEYWORDS. Internationalization, growth, knowledge-intensive firms, software business, born globals

INTRODUCTION

There is a tremendous amount of literature focusing on internationalization of small and medium-sized firms (SMEs, see e.g., reviews of Coviello and McAuley, 1999, and Rialp et al., 2005). Internationalization, therefore, has been studied from various perspectives, some of which are "stages" or incremental, and network, contingency and resource-based perspectives. The large number of perspectives or frameworks has both advantages and disadvantages. Regarding advantages, it is important to notice that there are studies which have analyzed different aspects of internationalization, such as the effect of collaboration for firms' internationalization as well as entry and operation modes used. A major disadvantage is that even today there are only a few studies on small firm growth and internationalization

Olli Kuivalainen is Professor of Business and Management, University of Kuopio, Finland (E-mail: olli.kuivalainen@uku.fi). Jani Lindqvist is a Researcher, Lappeenranta University of Technology, Finland (E-mail: jani.lindqvist@lut.fi). Sami Saarenketo is Professor of International Marketing, Lappeenranta University of Technology, Finland (E-mail: sami.saarenketo@lut.fi). Toivo Äijö is CEO, TSA International and Top Trainers Group, Antibes, France (E-mail: toivo.aijo@toptrainers.biz).

[Haworth co-indexing entry note]: "International Growth of Finnish Software Firms: Starting Points, Pathways and Outcomes." Kuivalainen, Olli et al. Co-published simultaneously in *Journal of Euromarketing* (International Business Press, an imprint of The Haworth Press, Inc.) Vol. 16, No. 1/2, 2006, pp. 7-22; and: *Contemporary Euromarketing: Entry and Operational Decision Making* (ed: Jorma Larimo) International Business Press, an imprint of The Haworth Press, Inc., 2006, pp. 7-22. Single or multiple copies of this article are available for a fee from The Haworth Document Delivery Service [1-800-HAWORTH, 9:00 a.m. - 5:00 p.m. (EST). E-mail address: docdelivery@ haworthpress.com].

from a *holistic* perspective (with some exceptions such as Melin, 1992; Andersen & Kheam, 1998; Fletcher, 2001; Bell et al., 2004).

In this paper our aim is to answer to the call of Coviello and McAuley (1999, p. 223) who pointed out the need for "future research based on more holistic approach to conceptual thought, empirical work and methodological development." Accordingly, one of the starting points here is that fact that internationalization cannot be seen as an isolated activity within growth-oriented SMEs. Furthermore, internationalization and growth are often intertwined, especially in knowledge-intensive industries such as the software industry. Thus, the aims of this research are: first, to present a conceptual growth and internationalization model with typical starting points, pathways and outcomes of international growth; and second, to try to demonstrate its validity with short case examples from the domain of software industry in Finland. Because of the special context, also the characteristics of the industry and the specific challenges software firms are facing are presented. Suggestions for future research directions are also given.

Software Business

During the last two decades, software industry has been one of the largest and fastest growing industries in the world. The latest available estimate by IDC (International Data Corporation) valued the worldwide Information Technology market as $2.1 trillion in 2005. The global market for software was about a $200 billion in 2005. Hardware and peripherals accounted for about $800 billion globally (about 200 million PCs were sold in 2005). Computer services were worth about $1 billion. Worldwide sales of chips grew to about $235 billion in 2005. The growth has also been rapid: for example, in the 1990s the growth of the packaged software product segment averaged 12% a year in the largest single market, the U.S. (SIIA, 2005). Along with the global growth of the software business, the Finnish software industry has also grown rapidly since the 1990s. According to a National Software Industry Survey, in 2003 the Finnish software product industry generated an overall revenue of around €1,000 M–of which €380 M came

from exports–and employed 12,000 professionals (Jokinen et al., 2005). However, Finnish and other European companies have lagged behind U.S. companies especially in the software product segment, due primarily to small and diverse home markets, as well as to the low degree of 'productization,' i.e., complete product development and internationalization.

Although the sales plummeted in the early 2000, expectations for industry growth have recently improved. However, there are many special needs and challenges typical of the software industry, which await a firm aspiring for a high-growth–high-risk internationalization strategy. The needs and challenges listed below are supported by evidence from numerous sources (e.g., McGrath, 1995; Etemad, 1999; Cusumano, 2004) and real-life experience:

- Constantly forming and growing new markets: innovators create new markets; new things can be enabled by software serving new converging technologies.
- Short and rapidly changing product lifecycles and at the same time a need for an above-average recovery of R&D costs.
- The law of increasing returns–initial costs are high but subsequent copies cost much less: hence the need for market leadership or being among the "top three."
- Network externalities–the value of the product and service often depends on the number of other users of the product: again the need for the market leadership.
- Need to harness emerging technologies–technologies should not only be applied to one's products, there is also a need for directing their development and force.
- Need to adapt to collapsing markets–a firm should be planning for the future product generations constantly, i.e., riding the "innovation stream." At the same time a firm should have a flexible structure to be able to adapt to new challenges.

These observations also apply largely to other high-technology markets such as telecommunications and digital media which also rely heavily on information systems and digital content. However, it is important to notice that software business is distinctive in a sense that most firms operating in this field face all these challenges at the same time, not only one or two of them.

Internationalization

Especially in software business, growth and internationalization are often intertwined. It is important to realize that internationalization is not an isolated activity in a firm's strategy. Internationalization is a way for a firm to achieve higher growth rates and is, in many cases, the only option to achieve growth. It does not mean only exporting but includes also other operations, such as importing and subcontracting. This is often referred to as "inward internationalization" as opposed to "outward internationalization" (see, e.g., Welch & Luostarinen, 1988). Importing of software has also often stimulated outward operations at a later stage. Bell (1995) notes that several Nordic firms obtained licenses from U.S. firms to distribute software in Norway or Finland, and subsequently "exported" products/services to other Scandinavian countries (with the agreement of the principal). One case example of such operations in Finland was Stonesoft who distributed Checkpoint's software in Nordic countries in 1990s and early 2000s.

Different definitions have been presented for internationalization. Here we adopt a broad definition: internationalization is a holistic learning process that results in increasing involvement in international operations (cf. also Welch & Luostarinen, 1988). More importantly, with respect to internationalization the following issues should be kept in mind:

- Internationalization is not a separate activity in the development and growth process of the firm.
- The internationalization process is a total gradual learning process, not simply a series of business operations, decisions and transactions.
- While "business is business everywhere," there are nevertheless specific challenges regarding internationalization.
- The internationalization process entails dealing with new types of customers who are located further away, and who may have different values needs and purchasing behavior.

- Higher cultural, linguistic, legal, institutional and regulatory barriers usually also exist.
- International activities may involve types of business arrangements, operations and transactions that are different from those practiced in the home market.
- In summary: international business operations are more demanding than domestic operations.

It would be impossible to present an internationalization planning model that would fit all situations. The contents and scope of planning vary in relation to the firm's life cycle, internationalization stage, organizational level, scope of planning, and competitive situation. Therefore, the first question that needs to be asked is: What is the strategic planning situation of the company and what are the special challenges of the company's situation or what is the starting point for internationalization?

The choice of the pathway represents an overall approach to internationalization. It is the preliminary or general phase of defining the strategic principles and strategic actions for achieving growth and internationalization. The choice of the pathway depends on the business model, on the basis of success that must lead to a perfect match between the firm's resources and capabilities and opportunities and challenges in the external environment.

Here we suggest that the real-life multitude of paths to growth and internationalization can be grouped into three distinct and more or less typical pathways. They are labeled here as *organic*, *collaborative* and *born global pathway*. In many ways the slow organic and accelerated born global pathways are the opposites of one another, at the two extreme ends of a spectrum. They also often represent the choice of going it alone, while in the collaborative path the firm resorts to different types of cooperation and partnerships in order to facilitate growth and internationalization.

The three pathways are presented here as an analytical and descriptive tool rather than a prescriptive model. As will be seen later, paths in real life often represent hybrid types, which also reflect the effects of contingencies (see, e.g., Crick & Spence, 2005). During the entire internationalization process, firms can also, at times, switch between the pathways. However, classification schemata presenting the basic pathway types and the requirements and challenges associated with them can help either practicing managers or researches to analyze internationalization processes of firms, and consequently, to study the possible options for the firms planning international activities. Hunt (1991, pp. 176-177) notices that "... they [schemata] are the primary means for organizing phenomena into classes or groups that are amenable to systematic investigation and theory development."

Figure 1 depicts our conceptual growth model that includes the following three categories of components:

- *Three archetypes of the starting situation* as firms contemplate internationalization challenge are on the left. These are described as a start-up, a small firm and an established larger firm.
- *Three typical pathways* through which a firm's internationalization process proceeds are presented in the middle. These are born global, collaborative, and organic pathway.
- *Three possible outcomes*, largely in terms of strategic or competitive postures, that firms reach after a successful initial internationalization are shown in the right-hand column. These include niche strategies, market specialist strategies (focus) and global generalist strategies.

STARTING POINTS

While recognizing the multiplicity of possible starting points, we have amalgamated them into three most generic types:

- *Start-up:* A new innovation or an innovative spin-off, with internationalization seen as an integral part of the business idea/concept.
- *Small firm:* An existing small domestic firm with (rapidly) saturating home market and potential markets abroad.
- *Established firm:* An experienced medium-size or large firm which starts internationalization with its whole business or with one single business unit.

These types have been here primarily defined in terms of four main dimensions. While there are countless, possibly relevant dimensions, we have focused on a narrow, more manageable set of important constructs. In general, these are very much related to the initial resource and competence conditions of the firm conducive to successful growth and internationalization.

Size and resources. Small size most typically means limited resources and competences. Size also correlates often (but not always) with the amount of general business experience or international experience. Traditionally, most research on international business has started with the premise that small and medium-sized businesses suffer from size disadvantages that prevent or limit their ability to compete internationally (Calof, 1993). While recent literature on born globals and international entrepreneurship has well documented the number of successful international expansions of smaller firms, the size still represents a major determinant when pursuing growth across borders.

Business experience. The length and amount of general (domestic) business experience usually implies general business and strategic management skills and competences. Indeed, the earlier research suggests that the capability to use strategic management practices appropriately is a function of the entrepreneur's previous experience (Bracker et al., 1988). Consequently, a high level of management and strategic competencies gained in previous experience is assumed, in most cases, to make subsequent internationalization easier.

International experience. The length and amount of international experience usually entails higher internationalization skills and competencies. Many studies suggest that earlier international experience is of great importance; and that an international experience of the top management team (TMT) of the firm is possibly its most critical (intangible) resource (Oviatt and McDougall, 1994; Reuber & Fischer, 1997). Reuber and Fischer (1997) found that the international experience of the TMT was positively related to the degree of internationalization of the firm.

FIGURE 1. The Internationalization Challenge–Starting Points, Pathways and Possible Outcomes

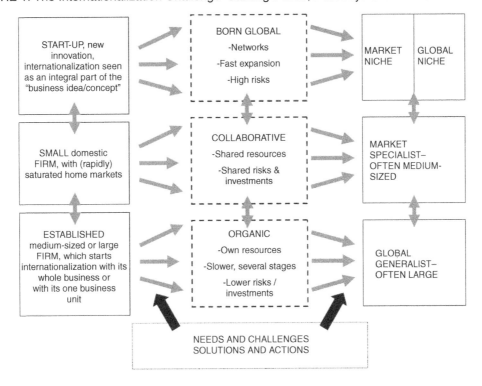

As learning takes place through experience, and both proficiency and contacts are developed, managers with prior exposure to international professions are likely to be more alert to the challenges and also to international profit opportunities than persons without such experience (Bloodgood et al., 1996). Previous literature (see, e.g., Reuber & Fischer, 1997; Saarenketo, 2004) also suggests that internationally experienced managers internationalize their companies *faster* than managers without such experience. Managerial orientation or mindset is also found to be an important determinant explaining internationalization of the firm (see, e.g., Nummela et al., 2004; Nummela et al., 2005).

Product and its prospects. This category includes such characteristics as the degree of newness/innovativeness, competitive strength, etc., of the products and business model. This is perhaps the most diffuse and analytically difficult category of factors. However, it is easy to argue, intuitively, that the less innovative and promising the product, the slower and harder the internationalization process. Or, con-versely, the more innovative and promising the product is, the better the prospects for international success. In the latter case such a firm would seem to be a good candidate for a fast high-risk high-yield born global pathway. A link between the importance of the first mover advantage and estimated turnover has been also found among small and medium-sized ICT firms (Kuivalainen, 2001).

Summarizing all the dimensions in combination, it can be concluded that small firms and start-ups have scarce resources and limited business experience, in particular as compared to more established firms. However, this may constitute also a strength in internationalization, as young firms, without established routines that hinder their learning opportunities in foreign settings, may be able to use their "learning advantage of newness" to grow more rapidly than their counterparts who wait longer to internationalize (Autio et al., 2000). The two other generic types of firms, small firms and larger established firms, that have operated domestically but whose home market is being saturated, are maybe in a better position in terms of resources, business practices, etc. Nevertheless, it may be more difficult for them to overcome their home-based routines and "domestic imprinting" (Autio, 2005).

INTERNATIONALIZATION PATHWAYS

The three internationalization pathways: born global, collaborative and organic, will be described below. The three main distinguishing dimensions used to define the pathways are (1) Speed; (2) Risk level; and (3) Degree of independence (mainly a dichotomy between going it alone or in cooperation). The dimensions and the pathways are depicted in Figure 2, where speed and risk level are combined into one dimension for the sake of two-dimensional presentation.

In real life, the level and types of cooperation vary considerably. A born global company is typically described as proceeding along a fast, high-risk pathway where cooperation, in the form of global networks and alliances, may play a significant role. To us it seems that most of the born global firms enable this type of strategy by operating through partnerships. However, some firms which operate in a narrowly defined global niche market and have only a limited number of customers may be able to sustain rapid international growth on their own. Thus, in the figure, the born global pathway is positioned in the middle in the degree of independency dimension and the collaborative pathway is a continuum, stretching from modest/limited to ambitious/extensive cooperation.

It is easier, however, to position a traditional organic growth path within the matrix: a firm following the organic pathway wants to attain independence and close control of its operations, and thus proceeds cautiously with lower risks. Next we will examine each of the three pathways in more detail.

Born Global

The born global phenomenon is by now rather well documented in the growing international entrepreneurship literature (for a review, see Rialp et al., 2005). It is thus acknowledged that firms on this pathway typically undergo

FIGURE 2. The Speed of Internationalization and Independency of the Firm in Different Pathways

		Speed/Risk-level	
		Slow/Low risk	Fast/High risk
Degree of independency	Cooperation	Collaborative	
			Born global
	Independent	Organic	

rapid and intensive growth through internationalization, almost from the first day of their establishment. However, despite the number of studies, there is still a limited amount of research focusing on the specific pathways that the firms adopt in pursuing early and rapid internationalization.

Evidently, the emergence of global markets with similar demand, new channels and shorter product/technology life cycles are among the main drivers that cause the firms to adopt an international outlook in spite of their young age and small size. The need to reach markets of sufficient size and to exploit first-mover advantages are also important drivers that lead firms to internationalize rapidly and to rely less on the small home market.

According to earlier research on born globals, the most common factors triggering this emergent phenomenon can be grouped as following (Rialp et al., 2005): (i) new market conditions in many sectors of economic activity, (ii) technological developments in the areas of production, transportation and communication, (iii) the increased importance of global networks and alliances, and (iv) more elaborate capabilities of people.

Born globals represent a special case of rapid internationalization. These typically operate in a narrowly defined market niche which makes it harder to thrive in a single, small (home) market. A high degree of specialization requires international expansion if the firm wants to achieve substantial sales growth. Furthermore, these firms often incur relatively high R&D costs, which occur "up front," i.e., before any sales are made. In order to survive, firms must quickly catch the growth track to cover these initial expenses. Finally, competition for typical born globals is very intense and their products may become obsolete rather quickly. If a company is to take full advantage of the market potential during its "window of opportunity," it may be forced to penetrate simultaneously all major markets.

While all of these aspects presented above are relevant in the case of software firms, there are some context-specific features that must be taken into consideration. Earlier research (see, e.g., Saarenketo, 2004; Jokinen et al., 2005) suggests that software firms following a born global pathway typically often share the following characteristics (the correspondence to the listing of Rialp et al., 2005 is provided in parentheses):

- Growth orientation, internationally experienced management team (iv).
- Innovation, core technology developed in-house (ii).
- Internationally experienced board members, systematic international networking (iii, iv).
- Packaged product and/or global niche market (i, ii).
- External financing (VC) (iii).
- Growth is often gained through networking/use of partners or acquisitions enabled by external financing (iii).

Collaborative

Due to the dynamic nature of the industry, it has been proposed that it is necessary for software companies to create both formal partnerships and informal collaborative networks. This is the main reason why we introduce a collaborative internationalization pathway separately from the born global and organic pathways. However, as mentioned earlier, in reality a collaborative approach to internationalization is not in any way exclusive of the other two pathways.

The reasons for creating cooperative relationships are diverse, for example: fixing a gap in the firm's own resources or competencies, reducing investments needed, sustaining growth, creating market penetration and accelerating the time to market (Hoch et al., 1999; Warsta et al., 2001; Äijö et al., 2005). Collaboration may occur in any area of business activity, such as product development, production, distribution, marketing, and financing to

name a few. Collaboration may take the form of a horizontal partnership with firms offering complementary products or a vertical partnership, when partners are suppliers, resellers or customers.

One specific factor that motivates software firms to take the collaborative pathway is the desire to complement business offering or product concept. Classifications of product concepts in software business have been presented by Hoch et al. (1999) as well as Nukari and Forsell (1999). Hoch et al. (1999) suggest three types of offerings: packaged mass-market software, enterprise solutions and professional services. Nukari and Forsell (1999) have specified four types of diverse offerings: tailored software, software products, software services, and embedded software (some authors include Internet-based services in this list; e.g., Hirvonen et al., 2000).

Tailored products and solutions as well as embedded software usually involve cooperation or co-development in projects with the (typically domestic) customer, and thus collaboration is inherent in firms involved in that type of business. Offering products created within projects promotes long-term oriented, interactive and multifaceted collaboration with the customer (Alajoutsijärvi et al., 2000). Furthermore, in the case of firms offering packaged software products, partnering and networking contributes to complementing the resource base of the firm, channel building in international markets, and to building alliances in the industry.

Collaborative pathway can be regarded as a special case implied by the network theories, but it is a concept which, to date, has not been adequately defined. As was mentioned above, the born global firms also tend to have a need for external resources from their partnership networks to internationalize rapidly. Thus, we need to distinguish the concept of typical collaborative pathway from the born global collaborative pathway. For this, we will briefly elaborate on the theories that contribute to our model: industrial network theory and the network approach to internationalization.

The basic assumption in industrial network theory is that firms operate in the context of interconnected business relationships, forming networks (Gadde et al., 2003). Industrial relationships can be divided in two major categories: organic and strategic. Organic networks are depicted to have evolved naturally from long-term buyer-seller relationships (Klint & Sjöberg, 2003). On the other hand, in strategic networks the relationships between firms have been organized with the aim of creating sustainable competitive advantage for the firms involved (Jarillo, 1988).

The network approach to internationalization, which was originally introduced in industrial systems by Johanson and Mattsson (1988), presents the internationalization process as being very complex and less structured than earlier (i.e., "stage" or "organic") models and theories have suggested. This implies that network relationships evolve in a dynamic manner, in some cases even creating incidents that may lead to rapid re- or de-internationalization decisions (Bell, 1995; Bell et al., 2001). In general, however, the networks a firm has purposefully created (strategic) or to which it belongs (organic) have an impact on its market expansion and development and thus, indirectly also on the decision-making concerning target markets and entry modes (Coviello & Munro, 1997).

On the basis of the network theory and the network approach to internationalization we have derived a definition for the collaborative pathway. In the collaborative pathway, collaboration is a strategic choice, where the focal firm is involved in partnerships and networks that are created to pursue long-term competitive advantage for all involved firms, and the partnerships are created to support market expansion and development. Nevertheless, collaborative pathway may lead the firm to enter markets reactively, whereas firms in born global pathway are more likely to search opportunistically for partners that will help them to reach particular markets (see also Coviello & Munro, 1997) in a faster and more dynamic manner.

To ground our concept to earlier research, we can note that Coviello and Munro (1997) have reported that a partnership with a larger firm early on in a software firm's growth path will ultimately influence both the future relationships and the internationalization process of the firm. The software firms on the collaborative pathway are thus typically small and

medium-sized companies developing tailored products and services for and with a specific customer, including those developing embedded software. Their internationalization is also affected by the partner's internationalization process as the focal company has developed dependency on one or few significant customers.

Firms in the software industry following the collaborative pathway typically share the following characteristics (see, e.g., Bell, 1995; Coviello & Munro, 1997):

- Lack of some key resource needed in internationalization (capital, marketing, distribution, etc.), which triggers the need for collaboration.
- Relatively experienced management with good local connections. These local connections may act as "bridges" to international connections and help the firm to go abroad by providing information about clients and markets.
- Systemic product, idea co-development with customers and/or suppliers.
- Ready cash flow and some public R&D funding.

Finally, it should be noted that the collaborative pathway is typically the least stable form of business that is rarely long-lasting, but typically a relatively brief phase in a firm's life-cycle leading to either born global or organic pathway. Most likely firms to follow it through are those developing embedded software in close collaboration with their customers.

Organic

Firms and their managers on this pathway do not typically have any prior international experience or knowledge and this fact contributes clearly to the following characteristic. There is a strong desire to protect the ownership of the company and to maintain close control of operations, and, at the same time, to minimize risks related to business (self-financing based on retained earnings). Growth and internationalization are achieved "internally" through a relatively slow process of "learning by doing." The lack of knowledge about foreign markets is also a major obstacle to speedy international operations. Therefore, firms typically focus first on their home markets and postpone entry into foreign markets until the perceived risks associated with the new investment are below the maximum tolerable risk level.

This pathway is most closely aligned with the traditional theories of internationalization, particularly the Uppsala-Model (Johanson & Wiedersheim-Paul, 1975; Johanson & Vahlne, 1977; 1990) and other stage models, i.e., the Process Theory of Internationalization. These theories can be summarized as follows: firms: (1) start and continue to invest in just one or a few neighboring countries, rather than in several countries simultaneously; and (2) as they carry out investments in a specific country very cautiously and while, concurrently, the firm's representatives operating in that market are learning as they go. Finally, firms on this pathway enter new markets characterized by greater and greater cultural and geographical distance.

Software firms following the organic growth pathway typically share the following characteristics (see, e.g., Saarenketo, 2004):

- Domestic management without international experience.
- Desire to exercise close control and minimize risks.
- "Learning by doing."
- Services, piloting tailor-made product.
- Cash flow and/or financing with retained earnings.

Having discussed the pathways, we will now examine the eventual outcomes regarding internationalization of the firm.

OUTCOMES

In this chapter, we will elaborate on the outcomes of the internationalization pathways. There are several ways for describing and categorizing the outcomes of successful internationalization. One rather natural approach would be to simply measure the degree of internationalization by using one or several widely-used metrics, such as proportion of sales from international markets, number of countries where the company is present, etc. Another possible option would be to focus on the ownership changes of the firm, i.e., has a firm stayed independent, has it become listed or has it been acquired by another firm, for example. Here we have taken a different approach and categorize the outcomes in terms of the strategic positioning of the firm in international markets.

In line with Sheth and Sisodia (2002), we propose that in mature global markets the competitive setup will ultimately consist of only few (three) major players (global generalists) together with a few medium-sized (market specialists) and several small niche players. This development has been long evident in other traditional industries, but it is increasingly valid also in software industry. In such a situation, the global generalists cover the mass markets and are able to dominate in terms of volume, cost efficiency, name recognition, etc. All other competitors will have to specialize. Market specialists refer to other large or medium-sized competitors who will have to specialize in specific product/technology types or in special customer/need segments. In this case, the segments are considerably larger than those of niche companies. Finally, the niche players specialize, by definition, in a similar fashion but in radically smaller niche segments. These segments can be either global or regional/local by nature.

Global Generalist

It is often proposed that in any industry, where there is a competitive, mature market, the top three firms rule 70% of the markets. These firms are characterized as volume-driven generalists, who provide a wide range of products and services for most segments. In software industry, so far, only Microsoft, IBM, and perhaps Oracle and SAP can be called as a pure full-line global generalist. Microsoft is in a position, where it has been (and still is) able to acquire start-ups with new products and business ideas, which it has integrated to its own offering (Sheth and Sissodia, 1998; 2002). Now it has products in all potentially large horizontal categories: desktop applications, desktop platforms, enterprise software and software products for consumer markets, which include embedded systems and software for mobile use (Cusumano, 2004). If ERP (enterprise resource planning) can be defined as a separate industry within industry, companies such as SAP and Oracle could also qualify as global generalists.

Market Specialist

Market specialists refer to other large or medium-sized competitors who cannot challenge the generalists and have to, therefore, specialize in a particular product/technology type or in special customer/need segments. In this case, the segments are considerably larger than those of niche companies. The markets can be defined according to geographical boundaries or demographic factors, or it can be one vertical market. A market specialist has typically a strong relationship with its market and serves its chosen market segment extensively. This enables it to recognize exact market needs and to utilize its brand in expansion of core business offering, e.g., by adding supplementary products to its portfolio. Thus, these companies typically diversify their product offerings or target markets. For example in ERP business, SYSPRO specializes in three global market segments: manufacturing, distribution and accounting, where it is competitive due to its customer focus against global generalist SAP.

Global Niche

A company that has adopted the global niche strategy focuses on a very narrow product/ technology or customer/need segment that is global by nature, i.e., there is already an existing market for the company's product offering globally. It is especially relevant for companies in software industry, due to the fact that a particular product or solution introduced to market may have a very limited number of potential users and the R&D costs need to be recouped through reaching all potential users. Additionally, in software industry, radical innovations emerge constantly from projects between developers and customers. Ultimately, as they create new markets, such solutions may have great potential for specific industrial users globally. Examples of global niches in

software industry are flight control and biotechnical systems, which require highly sophisticated and specialized software.

Market Niche

A company that implements a market niche strategy focuses on a very narrow product/ technology or customer/need segment that is regional or local by nature or that has not become global yet. Contributing to such positioning is the fact that the market can be constrained demographically or geographically due to cultural or legislative factors. For Finnish SMEs, it has been common to have a strong technological focus as well as geographical focus to Scandinavia, Baltic countries or Europe as a whole, as their own resources and skills have not been sufficient to reach global market coverage.

Even if these states are defined here as "the outcomes" of the internationalization pathways, they are by no means fixed "end results." Rather, they represent an interim stage or way-station in continued evolution. The companies may move between the outcomes through diversification, mergers and acquisitions, or through concentration. Due to the fast-changing nature of the industry the possibility for emerging full line generalists is still relatively high in software business (Sheth & Sisodia, 2002). There are nevertheless several barriers for free mobility between the groups, especially between generalist–specialist dimensions as a result of network effects and the different requirements in resources and skills. After outlining our conceptual model, we will try to demonstrate its validity with brief case examples from the domain of software industry in Finland.

RESEARCH FOCUS AND METHOD

The presented conceptual framework partially emerges from the earlier research conducted by the authors. For example, findings of the statistical study among small and medium-sized Finnish information and communication technology firms is reported elsewhere (Saarenketo et al., 2001; Kuivalainen et al., 2005). However, to be able to illustrate the internationalization and growth paths of Finnish software firms we developed case profiles, initially from the secondary sources such as the World Wide Web, databases/websites, and industry reports. One of the main sources was the database of Talentum, which is the leading Finnish business media publisher. In some cases the information was gained from the presentations of the personnel from the case companies.

For the purposes of this paper, five cases were selected for presentation on the basis that they comprehensively illustrate the starting points, pathways and outcomes suggested in our model. These particular case firms have been selected as they have had lengthy enough experience in international business so that their operations can be described and analyzed with our model. The screening of the case firms has been made on the basis of experience the authors have gained when conducting several surveys and interviews regarding internationalization of Finnish software firms. More specifically, the authors have been collaborating closely with case firms BG1, BG2 and COL1, whereas ORG1 and ORG2 have emerged as representative case examples from second-hand sources.

Case BG1: From a Start-Up to Market Niche and Subsequently to Merger Through Born Global Pathway

Formed in 1999, this Helsinki (Finland)-based firm produced mobile email and office solutions. In 1999, it was a start-up with four employees, and in late 2004 there were app. 40 employees in the offices in Helsinki, Cambridge (UK), Gothenburg, Munich and Singapore with an annual turnover of €0.2–0.4 million. This born global firm had an international orientation right from its foundation; from the very beginning, the language of operations was English and foreign employees were recruited to provide international business and market experience.

The firm's targeted end-users were small and medium-sized enterprises; all the technology was to be hosted and managed by the operator. Therefore, partners of the firm included a large number of ICT software and hardware producers as well as mobile operators. Although the firm had a presence in Asia, its main market was in Europe; this market niche situation lead to a merger with a U.S.-based competitor who acquired the firm in spring 2005. The management of the focal firm saw that a big market growth in mobile email and office solutions was going to occur that year and considered the company too small and scarce in resources to overtake heavy competition in North America. In addition, both the buyer and the focal firm saw this as an opportunity to create a leading provider of mobile email.

In summary, the firm had grown from a start-up to a medium-sized European market leader in five years. However, as it was still rather small and as there were expectations that the market was going to take off this born-global strategy ended in a merger. It can be seen that it acquired more experience in sales and marketing.

Case BG2: From a Start-Up to Global Niche Through Collaborative Born Global Pathway

This virtual prototyping and design-tool producer from Northern Finland was founded around the turn of 1997/1998. It was a spin-off of a medium-sized software service provider. The focal firm started its international operations from the beginning and it has followed a born global pathway; 80% of its revenues came from abroad in 1999. To a large extent, it has used cooperation and/or networks as enablers for its growth.

During the early days of its existence, the firm decided to have a clear customer-centric strategy; it analyzed all the largest mobile handset manufacturers and chose its primary targets among them, i.e., the firms which were ready to partner in their product development. Consequently, the case firm built its growth and internationalization strategy around these key targets. Even its main product is developed in cooperation with a large mobile handset producer and national research center. Through intensive product development the firm has become a virtual design and display software tool vendor for electronics and telecommunications industries, i.e., it has turned out to be a technology specialist for its own global niche segment.

Case COL1: From a Start-Up to Global Niche Through Collaborative International Pathway

Established in 1997 this "specialized" mobile software systems integrator and service provider has grown from a small web-designer to an international company with over 800 professionals and a turnover of €26 million. Although the firm had started its international operations earlier, the main seeds of its growth were sown in 2001 when it made a strategic decision to focus solely on smartphone software, components and products and integration services. Based on this decision, other business units or areas were sold. The firm built its international business within a partnership network; it is acting as a licensed competence partner and training partner of the producer of a well-known operating system. Consequently, the success of the firm is tightly knitted to the success of this software platform. Within this context, the firm has been actively seeking long-term collaborative partners and it is actually cooperating with two of the world's largest mobile handset manufactures by providing consulting, development services and training.

So far, the collaborative strategy has worked well. However, the firm has also enlarged its size through acquisitions, and eventually the firm's business scope widened again in 2005 as it merged with another Finnish software firm, mainly to achieve more size, economies of scale and credibility to attract and keep large multinational customers. In spite of this change, the smart phone division, which was the original focal firm, operates within a well-defined global niche segment in the software industry by collaborating closely with the manufacturers that use the mentioned operating system in their products.

Case ORG1: From Small Domestic Firm to Organic Pathway

This firm from Central Finland developed a range of enterprise resource planning solutions. Founded in mid 1980s, it had grown its business with a steady stream of revenue; it was a well-known firm in Finland and had a good position in the domestic market in its own segments. After almost twenty years of organic growth and some attempts at international operations, the firm went public in the late 1990s.

After the software industry growth plummeted in 2000, there were some signs of discomfort. For example, the focal firm had to furlough some of the workers for a few months in 2001 as the sales went down. At the end of 2001, it was announced that the firm would be taken over by a larger Nordic financial and business management software provider. One of the main reasons the owners decided to sell the firm was that, although it was relatively experienced in a business sense, its management saw internationalization as a problematic issue. They saw the new owner as a provider of resources and networks for future internationalization.

The CEO at the time stated that "together with the buyer we can grow more rapidly than alone." In summary, through the organic growth strategy the firm was not able to grow rapidly enough and was losing market share. The new company has more than 2,000 workers altogether and is active in more than 15 countries including the U.S. and many European countries.

Case ORG2: From Small Domestic Firm to Organic Pathway–and Through a Strategy Change–to Rapid Growth and Internationalization

This systems provider started its international operations in 1992. Founded in 1981 it had a long tradition of making tailor-made solutions before first foreign sales; it followed a traditional organic pathway in its internationalization. However, due to a clear change in its strategy in the mid 1990s, the firm started to grow more rapidly. For example, in 1999 it received 35% of its turnover from abroad by having operations in Finland, Estonia, Poland and Sweden. The key issues in the strategic orientation were the decision by the management and owners to focus on productization and clearly defined target market segments/industries such as energy, water supply and facility management. In addition, clear targets for growth were set.

The above-mentioned changes in the mindset, strategy and actual operations can be seen as particular "episodes" which have led to the firm's rapid international expansion (see Oesterle, 1997). Bell et al. (2001) notice that such "episodes" may lead to the "born-again global" behavior, i.e., a firm suddenly embraces rapid internationalization after many years of domestic operations. In the case of our focal firm it seems clear that partially the firm has jumped from the organic path to the born-global pathway. These types of firms often become acquisition targets. Consequently, the firm was acquired by a larger software provider in 2004.

An Overview of the Case Firms

All the firms studied focused on niche markets in their international operations. This type of strategy was chosen although starting points and internationalization pathways (rapidity, scale and scope of internationalization) differed from each other. A niche strategy may partially be a consequence of the smallness of the home market and limited resources available for internationalization. However, for born global cases, the niche was more global than for firms which internationalized in a more traditional sequential manner. This naturally relates to the products and their prospects in international markets. The case studies are summarized in Table 1.

Another interesting finding from our case analyses is that most of the Finnish small software firms whose internationalization has taken off have been acquired by other firms, either Finnish or foreign. One of the reasons for this development was being highlighted by the management of the BG1. In an interview, its former vice president stated that the merger was about "how to get enough resources for rapid U.S. market penetration." This is a valid question for Finnish software firms, as domestic market accounts for approximately 0.5% of the total world market whereas the main market–the U.S.–covers nearly 50% (Tekes, 2003).

DISCUSSION AND CONCLUSIONS

The purpose of this paper has been to present a conceptual growth model with typical starting points, pathways and outcomes of in-ternational growth. Furthermore, we have made an attempt to explore its validity with short case examples from the domain of software industry in Finland. Three archetypes of starting points presented in the paper include a start-up, a small firm and an established firm. We have examined these different starting situations with a set of dimensions important for the subsequent internationalization of the firm. Even if each software firm has a unique way to approach international markets, we have distinguished three types of internationalization pathways: born global, collaborative and organic. This kind of typology, even if simplified, has both heuristic and analytical value. It helps managers to map their position and look for alternatives, challenges and opportunities with regard to internationalization. They may need to ask, for example: "What should the company need to do to shift to another (faster) pathway?"

We have presented four possible outcomes, largely in terms of strategic or competitive postures, that firms reach after a successful initial internationalization. These include global generalist, market specialist, market niche and global niche strategies. While commonly ignored, we believe it is important to study and analyze the outcomes or strategic postures that the internationalization of a small firm leads to.

The illustrative five cases represented firms starting from different situations adopting diverse pathways and ending up initially as market niche players. Two of the case firms were classified as following the born global pathway, one as following the collaborative pathway and two as following the organic pathway. Even though collaboration is very common activity among small software firms, it proved to be a difficult task to identify cases that could purely be placed in this category. One possible reason for this could be the fact that it is difficult to create and maintain long-lasting strategic relationships during internationalization in such highly dynamic markets. Furthermore, the case firms supported the views on holistic growth strategies or "episodic" internationalization (see Bell et al., 2001; Crick & Spence, 2005) as they moved between pathways rather than systematically chose and stuck to one.

TABLE 1. Starting Points, Pathways and Outcomes of the Case Firms

	BG1	BG2	COL1	ORG1	ORG2
Starting point	Start-up	Start-up (spin-off)	Start-up	Established firm	Domestic firm
Pathway	Born global	Born global/ collaborative (product developed together with a MNC client)	Collaborative: –large Finnish multinationals –Partnership agreements	Organic	Organic → born global
Outcome 1	Market niche (Europe) (Target segment)	Market niche	Focused strategy four years after foundation Market niche	Market niche (mostly domestic)	Market niche
Outcome 2	Merger → global niche → future possibilities to become large generalists if the market takes off	Global niche	Global niche → merger → wider catalogue but still focus strategy	Taken over → subsidiary and the development center for the whole group	Merger → global niche?

As the most of the described case firms were small, it is only natural that the outcomes did not include global generalist or large multinational firms. However, as firms, technologies, products and markets mature, this type of strategic position is possible, although rare. There are only few (less than half a dozen) Finnish companies which can be said to be global generalists or among the top three players in any major industry. An example, closest to the software industry, is obviously Nokia Corporation. Its Nokia Mobile Phones subsidiary or division can be seen as having developed from the subsidiary of an established firm first to a market niche position through organic pathway, then to a global niche position, before the GSM technology and networks brought mobile phones to everybody's reach and helped make Nokia Mobile Phones a global generalist.

Public Policy Implications

Even if the number of global generalists remains low, the Finnish software cluster has ambitious vision and objectives. According to the industry vision by the year 2015, the cluster should have a turnover of over €15 billion, employ 60,000 persons, both domestically and internationally. At least 40 companies should have grown into global leaders and among top three in their field. Furthermore, by then a majority of these should have gone public internationally, e.g., on NASDAQ (Hietanen & Nurmi, 2005).

The above-mentioned growth objective is a challenge for public policy makers in charge of supporting the development of software industry. It is evident that industry characteristics create a need for firms to grow and internationalize rapidly. However, real international Finnish software success stories are limited. The reason for not "making it big" during the latter stages of the firm life cycle might relate to the fact that most of the Finnish software firms do not possess enough financial resources and market-specific knowledge for the full-scale "attack"; therefore often their destiny is to "fade away" or to be taken over by a large multinational firm. Bell (1997, p. 602) suggested that finance-related problems often pose the greatest difficulties for exporters and they "often intensify with increased international exposure."

The Finnish support system covers all the traditional support areas such as motivational and informational need. However, it is still somewhat confusing in its richness, and it does not always support those it aims to support (see, e.g., Ministry of Trade and Industry, 2005). Currently, the aim is to provide more support for growth-oriented firms. Accordingly, it is reasonable to argue that better targeted export assistance programs should be developed for internationalizing born global software firms. In line with Fischer and Reuber (2003), we suggest that the targeting could be improved by taking the experience of the managers as the supplementary basis for segmenting the services. The managers of born global software firms very often have prior international experience and this should be accounted for when developing new programs.

Areas of Further Research

There exist many avenues for further research. First, additional scholarly attention would be necessary to further elaborate the pathways, especially the collaborative pathway: What are the various forms of collaboration in different phases of internationalization and how does the collaboration typically evolve among small software firms? Second, the model depicted here reflects the situation in a small, open market where internationalization is thoroughly intertwined with the growth of the firm. Thus, it would be beneficial to validate the model statistically, longitudinally and with cross-national samples: Are the starting points, pathways and outcomes that we have suggested in the paper the most relevant ones for software firms in other countries or for firms in other industries? Finally, we hope that our effort, although explorative, to conceptualize the pathways of internationalizing software firms will encourage other researchers to investigate this both theoretically and managerially relevant issue.

REFERENCES

Äijö, T., Kuivalainen, O., Saarenketo, S., Lindqvist, J., & Hanninen H. (2005). *Internationalization handbook for the software business.* Espoo: Centre of Expertise for Software Product Business.

Alajoutsijärvi, K., Mannermaa K., & Tikkanen, H. (2000). Customer relationships and the small software firm: A framework for understanding challenges faced in marketing. *Information & Management,* 37(3), 153-159.

Andersen, O., & Kheam, L.S. (1998). Resource-based theory and international growth strategies: An exploratory study. *International Business Review,* 7(2), 163-184.

Autio, E. (2005). Creative tension: The significance of Ben Oviatt's and Patricia McDougall's article 'Toward a theory of international new ventures.' *Journal of International Business Studies,* 36(1), 9-19

Autio, E., Sapienza, H.J., & Almeida, J.G. (2000). Effects of Age at Entry, Knowledge Intensity, and Imitability on International Growth. *Academy of Management Journal,* 43(5), 909-24.

Bell, J. (1995). The internationalization of small computer software firms. *European Journal of Marketing,* 29(8), 60-75.

Bell, J. (1997). A comparative study of the export problems of small computer software exporters in Finland, Ireland and Norway. *International Business Review,* 6(6), 585-604.

Bell, J., Crick., D., & Young, S. (2004). Small Firm Internationalization and Business Strategy: An Exploratory Study of 'Knowledge-Intensive' and 'Traditional' Manufacturing Firms in the UK. *International Small Business Journal,* 22(1), 23-54.

Bell, J., McNaughton, R., & Young, S. (2001). "Born-again global" firms–An extension to the "born global" phenomenon. *Journal of International Management,* 7(3), 173-189.

Bloodgood, J.M., Sapienza, H., & Almeida, J.G. (1996). The Internationalization of New High-Potential U.S. Ventures: Antecedents and Outcomes. *Entrepreneurship Theory and Practice,* Summer, 61-76.

Bracker, J.S., Keats, B.W., & Pearson, J.N. (1988). Planning and Financial Performance Among Small Firms in a Growth Industry. *Strategic Management Journal,* 9(6), 591-603.

Calof, J.L. (1993). The Impact of Size on Internationalization. *Journal of Small Business Management,* 31(4), 60-69.

Coviello, N., & Munro, H. (1997). Network relationships and the internationalisation process of small software firms, *International Business Review,* 6(4), 361-386.

Crick, D., & Spence, M. (2005). The internationalisation of 'high performing' UK high-tech SMEs: A study of planned and unplanned strategies. *International Business Review,* 14(2), 167-185.

Cusumano, M.A. (2004). *The Business of Software–What every Manager, Programmer, and Entrepreneur Must Know to Thrive and Survive in Good Times and Bad.* New York: Free Press.

Etemad, H. (1999). Globalisation and the Small and Medium-Sized Enterprises: Search for Potent Strategies. *Global Focus,* 11(3), 385-104.

Fischer, E. & Reuber, A.R. (2003). Targeting export support to SMEs: Owner's international experience as a segmentation basis. *Small Business Economics,* 20, 69-82.

Fletcher, R. (2001) A holistic approach to internationalization. *International Business Review,* 10(1), 25-49.

Gadde, L.-E., Huemer, L., & Håkansson, H. (2003). Strategizing in industrial networks. *Industrial Marketing Management,* 32(5), 357- 364.

Hietanen, O., & Nurmi, T. (2005). *Ohjelmistotuoteliiketoiminnan klusterin visioprosessi.* Espoo: Ohjelmistotuoteliiketoiminnan osaamiskeskus.

Hirvonen, P., Sallinen, S., Seppänen, V., & Alajoutsijärvi, K. (2000). A conceptual tool for joint value creation in business relationships: A case from the software industry. Proceedings of the 16th Annual IMP Conference, Bath, UK, 7-9 September 2000. 13 p.

Hoch, D., Roeding, C., Purkert, G., & Lindner, S. (1999). *Secrets of Software Success: Management Insights from 100 Software Firms around the World.* Boston: Harvard Business School Press.

Hunt, S.D. (1991). *Modern Marketing Theory, Critical Issues in the Philosophy of Marketing Science.* Cincinnati: South-Western Publishing Co.

Jarillo, J.C. (1988). On strategic networks. *Strategic Management Journal*, 9(1), 31-41.

Johanson, J., & Mattsson, L.G. (1988). Internationalisation in industrial systems–A network approach. In N. Hood & J.-E Vahlne (Eds.), *Strategies in Global Competition* (pp. 287-314). London: Croom-Helm.

Johanson, J., & Vahlne, J-E. (1990). The Mechanism of Internationalization. *International Marketing Review*, 7(4), 11-24.

Johanson, J., & Vahlne, J.-E. (1977). The internationalisation process of the firm–A model of knowledge development and increasing foreign market commitments. *Journal of International Business Studies*, 8(1), 23-32.

Johanson, J., & Wiedersheim-Paul, F. (1975). The Internationalization of the Firm: Four Swedish Cases, *Journal of Management Studies*, October, 305-322.

Jokinen, J-P., Hietala, J., Mäkelä, M., Huurinainen, P., Maula, M., Kontio, J. et al. (2005). *Finnish Software Product Business: Results from the National Software Industry Survey 2004.* Helsinki University of Technology.

Klint, M.B., & Sjöberg, U. (2003). Towards a comprehensive SCP-model for analysing strategic networks/alliances. *International Journal of Physical Distribution & Logistics Management*, 33(5), 408-426.

Kuivalainen, O. (2001). Impact of Product Characteristics in the Internationalisation Process of the Born Globals–The Case of the Finnish Telecommunication and Information Technology Software Suppliers and Content Providers. In W.E. During, R. Oakey & S. Kauser (Eds.), *New Technology-Based Firms in the New Millenium* (pp. 26-41).

Kuivalainen O., Saarenketo S., & Puumalainen K. (2005). International Pathways Revisited–Towards a Longitudinal Analysis of Knowledge-Intensive SMEs, Proceedings of the UK AIB Conference, April 8-9, Bath, UK.

McGrath, M.E. (1995). *Product Strategy for High Technology Companies: How to Achieve Growth, Competitive Advantage, and Increased Profits.* USA: McGraw-Hill.

Melin, L. (1992). Internationalization as a Strategy Process. *Strategic Management Journal*, 13 (Winter), 99-118.

Ministry of Trade and Industry (2005). *A Development Track Adds Finnish Business Services to World Lead.* MTI Publications 19/2005.

Nukari, J., & Forsell, M. (1999). *Suomen ohjelmistoteollisuuden kasvun strategia ja haasteet.* Tekes. Teknologiakatsaus 67/99. Helsinki.

Nummela, N., Puumalainen, K., & Saarenketo, S. (2005). International Growth Orientation of Knowledge-Intensive Small Firms. *Journal of International Entrepreneurship*, 3(1), 5-18.

Nummela, N., Saarenketo, S., & Puumalainen, K. (2004). Global Mindset–A Prerequisite for Successful Internationalization? *Canadian Journal of Administrative Sciences*, 21(1), 51-64.

Oesterle, M-J. (1997). Time Span Until Internationalization: Foreign Market Entry as a Built-In Mechanism of Innovation. *Management International Review*, 37(2), 125-149.

Oviatt, B.M., & McDougall, P.P. (1994). Toward a theory of international new ventures. *Journal of International Business Studies*, 25(1), 45-64.

Reuber, A.R., & Fischer, E. (1997). The Influence of the Management Team's International Experience on Internationalization Behavior. *Journal of International Business Studies*, 28(4), 807-825.

Rialp, A., Rialp, J., & Knight, G.A. (2005). The Phenomenon of Early Internationalizing Firms: What Do We Know After a Decade (1993-2003) of Scientific Inquiry? *International Business Review*, 14(2), 147-166.

Saarenketo, S. (2004). Born Global Approach to Internationalization of High Technology Small Firms–Antecedents and Management Challenges. In: During, W., Oakey, R., & Kauser, S. (Eds.): *New Technology-Based Firms in the New Millennium, Volume III* (pp. 301-317). Oxford: Elsevier.

Saarenketo, S., Kuivalainen, O., & Puumalainen, K. (2001). Emergence of Born Global Firms: Internationalization Patterns of the Infocom SMEs as an Example. Proceedings of Fourth McGill Conference on International Entrepreneurship. Strathclyde International Business Unit. University of Strathclyde, Glasgow, UK, September 21-23, 2001.

Sheth, J.N., & Sisodia, R. (1998). Manager's Journal: Only the big three will thrive. *The Wall Street Journal*, Eastern edition. May 1, p. 1.

Sheth, J.N., & Sisodia, R. (2002). *The Rule of Three: Surviving and Thriving in Competitive Markets.* New York: Free Press.

SIIA (2005). [Software & Information Industry Association]. Packaged software industry revenue and growth. Available in http://www.siia.net/software/pubs/growth_software05.pdf.

TEKES (2003). Ohjelmistotuotteet SPIN 2000-2003–Teknologiaohjelmaraportti. 15/2003 (Software Products SPIN 2000-2003–Technology program report 15/2003), Helsinki.

Warsta, J., Lappi, M., & Seppänen, V. (2001). Screening of partner relationships in software business: From commencement to continuous assessment. Proceedings of the 17th Annual IMP Conference, Oslo, Norway, September 9-11, 2001. 23 p.

Welch, L.S., & Luostarinen, R. (1988). Internationalization: Evolution of a concept. *Journal of General Management*, 14(2), 36-64.

doi:10.1300/J037v16n01_02

What Makes Export Co-Operation Tick?
Analysing the Role of Commitment
in Finnish Export Circles

Niina Nummela
Tommi Pukkinen

SUMMARY. The objective of this study was to find out whether partner commitment to export co-operation leads to a higher degree of success. A distinction was made between commitment to internationalisation, to co-operation, and to the group, and the role of these factors in successful co-operation was examined. A Finnish promotion programme–export circles–was selected as the focus of the study. All of the participant firms from the years 1998-2002 were contacted in autumn 2003, and the majority of them agreed to take part: the response rate was 75 per cent. The findings indicate that the different types of commitment are related to success in export co-operation, particularly in terms of the achievement of financial objectives and the impact on the internationalisation process. doi:10.1300/J037v16n01_03 *[Article copies available for a fee from The Haworth Document Delivery Service: 1-800-HAWORTH. E-mail address: <docdelivery@haworthpress.com> Website: <http://www.HaworthPress.com> © 2006 by The Haworth Press, Inc. All rights reserved.]*

KEYWORDS. Export co-operation, commitment, success, export circles, export promotion

INTRODUCTION

Researchers and managers often point out the fact that companies operating on international markets encounter various problems that result in lower profits and higher risks than those operating on domestic markets. Helping them over this gap is probably the main justification for governmental export as-sistance (Czinkota, 1994; Kotabe & Czinkota, 1992). Governments in most developed countries encourage exporting (Stewart & McAuley, 1999; Weaver et al., 1998), but the form of assistance varies from sporadic intervention to more systematic support. Most export-promotion activities offer information services and market-research opportunities, and facilitate contacts on the target market through trade

Niina Nummela is Professor of International Business and Tommi Pukkinen is a Researcher, Turku School of Economics, Rehtorinpellonkatu 3, 20500 Turku, Finland (E-mail: niina.nummela@tukkk.fi).

The authors wish to thank Professor Lawrence Welch (Melbourne Business School), Professor Kaisu Puumalainen (Lappeenranta University of Technology) and Lecturer Satu-Päivi Kantola (Turku School of Economics) for their helpful and constructive comments on an earlier version of this paper.

[Haworth co-indexing entry note]: "What Makes Export Co-Operation Tick? Analysing the Role of Commitment in Finnish Export Circles." Nummela, Niina, and Tommi Pukkinen. Co-published simultaneously in *Journal of Euromarketing* (International Business Press, an imprint of The Haworth Press, Inc.) Vol. 16, No. 1/2, 2006, pp. 23-35; and: *Contemporary Euromarketing: Entry and Operational Decision Making* (ed: Jorma Larimo) International Business Press, an imprint of The Haworth Press, Inc., 2006, pp. 23-35. Single or multiple copies of this article are available for a fee from The Haworth Document Delivery Service [1-800-HAWORTH, 9:00 a.m. - 5:00 p.m. (EST). E-mail address: docdelivery@haworthpress.com].

fairs, for example, in order to advance the internationalisation of SMEs (Seringhaus & Rosson, 1990).

Export promotion could be broadly defined as public-policy measures aimed at enhancing exporting activities (Seringhaus & Rosson, 1990). These measures are usually realised in the form of various programmes focusing on key areas related to internationalisation, such as finance, knowledge of the business environment, company capabilities and access to target markets (for a review, see Globalisation . . ., 1997). However, in spite of considerable investments and the variation in assistance offered, little is known about the effectiveness of export-promotion efforts (Kotabe & Czinkota, 1992; Seringhaus & Rosson, 1990).

This paper evaluates the outcome of one form of export assistance, export co-operation, in the specific context of commitment. The objective is to find out whether partner commitment will improve the end result, i.e., lead to more successful co-operation. Seringhaus (1986) points out that it is probably better to concentrate empirical research on specific assistance programmes rather than on export promotion per se, and therefore a Finnish promotion programme was selected as the focus of the study.

EXPORT CO-OPERATION

Exporting inherently includes an element of co-operation–with customers and members of the distribution channel, for example. However, export co-operation as a deliberate, strategic action has not been extensively studied. It is understood here as an alternative strategy in small-business internationalisation and the focus is on co-operation among independent firms, which may be competitors or may offer complementary products. Their joint objective is to co-ordinate a set of activities in order to develop each partner's ability to operate on international markets (cf. Nummela, 2000).

Co-operation in exports offers partners several advantages, such as the possibility of combining and sharing information, resources and knowledge as well as of spreading the costs and risks related to internationalisation (Welch et al., 1998; Welch et al., 2000). From

the policy perspective, too, co-operation and network formation are attractive as they offer economies of both scale and scope when the export assistance is targeted on a group of firms instead of individual companies (McNaughton & Bell, 2001).

It is not surprising, therefore, that a wide range of export-promotion programmes supporting co-operation have been introduced worldwide in recent years (Welch et al., 1996; Welch et al., 1998). Empirical evidence also indicates that these programmes have been rather successful in stimulating the internationalisation of their participants (McNaughton & Bell, 2001). However, managing them, and particularly managing the groups, is a challenging task (Welch et al., 1996), not least because export co-operation requires SME managers to acquire novel skills related to decision-making, achieving consensus, maintaining commitment, coordinating and organising (McNaughton & Bell, 2001).

The above-mentioned skills are probably needed in any kind of co-operation, but export co-operation has its specific features. Perhaps the most significant of these is the strong connection with the internationalisation process of the company. Welch and Joynt (1987) used this as the basis of their argument that success in export co-operation depends on commitment both to the group and to the foreign market. Welch (1992) developed this thought further by suggesting that future success is determined by the partners' commitment to the co-operation and to internationalisation. Different levels of commitment lead to varying chances of success (see Figure 1).

According to Welch (1992), export co-operation has the best prospects if commitment to both internationalisation and co-operation is strong. It is also possible for the outcome to be favourable even if the partners' commitment to either of the basic elements is weaker, although in this case it would probably be mostly due to situational factors. It could also be asked why a company with weak commitment to internationalisation wishes to engage in export co-operation at all, since internationalisation should be the primary target. There may be tempting prospects, of course, and external influences (e.g., in the form of governmental support) could also encourage participation.

FIGURE 1. The Impact of Commitment on the Success of Co-Operation

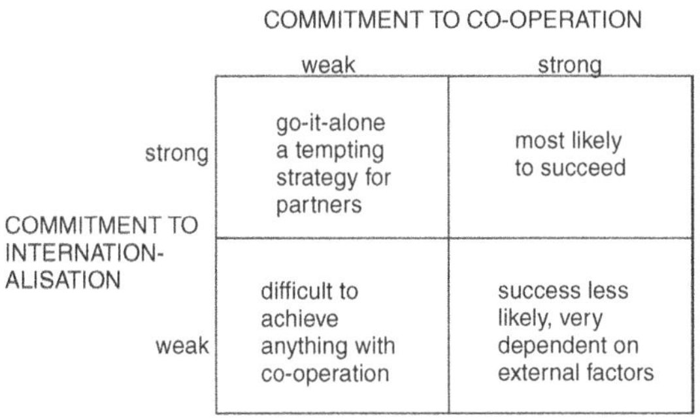

COMMITMENT TO CO-OPERATION

		weak	strong
COMMITMENT TO INTERNATIONALISATION	strong	go-it-alone a tempting strategy for partners	most likely to succeed
	weak	difficult to achieve anything with co-operation	success less likely, very dependent on external factors

(Adapted from Welch, 1992, 30)

These thought-provoking and logically sound arguments have never been empirically challenged. The aim in this study is to fulfil this gap by testing them on data from Finnish export circles.

RESEARCH DESIGN

In Finland, a considerable amount of export assistance is directed through the Export Circle Programmes offered by three semi-public organisations. Export circles are groups of independent firms (usually the number of firms varies from four to six), which jointly attempt to enter selected international markets offering complementary products. The circles usually do not include competitors. The firms do not create a separate organisation for co-operation, which often remains quite unstructured. They jointly employ an export manager who acts as the co-ordinator of this co-operative arrangement. He or she is selected by the companies and representatives of the semi-public organisation in question. The companies receive financial support from the Ministry of Trade and Industry for two or three years. In directing this support, the semi-public organisation acts as a middleman between the Ministry and the companies. Its representatives supervise the export co-operation and its outcomes, and the joint export managers are required to submit regular progress reports.

The majority of earlier studies on export co-operation (Chetty & Patterson, 2002; McNaughton

& Bell, 2001; Chetty & Blankenburg-Holm, 2000 and the various studies by Welch et al.) are qualitative in nature. The aim in this study was to present a more holistic picture of the phenomenon. In order to further this aim, a survey of all the firms who had participated in the programme during the years 1998-2002 was conducted during autumn 2003.[1] The study design thus resembled a census in that it took in all available units in a defined population. The registers included a total of 362 companies that fitted the criteria, but for technical and other reasons some of them had to be excluded (they had ceased to exist, or could not be traced, for example). The final sample thus comprised 300 firms. These firms were contacted by telephone and the respondents were asked to participate in a structured telephone interview that would take approximately 20 minutes. The person interviewed was the contact person in matters related to the export circle–in most cases it was either the managing director or the export manager. The majority of them (n = 226) agreed to participate in the study, which resulted in a response rate of 75 per cent.

The data was collected with the help of a structured questionnaire and analysed using the SPSS for Windows program. In order to increase the quality of the data, the questionnaire was pre-tested by two persons who had personal experience of export circles, since their firm had previously been involved in one. Comments were also elicited from the personnel of semi-public organisations. The original questionnaire was slightly altered as a result of the feedback. In order to further improve the quality of the responses, the questionnaire was kept relatively short and simple (the pre-test showed that it took approximately 20 minutes to complete).

Although many researchers claim that it is not possible to obtain a decent response rate in small-business research for several reasons, the response rate in this study (75 per cent) could be considered high. More important than a high response rate, however, is a demonstrated lack of response bias (Babbie, 1975). Although the number of non-respondents remained low, this potential bias was evaluated. The respondents who did not participate in the study were asked a few background questions.

Comparison between the respondents and non-respondents showed that the latter did not differ significantly from the former. The responses were carefully documented and coded, and unclear answers were coded following deeper examination. The data was entered into the computer program, and then double-checked with the help of frequency and spot checks for coding mistakes.

MEASURE DEVELOPMENT

Commitment to Internationalisation

Although commitment to internationalisation has been the focus of numerous studies, the concept itself has remained ambiguous (Stump et al., 1998). It first came under discussion in the 1970s, most prominently in the work of Johanson and Vahlne (1977), who stated that, during its internationalisation process, a firm successively increases its commitment to foreign markets. This could be interpreted as a growth process in which firms that are risk-averse gradually increase their stakes in foreign markets (cf. Penrose, 1959).

Commitment to internationalisation was called "market commitment" in Johanson and Vahlne's study, and interpreted as resources committed to a particular foreign market, including both the amount of resources committed and the degree of commitment. The degree of commitment was defined as "the difficulty of finding an alternative use for the resources and transferring them to it" (Johanson & Vahlne, 1977, 27). In other words, the more resources the firm has invested in internationalisation and the more focused the resources are on the specific market, the more committed the firm is. Market commitment is also connected to the acquisition of market knowledge: as a company collects information about the market, it becomes aware of the possibilities and decides to invest resources in it.

The allocation of resources to foreign markets has also been used as a measure of commitment to internationalisation in more recent studies. The perspective of these studies has usually been broader, and the focus generally on commitment to internationalisation and not only to a particular market. A large number of studies have analysed the internationalisation process as the sequence in which a firm implements various operation modes in foreign markets (Pedersen & Petersen, 1998). Other approaches to measuring resource commitment have also been developed. Philp (1998), for example, saw it in terms of concrete measures carried out in order to enhance exports, such as investigations of and excursions to export markets, the preparation of promotional material for foreign markets, and involvement in trade promotions. The more highly committed firms even ensured that they had the production capacity to meet the needs of foreign markets, familiarised themselves with foreign legal requirements, and adapted their products to the different standards and regulations.

To complement the dominant resource-oriented approach, some researchers added a more managerial perspective and related commitment to the attitudes and goals of top management. For example, if a company is operating quite satisfactorily in the domestic market, it may not be very motivated to internationalise. On the other hand, if the limited home market "pushes" a small firm into international markets, its motivation to internationalise increases significantly. Assessment of managerial commitment has sometimes been more vague than the measurement of resource commitment: Philp (1998), for example, described committed managers as "export minded," people who were interested in export sales and who discussed their plans frequently.

Stump et al. (1998) analysed attitudinal commitment by using measures such as management interest in the domestic market, willingness to expand onto international markets, and level of planning for exporting now and in the future.[2] Furthermore, Czinkota and Johnston (1983) pointed out that managerial attitudes also included the ability to recognise the differences between exporting and doing business locally. It seems that the better these differences are identified, the more committed the managers are. These measures of attitudinal commitment seem quite similar to the ones used in previous studies analysing managerial commitment. On the other hand, in analysing behavioural commitment Stump et al. (1998) tried to estimate how much time and financial resources were invested in export-related activities,[3] i.e., measures that had been used in analysing resource commitment.

On the basis of the literature review, we generated six items to measure company commitment to internationalisation. We considered multiple measures preferable, as they would give us a fuller understanding of the phenomenon. The response scale for each item was a five-point Likert scale (1 = disagree totally, 5 = agree totally). The items were worded as follows:

- The company management invests a lot of time in planning international operations.
- It is important for our company to internationalise rapidly.
- Our company has turned to international markets from the beginning.
- Domestic markets do not offer enough growth potential.
- We need to internationalise in order to succeed in the future.
- The company management sees the world as one big market place.

The reliability of the measure was assessed by computing Cronbach's alpha, which is the most widely used coefficient of equivalence (Gerbing & Anderson, 1988). The alpha value for the scale was considered acceptable (.703) as it exceeded the minimum level of .70 recommended by Nunnally (1978).

Commitment to Co-Operation

In the context of interfirm co-operation, the concept of commitment could be considered on three levels: the commitment of an individual, commitment to a relationship, and commitment to a network. Two types of co-operation have also been identified in previous literature according to the focus: it may be either internal (individual commitment) or external (commitment to a relationship/network) to the firm. Commitment of the individual and commitment to the network are relevant to this study.

The most popular perspective taken in previous research has been that of the individual, particularly in terms of organisational commitment. Since the role of the key individual,

the entrepreneur, is decisive in small-firm decision-making and operations in general, it is assumed here that research on the commitment of an individual actor is also applicable in the SME context. The commitment of individuals is the basis for the commitment of organisations, and as a generalisation, commitment in an organisation is the sum of the commitment of the individual actors that comprise it. For example, Björkman et al. (1991) state that the commitment of individuals has an effect on the commitment and future actions of the organisation of which they are members. People may have dual commitments (cf. Reichers, 1985), and it is assumed in this study that an individual may be differently committed to co-operation and to internationalisation.

On the other hand, evaluating commitment to a network is more complicated than evaluating commitment on any other level for several reasons. In spite of the contextual and situational differences, networks such as export circles usually share a few common characteristics. These networks often aim at offering or acquiring something jointly, in other words co-operation is a dominant feature. The underlying idea is for the partners to develop their own strategies in order to achieve the common goals (cf. Komppula, 1998). This, in turn, will increase their commitment to co-operation (cf. Welch et al., 2000).

Another issue that has to be considered is the increased complexity that the number of partners brings to the analysis. When studying commitment in a dyad, researchers usually evaluate it from the perspective of one partner, and sometimes also from the perspective of both. However, analysis of commitment in a network requires that the perceptions of several partners–if not all–are included. Naturally, the partners may all perceive the same reality differently. Just as commitment experienced by any individual may differ from that experienced by any other (e.g., Reichers, 1985), the commitment of partners co-operating in a network may also differ. Anderson and Weitz (1992), for example, claim that partners in dyads are likely to see the environment and co-operation in very different ways, and that the number of perspectives is multiplied in a network. Björkman et al. (1991) also mention that having a larger number of partners makes it difficult to reach any agreement. As a result, several decisions are compromises rather than best-possible solutions. What is even more important from the perspective of co-operation, the existence of a common goal cannot be taken for granted (Sevón, 1998); on the contrary, several partner-specific goals probably exist.

The desire for continuity is one of the key elements of co-operation in co-operative networks. Continuance has also often been considered the key criterion for success in export co-operation (Welch et al., 2000). However, continuity does not necessarily mean long-lasting co-operation, and may only apply until the objectives set have been achieved. The desire for continuity does not mean that all co-operative networks are successful–on the contrary, there are several examples of unsuccessful attempts. Some researchers claim that a lack of commitment has been one of the main reasons for ending co-operation in networks, possibly the most important one (Sevón, 1998; Murto-Koivisto & Vesalainen, 1995).

To conclude, previous literature assisted us in formulating three items to measure company commitment to co-operation. Again, multiple measures were considered necessary in order to capture a more multi-dimensional picture. The response scale used for each item was a five-point Likert scale with anchors 1 = disagree totally, 5 = agree totally. The items were worded as follows:

- Co-operation is a good way of operating for our company in the future.
- Interfirm co-operation is an effective way to work in exports.
- I am interested in co-operation with other companies.

Cronbach's alpha, which is the most widely used coefficient of equivalence (Gerbing & Anderson, 1988), was used to evaluate the reliability of the scale. The scale was considered acceptable as its alpha value (.714) exceeded the minimum level of .70 recommended by Nunnally (1978).

Success of Export Co-Operation

Commitment develops during the process of co-operation, which can be divided into three phases: start, implementation and evaluation. The partners express their commitment in different ways in different phases of the process (Nummela, 2000). The prevailing view is, however, that commitment mainly depends on performance, and dissatisfied partners will leave the co-operative venture. It is assumed here that this evaluation may lead the co-operation into either a positive or a negative cycle. In the positive cycle, satisfaction with the achievements leads to increasing attitudinal commitment, which then further leads to the demonstration of commitment through behaviour, and thus to increasing satisfaction. On the other hand, no attitudinal commitment to the network is established in the negative cycle because the partners are not satisfied with the outcomes of the co-operation. Decreasing attitudinal commitment leads to diminishing behavioural commitment, and thus in the course of time either one or several partners leave the co-operative arrangement (Nummela, 2000). In other words, during the process of co-operation the participants need tangible evidence that commitment is worthwhile (Welch et al., 2000).

The Uppsala school (e.g., Johanson & Vahlne, 1977) described the internationalisation of a firm as a process of increasing commitment and knowledge. In the case of export co-operation these two processes are strongly intertwined, and both have to be included in the measuring of success. Accordingly, success in export co-operation was evaluated in this study on three measures: achievement of goals (both financial and other) and impact on the company's internationalisation.

A strong joint goal has often been considered essential in overcoming problems of group dynamics (Welch et al., 2000), and goal achievement has also been a key criterion in evaluating the outcome of export co-operation in other countries (Welch et al., 1998). We assessed goal achievement by asking the respondents whether they had reached the financial and other goals set for export co-operation, and how satisfied they were overall with the export circle. Goal achievement was assessed on a five-point Likert scale ranging from 1 = the goals were not achieved at all, to 5 = the goals were achieved very well, and overall satisfaction on a seven-point Likert scale ranging from 4 = poor satisfaction to 10 = high satisfaction.

The question, "How much has the export circle advanced your company's internationalisation?" was asked in order to measure its impact on internationalisation, gauged on a five-point Likert scale (1 = not at all to 5 = very much). All four measures of successful export co-operation were subjective, reflecting the manager's perception of the outcome and impact of the export circle. The development of the measures and the literature review led to the generation of the following four propositions:

> *P1a: Companies with high commitment to internationalisation show better achievement in terms of the goals set for export co-operation.*

> *P1b: The impact on internationalisation is greater in companies with high commitment to internationalisation.*

> *P2a: Companies with high commitment to co-operation show better achievement in terms of the goals set for export co-operation.*

> *P2b: The impact on internationalisation is greater in companies with high commitment to co-operation.*

FINDINGS

The Respondents and the Key Measures

On average, the turnover of the companies was 10.3 million euros, the median turnover value demonstrating that in fifty percent of them it was 2.5 million euros or less. The company size is also reflected in the number of employees: fifty percent of the respondent firms employed 21 or fewer full-time workers. Company age also varied significantly, the youngest being recent start-ups and the oldest having been operating for almost a century.

The variance in the degree of internationalisation could not have been higher, as it ranged from no foreign operations to total dependence on foreign sales. Nevertheless, 88% of the respondents had some experience of international operations. The basic information on the companies is summarised in Table 1.

In terms of sectoral distribution, industrial companies dominated: they comprised over 50 per cent of the respondents (55%). Other major clusters included the service sector (25%), retail/wholesale (10%) and others (10%). Most of the respondents had had considerable exporting experience before participating in the export circles. Approximately one in ten (8%) had been exporting for less than five years, while the majority had been operating abroad for either 5-9 years (41%) or 10-19 years (32%), and even a history of over twenty years was not uncommon (19%).

The distribution of the key measures is summarised in Table 2. Half of the respondents had a high commitment to internationalisation, and the majority of them (73%) also had a high commitment to co-operation.[4] There was also a noticeable variance in success of export co-operation on the performance measures. It seems that the financial goals set for co-operation had not been achieved well, particularly compared with other goals. Almost half of the respondents (47%) felt that the export co-operation had not advanced their internationalisation to a noticeable degree.

The Role of Commitment in the Export Circles

The relationships between the types of commitment and success of export co-operation were studied according to the propositions presented earlier. The first step was to carry out a regression analysis. Four basic control variables were used, age of the firm, the number of employees, location, and industry. Table 3 gives the descriptives of the key variables as well as the regression models.

Proposition P1a suggested a positive relationship between the company's commitment to internationalisation and the achievement of goals set for export co-operation. As Table 3 indicates, our results gave partial support for this since the relationship between commit-

TABLE 1. Basic Information on the Respondents

	Mean	Median	S.D.	Min	Max	N
Turnover, € million	10.3	2.5	38.6	0.1	450	221
Company age	14.1	10.0	14.6	0	98	206
Number of employees	61.5	21.0	155.6	1	1500	220
Share of foreign turnover, %	32.3	23.0	30.8	0	100	216

TABLE 2. Descriptives of the Measures

	Mean	S.D.	Low (1-2)	Aver. (3)	High (4-5)	N
MEASURES OF COMMITMENT[7] . . .						
. . . to internationalisation	3.4	0.8	13%	37%	50%	215
. . . to co-operation	3.9	0.8	5%	22%	73%	218
MEASURES OF SUCCESS[8] . . .						
. . . achievement of financial goals	2.2	1.2	62%	20%	18%	161
. . . achievement of other goals	3.0	1.3	34%	27%	39%	168
. . . advancement of internationalisation	2.6	1.1	47%	34%	19%	222
. . . overall satisfaction with the export circle[9]	7.2	1.3	25%	26%	49%	224

TABLE 3. Logistic Regression on Commitment[10] and Success[11] of Export Co-Operation

	Regression Models (Exp(B) values presented)			
	S1	S2	S3	S4
Commitment to internationalisation (standardised)	1.882**	1.186	1.439*	1.225
Commitment to co-operation (standardised)	1.851**	1.994**	2.492***	1.757**
Location: Southern Finland (ref.)				
Western Finland	0.639	0.320	0.338	0.633
Eastern Finland	0.216*	0.865	1.183*	1.109
Northern Finland	0.327	0.550	0.829	0.576
Sector: Manufacturing (ref.)				
Retail/Wholesale	0.281	0.556	0.902	0.776
Services	0.739	0.564	0.232	0.334
Other	1.380	0.587	0.529	0.443
Company size (number of employees; standardised)	1.901	2.059	1.089	1.636
Company age (standardised)	0.913	1.074	0.934	0.996
Constant in Regression Model	1.048	3.791**	1.591	1.455
REGRESSION MODEL SUMMARY				
N	136	149	194	194
Model Sig.	< 0.01	< 0.05	< 0.001	< 0.05
Nagelkerke R Square	0.226	0.163	0.248	0.134
Hosmer and Lemeshow Test, Sig.	> 0.05	> 0.05	> 0.05	> 0.05
Total classification rate (%)	67.6	71.8	67.5	64.4
Classification rate for successful oriented group (%)	44.2	92.9	75.0	64.6
Classification rate for reference group (%)	82.1	30.0	58.9	64.3
Method of Analysis: Binary Logistic Regression, Enter				

***The regression coefficient is significant at the 0.001 level (2-tailed).
**The regression coefficient is significant at the 0.01 level (2-tailed).
*The regression coefficient is significant at the 0.05 level (2-tailed).

ment to internationalisation and financial goals seems to be significant. However, there was no such connection between commitment to internationalisation and the achievement of other objectives. Proposition P1b, in turn, claimed a positive relationship between commitment to internationalisation and the company's advancement in internationalisation. Our findings suggest that the impact on internationalisation was greater in the companies that were more committed to it. In other words, this proposition was supported but the relationship was not very strong.

The partial support for P1a suggests that there may be other effects that could not be tested in our study. The subjective measures of performance were constructed from perceptions of internationalisation and export co-operation. It should be borne in mind that the achievement of objectives and commitment to internationalisation are interrelated: companies with high commitment to internationalisation may set their objectives at a more ambitious level than those with lower commitment.

Proposition P2a implied that a relationship exists between a company's commitment to co-operation and the achievement of objectives set for export co-operation. This was also supported in the achievement of both quantitative and qualitative goals. According to Proposition P2b, commitment to co-operation would also be reflected in the advancement of internationalisation in the company: this was supported and the relationship was significant at the .001 level.

Our propositions were supported only in part, and thus further analysis was considered necessary. According to Welch (1992), commitment to internationalisation and to co-operation should be analysed together, and by combining these two concepts we were able to form a new four-category classification (cf. Figure 1). In order to test whether the classification logic would hold true, we compiled a new four-category measure.[5]

Furthermore, it could be said that commitment to co-operation generally and commitment to the group, i.e., the export circle in question, may differ because the role of the partners is crucial (cf. Welch & Joynt, 1987). In other words, co-operation as such might be a feasible strategy, but the partners in the export circle may not be optimal. Moreover, when there are several actors in a group, it is probable that successful co-operation requires the commitment of not one but of all the other companies involved. In order to take these aspects into consideration, we decided to add a new dimension to our analysis. For this purpose, we constructed an additional four-category measure based on the respondents' own commitment (scale 1-5) to the specific export circle and their perceptions of the partners' commitment (scale 1-5) to the same group.[6] The next step in the analysis was to carry out a regression analysis with the new measures (see Table 4).

The analysis suggests that the most committed companies had achieved the goals set for export co-operation better than those with lower levels of commitment. As Welch (1992) found, companies that were committed to both internationalisation and to co-operation achieved the best results. On the other hand, those that were committed to one or the other did not succeed any better than those with weak commitment. The findings also indicate that, in terms of success, companies' own commitment to the export circle is more significant than their perception of the commitment of others. Nevertheless, the most successful cases were the ones with the highest commitment of all types.

CONCLUSIONS AND IMPLICATIONS

The findings give empirical support to the ideas and typology put forward by Welch (1992). In other words, partner commitment seems to be related to the success of export co-operation. However, it also appears that the relationships between the key concepts are more complex and the phenomena more multifaceted than expected. For example, although commitment to both internationalisation and co-operation is apparently related to success, commitment to co-operation seems to be slightly more important. There are several possible reasons for this.

First, it is likely that a company with high commitment to internationalisation will try to advance the process by several means, not only through co-operation. These alternative

TABLE 4. Logistic Regression on Commitment[12] to and Success[13] of Export Co-Operation

	Regression Models (Exp(B) values presented)			
	S1	S2	S3	S4
General commitment to internationalisation (I) and co-operation (C)				
Weak I–Weak C (ref.)				
Strong I–Weak C	1.953	0.964	1.144	1.199
Weak I–Strong C	2.591	2.286	3.109*	2.595
Strong I–Strong C	13.911***	2.689	5.802**	3.971*
Commitment to the export circle: self (S) and perception of others (O)				
Weak S–Weak O (ref.)				
Strong S–Weak O	4.121*	8.080**	5.333**	6.005**
Weak S–Strong O	1.992	1.981	2.635	3.764*
Strong S–Strong O	4.891**	8.932***	5.987***	18.662***
Location: Southern Finland (ref.)				
Western Finland	0.637	0.404	0.947	0.608
Eastern Finland	0.159*	0.889	0.295	0.212*
Northern Finland	0.237	0.322	0.402	0.233*
Sector: Manufacturing (ref.)				
Retail/Wholesale	0.438	0.251	0.417	0.809
Services	0.821	0.618	1.090	0.904
Other	1.627	0.873	1.063	0.638
Company size (number of employees; standardised)	2.463	2.703	1.391	2.300
Company age (standardised)	0.890	1.001	0.842	0.919
Constant in Regression Model	0.142*	1.083	0.283*	0.229*
REGRESSION MODEL SUMMARY				
N	124	134	177	177
Model Sig.	< 0.01	< 0.01	< 0.001	< 0.001
Nagelkerke R Square	0.338	0.327	0.293	0.373
Hosmer and Lemeshow Test, Sig.	> 0.05	> 0.05	> 0.05	> 0.05
Total classification rate (%)	73.4	76.9	69.5	75.1
Classification rate for successful oriented group (%)	55.1	88.9	77.0	75.3
Classification rate for reference group (%)	85.3	52.3	59.7	75.0

Method of Analysis: Binary Logistic Regression, Enter

***The regression coefficient is significant at the 0.001 level (2-tailed).
**The regression coefficient is significant at the 0.01 level (2-tailed).
*The regression coefficient is significant at the 0.05 level (2-tailed).

activities compete for the same scarce resources within the company, and their success also affects the perceived importance and outcomes of export co-operation. Second, the data set included export circles in several phases–beginning, advanced and just terminated–and it is probable that well-functioning co-operation is the most visible in the early phases, thus the impact on success is also easier to observe. The findings also highlight–once again–the fact that performance is a very multifaceted and complex issue. How an export circle performs depends on numerous factors, and the

three types of commitment explain only a relatively small slice of it: this is indicated in the rather low strength of association, for example (in terms of Nagelkerke's R^2 ranging between 0.29 and 0.37 in Table 4).

There are also some limitations that should be discussed. On the one hand, the measures of the key concepts still need some elaboration. It should be noted that our measure for commitment to internationalisation excludes partner commitment to the particular market, even though the concept of market commitment has been recognised in earlier studies.

This could well have a role in export circles, as the partners might be highly committed to internationalisation, but the market selected as the focus of the circle may not be the one they would prioritise. On the other hand, so far our measure for commitment to co-operation only includes items measuring attitudinal commitment. It may be beneficial to include behavioural items in future studies.

The performance measures could also be improved. For example, the items related to other than financial objectives were not all related to internationalisation, and some were more general (e.g., interest in sharing risks, learning from partners), which might have been one reason why the relationship between the achievement of these objectives and commitment to internationalisation was not quite clear. Consequently, future studies could include more items that are specifically related to internationalisation in measures of the achievement of other, intangible objectives.

Another limitation is related to the research design. The study focused on dynamic concepts, such as commitment, which evolve over time, but the data was collected at one point in time, according to the cross-sectional research design. This bias is strengthened by the fact that the data set included companies in various phases of export co-operation, from circles that were just beginning, more advanced or already terminated. This naturally makes the comparison of partner commitment difficult, as it could be assumed to differ according to the phase of co-operation.

Consequently, we have some suggestions for further studies. First, future research should be based on a revised model that summarises the relationships between the key concepts (Figure 2). This model includes an additional variable, commitment to the export circle, which should contain items related to commitment to the particular markets and to the partners in this export circle. The feedback loop in the figure indicates the partners' changing commitment during the process.

Secondly, it could also be argued that a more dynamic research design should be utilised. We recommend researchers to try to collect longitudinal data at different phases of co-operation. In practice this would probably mean an ongoing process for two-three years,

FIGURE 2. Suggested Model for Future Studies

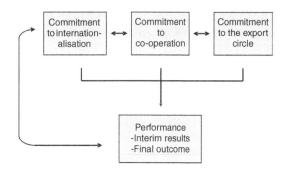

during which all co-operating firms would be contacted regularly. This would naturally require close co-operation with the semi-public organisations providing access to the companies.

All in all, the study adds to our knowledge of export promotion and its effectiveness in terms of one form of assistance. At the same time, it opens up new avenues for research, and identifies issues that need more elaboration.

NOTES

1. For a detailed description of the research process, see Nummela & Pukkinen (2004).

2. The measures for analysing management's attitude to exporting in SMEs were originally developed by Czinkota and Johnston (1983).

3. This operationalisation was used earlier by Kirpalani and Macintosh (1980) for analysing the international marketing effectiveness of technology-oriented small firms.

4. There were no differences (at the 5% risk-level) in commitment to either internationalisation or co-operation according to enterprise size (turnover, number of employees), industry, company age, company location, or starting year of export. On the other hand, the intensity of exports, in terms of regularity and share of turnover, were in positive association with commitment to internationalisation.

5. In this measure 1 = weak commitment to both internationalisation and co-operation, 2 = strong commitment to internationalisation, weak to co-operation, 3 = weak commitment to internationalisation, strong to co-operation, 4 = strong commitment to both of the concepts. The mean value of a measure was used as a cut-off point for each category, thus companies with higher-than-average commitment to internationalisation were coded into either category 2 or 4 (depending on the level

of commitment to co-operation). If the former was on the average or below-average level, the company was transferred into category 1 or 3. The same procedure was conducted in the case of commitment to co-operation.

6. The categorisation was operationalised as follows: 1 = low commitment to the export circle on the part of the respondent and the other group members, 2 = high personal commitment, low perceived commitment of others, 3 = low personal commitment, high perceived commitment of others, and 4 = high personal and other group members' commitment. In the categorisation the mean value of a measure was used as a cut-off point for each category, thus, companies with higher-than-average personal commitment to the export circle were coded into either category 2 or 4 (depending on the level of perceived commitment of other group members). If commitment to the group was on the average or below-average level, the company was transferred into either category 1 or 3. The same procedure was conducted in the case of the perceived commitment of other group members to the export circle.

7. Both measures of commitment are aggregates of separate items introduced in "Measure development"-section. A five-point Likert scale was used for each item, ranging between 1 and 5, where 1 = no commitment and 5 = strong commitment. Each aggregate measure was computed as an arithmetic mean for the group of separate items.

8. The measures of success were each single-item measures as described in "Measure development"-section. A five-point Likert scale was used for each measure, ranging between 1 and 5, where 1 = no success and 5 = great success.

9. A seven-point scale ranging from 4 to 10 was used, and recoded into three categories for the purposes of description: low (4-6), average (7), and high (8-10).

10. Commitment was assessed on two aggregate measures described in Table 2: internationalisation and co-operation on a scale from 1-5, where 1 = no commitment and 5 = strong commitment.

11. Success in export co-operation was assessed on four single-item measures described in Table 2: S1 = Satisfaction with financial goals, S2 = Satisfaction with other goals, S3 = Advancement in internationalisation, S4 = Overall satisfaction with the export circle. For the purposes of logistic regression each of the four measures was coded dichotomously: 0 (original values 1-2 for S1-S3 and 4-7,2 for S4) indicating no success and 1 (original values 3-5 for S1-S3 and 7,3-10 for S4) indicating success.

12. Commitment was assessed on the two aggregate measures described in Table 2 and in endnote 8.

13. Success in export co-operation was assessed on the four single-item measures described in Table 2 and in endnote 9.

REFERENCES

Anderson, E., & Weitz, B. (1992). The use of pledges to build and sustain commitment in distribution channels. *Journal of Marketing Research*, 29 (1), 18-34.

Babbie, E.R. (1975). *The practice of social research.* Belmont, CA: Wadsworth Publishing Co.

Björkman, I., Lindell, M., Salenius, B-M., Sevón, G., Währn, N. (1991). Creation and change of commitment to a collaborative R & D project–The case of Finnish EUREKA projects. *Publications of Swedish School of Economics and Business Administration*, Series Working Papers 219, Helsinki.

Chetty, S., & Blankenburg-Holm, D. (2000). Internationalisation of small to medium-sized manufacturing firms: A network approach. *International Business Review*, 9 (1), 77-93.

Chetty, S., & Patterson, A. (2002). Developing internationalization capability through industry groups: The experience of a telecommunications joint action group. *Journal of Strategic Marketing*, 10 (1), 69-89.

Czinkota, M.R. (1994). A national export assistance policy for new and growing businesses. *Journal of International Marketing*, 2 (1), 91-101.

Czinkota, M.R., & Johnston, W.J. (1983). Exporting: Does sales volume make a difference? *Journal of International Business Studies*, 14 (1), 147-153.

Gerbing, D.W., & Anderson, J.C. (1988). An Updated Paradigm for Scale Development Incorporating Unidimensionality and Its Assessment. *Journal of Marketing Research*, 25:2, 186-192.

Globalisation and small and medium enterprises (1997). Vol.1 Synthesis Report, Publications of the Organisation for Economic Co-operation and Development, Paris.

Johanson, J., & Vahlne, J-E. (1977). The internationalisation process of the firm–a model of knowledge development and increasing foreign market commitments. *Journal of International Business*, 8 (1), 23-32.

Kirpalani, V.H., & Macintosh, N.B. (1980). International marketing effectiveness of technology-oriented small firms. *Journal of International Business Studies*, 11 (3), 81-90.

Komppula, R. (1998). Commitment to what? Some aspects on commitment and co-operation in an issue-based network. Case North Karelia Tourism Network. *Proceedings of the 14th Industrial Marketing and Purchasing Conference*, Vol.1, Turku 3-5.9, 401-423.

Kotabe, M., & Czinkota, M.R. (1992). State government promotion of manufacturing exports: A gap analysis. *Journal of International Business Studies*, 23 (4), 637-658.

McNaughton, R.B., & Bell, J. (2001). Competing from the periphery: Export development through hard business network programmes. *Irish Marketing Review*, 14 (1), 43-54.

Murto-Koivisto, E., & Vesalainen, J. (1995). Pktyritysyhteistyön kehittyminen ja tuloksellisuus.

Seurantatutkimus yhdeksästä yhteistyöryhmästä (Development and profitability of SME co-operation. A follow-up study of nine co-operative arrangements). *Research reports of the Finnish Ministry of Trade and Industry*, No.105/1995, Helsinki.

Nummela, N. (2000). SME commitment to export co-operation. *Publications of the Turku School of Economics and Business Administration*, Series A-6:2000, Turku.

Nummela, N., & Pukkinen, T. (2004). Nopeammin, tehokkaammin ja kauemmas? Vientirenkaat kansainvälistymisen tukena (Faster, further and more effectively? Export circles as facilitators of internationalisation). *Publications of the Finnish Ministry of Trade and Industry*, Series Studies and Reports No. 1/2004, Helsinki.

Nunnally, J.C. (1978). *Psychometric theory.* 2nd edition. New York: McGraw-Hill.

Pedersen, T., & Petersen, B. (1998). Explaining gradually increasing resource commitment to a foreign market. *International Business Review*, 7 (5), 483-501.

Penrose, E. (1959). *The theory of the growth of the firm.* London: Basil Blackwell.

Philp, N.E. (1998). The export propensity of the very small enterprise (VSE). *International Small Business Journal*, 16 (4), 79-93.

Reichers, A.E. (1985). A review and reconceptualization of organizational commitment. *Academy of Management Review*, 19 (3), 465-476.

Seringhaus, F.H.R. (1986). The impact of government export marketing assistance. *International Marketing Review*, 3 (2), 55-66.

Seringhaus, F.H.R., Rosson, P.J. (1990). *Government export promotion. A global perspective.* London: Routledge.

Sevón, G. (1998). The "joints" in joint R&D ventures. In Sevón, G. & K. Kreiner (Eds.), *Constructing R&D collaboration* (pp. 65-83). Copenhagen: Copenhagen Business School Press.

Stewart, D.B., & McAuley, A. (1999). The Effects of Export Stimulation: Implications for Export Performance. *Journal of Marketing Management*, 15 (6), 505-518.

Stump, R.L., Athaide, G.A., & Axinn C.N. (1998). The Contingent Effect of the Dimensions of Export Commitment on Exporting Financial Performance: An Empirical Examination. *Journal of Global Marketing*, 12 (1), 7-25.

Weaver, K.M., Berkowitz, D., & Davies, L. (1998). Increasing the Efficiency of National Export Promotion Programs: The Case of Norwegian Exporters. *Journal of Small Business Management*, 36 (3), 1-11.

Welch, D., Welch, L., Wilkinson, I.F., & Young, L.C. (1996). Network analysis of a new export grouping scheme: The role of economic and non-economic relations. *International Journal of Research in Marketing*, 13 (5), 463-477.

Welch, D.E., Welch, L.S., Young, L.C., & Wilkinson, I.F. (1998). The importance of networks in export promotion. *Journal of International Marketing*, 6 (4), 66-82.

Welch, D., Welch, L., Wilkinson, I., & Young, L. (2000). An export grouping scheme. *Journal of Euromarketing*, 9 (2), 59-84.

Welch, L.S. (1992). The use of alliances by small firms in achieving internationalization. *Scandinavian International Business Review*, 1 (2), 21-37.

Welch, L.S., & Joynt, P. (1987). Grouping for export: An effective solution? In Rosson, P.J. & S.D. Reid (Eds.), *Managing export entry and expansion. Concepts and practice* (pp. 54-70). New York: Praeger Publishers.

doi:10.1300/J037v16n01_03

Variety in International New Ventures–
Typological Analysis and Beyond

Johanna Hallbäck
Jorma Larimo

SUMMARY. Different from the earlier research with its tendency towards a rather homogenous view on International New Ventures (INVs), the contribution of this study is the identification and understanding of the possible variety among INVs. The study aims at exploring the following: (1) Are INVs different from one another in terms of their international development? and (2) If they are, how and why are the differences manifested in these firms? The pioneering INV-framework by Oviatt and McDougall (1994) is applied, accompanied by a long-term perspective on their development and inclusion of several factors as possible agents of the differences. Based on the analysis of eight INVs, the results highlight the importance of the founding conditions, the internationalization motives and the international experience of the founding managers on the INV's development in the early phase. Both initial and subsequent development of the INVs varied with regard to geographical breadth and type of operations abroad, and the results call for a framework that goes beyond typological categorization and includes various situational factors. The implications for theory and practice are provided. doi:10.1300/J037v16n01_04 *[Article copies available for a fee from The Haworth Document Delivery Service: 1-800-HAWORTH. E-mail address: <docdelivery@haworthpress.com> Website: <http://www.HaworthPress.com> © 2006 by The Haworth Press, Inc. All rights reserved.]*

KEYWORDS. International new venture, international entrepreneurship, internationalization, born global

The research conducted during the last ten years shows new interesting patterns of international development of SMEs. Results in several studies indicate an increasing amount of young, small firms that initiate international operations soon after establishment. This phenomenon was identified in different parts of the world, especially in the last fifteen years

Johanna Hallbäck and Jorma Larimo are affiliated with the Department of Marketing, University of Vaasa.

Address correspondence to: Johanna Hallbäck, University of Vaasa, Department of Marketing, P.O. Box 700, 65101 Vaasa, Finland (E-mail: johanna.hallback@uwasa.fi or johhal@uwasa.fi).

This research project was part of a national LIIKE-programme. The authors thank the Academy of Finland, the National Technology Agency of Finland and the University of Vaasa for the financial support for this research. The authors are also thankful for the valuable comments made by Professors Kjell Grönhaug, Niina Nummela and Per Servais, as well as the anonymous reviewers and the commentators of the EIBA and Vaasa IB Conferences.

[Haworth co-indexing entry note]: "Variety in International New Ventures–Typological Analysis and Beyond." Hallbäck, Johanna, and Jorma Larimo. Co-published simultaneously in *Journal of Euromarketing* (International Business Press, an imprint of The Haworth Press, Inc.) Vol. 16, No. 1/2, 2006, pp. 37-57; and: *Contemporary Euromarketing: Entry and Operational Decision Making* (ed: Jorma Larimo) International Business Press, an imprint of The Haworth Press, Inc., 2006, pp. 37-57. Single or multiple copies of this article are available for a fee from The Haworth Document Delivery Service [1-800-HAWORTH, 9:00 a.m. - 5:00 p.m. (EST). E-mail address: docdelivery@haworthpress.com].

(OECD, 1997; Moen, 2002). The first reference to the concept of "born global" was made by McKinsey and Co. (1993) but a few references to rapid internationalization were earlier made. While these mainly referred to *exceptions* in international development among firms with for example high-tech, narrow niche or differentiation focus (Hedlund & Kverneland, 1985; Bonaccorsi, 1992), the overall reduction of the time-lag from the start-up of the firm to the start of export activity was clearly evidenced among Danish SMEs in the late 80s (Christensen, 1991). The firms confronted with the phenomenon of accelerated internationalization have been termed "born globals" (Rennie, 1993; Knight & Cavusgil, 1996), "international new ventures" (Oviatt & McDougall, 1994), "global start-ups" (Oviatt & McDougall, 1995) and "infant multinationals" (Lindqvist, 1991). While the literature on these firms is increasing fast, the variety of the terms and the inconsistency of the definitions employed are strongly present in the research (see the conceptual and methodological discussion by Coviello and Jones, 2004; and Hurmerinta-Peltomäki, 2004). In many instances, the high-technology character of the phenomenon was stressed (cf. concept high-technology start-ups), but researchers have identified increasing evidence of the phenomenon also in other industries (Madsen & Servais, 1997; Rialp, Rialp & Knight, 2005). In this study, the concept of international new ventures (INVs) is adopted to refer to firms characterized by early internationalization of business, with no industry limitations.

Several trends may be identified in the business environment as triggers for the phenomenon and new ways of internationalization among firms established after 1990s (see Knight & Cavusgil, 1996; Knight, 1997; Madsen & Servais, 1997; Shrader, Oviatt & McDougall, 2000).[1] In combination with these triggers, the inherent advantages of small firms (such as faster decision-making, quicker response time, adaptability and flexibility) increase the possibilities of internationalization among new, small firms. This type of development clearly calls for research, since creating an understanding of the firms confronted with the phenomenon, their economic role and of how to relate to them is of increasing importance.

Followed by the vast increase of research on these young, international enterprises (Rialp et al., 2005), also a research stream named international entrepreneurship has emerged (positioned somewhere between international business and entrepreneurship) (Dana, Etemad & Wright, 1999; Oviatt & McDougall, 2000). Earlier research has taken different approaches, from which the most general have been either to explore and explain the rational behind domestic versus international new ventures or to research the INVs in relation to traditional, gradually internationalizing firms (often larger firms). However, more research is needed to analyze the different types of INVs rather than to treat these as a homogenous group different only from the domestic or gradually internationalizing firms. Consequently, this paper is focused on exploring two research questions: (1) Are INVs different from one another in terms of their international development of operations? and (2) If they are, how and why are the differences manifested in these firms? Oviatt and McDougall's (1994) typological INV-framework serves as the basis for the analytical apparatus of the present research because it offers an appropriate starting point for the analysis of differences in this firm context. In order to understand the reasons behind possible differences, the features related to the founding conditions, initial internationalization motives, the early entrepreneurial and managerial characteristics as well as the core competencies of the ventures will be analyzed. The empirical analysis is based on eight illustrative cases of Finnish-based INVs. The contribution of the study is based on the identification and understanding of the variety among INVs as well as on the empirical application and development of the INV-framework by Oviatt and McDougall (1994). Despite their work being one of the pioneering and most cited ones in the INV and international entrepreneurship literature, it has rarely been applied to an empirical analysis. The application of the framework is accompanied by a dynamic, long-term view by analyzing the aspects of background characteristics of the foundation, the early-phase and subsequent international development of the firms. In the following, the article presents the theoretical background for the study, the method and results of the empirical analysis. The article concludes with a discussion of the findings in terms of their theoretical and managerial implications.

THEORETICAL BACKGROUND

Typological approach to INVs. At the same time with significant opposition to the use of types and classifications in methodological and ideological discussion, different typological approaches have characterized a considerable part of the history of social sciences, including business studies (Tiryakian, 1968). Examples in business strategy literature are that of Porter's (1980) typology on generic strategies and Miles and Snow's (1978) typology on strategic orientations/business unit strategies. Similarly, examples of typologies that emerged in international business literature are the Perlmutter's (1969) typology on overseas marketing orientations and Bartlett and Ghoshal's (1991) organizational typology on organization forms of international business. While the risk of general modeling resides in the tendency to leave marginal firms and disparities aside, the relevance of typologies in the depiction of business phenomena is arguable taking account their significance in the literature. In the INV-context, few typological approaches may be identified (Madsen, Rasmussen & Servais, 2000; Servais & Rasmussen, 2000; Bell, McNaughton & Young, 2001; Knight & Cavusgil, 2005). In the present study the approach by Oviatt and McDougall (1994) is applied for its appropriateness of the objectives of this study and significance as a pioneering study in the field. The typologies introduced in later studies[2] do not comprehensively elaborate the understanding of INVs as a heterogeneous group of firms.

Early INV-framework by Oviatt and McDougall (1994) presents an alternative explanation to firm internationalization in the situation where technology, specific industry environments and firm capabilities contribute to a faster internationalization. The framework applies a multidimensional definition of INV as "*a business organization that, from inception, seeks to derive significant competitive advantage from the use of resources and the sale of outputs in multiple countries*" (p. 49). The underlying view is value added, not assets owned. In integrating two research streams, entrepreneurship and international business, the authors fused very different research interests . . . Oviatt's interest in transaction cost theory and organizational risk and McDougall's background in strategic management, new ventures and entrepreneurship (Oviatt & McDougall, 2005a). The authors name four necessary and sufficient elements for sustainable INVs but conclude that these elements manifest in the firms in different ways as indicated by the four types of INVs (see Figure 1).

The first element of sustainable INV, *internalization of some transactions* explains the formation of all organizations; organizations form within market imperfections. The second element, *reliance on alternative governance structures* distinguishes the economic transactions of new ventures from those of other organizations. Since new ventures typically have limited resources to control assets by ownership, they have to take greater advantage of other ways of controlling such as licensing, franchising or even networking. While this may strengthen the focus on key competencies, it also brings along the risk of leakage. To separate an INV from the domestic counterpart, the authors introduce a third parameter, *the existence of foreign location advantage* in transferring resources across national borders. The most probable alternative for INVs to overcome the disadvantages brought by trade barriers as well as the lack of knowledge of the language, laws and practices and to have an advantage over local firms is the possession of tacit knowledge. Due to advances in communication technology, knowledge can be transferred and reproduced easily and with a minimal marginal cost across countries (cf. the importance of knowledge-intensive industries in the research of INVs). Finally, competitive advantage through *unique resources* differentiates a sustainable from the short-lived INV. Again, knowledge as a source of competitive advantage is emphasized. This may encounter challenges for sustainability due to the easy dissemination of knowledge and INV might rely on patents or copyrights, focus on the type of knowledge with imperfect imitability (such as management style), or uti-

FIGURE 1. Types of International New Ventures (Oviatt & McDougall, 1994: 59)

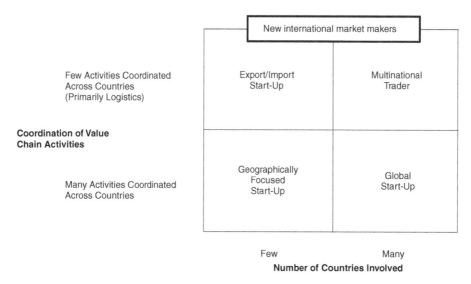

From "Toward a Theory of International New Ventures" by B.M. Oviatt and P.P. McDougall, 1994, *Journal of International Business Studies* 25(1), p.59. Copyright 1994 by the Academy of International Business. Reprinted with permission of Palgrave Macmillan.

lize the network structure with high personal relations contributing to internal control of risk.

Based on the manifestation of above elements, Oviatt and McDougall (1994) formulate four INV types which differ from one another in terms of geographical scope of business and coordination of value chain activities (based on Porter, 1980). *New international market makers* are traditional firms concentrating their international activities primarily on exporting or importing either in few (*export/import start-ups*) or multiple countries (*multinational traders*). Whereas their key value chain activities (i.e., inbound and outbound logistics) tend to be internalized, other activities usually rely on alternative governance structures with the direct investments being minimized. Their location advantage lies in discovering resource and market price imbalances between countries, and sustainability in the ability to act on emerging opportunities as well as in knowledge of markets and suppliers. *Geographically focused start-ups* typically focus on serving a special need of narrow customer group located in a particular part of the world. In the geographical area in question, the value chain activities such as technology development, human resources and produc-

tion are highly coordinated across different nations. The tacit knowledge involved in the coordination and its difficult imitation may contribute to a competitive advantage over rivals. *Global start-ups* can clearly be characterized as "born global." These firms proactively utilize the market opportunities to acquire resources and sell products globally. They are likely to be the most sustainable, since they gain competitive advantage by a combination of highly inimitable resources, by coordinating multiple business activities across borders usually through close network alliances.

After the pioneering study, Oviatt and McDougall have published several articles in the INV and international entrepreneurship research, but so far they have not empirically applied the framework. Their later findings imply that the use of licensing and network alliances may be less common than expected (Shrader et al., 2000; Shrader, 2001), as well as that the role of the founder deserves more attention in the research of INVs (Oviatt & McDougall, 1995). Finally, striving to be more consistent with the emphasis of the entrepreneurship discipline on opportunity recognition, the recent definition of international entrepreneurship by Oviatt and McDougall (2005b) goes beyond new venture internationalization by interpreting it in terms of "discovery, enactment, evaluation, and exploitation of opportunities–across national borders–to create future goods and services."

A rapidly developing research trend began to rise around the phenomenon of accelerated internationalization after the mid 1990s (see Rialp et al., 2005). In spite of the emphasis on the variety of INVs in the pioneering framework as well as a few other studies, the majority of later inquiries have often treated INVs as more homogenous group in identifying their key characteristics in individual, organizational and environment/industry-level. While the framework of Oviatt and McDougall is conceptualized at the firm-level, the later studies have stressed the role of the entrepreneur and management team for explaining INVs (as will be discussed below). In their recent framework, for example, Jones and Coviello (2005) add the individual-level (entrepreneur) as a variable that influences the behavior and the internationalization process of INVs. Earlier research has placed only little attention to the wider understanding of the founding conditions of the new ventures as possible explanation behind internationalization.

Founding conditions refer to situational factors in the founding phase and the first operational years of the business, i.e., to the background of the business idea, the internationalization rate of the industry, as well as the state of development and knowledge- and technology intensity of the industry. Additionally, the characteristics of the founders and the early management are important internal conditions at the founding phase. In prior research, some implications of the founding phase entrepreneurial team, the resources and the technology for new venture survival in general have been reported (see, e.g., Aspelund, Berg-Utby & Skjevdal, 2005). However, earlier research has placed minor attention on these conditions in the context of new venture internationalization.

Regarding the business idea for the new venture, different alternatives may be identified (cf. the different entry wedges by Vesper, 1990). Business ideas stemming from innovation, R&D project, franchising, management-buyout or bankrupt of former employer are likely to determine different trajectories of the venture development. Similarly, the venture established in an industry characterized by international-level networks and high internationalization rate may develop differently from the one established in an industry with more local networks in inward and outward operations. Also ventures entering competition in a different state of the industry development (at its introduction, growth, maturity or decline phase) have different kind of business environments to cope with. Finally, the technology-level and knowledge-intensity of the industry may impose different types of internationalization paths. Vast majority of INV research has focused on the high-technology and knowledge-intensive fields, often assuming a stronger link between the phenomenon and these particular industries (e.g., Burgel & Murray, 2000; Coviello & Munro, 1995, 1997; Crick & Jones, 2000; Jones, 1999; Lindqvist, 1991). However, a growing number of later studies concentrated on other industries or had no industry limitations at all (e.g., Knight, 2000; Larimo & Pulkkinen, 2002; Madsen & Servais, 1997; Moen, 2002) and the results imply the increase of INVs both in manufacturing and service industries (Larimo & Pulkkinen, 2002), as well as in industries of both high and low knowledge-intensity (Knight, Bell & McNaughton, 2001). Little attention was paid so far to understanding the findings of these analyses. Going further on situational conditions, in the context of start-up growth, the results on metal-based manufacturing and business service SMEs suggest that the high-growth firms differ from the low-growth firms in their motivations for start-up (Littunen & Tohmo, 2003). Internationalization can be seen a strategy for firm growth and the firms pursuing rapid international growth may be expected to differ from local new ventures in their motivations regarding start-up establishment as well as internationalization.

Entrepreneur(s) and early management of INVs have been characterized in several studies by strong international orientation. The issue was investigated through various aspects and concepts. The findings suggest the managers of INVs to be growth-oriented with a strong international vision, emphasize proactive approach and high commitment to international markets as well as responsiveness to customers' needs, and to possess high competence in conducting international marketing activities (Rennie, 1993; Oviatt & McDougall, 1995; Knight, 1997; Nummela, Saarenketo & Puumalainen, 2004). For the new venture to deepen its international behavior, the ability to diffuse the international orientation throughout the organization is likely to become essential. Many authors also argue the earlier international experience and contacts of these decision-makers to be the crucial driving forces of accelerated internationalization and global mindset (e.g., Madsen & Servais, 1997; Oviatt & McDougall, 1995, 1997; Harveston et al., 2000; Pulkkinen, 2006). Oviatt and McDougall (1994) acknowledge the internationally experienced founding team as the most common condition for utilizing the network relationship for the protection of unique knowledge. Nevertheless, the research on this issue in INV context lacks profoundness and unified findings. INV as a *firm* is likely to go international before even having gained experience on the domestic market, and due to its small size it may lack financial resources to acquire external professional advice. The individual-level international experience gained for example through previous assignments increase the knowledge, abilities and the courage in international markets and may significantly affect the ability to formulate and implement strategies at international level. The experience in a similar industry may explain why for example the foreign sales do not necessarily start with just a few occasional export orders but are more regular from the beginning.

Firm-level characteristics refer to the resources, competencies and the competitive advantages as well as the market and operation behavior of INVs. In line with the INV-framework, later findings indicate the core resources of an INV to be often intangible and knowledge-intensive with the competitive advantage deriving from the unique knowledge held by the firm's key personnel (Oviatt & McDougall, 1997; Rialp et al., 2005). These firms are argued to compete on differentiated products with regard to quality and value created through innovative technology, product design (Rennie, 1993; Knight, 1997) or marketing, with these usually exceeding the importance of price

in the competitiveness. Knight and Cavusgil (2005) found that INVs use differentiating, cost leadership as well as focus strategies, and that employing an appropriate set of the three strategies was likely to lead to higher performance abroad. INVs may differ from other types of SMEs especially displaying a higher technological advantage (ibid., Moen, 2002; Larimo & Pulkkinen, 2002). Based on the literature review, Rialp, Rialp and Knight (2005) also argue that the use of personal and business networks, market knowledge, the narrow customer groups with close relationships, and the flexibility towards changing external conditions are critical for INVs.

Previous research indicates INVs to target global niche markets (Rennie, 1993; McDougall, Shane & Oviatt, 1994; Knight, 1997; Moen, 2002). Employing such strategy, the resources can be devoted to serving markets in which the firm has special competence and to be more efficient than the competitors, which operate on broader markets. INVs are likely to expand simultaneously into several new countries (Lindqvist, 1991; Crick & Jones, 2000; Shrader et al., 2000), most commonly due to the niche strategy (Burgel & Murray, 2002; Moen, 2002). The essence of rapid internationalization is managing the risks of foreign entries in the light of the resource-restrictions of the firm as well as ensuring flexibility in the changing market conditions (Shrader et al., 2000). The most important entry modes are argued to be exporting through independent distributors and agents and direct exporting to end-customers (Lindqvist, 1991; Knight, 1997; Burgel & Murray, 2000; Burgel, Murray, Fier & Licht, 2000). The risk of technological leakage, the need to offer service close to the customer, or the high growth objectives may determine the use of firm-owned channels such as subsidiary, especially among medium-sized INVs (Lindqvist, 1991; Crick & Jones, 2000; Shrader et al., 2000). Besides that, the combination of different modes and use of co-operative arrangements has found to be significant (Crick & Jones, 2000), due to the limited possibilities for high investments, and justified by the need to acquire supplementary skills (Oviatt & McDougall, 1995). The use of modes such as R&D joint ventures or licensing has been linked to high technology-level, substantial R&D efforts and short product life cycles (Lindqvist, 1991; Crick & Jones, 2000).

In the empirical part, the international development of the chosen firms will be analyzed applying the INV-framework by Oviatt and McDougall (1994) and taking into consideration the founding conditions, the initial internationalization motives and the individual- and firm-level factors as possible agents for development.

METHOD

The research methodology used in this study is a multiple case study of eight INVs. A comparative case-study approach and descriptive analysis within themes are adopted for the empirical data. Oviatt and McDougall (1997) suggest the key defining dimension of INVs to be the significant percentage of foreign sales, since obtaining international sales is likely to be more challenging than obtaining international inputs and most of the other international dimensions are usually associated with the initiation of sales (see also Lindqvist, 1991; Knight, 1997; Harveston et al., 2000). Altogether, the firms were required to meet the following criteria: (1) International sales three years after establishment to weight at least 25% of the total sales; (2) Growth tendency in international sales, being at least 50% of the total sales in 2001; (3) Sufficient number of foreign countries in which the firms have sales (at least six); (4) Firm establishment after 1985 (an earlier date would impede on the data collection of the early international development of the firm); (5) The majority of the selected firms is not owned by any single larger Finnish or foreign group (cf. independency of operations and decision-making).

Identifying the case firms started by screening the firms that participated in a large mail survey conducted in 2001-2002. Among 486 exporting Finnish SMEs only 25 firms fulfilled the above criteria. To further identify the case firms, the earlier surveys made by other authors and articles in Finnish business magazines were used. On a closer look, eight INVs representing different manufacturing industries were selected as appropriate for the empirical

study. In addition to the survey questionnaire, the information from the firms was collected through personal contacts by phone and e-mail using a semi-structured questionnaire as well as through documentary information and archival records (firm reports, newspaper and journal articles, also Larimo, 2003). The basic information of the selected firms is presented in Table 1. All of these sell products to industrial customers, except for Finnlamelli which has also end-consumers.

The INV-framework by Oviatt and McDougall (1994) is concerned with start-ups, while the case firms are established between 1988 and 1997, thus having an age range between 6 and 15. Consequently, as compared to the original framework, we have applied a more dynamic view, by first looking into the firm activities within the first six years of existence and then their subsequent development (the limit of six years has been used to define new venture also by Shrader et al., 2000). Finally, the fact that Oviatt and McDougall (1994) offer no operationalization of the typology impedes its application. The criteria used in this study are presented in the following.

TYPOLOGICAL ANALYSIS AND THE RESULTS BEYOND

The individual description of the case firms in terms of venture establishment, founders and early management as well as venture competitiveness are presented in Appendix 1.

Reviewing the results of the development of international operations. In applying the typology, we have used two main classification criteria: (1) The international coordination of value chain activities: in addition to sales activities (including own export, marketing co-operation, sales subsidiaries), less or more than two of the other value chain activities (purchasing, manufacturing, R&D activity, financing) coordinated across countries; and (2) The number of countries with value chain activities: sales activities in less or more than 20 countries, level of market concentration higher or lower than 60% and number of countries with activities other than sales. (For information used in the classification, see Appendix 2.) The development within first

TABLE 1. Basic Information on the Case Firms

Firm name	Founded	Main products	Number of personnel[1]	Turnover[1]	Turnover change[4]	Starting year of export	Share of exports[1]
Finnlamelli	1996	Laminated log houses	76	12,9 Meur	47,4%	1996	60%[3]
Logset	1992	Light forest machines	50	12 Meur	18,9%	1992	75%
Stick Tech	1997	Fiber reinforcements	15	0,4 Meur[2]	328,6%	1999	58%[3]
Vacon	1993	Frequency converters	426	97,5 Meur	120,1%	1995	82%[3]
Biohit	1988	Liquid handling, diagnostic tests	303	25,4 Meur	23,6%	1990	97%
Selka-Line	1992	Public space furniture	28	4,1 Meur	22,0%	1992	50%
Cross Wrap	1994	Square bale wrapping systems	13	1,4 Meur	50,0%	1994	95%
Nowo	1994	Machinery for textile industry	13	2,4 Meur	42,9%	1996	98%

Note. [1]in 2002; [2]in 2001; [3]in 2001-2002, [4]growth of turnover between 1999-2002, except for Stick Tech and Cross Wrap between 1999-2001

six years implies the initial positioning in the typology, whereas the development of firms within the typology after six years of operation is also illustrated (see Figure 2). In many respects the INV-framework and its arguments are well suitable for the characteristics of a small open economy such as Finland. This is especially valid considering the emphasis on unique knowledge and knowledge-intensity as a source of competitiveness both in the employed theory and in the Finnish business environment. The global competitiveness of the Finnish firms is increasingly relying on unique knowledge and in many cases advances on high-technology. In relation to the population, only in Japan, Germany and USA are more patent applications made than in Finland, which also receives world's most numerous patent applications on high-technology (National Board of Patents and Registration of Finland, 2002).

Looking at the operations within the first six years of the firms' existence, except for the export start-up and one multinational trader, six of them had, in addition to sales, also foreign supply partners right from the beginning. Seven firms had also conducted international R&D co-operation with customers, suppliers or other partners. This emerged characteristic especially of global and geographically focused cases. Instead in the multinational trader cases the operations in marketing, sales and logistics were coordinated internationally while the majority of inward operations were especially at start-up phase handled within the domestic market. As an example, Cross Wrap

was able to rapidly initiate sales in Europe, USA, Asia and Middle-East. However, while 75% of its production was outsourced, no foreign sub-contractors were used. Global and two geographically focused start-ups had brand label and/or Original Equipment Manufacturer (OEM)-customers, and especially in the global start-ups they had a significant role in the marketing and to some extent in the product development. The marketing of products was efficiently coordinated at international level right from the start. Not only traditional exports, but also different relationships were utilized and, for example, through distributor partners, joint venture partners, OEM-customers, and licensing (in Biohit), the firms were able to gain visibility and sales volume in many countries faster than would have been possible alone.

Only three of the firms had, until 2002, invested in their own sales subsidiaries. Furthermore, none of the firms had made its own manufacturing unit investments abroad.[3] In many firms outsourcing played a critical role in the production. In two geographically focused start-ups a large part of the production was outsourced to the most efficient subcontractors in different locations of the world, while in other cases the production was largely concentrated in the hands of domestic subcontractors. All these results support Oviatt and McDougall's (1994) notion of usage of alternative governance structures and hybrid structures of ownership and control as distinctive characteristic of new ventures. While Oviatt and McDougall considered the licensing, fran-

FIGURE 2. The Positioning of Case Firms in the INV-Typology (Arrows Imply the Development After Six Years of Foundation)

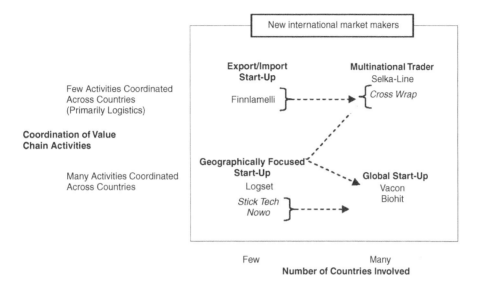

chising and networking as important, the case results indicate the informal networking, R&D and marketing co-operation with various partners as well as outsourcing to be more poignant in illustrating the ways of operation in most of these INVs. Instead the more formal networking, alliances and JVs are typical in early years only in the global new ventures.

In line with the typology, the results on market strategies suggest that despite that all firms had sales in very different locations, the differences were structured in terms of geographical diversification vs. concentration. In five firms the majority of the sales was concentrated on a few key markets (varying from 55 to 75% of all sales). In global player and multinational trader cases there was more diversification (e.g., in the multinational trader the three main markets formed 35% of foreign sales). Notable is that the INV-typology does not elaborate the physic or psychic distance of the markets that the INV operates in. Later studies have emphasized the importance of differentiating between operations on for example the home continent from those on other continents in order to illustrate the in-

ternational or global level of activities (e.g., Gabrielsson, Sasi & Darling, 2004). All the case firms operated both on and outside the European continent, but the commitment in these entries and later operations varied. The entry in the market outside the home continent was carried out instantly in the establishment year in the case of most of the firms, except two that were characterized as geographically focused players in the first years of their existence.

Further results on the varieties in internal and external characteristics. Looking at the findings on background characteristics of the venture foundation and the early management, the industries involved, the initial internationalization motives, as well as the core competencies and the unique resources of the firms, allows us to go beyond the typological results and reveal some influence mechanisms behind the development paths.

Founding conditions. The founding conditions prove to be rather determinant for the early development of the ventures and also to imply a clear connection to instant international operations. However, the variety does

not often fall in line with the typological results. In three INVs (representing different
types) the foundation stems from inventions
made by the founder(s). In turn, the background of two geographically focused start-ups
and one multinational trader stems from the
bankruptcy of the former employer of founders and managers in the same field. Of these
firms, in the other geographically focused
start-up the era of product and technology development with new subcontractors and partners was initiated and new product designs
were introduced soon after establishment
while on the other a new service and product
category was added. In the later development
of the ventures, the findings imply that those
having innovation or strong R&D emphasis in
the background of their founding (four such
firms were identified) were more likely to develop into a global player. Biohit was characterized by global operations very soon after
founding, while the other three companies
were heading towards global type of ventures
in their later phases of development. The two
remaining companies exhibit, in spite of their
very different international development, slightly
similar foundation background. While the export start-up was founded by the former employees of a company in the field as it was sold
and merged to a bigger corporation, the foundation of the global start-up traces back to a
change in strategy of the former employer of
the founders, as the entered business line was
moved to another location.

In conclusion, none of the ventures were set
up from scratch in the sense that the founders
had some type of international networks established around the business idea. While in some
cases these networks stemmed from research
activity, in the other the networks were already partly established in the sales and/or
purchasing side of their business. In most of
the cases these latter types of relationships
were based on the informal contacts established during the former work, but for example, in Logset they were more formally passed
on from the former company in the buyout. In
some other cases, where the former employer
was from the same field and continued its
business, establishing new contacts was more
crucial.

Regarding the findings on the nature of the
industry, the global start-ups as well as two
geographically focused INVs were characterized by extremely international networks,
whereas the networks in the industry of the export start-up were rather domestic. This finding
indicates a connection with the international
level coordination of value chain activities.
Generally, the firms under scrutiny are operating on global niche markets, having a special
type of products for the markets where the
potential is narrowly spread across several
countries. Three of the firms (global and two
geographically-focused start-ups) were established in an industry characterized by extreme
technology intensity, whereas two firms (export start-up and multinational trader) entered
more traditional industries (see also results of
product characteristics). The lower technology level of the industry was associated with
lower coordination of inbound and outbound
activities across countries both in the first
years and later phases of their development.
Finally, one firm was established within an industry at its mature phase. This geographically
focused start-up had in later years developed
into a global player. The maturing phase of the
industry may partly explain the need for global
expansion. Four of the firms, all characterized
by different initial (and partly later) type of development were established in an industry at
its growth phase. Two firms, sharing many
similarities, entered the industry by pioneering
in a new growth segment while the last firm
part of our case studies entered the industry in
its introduction state. These three firms, initially characterized by different types of development of international operations, were
all in later phase representative of the global
player in the typology.

*Characteristics of the entrepreneur(s) and
early management.* The founding conditions
and characteristics of the entrepreneurs and
early management are in all cases interlinked
and these backgrounds underline similarities
as well as differences. In five of the firms under scrutiny, the international orientation was
high, and in two global players it can be regarded as extremely high. The previous *industry* experience and the established contacts of
the founders and early management were extremely high in four and rather high in three

cases. Even in the case of the eighth firm, the founder had worked in the same field, but only for a shorter period. On a closer look, the industry experiences differ between firms in their functional areas, a finding which may be considered as an important factor behind certain–and different–types of development paths of the firms. Illustrative of this point is Stick Tech, a firm in which the industry experience was concentrated mainly on the R&D functions in the industry, whereas conducting marketing operations in the specific industry was almost an unknown area to the firm's personnel. The variety among cases was also rather strong, regarding the previous international experience of the focal actors. In all cases there was some earlier experience from working in international assignments home or abroad, from studying abroad or in some cases from the research field at international level. However, this experience varied significantly with regard to duration and number of persons involved. When considering both industry and international experience, the size of the enterprise and especially the founder/management team thus needs to be taken into account. Moreover, the nature of the key person's international experience in terms of its functional area and industry appears rather decisive to the firm's international development. In some cases the founders were former managers of multinational company in the same industry and thus familiar with the international business in the field. In other cases, such as one geographically focused player, the managers were also internationally experienced, but in different fields of business. In this case, the marketing side of the new enterprise was the primary problem due to the lack of beneficial experience and established sales contacts abroad. Different than the aforementioned, in firms with higher international industry experience, the management had established international customer relations and other contacts which helped the starting phase of international sales. In their case, of greater concern was to keep up with the technology and the product development in their respective industry.

Internationalization motives. While the founding conditions and entrepreneurial and early management characteristics reflect some of the reasons behind internationalization, the impact of other types of factors in the initiation of international operations in the selected firms is analyzed in the following, so that to gain a deeper understanding of the differences in internationalization (see Table 2). Some of the motives may be regarded as more proactive, while others imply more reactive behavior towards changes in the environment. In the case ventures both types of motives were considered to be important for initial internationalization. Except for an export start-up, the fact that the firm had never considered Finland as the only market was rather strongly supported by the managers. The non-exclusive view on the home market supports the finding that firm managers shared a global orientation towards business. Additionally, the management's prior international experience and interest towards internationalization, as well as the inadequate domestic demand were rather strong motives in all cases. The enquiries received from the foreign customers played an important role especially in the ventures that were focused on fewer countries.

The subsidies received for international operations, the contacts from export supporting organizations or the lack of subcontractors in the home market did not generally impact on the decision to initiate international operations. On the other hand, the access to competitive foreign subcontractors was an important internationalization motive only for two geographically focused INVs, which both have carried out major international sourcing operations (40-50%) from the beginning. The connection between the international development and the variation of the remaining motives was more difficult to asses. The motives emphasized by the export start-up indicated a rather reactive behavior, whereas some reasons underlined as important by other types of INVs (e.g., managers' international experience and view on their respective market area) did not have a major impact on its internationalization decisions. The motives of one geographically focused INV and of one multinational trader were rather similar to the export start-up, with the notable exception that the emphasis was put on the global view on the market, while the competition on the home market was rendered unimportant. In conclusion, while some simi-

TABLE 2. Internal and External Varieties of Eight Finnish INVs

NAME OF THE FIRM	Finn-lamelli	Cross Wrap	Selka-Line	Logset	Stick Tech	Nowo	Vacon	Biohit
INV-TYPE AT START-UP	Export Start-Up	Multinational Start-Up		Geographically Focused Start-Up			Global Start-Up	
FOUNDATION								
Innovation/R&D-project	−	++	−	−	++	+	−	++
Bankrupt/MBO	−	−	++	++	−	++	−	−
Within change of former employer	++	−	−	−	−	−	++	++
FOUNDER(S) & MGM								
International orientation	+/−	+	+	+	+	+	++	++
International experience	+/−	+/−	+/−	+	+	+	++	++
Industry experience	++	+	+/−	++	+	+	++	++
Entrepreneur experience								
INDUSTRY								
International industry networks	−	+	+	++	++	+	++	++
High-technology	+/−	+	−	+	++	++	++	+
Industry state of development	Growth	Introduct.	Growth	Growth	Growth[4]	Maturity	Growth	Growth[4]
MOTIVES FOR INITIATING INTERNATIONALIZATION								
Int'lization of customer	+	+/−	−	−	−	++	+/−	−
Int'lization of competitor	+	++	−	+	−	++	+/−	−
Int'l success of competitors	++	+/−	−	+	−	+/−	−	−
MgM's interest in int'lization	++	+	++	++	+	++	−	++
MgM's int'nal experience	+/−	+	+/−	++	+	++	+	++
Competitive foreign subcontractors	−	−	−	+	−	+	−	−
Inadequate domestic demand	+	+	++	+	++	++	++	++
Increasing domestic competition	++	−	+	+	−	+/−	−	−
Foreign enquiry	++	+	+/−	+	++	++	−	+/−
Lack of domestic subcontractors	−	−	−	−	−	+/−	−	−
Export/int'lization subsidies	−	−	+	+/−	+/−	−	−	−
The company has never considered its home market as the only market	+/−	++	++	+	++	++	++	++
PRODUCT								
Product-service/software/education	+/−	+	−	+	++	++	++	+
Physical product	++	++	++	++	+	++	+	+
High-technology (R&D costs)	+/−	++	+/−	+	++	+/−	++	++
CORE COMPETENCE & COMPETITIVENESS								
Role of patents	−	++	+/−	+/−	++	++	−	++
Customer-adaptation	+	+	+	+	+/−	+	++	+/−
Product-based differentiation	+/−	+	+	+/−	++	++	+/−	++
Marketing-based differentiation	−	+	++	+/−	++	++	+	++
Global niche strategy	+	+	+	+	++	++	+	++
CO-OPERATION								
Role of strategic alliances	+/−	+	+/−	+	++	+	++	++
Role of outsourcing	+/−	++	+	++	+	++	++	+
Role of OEM/Brand Label partners	−	−	−	−	+	+	−	++	+
MAJORITY OWNERSHIP	Eight persons	Family-owned	Family-owned	Three founders	Capital investors[3]	Family-owned	Capital investors[1]	Family-owned[2]

Note. ++ = extremely characteristic/very high role; + = characteristic/high role; +/− = moderately characteristic/limited role; − = not present/no role
[1]Public limited company since 2000, management holds about 10% ownership, 80% of employees hold an ownership share.
[2]Public limited company since 1999.
[3]Minority owned by private persons, including one firm manager.
[4]Growth segment in rather mature industry.

larities were found in the motives behind all ventures, there was also place for differences. The variances displayed did not often fall in line with the INV-typology. Nevertheless, the differences in the motives between the two opposite ventures (export vs. global start-ups) reveal some links between the motivational backgrounds and international development.

Product-related characteristics. The analysis of their competitiveness and resources suggest that in many of the firms the sustainability is ensured by patent rights protecting the unique knowledge on technology, production method, design or alike. Six of the firms possessed a few or several patents and one firm had design and utility model protections. In four firms the patented innovations played a significant role in their overall competitiveness. In general, there was rather great emphasis on the R&D operations in all studied INVs, reflecting the salience of high-technology features among them. However, when looking at the R&D expenditure share of turnover in 2000-2002, five firms may be characterized as high-tech and two as more low-tech oriented. The latter firms were characterized by more home-oriented coordination of activities. These results, especially the role of patents support Oviatt and McDougall's (1994) emphasis on the private knowledge, and not the scale, as the source of foreign location advantage and unique resources. With great mobility, knowledge-intensive services and products are advantageous to internationalization. Oviatt and McDougall (1994) argue this to be valid in the case of ventures offering software-components. In general, the results of this study indicate the degree of *mobility* of the offering to be somewhat consequential to the level of international operations. The global players display a greater mobility in offerings while the export start-up is offering the less mobile products, although still based on high knowledge in production technology. However, the variety in the role of software was found greater. None of the firms offer purely software products. While some firms have products with software as their key component (e.g., Vacon), others offer products that are less mobile (e.g., Finnlamelli). Finally, in some cases the mobile component of the product consists of education or other type of service (e.g., Stick Tech) along with the product.

The uniqueness of the INVs either in their pioneering position in the industry[4] or success in internationalization[5] and growth[6] is reflected in the numerous awards they were conferred. Despite common features the firms have achieved their growth in a variety of ways (see Table 2).

CONCLUSIONS

The aim of this study was to understand the possible heterogeneity among INVs by exploring two research questions: (1) Are INVs different from one another in terms of their in-

ternational development? and (2) If they are, how and why the differences are manifested in these firms? For this purpose, the study has analyzed the development paths of eight INVs from different manufacturing industries, monitoring them from their inception until to their current stage and assessing the founding conditions (background of foundation idea, industry nature), the founders and management team, initial internationalization motives and core competencies as possible agents for the differences in their international development. This study was among the first ones to offer an empirical application of the widely-cited[7] INV-framework by Oviatt and McDougall (1994). In addition to concretization of the framework, it is accompanied by a long-term perspective to the analysis.

Looking at the operations and market strategies within the first six years of existence, the firms were classified into four different types. The ventures under scrutiny differed significantly from another in their operations in terms of the value chain activity types and level of commitment employed in the international level. Despite that all firms had activities in many different locations, the differences in the market strategies were structured in terms of geographical diversification vs. concentration. When studying their later evolution, no typical paths of development could be identified. The classification of ventures into types as suggested by Oviatt and McDougall (1994) was somewhat complex, due to the natural dynamism in the organizational and operational behaviour. Indeed, the fast pace of development and the differences in both early and later changes in at least some of these firms suggest that, as compared to the typology in the early INV-framework, a more dynamic theory for analyzing the different development paths of INVs is needed.

Going beyond typological analysis in using the theoretical description provided by Oviatt and McDougall's framework, the present study aimed to find which factors impact on the coordination of value chain activities on international level. The results imply some similarities with regard to the background of foundation (often linked to changes in another firm), the high international orientation and previous industry experience of the founders and management, the nature of the product or service market (globally spread niche markets targeted with highly special offerings), and finally, the high use of patent rights to ensure the sustainability by protecting the knowledge on technology, production method, design or alike. However, further analysis identifies various influential factors behind international development. From the resource-perspective, the previous international experience varied significantly with regard to duration and number of persons involved. Besides that, the industry experience was found consequentially different with regard to functional areas. Although the background of foundation was often linked to change in another firm, some differences could be identified as well. The founding stemming from innovation or intensive R&D project indicated a more global development of all operations, especially in later phases of the firm. While some similarities were found in the motives for initiating international operations behind most ventures (management's international experience and interest towards internationalization, management's view on the venture's market area, inadequate domestic demand and enquiry from abroad as important motives, whilst subsidies received for international operations or lack of subcontractors in the home market as less important motives), there was also a significant variance among the triggering motives for the internationalization of the analyzed enterprises. Overall, this study identified the founding conditions of the venture (background of the foundation idea, internationalization and technology level of the industry entered), the entrepreneur and the management team characteristics (especially degree and functional area of the international industry experience), the nature of the initial internationalization motives (whether they were proactive vs. reactive and backward vs. forward oriented), and degree of mobility of the venture's offering as important influencing factors on the international firm-level development of the value chain activities. Although these characteristics were major determinants of development of the ventures and implied a clear connection to their internationalization behavior, the variances displayed (especially in the founding conditions and initial international-

ization motives) did not often fall in line with the typology. These results suggests that to grasp the complexity of the phenomenon–the different development paths and speed of changes in the development–the theoretical framework for INVs needs to go beyond typological categorization and include the various situational factors and influence mechanisms behind such level of complexity.

When dividing the firms in terms of the number of countries in which they are present, Oviatt and McDougall (1994) ignore the (physic and psychic) distance of the markets that the INVs operate in. As suggested by the results of this study, the INVs display a great difference from another in terms of geographical dispersion of the activities. To identify such differences, it is important to differentiate between firms operating in close markets and home continent and those operating in more distant markets (see Servais & Rasmussen, 2000; Gabrielsson et al., 2004). This study used both the number of countries and level of concentration into certain markets as indicators of the geographical expansion of the firms. The findings imply that except for one firm, the three first entries by INVs were into other European countries. Although all the firms expanded their operations also into other continents, in later phases only two global start-ups generated more than 25% of their sales from outside Europe.

Finally, assessing the usability of the framework provided, it can be noted that it has four dimensions. The first two are concerned with all new ventures (domestic and international), while the latter two especially with international new ventures. More emphasis and tools to analyze the last two dimensions, i.e., source of foreign location advantage and unique resources need to be developed. The framework does not elaborate why the new venture is either domestic or international, i.e., why there is a foreign location advantage, and more importantly why this advantage is seen and utilized varyingly as illustrated by the differences in the international operations, market entries and intensity of international activity of the INVs. For these factors to be understood, the research should identify the various influence mechanisms and their dynamics. For this purpose, this study has identified several important situational factors in the industry-, firm- and individual level in both the foundation and subsequent phases of the venture development. The early framework is conceptualized at the firm-level, but in this study it is argued that in the case of small new firms, the question to be considered is "why *entrepreneurs and venture managers* see the advantage in foreign markets."

With regard to the managerial implications of this contribution, the growth of turnover and financial performance (such as annual net profit) varied considerably in the case firms. While this study revealed no single success formula for the market or operation modes, some important notes may be highlighted when looking at the highest performing ventures. Entry into new countries is in these firms based on earlier contacts of the firm managers (especially in the first entries) as well as on strategic issues rather than on "psychic proximity" (also Lindqvist, 1991; Crick & Jones, 2000). Along with the sales potential, also the R&D and marketing co-operation prospects in the markets play an important role in the entry decisions. The so called lead markets such as USA, Japan and Germany are of strategic importance to many knowledge-intensive INVs (see also Bell et al. 2001). In the case of a new venture with limited resources, the entry into these markets and the realization of their potential (in terms of sales and product development) might be best executed using various parallel sales channels and partners such as local distributors and OEM- and Brand Label-customers that have a strong presence in the market. The case firms were all focused on serving special niche markets that were narrowly spread across countries. While the operations were often based on one core product and/or technology idea, the range of offerings was widened through different modifications and adaptations of the core package (for example, through software). Regarding the policy implications, the subsidies received for export operations seem less relevant triggers for internationalization of new ventures. The variety of international entry and expansion operations calls for a more versatile assistance from the government.

FUTURE RESEARCH AVENUES

There are several possible ways to deepen the research agenda focusing on INVs. First, a more theoretical elaboration of the INV-concept and its related concepts is needed in order to unify the research field. The results discussed here highlight the importance of developing conceptually more sophisticated yet flexible definition of INVs, the one which includes the INVs' differences in the international level of value chain activities (Porter, 1980) (not limiting only to primary activities such as outward operations and logistics, but also procurement, R&D, financing and other support activities) and the geographical dispersion of these activities, as well as which takes a wider time horizon to incorporate and differentiate between the pre-founding, early and subsequent internationalization phases of the INV. Also the inclusion of the industry internationalization rate into the definition might serve some comparative purposes. However, some authors have claimed that it might prove difficult to employ, since many INVs are in fact operating in many industries at the same time.

Second, this study analyzed eight firms giving descriptive information of the internationalization paths of these INVs; a further step would entail a bigger sample size of the firms, so that to offer further information and more generalizable results about the development paths and difference in INVs as well as their impact to the INV-theory.

A third possible research avenue is a study of the impact of the industry. Different industries (such as manufacturing vs. service sectors, low vs. high-tech industries) might impact on the development paths of firms and results of the application of the INV-theory. Originating from different field of the industry and both high and low/medium technological industries, the case firms of the present study allow some research findings on this issue. However, all the analyzed firms were from the manufacturing sector so in the future the service firms could also be included in the analysis. Indeed, the INV and international entrepreneurship research has been argued to suffer from the lack of service sector research (Coviello & Jones, 2004).

Fourth, already in an early INV-framework (Oviatt & McDougall, 1994), the emphasis was put on controlling assets through alternative governance structures and networks, instead of owning them. The present research showed that controlling marketing, manufacturing and technology development through networks and different forms of co-operation (such as alliances, joint venture partners, OEM-partners and subcontractors) is an evident attribute of many INVs. However, for future research, as an interesting challenge remains to investigate the optimum formation of the INV organization (i.e., which resources are best utilized with the ownership and which resources through networking?).

Finally, the link to performance is of interest to a wide audience among researchers and practitioners. In the context of INVs, once internationalized the successful management of high growth sets a major challenge and has been less investigated. Knight and Cavusgil (2005) found faster internationalization to correlate with better ultimate performance in foreign markets. On the other hand, in the study by Oviatt and McDougall (1995), three out of twelve INVs have failed, one was in the process of ceasing operations, and an additional three were acquired by larger corporations. Similar stories exist in, for example, many high-tech fields such as ICT, which also are strongly characterized by increase in globalization and INVs. Consequently, it might be fruitful to investigate the factors that have contributed to successful international development and also to consider the factors that may have inhibited the sustainable development of some firms. In the previous research, the success has been defined differently and with different accuracy, depending on the approach. As the research has typically focused on successful internationalization, the success has often been linked to growth of percentual foreign sales, while other elements of success have been rather neglected.

easier access to means of internationalization (knowledge, technology, tools, facilitating institutions) and wider range of supporting institutions (within, e.g., European Union) for internationalization of business and cooperation of SMEs, increased international financing opportunities, and trend towards international networks.

2. Madsen et al. (2000) suggest a typology that classifies firms and differentiates born globals from other types of exporters (such as experimental and traditionally evolved exporters). In a similar vein, Bell et al. (2001) propose a classification of international SMEs into born-global, born-again global and traditional ones. The typology by Servais and Rasmussen (2000) classifies INVs based on the year of foundation and number of employees and is thus different from the INV-framework by Oviatt and McDougall (1994) which focuses on analyzing INVs in relation to their differences in international operations, while the size of the firm is rendered irrelevant. The results by Servais and Rasmussen (2000) imply that the majority of Danish INVs (born globals) do not in fact grow in terms of employees. Finally, Knight and Cavusgil (2005) developed a taxonomy, where four clusters of US-based born-globals were identified on the basis of entrepreneurial orientation, technological leaderships and Porter's (1980) generic strategies. The firms in one cluster initiated exports more than four years after foundation, thus being less representative of the born globals. The differences between the clusters were analyzed in terms of the firm performance abroad, while the differences in internationalization paths among clusters were not reported.

3. Until 2005, only one case firm (Vacon) had invested in own manufacturing unit abroad.

4. Stick Tech received in 2002 the INNOFINLAND Award from the President of Finland and Biohit in 2002 was awarded by the National Board of Patents and Registration of Finland for having most domestic patents in the country.

5. Biohit (in 1994) and Vacon (in 1998) were awarded by the President of Finland with the Finnish Export Award.

6. Between 1998-2000 Finnlamelli, Vacon, Biohit and Nowo were listed (once or twice) among the 50 fastest growing Finnish firms in Finland's leading business magazine and in 2000 Vacon already achieved a position among the 500 biggest Finnish firms; in 1999 Cross Wrap and Stick Tech were acknowledged by another Finnish business magazine as among the ten domestic high-tech growth firms with possibilities to multiply their turnover in the near future.

7. The significance is also illustrated by the *Journal of International Business Studies* Decade Award conferred to the aforementioned study in 2004.

NOTES

1. Such as the globalization of markets, increased niche markets, advances in process and communication technology, increased international mobility of people,

REFERENCES

Aspelund, A., Berg-Utby, T., & Skjevdal, R. (2005). Initial resources' influence on new venture survival: A longitudinal study of new technology-based firms. *Technovation*, 25:11, 1337-1347.

Bartlett, C.A., & Ghoshal, S. (1991). Managing Across Borders: The Transnational Solution. Boston (MA): Harvard Business School Press.

Bell, J., McNaughton, R., & Young, S. (2001). 'Born-again global' firms: An extension to the 'born global' phenomenon. *Journal of International Management,* 7, 173-189.

Bonaccorsi, A. (1992). On the relationship between firm size and export intensity. *Journal of International Business Studies* 23:4, 605-635.

Burgel, O., & Murray, G.C. (2000). The international market entry choices of start-up companies in high-technology industries. *Journal of International Marketing* 8:2, 33-62.

Burgel, O., Murray, G.C., Fier, A., & Licht, G. (2000). Research Report. The Rapid Internationalisation of High-Tech Young Firms in Germany and the United Kingdom [online]. Available from World Wide Web: <URL: http://intsme.zew.de/ExecSumm.pdf>

Christensen, P.R. (1991). The small and medium-sized exporters' squeeze: Empirical evidence and model reflections. *Entrepreneurship & Regional Development,* 3, 49-65.

Coviello, N.E., & Jones, M.V. (2004). Methodological issues in international entrepreneurship research. *Journal of Business Venturing,* 19:4, 485-508.

Coviello, N., & Munro, H. (1995). Growing the entrepreneurial firm: Networking for international market development. *European Journal of Marketing* 29:7, 49-57.

Coviello, N., & Munro, H. (1997). Network relationships and the internationalization process of small software firms. *International Business Review* 6:4, 361-386.

Crick, D., & Jones, M.V. (2000). Small high-technology firms and international high-technology markets. *Journal of International Marketing* 8:2, 63-85.

Dana, L-P., Etemad, H. & Wright, R.W. (1999). Theoretical foundations of international entrepreneurship. *Research in Global Strategic Management* 7, 3-22.

Gabrielsson, M., Sasi, V., & Darling, J. (2004). Finance strategies of rapidly-growing Finnish SMEs: Born internationals and born globals. *European Business Review,* 16:6, 590-604.

Harveston, P.D., Kedia, B.L., & Davis, P.S. (2000). Internationalization of born global and gradual globalizing firms: The impact of the manager. *Advances in Competitiveness Research* 8:1, 92-99.

Hedlund, G., & Kverneland, A. (1985). Are strategies for foreign markets changing? The case of Swedish investment in Japan. *International Studies of Management and Organization* 15:2, 41-59.

Hurmerinta-Peltomäki, L. (2004). Conceptual and methodological underpinnings in the study of rapid internationalizers. In M.V. Jones & P. Dimitratos (Eds.), *Emerging Paradigms in International Entrepreneurship* (pp. 64-88). Cheltenham: Edward Elgar.

Jones, M.V. (1999). The internationalization of small high-technology firms. *Journal of International Marketing* 7:4, 15-41.

Jones, M.V., & Coviello, N.E. (2005). Internationalisation: Conceptualising an entrepreneurial process of behavior in time. *Journal of International Business Studies* 36:3, 1-20.

Knight, G.A., & Cavusgil, S.T. (1996). The born global firm: A challenge to traditional internationalization theory. In S.T. Cavusgil (Ed.), *Advances in International Marketing* (Vol 8, 11-27). Greenwich, CT: JAI Press

Knight, G.A. (1997). *Emerging Paradigm for International Marketing: The Born Global Firm.* Doctoral dissertation. Michigan: UMI Dissertation Services.

Knight, G.A. (2000). Entrepreneurship and marketing strategy: The SME under globalization. *Journal of International Marketing* 8:2, 12-32.

Knight, G.A., & Cavusgil, S.T. (2005). A taxonomy of born-global firms. *Management International Review,* 12:3, 15-35.

Knight, J., Bell, J., & McNaughton, R. (2001). "Born globals": Old wine in new bottles? Paper presented in the ANZMAC Confrence in Auckland, New Zealand (conference proceedings).

Knight, G.A., Madsen, T.K., & Servais, P. (2003). An inquiry into born-global firms in Europe and the USA. *International Marketing Review,* 21:6, 645-665.

Larimo, J. (2003). Internationalization of SMEs–Two case studies of Finnish born global firms. In A. Blomstermo & D. Sharma (Eds.), *Learning in the Internationalization Process of Firms* (pp. 258-280). Cheltenham: Edward Elgar.

Larimo, J., & Pulkkinen, J. (2002). Global orientation, competitive advantages and export strategies of different types of SMEs: Empirical evidence from Finland. Paper presented in the 28th EIBA Conference in Athens, Greece (conference proceedings).

Lindqvist, M. (1991). *Infant Multinationals. The Internationalization of Young, Technology-Based Swedish Firms.* Doctoral dissertation. Stockholm: Institute of International Business (IBB), Stockholm School of Economics.

Littunen, H., & Tohmo, T. (2003). The high growth in new metal-based manufacturing and business service firms in Finland. *Small Business Economics,* 21, 187-200.

Madsen, T.K., & Servais, P. (1997). The internationalization of born globals: An evolutionary process? *International Business Review* 6:6, 561-583.

Madsen, T.K., Rasmussen, E., & Servais, P. (2000). Differences and Similarities between Born Globals and Other Types of Exporters. In S.T. Cavusgil (Ed.), *Advances in International Marketing* (Vol 10, pp. 247-265). Amsterdam: JAI Press.

McDougall, P.P., Shane, S., & Oviatt, B.M. (1994). Explaining the formation of international new ventures: The limits of theories from international business research. *Journal of Business Venturing* 9:6, 469-487.

McKinsey & Co. (1993). Emerging Exporters: Australia's High Value-Added Manufacturing Exporters. Australian Manufacturing Council, Melbourne.

Miles, R., & Snow, C. (1978). *Organizational Strategy, Structure, and Process.* McGraw-Hill: New York.

Moen, O. (2002). The born globals: A new generation of small European exporters. *International Marketing Review* 19:2, 156-175.

National Board of Patents and Registration of Finland (2002). *Tunnustusta keksijöille* [online]. Helsinki: National Board of Patents and Registration of Finland [cited 16.6.2003]. Available from World Wide Web: <URL: http://www.prh.fi/fi/uutiset /36.html>.

Nummela, N., Saarenketo, S., & Puumalainen, K. (2004). Global mindset–A prerequisite for successful internationalization? *Canadian Journal of Administrative Sciences*, 21:1, 51-64.

Organization for Economic Co-operation and Development (1997). Globalisation and small and medium enterprises (SMEs). Paris: OECD Publications.

Oviatt, B.M., & McDougall, P.P. (1994). Toward a theory of international new ventures. *Journal of International Business Studies* 25:1, 45-64.

Oviatt, B.M., & McDougall, P.P. (1995). Global start-ups: Entrepreneurs on a worldwide stage. *Academy of Management Journal* 9:2, 30-43.

Oviatt, B.M., & McDougall, P.P. (1997). Challenges for internationalization process theory: The case of international new ventures. *Management International Review* 37:2, 85-99.

Oviatt, B.M., & McDougall, P.P. (2000). International entrepreneurship: The intersection of two research paths. *Academy of Management Journal* 43:5, 902-906.

Oviatt, B.M., & McDougall, P.P. (2005a). Retrospective–The Internationalization of entrepreneurship. *Journal of International Business Studies*, 36:1, 2-8.

Oviatt, B.M., & McDougall, P.P. (2005b). Defining international entrepreneurship and modeling the speed of internationalization. *Entrepreneurship Theory & Practice*, 29:5, 537-553.

Perlmutter, H.V. (1969). The Tortuous Evolution of the Multinational Corporation. *Columbia Journal of World Business*, January-February, 9-18.

Porter, M.E. (1980). *Competitive Strategy.* New York: The Free Press.

Pulkkinen, J. (2006). Internationalization of New Ventures–Mediating Role of Entrepreneur and Top Management Team Experience. In F. Poulfelt & R. Christensen (Eds.), *Managing Complexity and Change in SMEs: Frontiers in European Research 2005.* Cheltenham: Edward Elgar Publishing.

Rennie, M.W. (1993). Global competitiveness: Born global. *The McKinsey Quarterly* 4, 45-52.

Rialp, A., Rialp, J., & Knight, G.A. (2005). The phenomenon of early internationalizing firms: What do we know after a decade (1993-2003) of scientific inquiry? *International Business Review*, 14:2, 147-166.

Servais, P., & Rasmussen, E. (2000). Different types of international new ventures. Paper presented in the AIB Annual Meeting, Phoenix, Arizona.

Shrader, R.C. (2001). Collaboration and performance in foreign markets: The case of young high-technology manufacturing firms. *Academy of Management Journal*, 44:1, 45-60.

Shrader, R.C., Oviatt, B.M., & McDougall, P.P. (2000). How new ventures exploit trade-offs among international risk factors: Lessons for the accelerated internationalization of the 21st century. *Academy of Management Journal* 43:6, 1227-1247.

Tiryakian, E.A. (1968). Typologies. In D.L. Sills (Ed.) *International encyclopedia of the social sciences* (Vol. 16, 177-186). New York: MacMillan and Free Press.

Vesper, K.H. (1990). New venture strategies. Englewood Cliffs, N.J.: Prentice Hall.

doi:10.1300/J037v16n01_04

APPENDIX 1. Individual Descriptions of the Case Firms

Finnlamelli is manufacturing laminated log houses. The firm is located in the Western part of Finland, in an area that has strong tradition in the industry. Finnlamelli was established in 1996 by former employees of another log construction firm as it was sold and merged to a bigger corporation. At the time of foundation, the markets were slightly recovering from the recession and the industry was in its growth phase. The founders and managers possessed long experience and tradition in the field and many were experienced from international assignments in the former firm. The main competitors of Finnlamelli are other domestic manufacturers, consisting of about 100 players with a quarter being industrial manufacturers. Finnlamelli is among the four biggest competitors in the country. Finnlamelli's core competencies lie in production and technology know-how as well as knowledge of the industry. In December 1999, Finnlamelli began using a new radio frequency gluing line, which is the first one of its kind in Finland dimensioned for the production of log houses.

Selka-Line is specialized in public space furniture and components. The Selka-Line concept is a product of nearly 30 years of development work, since the firm was established in 1992 to market the products of another furniture firm, Selkate Ltd., and to develop marketing material and public space furniture. The founder had gained previous experience from working in Europe, Australia and Canada. In addition, the firm manager possessed previous experience from working as a CEO in the firm from which Selkate Ltd. was founded. Too years later, Selkate was bankrupted and Selka-Line acquired its activities and moved to the ownership of the founder family. The core competencies of Selka-Line are efficient coordination of operations and good knowledge of the industry and customers. The firm's main competitors are from foreign countries.

Cross Wrap is specialized in square bale-wrapping systems and waste handling equipment. The firm was established in 1994 by one family, followed by the invention of new square bale waste handling method. The founder innovator was experienced from working in the field in selling to international markets and knew the customers. Instead of existing round bale wrapping lines, there was demand for the invented new square bale-wrapping product. Initial market potential for the product was located to Europe and New Zealand, where part of the product development and first marketing operations were conducted in the foundation year. The firm has wide global networks as well as good knowledge of the customers and the industry–all reflecting the strong role of the founder's background in the industry. The method innovation is difficult to imitate and widely protected by patent right. Also due to the EU-directive on waste-energy utilization, the future prospects in Europe are positive.

Logset is specialized in light forest machines (harvesters and forwarders). It was founded in 1992 as the three managers of a bankrupt forest company bought its assets and product rights and continued its forest machine manufacturing operations. The former company had been among the three biggest players in the Finnish market, with these firms possessing over 90% of the market share. Logset started operating with one-third of the former workforce and broadened its operations in repair and sale of second-hand forest machines. The managers possessed vast industry experience and knowledge on conducting international business in the field. One manager had also worked abroad. The firm has approximately five domestic and ten foreign competitors. As compared to main large competitors (all foreign-owned), the firm's forest machines are light-structured and environmental friendly. In addition to technology know-how, it possesses good knowledge of the customers and industry as well as two patents.

Stick Tech, established in 1997, is specialized in fiber reinforcement products. The firm evolved from the biomaterials research project at the university. After years of intensive research the project resulted to invention of new, patented fiber reinforcement technology, which is now the basis of Stick Tech's operation and its pioneering position in the new, growing industry segment. In addition to main innovator, the project included one founder member and few employees of Stick Tech. Altogether the firm management consists of five highly educated members, with most of them possessing earlier international experience from business, research or education. However, despite experience in research of fiber reinforcement technology, none of them had been active in marketing in this field, meaning that distributor and customer, as well as supply contacts, had to be built from the start. The commercialization was complicated since the product was new for the practices of the customers. Every market entry is indeed preceded by co-operation in research and training of dentists and technicians to use the new technology. The competitiveness of the firm is based on its technology offering unique bonding resistance, customer friendliness and application ability.

Nowo (Textile Machinery) was established in 1994 for designing and manufacturing textile machinery (bale openers, ball fiber machines, pillow filling, quilting lines, etc.). In the background of Nowo is bankruptcy of another firm, which had been marketing machinery for similar purposes since 1990 but failed its key product development project. The new firm was founded by one manager of the former firm, with two former employees continuing in the new firm. In addition to industry experience, the management had gained international experience from working in domestic and foreign firms. At the time of foundation the industry markets were already rather mature. However, a need for modern and more efficient production technology was identifiable in the industry and Nowo's strategy was to target these new markets. The firm started with new subcontractor partners and launched new designs for the market. It is Europe's market leader in the ball fiber and pillow filling machine markets and is among the three biggest competitors in the other products. Its core competencies are technological know-how, efficient coordination of operations and knowledge of the industry. In 1998 the firm patented new ball fiber machines, having altogether four patents.

Vacon is a manufacturer of frequency converters. The world market consists of about 80 competitors, with the seven biggest sharing 57% of the market. The biggest player, ABB, has 13% share and Vacon 2,3% share. The firm was established in 1993 by a group of former managers of ABB followed by its strategic change and move of its frequency converter business to another location. The founders saw positive prospects for starting the business with technological knowledge, over 150 man-years' business experience in the field and large international network with customers, suppliers, financiers and other parties as well as advantages of smaller organization. The distinguishing feature of Vacon is the efficient coordination of global activities, utilization of the network structure and close back-and-forward integration. Tight co-operation with the firm's interdependent supplier network allows it to concentrate on the highest value added parts of production and to exploit new technologies faster.

Biohit manufactures liquid handling products and accessories and develops diagnostic test systems for use in research, health care and industrial laboratories. It has a 60% share of the global electronic pipettor markets and about 1,5% share of disposable pipettor tips. In the mechanical pipettor markets it is the fourth largest producer in the world. Biohit was founded in 1988, mainly by one advanced researcher and innovator in the field. The background stems from another firm established by him in 1971, specializing in mechanical pipettors and laboratory equipment. The founder was also the chairman, president and main innovator of both, that firm, and since 1978 a Finnish-American joint venture firm. During 1971-1986 the firms had some 100 inventions and over 200 patents in different countries, and in mid-80s already about 700 employees, over 35 million euros turnover and 10 foreign subsidiaries. In late 1986 Finnish bank took over the firms after which the founder left them, followed by several trials on the rights and compensations. The first two years of Biohit were mainly dedicated to product development. The introduction of a new electronic pipettor was made in 1990, followed by the launch of three new types of pipettors in the next few years. New innovations and patents have had a key role in the competitiveness all the time.

APPENDIX 2. International Development of the INVs

	Finnlamelli	Selka-Line	Cross Wrap	Logset	Stick Tech	Nowo	Vacon	Biohit
Timelag from foundation to initiation of foreign operations (years)								
Sales	< 1	< 1	< 1	< 1	2	2	2	2
Purchasing	Not initiated	2	Not initiated	After exports	3	2	1	2
Co-operation[1]	Within 6 years	Within 6 years	2	Within 6 years	2	Within 6 years	3	3
International level of value chain activities								
International operations within first 6 years	See below	Sales, purchasing (5%), marketing co-operation (distributors)	Sales, marketing and R&D co-operation with customers	Sales, purchasing (40%), one R&D partner, seven marketing partners	See below	Sales (direct export, foreign agents), four European marketing partners, purchasing (50%), pilot plant	Sales (direct export, distributors, JV-subsidiary, subsidiaries, OEM, brand label), purchasing, R&D co-operation	Sales, four subsidiaries, licensing, JV in Japan, purchasing (5%)
International operations in 2001-2002	Sales (direct export, 30 distributors (importers)), R&D co-operation in Japan (earlier), marketing co-operation (design & sales) in Germany and France	Sales (some direct export, 80 distributors), purchasing (5%), R&D co-operation with customers and suppliers, marketing co-operation (sales)	Sales (direct export, distributors, marketing partners, one sales subsidiary in Austria), product development with customers, universities and research institutes, marketing co-operation (sales)	Sales (some direct export, distributors, one sales subsidiary in Great Britain), purchasing (40-50%), product/ technology development with one customer and one supplier	Sales (distributors, brand label, via Internet), purchasing (5%), R&D and training co-operation with research institutes, opinion leaders, customers and suppliers, alliances in USA and Japan, financing	Sales (direct export, foreign agents), marketing co-operation, purchasing (34%), product & technology co-operation with customers. Planning a JV in India.	Sales (direct export, distributors, 15 subsidiaries, OEM, brand label), some purchasing, R&D co-operation with suppliers and customers, JVs, financing	Sales (direct export, > 60 distributors, seven subsidiaries, private label, licensing), JV in Japan, purchasing (5%), acquisitions in Russia and USA (2000), product development co-operation
Foreign sales in (1) in the sixth year (2) in 2001-2002	60% 60%	50% 50%	98% 95%	70% 75%	– 50%	97% 98%	82% 82%	94% 97%
Foreign purchasing (1) in the sixth year (2) in 2001-2002	0% 0%	5% 5-10%	0% 0%	40% 50%	5% 5%	50% 34%	< 20% NA	5% 5%

Geographical dispersion of value chain activities

First export countries	Germany, Netherlands, Japan	Germany, Sweden, Great Britain	Great Britain, Germany, the Netherlands	Germany, Great Britain, Sweden	Sweden, Great Britain, Denmark	Sweden, Germany, Portugal	Sweden, Germany, Switzerland	Sweden, Denmark, Norway
Entry outside Europe	1996	1992	1996	1995	1997	1997	1996	1992
Sales market concentration								
Three key countries	Germany, Japan, France	Russia, Great Britain, Sweden	Italy, Norway, the Netherlands	Germany, Great Britain, France	Denmark, Italy, Great Britain	Italy, Poland, Germany	USA, Germany, Italy	USA, France, Great Britain
Share of three key countries	75%	35%	55%	60%	55%	65%	40%	50%
Share of sales outside Europe	≤ 25%	≤ 25%	≤ 25%	≤ 25%	≤ 25%	≤ 25%	> 25%	> 25%
No. of foreign countries (beginning → 2001-2002)								
Sales	17	20-25 → 20-25	16 → 22	11 → 13	13	25 → 30	Several → 100	Several → 70
Purchasing	No	5 → 5	0 → 0	4 → 6	2	7 → 7	Few → 6	Several
Other operations	3	NA	8 → Several	7 → NA	Several	7	Several	Several
Future expectations								
Foreign sales	No change	Increase (10%)	No change	Increase (5%)	Increase (15%)	Slight increase	Increase (10%)	No change
Foreign sales countries	Increase (2)	Increase (2)	Increase (5)	Decrease (2)	Increase (4)	Increase (2)	Increase	No change

Note. ¹Marketing, R&D and/or production co-operation

Profitability of Rapid Internationalization: The Relationship Between Internationalization Intensity and Firms' Export Performance

Olli Kuivalainen
Sanna Sundqvist

SUMMARY. Internationalization is seen as a critical ingredient in the strategy of firms to achieve growth and superior performance. Although this has been a subject of intensive research during the last few decades, there is still a scarcity of empirical research to determine when rapid, accelerated internationalization, in other words, increase in export intensity is profitable. In this paper we study a sample of 783 Finnish exporting firms and explore the relationship between export intensity and different types of performance by structural equation modeling (SEM) analysis. Our base model does not show any significant relationships between these two constructs. However, when studying small and large firms separately, the results differ. For small firms higher internationalization intensity means better sales performance, better profit performance and indirectly also better efficiency performance, whereas for large firms higher internationalization intensity reflects only better profit performance. doi:10.1300/J037v16n01_05 *[Article copies available for a fee from The Haworth Document Delivery Service: 1-800-HAWORTH. E-mail address: <docdelivery@ haworthpress.com> Website: <http://www.HaworthPress.com> © 2006 by The Haworth Press, Inc. All rights reserved.]*

KEYWORDS. Accelerated, rapid internationalization, export/internationalization intensity, export performance, Structural Equation Modeling

INTRODUCTION

Being an international firm in the current dynamic, complex and competitive market environment is often perceived as a critical ingredient of a firm's strategy to achieve growth, sustainable competitive advantage and above-the-average financial performance. This tenet is one of the reasons behind the increasing economic importance of small entrepreneurial ventures in international business. Consequently, there is more and more empirical evidence on small firms which start to export almost immediately after being established (see, e.g., Knight & Cavusgil, 1996; Oviatt & McDougall, 1994). Unfortunately, a large share

Olli Kuivalainen is Professor, International Business of SMEs, Department of Business and Management, Faculty of Business and Information Technology, University of Kuopio, P.O. Box 1627, FI-70211 Kuopio, Finland (E-mail: olli.kuivalainen@iki.fi). Sanna Sundqvist is Professor, International Marketing, Department of Business Administration, Lappeenranta University of Technology, Lappeenranta, P.O. Box 20, FI-53851 Lappeenranta, Finland (E-mail: sanna-katriina.asikainen@lut.fi).

[Haworth co-indexing entry note]: "Profitability of Rapid Internationalization: The Relationship Between Internationalization Intensity and Firms' Export Performance." Kuivalainen, Olli and Sanna Sundqvist. Co-published simultaneously in *Journal of Euromarketing* (International Business Press, an imprint of The Haworth Press, Inc.) Vol. 16, No. 1/2, 2006, pp. 59-69; and: *Contemporary Euromarketing: Entry and Operational Decision Making* (ed: Jorma Larimo) International Business Press, an imprint of The Haworth Press, Inc., 2006, pp. 59-69. Single or multiple copies of this article are available for a fee from The Haworth Document Delivery Service [1-800-HAWORTH, 9:00 a.m. - 5:00 p.m. (EST). E-mail address: docdelivery@haworthpress.com].

of the available research has been descriptive by nature, lacking a well-developed theoretical framework (Madsen & Servais, 1997).

Although internationalization and its effect on firms' performance have been a subject of intensive research throughout the last three decades (see, e.g., Annavarjula & Beldona, 2000; Grant, 1987; Ruigrok & Wagner, 2003; Sullivan, 1994),[1] there is a scarcity of empirical research to determine when rapid, accelerated internationalization is actually profitable. Lu and Beamish (2001) note that the scarcity of studies concentrating especially on the effects of internationalization on small and medium-sized firms' performance is primarily due to the fact that detailed information is hard to obtain. Another problem is the actual measurement of performance, i.e., how the performance of the firm should be measured in rapid internationalization. Focusing on this gap, these questions form the main research target of this paper. We study the relationship between export intensity and profit, sales and efficiency performances using a cross-industrial sample of Finnish exporting firms. The paper focuses on the following three issues:

- Are the commonly used export performance measures useful?
- Is rapid internationalization (increase in export intensity) profitable?
- Does the relationship between internationalization intensity and a firm's export performance differ across firms with different resources (i.e., the effect of the size of the firm)?

The rest of the paper consists of six sections. First, the conceptual foundations regarding internationalization theories and Born Globals are discussed. This is followed by the discussion of operationalization of rapid internationalization. In the following chapter, the focus is on internationalization-performance linkage, and all these discussions are then followed by the development of the structural model of the role of rapid internationalization on firms' export performance. These theoretical issues are followed by a description of the methodology employed and the analytical methods applied. The findings and their implica-

tions for future research and managerial action are discussed in the final section of the paper.

INTERNATIONALIZATION THEORIES AND BORN GLOBALS

The theory of internationalization is a research tradition with a lot of research in the area and with various definitions by different researchers. For example, Calof and Beamish (1995) define internationalization as "the process of adapting firms' operations (strategy, structure, resource, etc.) to international environments." Welch and Luostarinen (1988) explain internationalization as "the process of increasing involvement in international operations." After several decades of research the concept of internationalization is still elusive. Johanson and Vahlne (1977; 1990) assume that within the frame of economic and business factors, the characteristics of the learning process regarding knowledge about international markets influence the pattern and pace of the internationalization of firms.

Several studies on international business have indicated that the internationalization of firms is a process in which firms gradually increase their international involvement. According to these, so-called incremental internationalization theories (e.g., Bilkey & Tesar, 1977; Johanson & Vahlne, 1977; 1990), a firm commits itself through temporal and operational "stages" to international operations as the gained market knowledge and market commitment affect the commitment decisions and the way/extent they are performed.

However, in the current business environment this does not necessarily hold true, as firms might already be global in a very early phase of their life cycle (see, e.g., Saarenketo et al., 2001). Recently there has been more evidence of and research on the internationalization of small- and medium-sized firms, and many service intensive or knowledge-intensive firms seem not to follow the incremental internationalization patterns of starting in a few neighboring countries and gradual extension of the markets (see, e.g., Bell, 1995; Knight & Cavusgil, 1996; Oviatt & McDougall, 1997; Rennie, 1993). Knight and Cavusgil

(1996) define these firms as Born Globals, which are "small, technology oriented companies that operate in international markets from the earliest days of their establishment." The focus of earlier research on such firms can be divided into four groups: (1) extent/degree of internationalization, (2) speed, and (3) scope (i.e., number of target markets) (Zahra & George, 2002), and (4) antecedents (e.g., managerial and firm characteristics) of rapid internationalization (see, e.g., Bloodgood et al., 1996; Knight & Cavusgil, 1996; 2004).

There seems to be a consensus among researchers that incremental internationalization theories cannot alone explain the dynamics of internationalization of small knowledge intensive firms (see, e.g., Coviello & McAuley, 1999; Oviatt & McDougall, 1997). However, there are problems within the definition of rapid, accelerated internationalization and in its operationalization.

OPERATIONALIZATION OF RAPID INTERNATIONALIZATION

Born Globals have generally been assessed by three characteristics: (1) the rapidity of internationalization or exporting (a common criterion is that a firm has to begin exporting within two years of its establishment), (2) the amount of turnover derived from international operations (at least 25 percent), and (3) the number of countries the firm does business in (at least 2 countries). Bell (1995) found out that the commitment of the management played an important role in the rapid internationalization process. The study by Rennie (1993) revealed that Born Globals are very close to their customers, they are flexible and are able to adapt their products to quickly changing needs and wants, i.e., Born Globals fulfill the description of customer oriented companies, which is a characteristic of export market oriented firms (Narver & Slater, 1990). Furthermore, Born Globals are said to possess the following characteristics: managerial characteristics, like emphasis on internationalization and propensity to export early, and a relatively wide scope of export countries or regions already from the very beginning of their operation. Knight and Cavusgil (1996) believe

that the most distinguishing feature of Born Global firms is that they tend to be managed by entrepreneurial visionaries who view the world as a single, borderless marketplace. The emerging research on international entrepreneurship[2] (see, e.g., Oviatt & McDougall, 1994; Zahra & George, 2002) is linked with these findings. Entrepreneurial and international entrepreneurial orientation (often associated with risk taking, proactiveness and innovativeness, see, e.g., Dess et al., 1997) can be seen as determinants which may explain the growth strategy and performance differences within the new firms.

The characteristics or measures of rapid internationalization, like the number of countries (Saarenketo et al., 2001), percentage of turnover derived from international operations (Knight & Cavusgil, 1996; Madsen et al., 2000), and the rapidity of international operations, i.e., the time lag between years in business and years practicing international operations (Knight & Cavusgil, 1996; Madsen et al., 2000) have been identified by existing research. However, there is little empirical research into the relationship between the rapid internationalization or globalization of firms and the actual performance or success.

EXPORTING, INTERNATIONALIZATION AND PERFORMANCE

Exporting is one possible growth strategy for a firm. There are empirical research results suggesting that exporting firms have higher level of sales and productivity than non-exporters, and that firms that increase their share of exports in their total sales experience a further increase in productivity and sales (see, for example, the research conducted at Nottingham University based on longitudinal data from ca. 9000 firms (Trade Partners UK, 2002)). The premise of international business studies is based on the assumption that increased multinationality is good for a firm's performance (see, e.g., Contractor et al., 2003; Tallman & Li, 1996). Venkatraman and Ramanujam (1986) note that corporate performance can be conceptualized on two dimensions, i.e., financial and operational. Common performance measures include financial goals (profit-related, sales-related and market-share related, for example, the ratio of foreign sales to total sales, see, e.g., Grant, 1987). Operational, non-financial measures have also been used, including, for example, managers' satisfaction with the fulfillment of export objectives or objectives related to the market and the product (see Cavusgil & Zou, 1993; Leonidou et al., 2002 for practical examples).

However, there is still a limited number of uniform, reliable and valid international or export performance measures (Matthyssens & Pauwells, 1996), and export performance has been found to be a complex and multifaceted construct (see, e.g., Leonidou et al., 2002; Sullivan, 1994). One of the problems in the measurement is that in many cases the measures are partly financial and partly actually strategic or processual outcomes of the internationalization (e.g., number of target markets served). In addition, there are practical problems in measuring export performance, as for example, accounting standards and currency fluctuations can affect the measurement.

EXPORT INTENSITY
AND RAPID INTERNATIONALIZATION

Export intensity can be measured as the proportion of export sales of the firm's sales (see, e.g., Cooper & Kleinschmidt, 1985; Verwaal & Donkers, 2002). However, this approach may prove to be problematic as the growth of intensity can be sporadic and not linear. As Figure 1 illustrates, firms A and B may have started exporting at the same rapidity, but after that their speed and intensity have differed: firm A has reached the same intensity level (35% of turnover derived from international operations) much faster than firm B. Thus, export intensity should be measured by proportioning to the time. This also applies, for example, to the intensity related to the number of target markets the firms operate within. Moen and Servais (2002) found that in terms of export intensity Born Globals outperform those firms that waited for several years before starting to export.

Based on the discussion above, we propose a model (see Figure 2) which considers also

FIGURE 1. The Effect of Time on the Rapidity and Intensity of International Operations

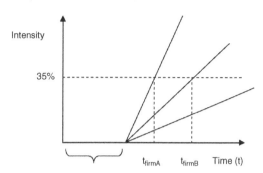

Time between establishment of the firm and beginning of international operations

the effect of the export intensity, and explore whether intensive internationalization has an effect on the firm's profit, sales and efficiency performances.

METHODOLOGY

Sampling Issues

We used a mail survey to generate data for testing the model. The sampling frame consisted of 1,205 Finnish exporting firms. In order to obtain responses, we first contacted all the firms on the database (purchased from Kompass Finland) by telephone to determine eligibility and then elicited their cooperation in the study. A questionnaire was mailed to the export manager of the firm agreeing to participate. Ten days after this mailing, a reminder card was sent to each non-respondent, and seven days after this, a second questionnaire was mailed to the remaining non-respondents. In total, 237 firms were deemed ineligible (e.g., the firm had never exported, the firm had stopped exporting, the firm was listed more than once), a further 21 declined to participate, and 783 returned completed questionnaires, corresponding to a response rate of 81% (i.e., 783/968). Non response bias was not considered to be an issue for two reasons: (a) the relatively high response rate reduces the risk of response bias, and (b) a comparison between early and late respondents on all variables of interest demonstrated that no significant

FIGURE 2. Model of the Relationships Between Internationalization Intensity and Performance

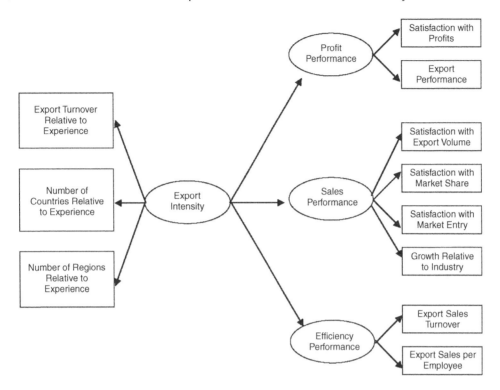

differences existed (Armstrong & Overton, 1977).

Measurement

Following the recommendations of Cavusgil and Zou (1993) and Matthyssens and Pauwels (1996), among others, we measured the aspects of the firm's export sales, export profits and export efficiency. Our "sales performance" measure contained items to capture (a) the firm's sales growth relative to the industry average, (b) the firm's degree of satisfaction with its export volume, (c) the firm's degree of satisfaction with its market share in its export markets, and (d) the firm's degree of satisfaction with its rate of new market entry. Our "profit performance" measure captured (a) the firm's degree of satisfaction with its export profits over the last three years, (b) the firm's degree of satisfaction with its market share in its export markets, and (c) an overall assessment of the profitability of the firm's exporting operations during the last financial year. The last performance measure "efficiency per-

formance" captured (a) the ratio of the firm's total annual export sales turnover to the total number of employees working in the firm, and (b) the ratio of the firm's total annual export sales turnover to the total number of countries the firm exported to.

Export intensity was measured with three items: (a) the number of regions exported to proportioned to the firm's experience with international operations, (b) the number of countries exported to relative to the firm's experience with international operations, and (c) export turnover relative to the firm's experience with international operations.

On average, the firms in the sample had been doing business for 53 years, their turnover was 202 million euros and they employed 866 persons. The firms were exporting to almost 23 countries and to almost four regions (e.g., Asia, Europe, North America and South America), their exporting experience was on average 27 years and they derived almost 49 percent of their sales from international markets. The characteristics of the firms in the sample are summarized in Table 1.

TABLE 1. Firm Characteristics

Variable	N	Mean	Std. Dev.
Years in business	768	53.16	47.44
Percentage of sales derived from exporting	777	48.62	31.31
Export experience (years of exporting)	775	27.31	37.36
Number of countries exported to	769	22.53	24.70
Number of regions exported to	781	3.94	2.30
Export intensity	766	25.76	33.38
Size of the firm (number of employees)	777	865.53	3818.51
Size of the firm (turnover– million €)	769	201.58	1032.62

Measurement Assessment and Construction

In order to comment on the validity and reliability of the measures used, all multi-item scales were entered simultaneously into an exploratory factor analysis. Following this, confirmatory factor analysis (CFA), using LISREL 8.50 (Jöreskog & Sörbom, 1996) was undertaken. The final model fit indexes obtained for the CFA were good: $\chi^2 = 120.22$, d.f. = 38 (p < .001); Root Mean Square Error of Approximation (RMSEA) = .039; Goodness of Fit Index (GFI) = .967; Nonnormed Fit Index (NNFI) = .974; Comparative Fit Index (CFI) = .982.

Having confirmed that the items used to test the model were unidimensional, single scores were then created for each of the concepts of interest. Specifically, a single score was obtained for profit performance by averaging across the scale items; the same was undertaken for the sales performance, efficiency performance and export intensity scales. However, for the export intensity and efficiency performance the individual items underlying the scale were first standardized (to remove the units of measurement), and then summated to create single scores of export intensity and efficiency performance.

Analyses

We tested our hypothesis by applying the structural equation modeling technique (i.e.,

LISREL 8.50) for the validation of the model proposed in Figure 2. Our final[3] model returned an excellent fit, as the following fit indexes show: $\chi^2 = 2.00$, d.f. = 1 (p = .157); RMSEA = .039; GFI = .998; NNFI = .986; CFI = .998 (see also Figure 3). The standardized path estimates are presented in Table 2.

As Table 2 shows, export intensity was not significantly related to the export performance variables. However, our measurement model returned an excellent fit and provided us with sound measures for both export intensity and different dimensions of export performance.

As our interest was to study also whether the size of the firm would have an effect on the hypothesized relationships, we took a step further and tested the model separately for small and large firms. We used turnover to indicate the firm size and classified the firms into two groups: large firms whose turnover was over 82.4 million euros and small firms whose turnover was under 10.5 million euros. The classification was based on the upper and lower quartiles of the firms' turnover.

Our model for large firms returned a good fit, as the following fit indexes show: $\chi^2 = 9.70$, d.f. = 2 (p = .008); RMSEA = .155; GFI = .971; NFI = .940; CFI = .946. We specified the path from profit performance to sales performance "post-hoc" after examining the modification indexes (see Figure 4). Although the proposed model was not significant when looking at the likelihood-ratio χ^2 statistics (p = .008), the model can be considered useful as the values of the other measures of fit were good.[4] Also some of the proposed relationships between internationalization intensity and firms' performance returned a significant fit. Our results indicate that for large firms high internationalization intensity leads towards better profit performance. Rapid internationalization affects also indirectly the sales performance, as the path from profit performance to sales performance was significant.

Also, our model for small firms returned a good fit, as the following fit indexes show: $\chi^2 = 6.83$, d.f. = 2 (p = .033); RMSEA = .122; GFI = .979; NFI = .961; CFI = .971. We specified the path from profit performance to efficiency performance "post-hoc" after examining the modification indexes (see Figure 5).

FIGURE 3. Basic Model with Standardized Solutions (N.B. the Paths from Profit Performance to Sales Performance and to Efficiency Performance Have Been Specified 'Post-Hoc'–After Examining the Modification Indexes)

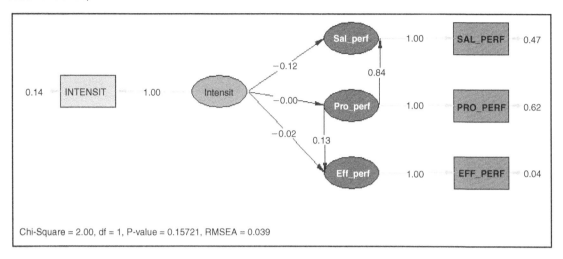

Chi-Square = 2.00, df = 1, P-value = 0.15721, RMSEA = 0.039

TABLE 2. Standardized Path Estimates for the Structural Model

Dependent variables	R^2	Independent variables	Standardized parameter estimates	t-values
Sales Performance	.795	Export Intensity	−.08	−2.175
		Profit Performance	.87***	21.668
Profit Performance	.759	Export Intensity	−.00	−.03
Efficiency Performance	.949	Export Intensity	−.02	−.47
		Profit Performance	.224**	5.104

*p < .01; **p < .05; ***p < .001; one-tailed significance test.

Interestingly, these two models differ. For small firms higher internationalization intensity means better sales performance, better profit performance and indirectly also better efficiency performance, whereas for large firms higher internationalization intensity reflects only better profit performance.

DISCUSSION AND FURTHER RESEARCH

The relationship between export intensity (or international expansion/degree of internationalization) and performance is often context specific and there are contradictory results. Some authors suggest that highly dispersed international operations increase management constraints and costs, and thus make the performance benefits smaller (see, e.g., Egelhoff, 1988; Grant, 1987).

The seminal study conducted by Ayal and Zif (1979) hypothesized that for each firm there may be an optimum number of export countries, and the strategies how to reach this optimum can be different and even opposing. There are only a few studies which have examined the role of countries or regions in the internationalization process of small entrepreneurial firms (one of them being Reuber & Fischer, 1997). In many Born Global studies it is only noted that Born Globals often derive their turnover from multiple countries (see, e.g., Knight & Cavusgil, 2004; Oviatt & McDougall, 1994) but this "country effect" has been excluded from the empirical work. Thus,

FIGURE 4. The Effect of Internationalization Intensity on Large Firms' Performance (N = 161)

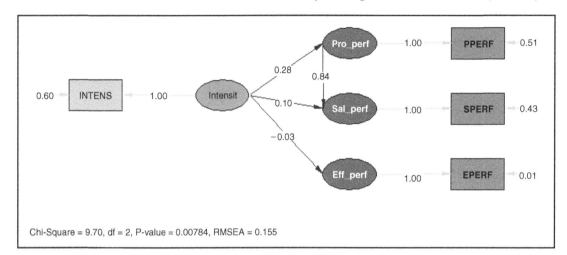

Chi-Square = 9.70, df = 2, P-value = 0.00784, RMSEA = 0.155

FIGURE 5. The Effect of Internationalization Intensity on Small Firms' Performance (N = 163)

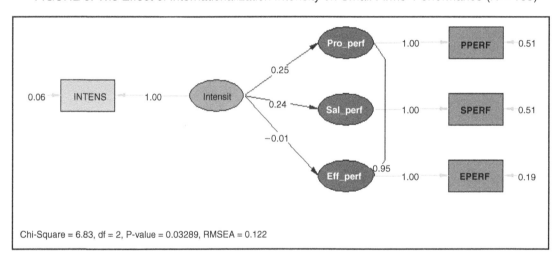

Chi-Square = 6.83, df = 2, P-value = 0.03289, RMSEA = 0.122

it seems that we have not known what the performance consequences of rapid and dispersed internationalization really are.

In our study we studied export intensity with a three-dimensional measure consisting of the number of regions and countries a firm exported to, and the export turnover relative to the firm's experience with international operations, namely exporting. The results of our base model revealed that export/internationalization intensity did not have a direct positive effect on a firm's export performance. Instead, the results suggested that the relation-

ship between export intensity and export performance can be negative. Conversely, within our sample there were significant differences between small and large firms. For small firms it can be said that the higher the extent of internationalization, the better the performance. Partial support for this result can be found in earlier literature. Bloodgood et al. (1996) found out that for new U.S. ventures, the higher levels of internationalization were significantly related to income but not related to sales growth. They concluded that their results could not prove that rapid internationalization would lead to better performance (or worse, either). On the basis of our sample we can say that for some firms higher export intensity means better performance. For smaller firms there were more significant relationships between export intensity and performance than for larger firms. However, we cannot make any strong generalizations regarding rapid internationalization on the basis of these results, as our analysis was based on a sample of Finnish exporters and because we did not examine contingency factors (like the effect of internationalization mode or the differences across industries), which may have a significant effect on the model. There were also different results from different market areas, and adjustment to geographic/cultural proximity could develop more sophisticated measures of multinationality (see Gomes & Ramaswamy, 1999). This might be useful also in the case of export intensity for small firms.

Implications of the Research

It seems that the size of the firm made a difference in our results. The smaller and larger firms enjoyed better performance export intensity than the firms which were "stuck in the middle." As we did not study the strategy of the firms, strong conclusions cannot be drawn regarding this result. However, we can speculate that the size of the firm is related to the competitive strategy of the firm: smaller firms often follow niche strategies and are closer to their customers, which in turn may lead to performance consequences. Some of the key questions (cf., e.g., Bell et al., 2004; Oviatt & McDougall, 1994) discussed here which form avenues for future research are:

- What factors and strategic choices made by small exporting firms, in their early growth years, create above-the-average performance in the later stages of the firm's life-cycle?
- What is the role of rapid internationalisation for the later performance of the firm?

The focal area in our research was export intensity. Incorporating contingencies, such as corporate strategy, the target country selection and the operation mode to our study would

provide a good platform for further research and put our export intensity measures to use. In future more research should also be focused on the nature of business, which is probably related to internationalization costs. In traditional industries the costs of internationalization may be much higher than the costs of internationalization of knowledge intensive firms selling for example digital products, such as software and audiovisual products.

There are often limitations in research, and the present study is no exception. On the other hand, limitations also offer opportunities for further research.

Firstly, the study focused on a single-country sample as the data was collected in Finland. It is possible that the internationalization of firms in Finland differs from that of other countries, since the size of Finnish home markets is relatively small compared to the markets of other European countries, for example. Secondly, the fact that our sample consisted only of exporting firms is a limitation, and future research should also study all internationally active firms regardless of the operation mode. Naturally this may have an effect on the internationalization intensity-performance curve. Thirdly, the fact that our analysis was based on cross-sectional empirical data can be seen as some kind of limitation. When measuring and analyzing the effects of internationalization longitudinal data would provide us with valuable insights.

Managerial Implications

The managers of exporting firms could benefit from a better understanding of the performance implications of export intensity. This would call for a detailed understanding of the nature of the firm's business, internationalization options (e.g., what is the suitable strategy for a firm on the basis of the available opportunities and resources) and clearly set performance goals and objectives. As our results imply that smaller export intensive firms enjoyed all performance effects (i.e., sales, profit and indirectly efficiency) it seems that a more geographically wide market spread might be beneficial for these firms. This kind of result has been found also elsewhere, e.g., Madsen (1989) found that it would actually be better for very small firms to spread their efforts over several markets, as they may not have the resources to follow a market concentration strategy successfully.

In general, both practicing managers and researchers alike should focus more on the performance implications of rapid internationalization among small exporting firms and study in a more in-depth manner all factors and key issues which may affect the performance benefits.

NOTES

1. Most of the early research suggested a positive linear relationship of the internationalization-performance relationship, but the findings were often inconsistent and conflicting (see Ruigrok & Wagner, 2003). Such findings have led researchers to study the effects of the degree of internationalization and the costs associated with internationalization (for example costs from the change of the operation mode) and suggest for example J-shaped or S-curved links between internationalization and performance (e.g., Sullivan, 1994; Gomes & Ramaswamy, 1999; Riah-Belkaoui, 1998). Although the shape of the curve tells us more regarding the patterns of growth, there is still a problem of time, what is the "right time" to conduct the measurement of performance and make the comparison.

2. Zahra and George (2002, p. 261) define international entrepreneurship as "the process of creatively discovering and exploiting opportunities that lie outside a firm's domestic markets in the pursuit of competitive advantage."

3. We first tested a model without paths between different performance dimensions. The model returned an excellent fit but the χ^2 value was not significant. Thus, on the basis of modification indexes and after studying the literature, two paths were added to the model.

4. For example Metsämuuronen (2001) and Hair et al. (1998) note that χ^2 is quite sensitive to differences in sample sizes and encourage researchers to complement χ^2 with other goodness-of-fit measures. As the values of Normed Fit Indexes (NFI) in all the models are above .90, it can be seen that the χ^2 measure is sensitive to our sample and the use of other measures is justified.

REFERENCES

Annavarjula, M., & Beldona, S. (2000). Multinationality-performance relationship: A review and reconceptualization. *The International Journal of Organizational Analysis*, 8 (1), 48-67.

Armstrong, S. J., & Overton, T. S. (1977). Estimating non-response bias in mail surveys. *Journal of Marketing Research*, 14, 396-402.

Ayal, I., & Zif, J. (1979). Marketing expansion strategies in multinational marketing. *Journal of Marketing*, 43, 84-94.

Bell, J. (1995). The internationalization of small computer software firms–A further challenge to "stage" theories. *European Journal of Marketing*, 29 (8), 60-75.

Bell, J., Crick, D., & Young, S. (2004) Small firm internationalization and business strategy: An exploratory study of 'knowledge-intensive' and 'traditional' manufacturing firms in the UK. *International Small Business Journal*, 22, 23-56.

Bilkey, W. J., & Tesar, G. (1977). The export behavior of smaller sized Wisconsin manufacturing firms. *Journal of International Business Studies*, 8, 93-98.

Bloodgood, J. M., Sapienza, H., & Almeida, J.G. (1996). The internationalisation of new high-potential U.S. ventures: Antecedents and outcomes. *Entrepreneurship: Theory and Practice*, 20 (4), 61-76.

Calof, J. L., & Beamish, P. W. (1995). Adapting to foreign markets: Explaining internationalization. *International Business Review*, 4, 115-131.

Cavusgil, S. T., & Zou, S. (1993). Product and promotion adaptation in export ventures: An empirical investigation. *Journal of International Business Studies*, 24, 479-507.

Contractor, F., Kundu, S. K., & Hsu, C-C. (2003). A three-stage theory of international expansion: The link between multinationality and performance in the service sector. *Journal of International Business Studies*, 34, 5-18.

Cooper, R. G., & Kleinschmidt, E. J. (1985). The impact of export strategy on export sales performance. *Journal of International Business Studies*, 16, 37-55.

Coviello, N. E., & McAuley, A. (1999). Internationalisation and the Smaller Firm: A Review of Contemporary Empirical Research. *Management International Review*, 39 (3), 223-256.

Dess, G., Lumpkin, G., & Covin, J. (1997). Entrepreneurial strategy making and firm performance: Test of contingency and configurational models. *Strategic Management Journal*, 18, 2-23.

Egelhoff, W. G. (1988). Strategy and structure in multinational corporations: A revision of the Stopford and Wells model. *Strategic Management Journal*, 9, 1-14.

Gomes, L., & Ramaswamy, K. (1999). An empirical examination of the form of the relationship between multinationality and performance. *Journal of International Business Studies*, 30, 173-188.

Grant, R. M. (1987). Multinationality and performance among British manufacturing companies. *Journal of International Business Studies*, 22, 249-263.

Hair, J. F., Anderson, R. E., Tatham, R. L., & Black, W. C. (1998). *Multivariate Data Analysis* (5th ed.). New Jersey: Prentice Hall.

Johanson, J., & Vahlne, J-E. (1977). The internationalization process of the firm: A model of knowledge development and increasing foreign market commitments. *Journal of International Business Studies*, 8, 23-32.

Johanson, J., & Vahlne, J-E. (1990). The mechanism of internationalization. *International Marketing Review*, 7 (4), 11-24.

Jöreskog, K., & Sörbom, D. (1996). *LISREL 8: User's reference guide*. Chicago: Scientific Software International.

Knight, G. A., & Cavusgil, S. T. (1996). The born global firm: A challenge to traditional internationalisation theory. *Advances in International Marketing*, 8, 11-26.

Knight, G. A., & Cavusgil, S. T. (2004). Innovation, organizational capabilities, and the born-global firm. *Journal of International Business Studies*, 35, 124-141.

Leonidou, L. C., Katsikeas, C. S., & Samiee, S. (2002). Marketing strategy determinants of export performance: A meta analysis. *Journal of Business Research*, 55, 51-67.

Lu, J. W., & Beamish, P. W. (2001). The internationalization and performance of SMEs. *Strategic Management Journal*, 22, 565-586.

Madsen, T. K. (1989). Successful export marketing management: Some empirical evidence. *International Marketing Review*, 6 (4), 41-57.

Madsen, T. K., Rasmussen, E., & Servais, P. (2000). Differences and similarities between born globals and other types of exporters. *Globalisation, the Multinational Firm*, 10, 247-265.

Madsen, T. K., & Servais, P. (1997). The internationalization of born globals: An evolutionary process? *International Business Review*, 6, 561-583.

Matthyssens, P., & Pauwels, P. (1996). Assessing export performance measurement. In S. T. Cavusgil & T. K. Madsen (Eds.), *Advances in International Marketing* (pp. 85-114). Greenwich, CT: JAI Press.

Metsämuuronen, J. (2001). *Monimuuttujamenetelmien perusteet SPSS-ympäristössä*. Metodologia-sarja 7. Estonia: International Methelp Ky.

Moen, O., & Servais, P. (2002). Born global or gradual global? Examining the export behavior of small and medium-sized enterprises. *Journal of International Marketing*, 10 (3), 49-72.

Narver, J. C., & Slater, S. F. (1990). The effect of a market orientation on business profitability. *Journal of Marketing*, 54 (4), 20-35.

Oviatt, B. M., & McDougall, P. P. (1994). Toward a theory of international new ventures. *Journal of International Business Studies*, 25 (1), 45-64.

Oviatt, B. M., & McDougall, P. P. (1997). Challenges for internationalization process theory: The case of international new ventures. *Management International Review*, 37 (2), 85-99.

Rennie, M. W. (1993). Global competitiveness: Born global. *The McKinsey Quarterly*, 4, 45-52.

Reuber, A. R., & Fischer, E. (1997). The influence of the management team's international experience on the internationalization behaviors of SMEs. *Journal of International Business Studies*, 28, 807-825.

Riah-Belkaoui, A. (1998). The effects of the degree of internationalization on firm performance. *International Business Review*, 7, 315-321.

Ruigrok, W., & Wagner, H. (2003). Internationalization and performance: An organizational learning perspective. *Management International Review*, 43 (1), 63-83.

Saarenketo, S., Kuivalainen, O., & Puumalainen, K. (2001). Emergence of born global firms: Internationalization patterns of the infocom SMEs as an example. Paper presented at 4th *McGill Conference on International Entrepreneurship*, 21-23 September, University of Strathclyde, Glasgow, UK.

Sullivan, D. (1994). Measuring the degree of internationalization of a firm. *Journal of International Business Studies*, 25, 325-342.

Tallman, S., & Li, J. (1996). Effects of international diversity and product diversity on the performance of multinational firms. *Academy of Management Journal*, 39 (1), 179-196.

Trade Partners UK (2002). *Exporting and business performance. A report for Trade Partners UK*. Retrieved May 23, 2003, from http://www.tradepartners.gov.uk/files/export_performance.pdf.

Venkatraman, N., & Ramanujam, V. (1986). Measurement of business performance in strategy research: A comparison of approaches. *The Academy of Management Review*, 11, 815-827.

Verwaal, E., & Donkers, B. (2002). Firm size and export intensity: Solving an empirical puzzle. *Journal of International Business Studies*, 33, 603-613.

Welch, L. S., & Luostarinen, R. (1988). Internationalization: Evolution of a concept. *Journal of General Management*, 14 (2), 36-64.

Zahra, S. A., & George, G. (2002). International entrepreneurship: The current status of the field and future research agenda. In M. Hitt, D. Ireland, D. Sexton & M. Camp (Eds.), *Entrepreneurship: Creating an integrated mindset* (pp. 255-288). Blackwell Publishers.

doi:10.1300/J037v16n01_05

Faster and More Successful Exporters:
An Exploratory Study of Born Global Firms
from the Resource-Based View

Alex Rialp

Josep Rialp

SUMMARY. In this paper, we develop a resource-based model for analyzing the effect of several firm resources, more concretely those of an intangible character, on the born global nature of an exporting firm. We test then whether several intangible resources may have influenced the fact that a firm started its export activity almost from inception, and also whether the results achieved from this activity (as measured through the export intensity ratio) are indeed better than those obtained by other firms that were not exporting from inception. The model has been empirically tested among a representative sample of Spanish exporting manufacturers. Results seem to confirm that basically both human and organizational capital resources show a significant impact on those firms being considered as highly successful born globals. Relevant conclusions and implications for future researchers in this field are derived from these findings. doi:10.1300/J037v16n01_06 *[Article copies available for a fee from The Haworth Document Delivery Service: 1-800-HAWORTH. E-mail address: <docdelivery@haworthpress.com> Website: <http://www.HaworthPress.com> © 2006 by The Haworth Press, Inc. All rights reserved.]*

KEYWORDS. Born globals, intangible firm resources, empirical analysis, Spanish exporters

INTRODUCTION

Traditionally, the internationalization process of a firm has been conceived as a gradual, on-going process, taking place in incremental stages and over a relatively long period of time (Johanson and Vahlne, 1977, 1990). However, when the most critical theoretical prescriptions of the internationalization process models have been empirically examined, several paradoxes and major disagreements have seemed to emerge (Christensen, 1991). Some authors, as for example, Andersen (1997), have even questioned their adequacy as good theories, concluding that their theoretical boundaries, explanatory power, and operationalization had to be radically improved. Other researchers have also accused the stages models for being too deterministic and basically mechanistic in nature (Reid, 1983). Conse-

Alex Rialp (E-mail: alex.rialp@uab.es) and Josep Rialp (E-mail: josep.rialp@uab.es) are both affiliated with the Department of Business Economics (B Building), Autonomous University of Barcelona, 08193 Bellaterra (Barcelona), Spain.

[Haworth co-indexing entry note]: "Faster and More Successful Exporters: An Exploratory Study of Born Global Firms from the Resource-Based View." Rialp, Alex, and Josep Rialp. Co-published simultaneously in *Journal of Euromarketing* (International Business Press, an imprint of The Haworth Press, Inc.) Vol. 16, No. 1/2, 2006, pp. 71-86; and: *Contemporary Euromarketing: Entry and Operational Decision Making* (ed: Jorma Larimo) International Business Press, an imprint of The Haworth Press, Inc., 2006, pp. 71-86. Single or multiple copies of this article are available for a fee from The Haworth Document Delivery Service [1-800-HAWORTH, 9:00 a.m. - 5:00 p.m. (EST). E-mail address: docdelivery@haworthpress.com].

quently, future research in this field must seek completely new paths.

Such a research gap could be well filled by an emerging topic centered on the so-called international new ventures (INVs) and/or born-globals (Knight and Cavusgil, 1996; Oviatt and McDougall, 1997). The emergence of this type of firm characterized by becoming international at founding or very shortly thereafter, becomes a sign that important dimensions of the internationalization process may have changed since two decades ago, when much of the current popular theory about the firm internationalization process was developed.

In spite of the increasing amount of research being currently conducted on such type of ventures (Moen, 2002; Rialp et al., 2005), a more accurate assessment of the strategically valuable resources and capabilities managed and/or controlled by a firm, as a key antecedent for it to become a successful born global is still needed. In this context, this research is aimed at investigating a firm's export adoption and performance by adopting, as an increasingly accepted theoretical framework, the resource-based view of the firm (RBV). In particular, the relevance of different resources, mainly intangible ones, in the development of specific capabilities to conduct earlier export activities becomes our main research interest. Moreover, and following Barney (2001), the way in which the resource-based perspective should be applied in analyzing these relationships depends mostly upon the empirical context of the application itself. Consequently, in this paper we analyze the possible relationship existing between firm-specific intangible assets and the fact of being, or not, a successful born global company in the Spanish industrial setting.

With this goal in mind, this paper is organized as follows: the next section offers an overview of the born-global firm literature. Then, a resource-based model and several testable hypotheses on the expected relationships between the firm's endowment of intangible resources and its potential born global character are established. The following section shows the empirical methods and operational variables being used for empirically verifying the model. Then, we present and discuss our empirical results. Finally, several conclusions

and implications are derived from these findings.

LITERATURE REVIEW OF BORN GLOBALS

The so-called stage models of internationalization (Johanson and Vahlne, 1977) have traditionally conceptualized internationalization of the firm as an incremental process involving a varying number of stages. This stream of research contends that firms become international in a slow and incremental manner. Although sometimes the empirical data have indeed supported the notion that firms often internationalize incrementally, in many other cases, these stages models have been found to be of rather limited value. In fact, quite convincing evidence of the limitations of the stages models has appeared in the literature (Welch and Luostarinen, 1988). Thus, there is increasing evidence that such a traditional view of risk-averse, incremental firm internationalization may be considered conceptually weak, and that changing internal and external conditions are challenging its relevance and casting doubt on its future applicability (Oviatt and McDougall, 1997; Rialp and Rialp, 2001).

More recently, other studies have identified an increasing number of firms which, instead of following the traditional stages pattern, choose to be extensively present in international markets right from–or almost from– their birth. These firms have been labeled quite differently from one study to another: Born Globals (Knight and Cavusgil, 1996; Madsen and Servais, 1997; Aspelund and Moen, 2001; Moen, 2002), Global Start-ups (Oviatt and McDougall, 1994), and International New Ventures–INVs (Oviatt and McDougall, 1994; McDougall et al., 1994; Oviatt and McDougall, 1997), among others. Regardless the specific term used for calling them, the emphasis has generally been put on identifying and characterizing these firms, which become international approximately from the time of their formation, and for which the generally accepted theories of international business clearly fail to explain their existence (McDougall et al., 1994).

From the theoretical standpoint, several frameworks concerning born globals and/or INVs have been recently established in the literature. Oviatt and McDougall (1994) proposed a theory integrating international business, entrepreneurship, and strategic management theory. In their opinion, quite more elemental sources of advantage than merely size/scale issues make these new ventures possible. More concretely, their theoretical approach describes four necessary and sufficient elements for explaining the existence of sustainable INVs: (1) organizational formation through internalization of some transactions; (2) strong reliance on alternative governance structures to access resources; (3) establishment of foreign location advantages; and (4) control over unique resources. Later on, Madsen and Servais (1997) also conceived this emerging phenomenon as being in strong opposition to the traditional models of internationalization. However, their rigorous theoretical and empirical review lead them to conclude that these firms grow in a way which may be in a certain degree of accordance with evolutionary thinking. Their argument basically offers a new conceptualization of this research issue by means of establishing its links to the original Uppsala-Model and other approaches such as the International Network approach (Johanson and Mattsson, 1988). From those links, they also derive some propositions about the antecedents of as well as the necessary and sufficient conditions for the continued rise of this emerging issue. Also, from the empirical standpoint, Born Globals/INVs had been almost ignored until recently. However, since the early 1990s, several reports based mostly but not only on case studies, have begun to appear, thus indicating that the born global phenomenon is indeed challenging the stages theory of internationalization (see a very detailed review of empirical studies on this issue in Rialp et al., 2005).

A RESOURCE-BASED MODEL ON BORN GLOBALS AND HYPOTHESES

The *resource-based view of the firm* (RBV) has become, since the early eighties, a very popular theory of competitive advantage in the strategic management literature (Wernerfelt, 1984, 1989; Dierickx and Cool, 1989; Reed and DeFillippi, 1990; Barney, 1991; Conner, 1991; Grant, 1991; Mahoney and Pandian, 1992; Peteraf, 1993). Basically, this theoretical framework emphasizes the importance of firm specific resources and capabilities in the generation and maintenance of sustainable competitive advantage which allows a firm to earn above normal economic profits (*ricardian rents*). The resource-based approach is developed from the assumption that resources are heterogeneously distributed across firms and that these differences may be long lasting (Barney, 1991). Thus, by identifying specific sources of sustained competitive advantage, the RBV provides a more clear understanding of why some firms can consistently outperform their rivals in the marketplace.

Although the lack of a generally accepted model of the determinants of the export behavior and performance still remains as a clear concern in the field of export literature, a certain number of studies seem to identify several firm resources and capabilities (i.e., demographic, structural, organizational, and managerial ones) as major determinants of this export behavior and export performance (Louter et al., 1991; Moen, 1999; Fahy, 2002).

Accordingly, we believe that also for obtaining a better understanding the born global phenomenon, a certain match between a firm's resource base and its potential born global character is needed. The challenging capability of performing internationally from inception could depend highly on the level of resources of the firm and, more precisely, on the prevalence of key intangible resources. However, in spite of its strong theoretical content, to date, there has been relatively little validation of key propositions of the RBV and, more precisely, of the challenges involved in identifying and measuring key firm and managerial resources together with their incidence on international performance (Fahy, 2002).

In this section, we develop a basic resource-based model of sustainable competitive advantage which is regarded in terms of sustained export activity (see Figure 1). This model encompasses the hypothetical linkages existing between the essential elements of the

FIGURE 1. A Resource-Based Model of the Antecedents of the Born-Global Nature of the Firm

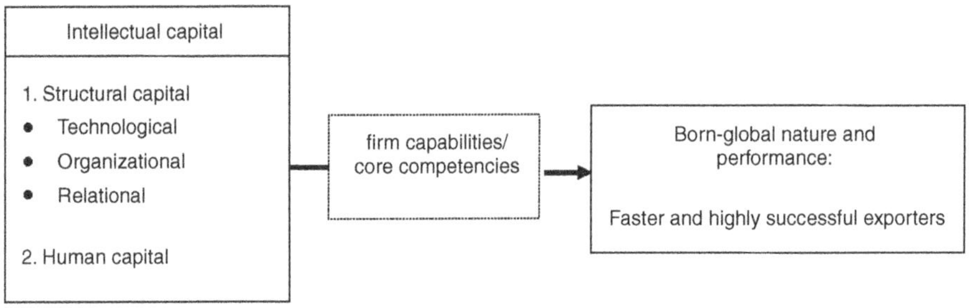

resource-based perspective and the born-global condition of a firm. More concretely, it highlights that a firm's intangible resource and capabilities base may be of the highest relevance in determining such a born global character, which is basically understood here as an earlier and/or faster enrollment in exporting, together with a more successful development as an exporting firm, as compared to the more traditional pattern shown by non born-globals.

Forming part of a firm's stock of *intellectual capital*, intangible resources are, by nature, relatively resistant to duplication efforts by other competitors due to the inherent complexity and specificity of their accumulation process which hinder imitability and substitutability in the short/medium term (Fahy, 2000). They include both people dependent–human capital, and people independent intangible resources: organizational capital, technological capital, and relational capital (Hall, 1992; Fernández et al., 2000).

Human capital is basically defined as generic and specific knowledge, inseparable from its bearer, which increases his/her productivity. Thus all forms of individual intelligence, skills, personal contacts and relations, training, experience, insight, and motivation of individual managers and workers of a firm can be included here. *Organizational capital* embraces norms, procedures, and guidelines, as well as internal organizational structures, corporate culture, company networks and databases, and its formal and informal planning, controlling, and coordinating systems. The firm's stock of *technological capital* includes knowledge related to the internal or external access, assimilation, use and innovation of production techniques and product technol-

ogy. It basically consists of several forms of intellectual property and regulatory protection such as copyrights and trademarks, patents, and trade secrets, among others. Finally, *relational capital* consists of those intangible resources more directly related to the marketplace. It logically includes brands and company reputation, customer loyalty, long-term customer relationships, and distribution channels, among others.

Firm capabilities have proved even more difficult to be analyzed. Thus, in the context of strategic management research, firm-specific capabilities have been regarded as rather "unobservable," path-dependent assets because their accumulation process is characterized by high levels of tacitness and causal ambiguity (Lippman and Rumelt, 1982; Reed and DeFillippi, 1990). Essentially, they are, in part, the result of combining the intangible resources of the firm as capabilities encompass complex interactions of individuals, groups, and organizational routines through which all the firm's resources are coordinated (Wernerfelt, 1984, 1989; Grant, 1991). Thus, firm capabilities are particularly complex in their development and valuation because their usually tacit character make them difficult to be observed by others and do not have clear property rights.

Accordingly, a firm's stock of intellectual capital (integrating several types of intangible resources and firm-specific capabilities) seems to include a strategically more relevant list of resources as compared to those of a purely tangible nature. Most of these intangible resources can only be developed over long periods of time (i.e., path-dependence), it may be not always clear how to develop them in the short-medium term (mostly because of social complexity) and/or cannot be easily transferred among firms or internally replicated by others (due to intrinsic causal ambiguity). On the other hand, according to the theoretical assumptions of the RBV, intangible resources (human, organizational, technological, and relational capital) are heterogeneously distributed among different (exporting) firms. Moreover, the level accumulated of intellectual capital by a firm is difficult to replicate by other competitors at least in the short-medium term.

Therefore, the amount and type of intangible resources might well influence the born global condition of the firm (i.e., having been a faster and currently a highly successful exporter). Thus, if we empirically define born global firms as those accomplishing at least two critical characteristics: (a) becoming international approximately from the time of inception (McDougall et al., 1994), and (b) being currently exporting more successfully (i.e., above the export intensity level shown, in average, by the rest of firms contained in the reference sample at a specific moment in time); then we could hypothesize that those firms showing a wider variety of components of intellectual capital would also have a higher probability of being considered as such born globals. More concretely, we will test in this paper whether:

> *H1: Those firms with a greater amount of human capital have a higher probability of being born globals than those firms lacking such human capital resources.*

> *H2: Those firms with more organizational capital have a higher probability of being born globals than those firms without such organizational capital.*

> *H3: Those firms with a higher level of technological capital have a higher probability of being born globals than those firms without such level of technological capital.*

> *H4: Those firms with a certain degree of relational capital have a higher probability of being born global than those firms lacking such relational capital.*

RESEARCH METHODOLOGY

Sampling Issues and General Description of the Database

The empirical part of this study is based on a survey conducted in 1996 among a representative sample of manufacturing firms registered as exporters in the database OFERES obtained from the ICEX (Spanish Institute of Foreign Trade), in any one of the years 1991-1993. This sample has been already used in previous studies about Spanish exporters (Alonso and Donoso, 1997). For determining the concrete unit of analysis contained in the sample, a random stratified sampling method was implemented. Three different criteria of stratification were considered: the industrial sector where the firm belongs (9 sectors were distinguished), the size of the firm (measured in terms of export volume), and its relationship with the international markets (this is, if the firm was a regular or a sporadic exporter). The total number of firms in the sample was 1,102. This number guaranteed a sampling error of $\pm$ 3%, at a confidence level of 95%. In addition, a personal survey technique was performed from May 1996 through October 1996, addressed to the export manager of the firm.

Independent Variables

In Table 1, we show the variables that were considered as intangible resources indicators in our analysis as well as their basic descriptive statistics. As can be seen, these variables have been classified according to each specific type of intangible resources.

Technological capital: Several studies have previously investigated the relationship between technological innovation and export behavior/performance usually confirming a positive relation between them (Wakelin, 1998; Lefebvre et al., 1998). Although no generally accepted approach to the measurement of technological (knowledge) intensity has yet been developed (Autio, Sapienza and Almeida, 2000), some objective indicators, such as R&D spending or patents, have been mostly preferred. In this research, the firm's stock of technological capital was captured through the amount invested

TABLE 1. Independent Variables in the Analysis

INTANGIBLE RESOURCES	%
TECHNOLOGICAL CAPITAL	
Technological intensity: (% of R&D expenditures/total sales) 1. 0% 2. > 0%	18.6 81.4
ORGANIZATIONAL CAPITAL	
Organizational arrangements for exporting: Foreign Trade/Export Department existence inside the firm . . . 1. Yes 2. No	54.1 45.9
Foreign market knowledge: 1. Foreign market research is systematically performed by means of several sources of information 2. No foreign market information is systematically collected	17.8 82.2
Export planning systems: 1. No formal planning for exporting 2. Export activity is formally and systematically planned	66.8 33.2
HUMAN CAPITAL	
Level of quality of employees: (% of total employees with higher studies) 1. Less than 10% 2. Between 10%-20% 3. More than 20%	24.9 44.8 30.3
Perceived relative export profitability: export sales profitability versus domestic sales profitability is perceived by managers as being generally . . . 1. Higher 2. Equal 3. Lesser	37.6 43.4 19.1
RELATIONAL CAPITAL	
Post-sale service performance to foreign clients: 1. Performed 2. Not performed	45.0 55.0
Contractual agreements with foreign firms: 0. No 1. Yes	69.0 31.0

by each firm in R&D activities in terms of its total sales (% expenditures in R&D/total sales), thus distinguishing between those exporting firms which devoted part of their efforts to the improvement of products and/or processes quality and degree of technical sophistication, and those which did not at least in a regular basis.

Organizational capital: According to the previous section, this category of intangible assets includes, among others, a firm's procedures and guidelines, as well as internal structures, company databases, formal and/ or informal planning and coordinating systems, etc. In the specific case of exporting firms, such organizational resources may well refer to the existence of export-specialized units inside the firm, as well as export planning systems, decision-making processes related to this activity, and mechanisms for conducting systematic foreign market research. Some authors

have predicted a gradual increase in a firm's resource commitment towards international operations (Johanson and Vahlne, 1990), where the higher the level of export involvement by the firm, the higher the allocation of infrastructural resources. Moreover, several studies have empirically attributed a higher level of export performance to those firms making major use of systematic mechanisms for gaining foreign market knowledge. Similarly, the existence of foreign trade departments inside the firm is also more likely as it approaches exporting in a more proactive and successful manner (Aaby and Slater, 1989).

In this research, organizational capital could be measured in terms of three distinct variables, it being our expectation that they were highly correlated with the firm's level of export capability and, consequently, export performance. One of them, labeled "organizational arrangements for exporting," revealed the existence of an export department inside the firm's organizational formal structure. Another variable, "export-planning systems," provided information about whether export activity was formally and systematically planned by the firm or, contrarily, such a formal planning system for exporting simply did not exist. Finally, the variable "foreign market knowledge" measured the degree in which foreign market research was systematically performed by means of several sources of information, versus the opposite situation where no foreign market information was systematically collected by the exporting firm. This more formally planned, systematic, and highly structured exploration of business opportunities abroad should theoretically correlate with a more proactive export behavior. However, as some degree of relationship could be expected between the presence of a trade/export department and a more systematical plan for exporting as well as with conducting foreign market research, we first analyzed these possible relationships through contingency tables. As can be observed in Table 2, of those firms having an export department, 32.9% systematically conducted foreign market knowledge activities, while none firm did it if it had not such export department. In the same vein, of those firms with an export department, 47% also developed a formal export planning, while considering the total sample, only 32.2% systematically conducted foreign market research (see Table 2). Therefore, the model was finally estimated without these two mutually dependent variables.

Relational capital: This class of intangible resource is conceptualized as those assets of a firm that are directly related to the marketplace (Fernández et al., 2000). Due to the lack of information in our database concerning aspects such as brand and company reputation, customer loyalty, and so on, we could rely only on one proxy variable estimating the firm's long-term relationships with both customers and distribution channels. Such relationships usually demand care, confidence, regularity, and frequent communication on behalf of each party, but can also help increase exports significantly (Miesenböck, 1988). Our variable, labeled "performance of complementary, post-sales service to foreign clients" basically informed us whether the exporters in our sam-

ple were able to offer sale services directly to their customers abroad or not. Very often, this possibility is also related to the use of wholly-owned distribution channels abroad, i.e., direct export channels established by the firm itself (such as sales subsidiaries, sales branches, etc.), instead of relying on export agents and foreign distributors (external networks) who usually lack customer service capabilities. However, and due mostly to financial restrictions, some firms usually decide to select, as their first best for offering sales services to foreign customers, to implement co-operation agreements. Thus we have also considered if a firm had established this strategic collaboration tool or not.

Human capital: It refers to both generic and specific knowledge that is rather inseparable from its bearer and increases individual productivity. It may then include all those forms of personal knowledge, skills, experiences, training, and even attitudes or perceptions of both managers and employees. Several studies have already attributed a higher level of export performance to those firms having highly qualified and better motivated staffs. Similarly, the assignment of more qualified personnel into foreign trade departments, as well as their corresponding levels of motivation, technical training and command of foreign languages, for instance, usually correlates highly with a more successful export performance (Aaby and Slater, 1989). Also, key managers and/or decision-makers' influences on the firm's export behavior have been widely investigated in the SMEs' export literature (Dichtl et al., 1990). Thus, the nature of key managers' expectations and attitudes, including their export-related success perception, generally affect both export behavior and performance (Aaby and Slater, 1989; Louter et al., 1991; Leonidou and Katsikeas, 1996). Clearly, those firms whose management seems to show higher–but realistic–expectations toward export activities will likely be less reluctant to allocate resources to such operations. Moreover, further resource commitment decisions can be also reinforced by an *ex-ante* perception of some degree of success in evaluating current export performance. Consequently, human capital resources were measured in this research at these two different levels inside the firm: em-

TABLE 2. Relationships Between Export Department, Foreign Market Knowledge, and Export Planning System

	Foreign market knowledge		Export planning system		**Total**
Export department	No systematically collected	Systematically performed	No formal planning	Formal export planning	
No	100%		83%	17%	506
Yes	67.1%	32.9%	53%	47%	596
Total	82.2%	17.8%	66.8%	32.2%	1,102
Chi square	202.4***		110.91***		

***Sig. < 0.01

ployees and export managers. At the employees-level, the level of quality of these human resources was inquired by computing the percentage of total employees with higher studies/specialized training in each firm. At the export management level, we took into account Bilkey's (1982) previous finding that a higher estimation of export versus domestic profitability constitutes a potential export success factor. Thus, export managers were also asked about the perceived level of profitability resulting from export versus domestic sales.

Control Variables

Firm size: Firm dimension has usually been taken as a possible determinant of export behavior (Bonaccorsi, 1992; Calof, 1994). Generally speaking, insufficient size is seen as a critical handicap for starting and/or conducting export business in a more regular basis (Miesenböck, 1988). Thus, a certain critical mass seems to be necessary before reasonable export results can be reached. However, in spite of the great empirical attention paid to this variable in the last decades, not much agreement still seems to exist on its observed impact on export performance (Moen, 1999). This lack of consensus in research results calls for the use of several criteria for measuring size. Consequently, in this research we also introduced, as a control variable, firm size as measured by the number of total employees (with 100 employees as a cut-off value for distinguishing between larger and smaller firms), and total sales volume (in logarithmic form).

Sector: The type of industry in which the company competes can also have an impact on its export performance. Actually, the development of firm-specific, competitive advantage takes place within a particular sector or segment. Thus, the generic class of product or service offered by the company usually becomes another relevant issue in its internationalization process as industries themselves vary in competitiveness and international opportunities (Miesenböck, 1988; Johanson and Mattsson, 1988). Certain manufacturing activities are more likely than others to require adaptations to enable export operations. Interestingly, many empirical studies have not considered this factor explicitly due mostly to their sector-specific character. However, when this variable has been included in previous studies of firm's export behavior (Louter et al., 1991; Alonso and Donoso, 1997), some differences have been systematically detected, thus confirming its potential influence on the level of export success finally achieved by the firm. Thus, taking this into account, the general product class of the exporters in the sample was also used as another control variable.

Export experience: Finally, as the number of years that a firm has been exporting could also have an impact on its level of export performance (Bloodgood et al., 1996; Aspelund and Moen, 2001), we also included such export experience as another control variable in our analysis. In Table 3 some descriptive statistics on these three control variables are shown.

Dependent Variable

Born global firms are, by theoretic definition, international at inception. Thus, for our purposes, both the year of start up of the firm and the year in which it began to export were,

TABLE 3. Control Variables

CONTROL VARIABLES			
Product class:		5. Non-metal products	7.0%
1. Agriculture and Food	11.6%	6. Iron and Mining	10.9%
2. Clothes, Shoes and Leather	19.1%	7. Electronics and Telecommunications	14.9%
3. Paper, Wood, and Furniture	9.7%	8. Cars and other vehicles	7.4%
4. Chemicals	11.7%	9. Construction	7.8%
Firm size: (measured by number of employees)			
1. Up to 25			36.2%
2. From 26-50			25.0%
3. From 51-250			26.1%
4. More than 251			12.7%
Export experience: (measured by number of years exporting)			16.56 years (average)

of course, crucial variables, and both were contained in the database. However, any conceptual definition of born global firms seems to carry on several problems of empirical operationalization. Actually, there is neither general resolution to the ambiguity concerning the point at which a venture is considered really formed, nor a satisfactory operational definition of the term "global" itself. For instance, Oviatt and McDougall (1997) suggested that an INV/born global should be operationally defined as a firm that makes observable foreign commitments (e.g., sales efforts, specific investments) within a "conventionally accepted" short period after establishment. In their opinion, if internationalization takes place during the first six years period, it is likely to have occurred during the venture's formative stage. However, the selection of any particular period is, in our opinion, somehow arbitrary, and rather the two-to-three years from birth convention seems to have been basically adopted as the standard in the literature (Christensen, 1991; Moen, 2000; Madsen et al., 2000).

Consequently, in this paper, those firms exporting not later than two years after their start-up, regardless the period in which such a birth took place, were tentatively considered as potential born globals. Furthermore, following the results obtained by different authors (McDougall and Oviatt, 1996; Autio, Sapienza and Almeida, 2000), we believe that the empirical definition of a born global firm would be better adjusted if it was completed with the condition of reaching some level of exports at a certain point in time. Therefore, we also added a second relevant condition for a firm to be considered a born global one: the

level of exports over total sales should have reached, at least, the level obtained, in average, by the total number of firms in the sample when data were collected in 1996 (39.47%).

Accordingly, the number of Spanish manufacturing firms that started exporting before two years since their foundation increases significantly, in average, along time (Table 4). Thus, although a certain number of firms exporting not longer than two years from inception have traditionally existed before, their raise in number is clearly increasing, mainly among those exporters born after 1987.

Moreover, considering the group of exporters that were born before 1961, only 7% of these firms can be considered as being born global according to our operational criteria, whereas 50% of the companies born after 1987 meet our empirical definition of born-globalness. Therefore, born global firms have systematically existed since long time ago, though their relevance in number has clearly risen in the last several years. Therefore, in our opinion, the born global issue cannot be considered only a new phenomenon of the nineties, although we acknowledge a huge increase of such type of firms in the last decade.

In Table 5, we also analyze the existence of born globals according to the industrial sector where they belong. Again, some statistically significant relationships were found. The percentage of born globals, considering the total number of firms in the sample, reaches almost 23%. However, if we focus on some specific sectors (i.e., clothes, shoes and leather, cars and other vehicles, construction or non-metal products), the percentage of firms which accomplish the born global operational defini-

TABLE 4. Operational Definition of Born Globals (Year of Export − Year of Start Up ≤ 2 and % of Export Intensity ≥ 39.47% = Total Sample Average)

For those firms which started up . . .	N	Mean (%)	Standard Deviation
< 1961	315	7	0.26
1961-1980	403	21	0.40
1981-1987	241	30	0.46
> 1987	143	50	0.50
Total	1,102		
F test		41.18***	

***Sig. < 0.01

TABLE 5. Distribution of Spanish Born-Global Firms by Sector of Activity

	Born global (dif ≤ 2 and % exports ≥ 39.47%)		
	No	Yes	**Total**
Agriculture, Food	77.3%	22.7%	128
Clothes, Shoes, Leather	67.1%	**32.9%**	210
Wood, Paper, Furniture	83.2%	16.8%	107
Chemicals	81.4%	18.6%	129
Non-metal products	75.3%	24.7%	77
Iron and Mining	88.3%	**11.7%**	120
Electronics and Telecommunications	78.0%	22.0%	164
Cars and other vehicles	74.1%	25.9%	81
Construction and other	74.4%	25.6%	86
Total	77.1%	22.9%	1,102
Chi square		24.97***	

***Sig. < 0.01

tion is significantly higher. There could be some specific characteristics in these sectors (such as scale economies, other global competitors, entry barriers, etc.) that imply the convenience of acting in a global way from the very beginning. In addition, a large number of a venture's customers and/or competitors are already global in these industries. In this context, smaller exporters try to distinguish themselves by means of producing leading edge technology products oriented toward international niche markets. On the other hand, the percentage of born global firms in sectors such as iron and mine, wood, paper, and furniture, and also chemistry is significantly smaller than

the average percentage at the total sample level for the Spanish case.

Statistical Procedures

In order to check the relationship apparently existing between the firms' resource endowments and the possible born global condition of each firm in the sample, a logit regression model was applied. The dependent variable distinguished between the born global (1) versus non born global (0) status of each firm, and the independent variables allowed us to characterize the different types of intangible resources of these firms as discussed above. Several estimations of our conceptual model took place at different stages according to the different number of independent and control variables included in the analysis and a further refinement of the empirical definition of the born global condition being used.

RESULTS AND DISCUSSION

Model #1

As can be seen in Table 6, hypothesis 1 was partly confirmed in the first model ("Model 1"). The two variables used for testing this hypothesis showed the expected sign and were significant. With qualitative variables, as this was the case, one category of the variable becomes the reference category so the effects–i.e., the signs–and their significance, should be interpreted in terms of this omitted category. Therefore, the level of quality of employees was computed attending to the percentage of employees with higher studies. This variable had three categories. The omitted one was the last one: the percentage of total employees with higher studies is higher than 20%. So, the signs for the other two categories were expected to be negative, meaning that the higher the percentage of employees with higher training, the higher the probability of being a successful born global firm. With our data, the coefficient for the first category presents the right sign but was not significant, while the coefficient for the second category was negative and statistically significant. Concerning the results for the second variable measuring the

TABLE 6. Logit Estimations

TECHNOLOGICAL CAPITAL	Model 1	Model 2	Model 3	Model 4
Technological intensity: % of R&D expenditures/total sales > 0%	−0.565**	−0.556**	−0.475**	−0.537**
ORGANIZATIONAL CAPITAL				
Organizational arrangements for exporting: Foreign Trade/Export Department exists inside the firm	0.493**	0.492**	0.568***	0.466**
HUMAN CAPITAL				
Level of quality of employees: % of total employees with higher studies less than 10%	−0.335	−0.342	−0.206	−0.376
Level of quality of employees: % of total employees with higher studies: 10-20%	−0.571***	−0.559***	−0.455**	−0.588***
Perceived relative export profitability: export sales profitability is perceived as being generally higher versus domestic sales profitability	0.965***	0.951***	0.917***	0.965***
Perceived relative export profitability: export sales profitability is perceived as being generally equal versus domestic sales profitability	0.469*	0.418	0.371	0.423
RELATIONAL CAPITAL				
Post-sale service performance to foreign clients: 1. Yes; 2. No	−0.177	−0.139	−0.118	−0.155
Agreements with foreign firms: 0. No; 1. Yes	−0.022	−0.073	−0.031	−0.110
CONTROL VARIABLES				
Agriculture and Food	0.093	0.185	0.265	0.135
Clothes, Shoes and Leather	0.780**	0.836**	0.841**	0.865**
Paper, Wood, and Furniture	−0.160	−0.016	0.034	−0.032
Chemicals	−0.001	0.167	0.262	0.148
Non-metal products	0.346	0.440	0.478	0.459
Iron and Mining	−0.685	−0.587	−0.494	−0.579
Electronics and Telecommunications	0.188	0.179	0.215	0.192
Cars and other vehicles	0.520	0.492	0.567	0.519
26-50	0.086	0.097		0.064
51-250	0.095	0.102		0.048
> 250	0.045	0.096		0.020
Ln of revenues			−0.063	
Number of years exporting				0.01*
Constant	−1.51***	−1.594***	−1.335**	−1.714***

Model 1:	−2 loglikelihood: 834.995	*Chi squared: 57.135***
Percentage of correct classification: 64%		• Percentage of correct classification of born global: 66.1% • Percentage of correct classification of non-born global: 63.4%
Model 2:	−2 loglikelihood: 826.934	*Chi squared: 55.27***
Percentage of correct classification: 63.7%		• Percentage of correct classification of born global: 61.9% • Percentage of correct classification of non-born global: 70.3%
Model 3:	−2 loglikelihood: 819.610	*Chi squared: 53.068***
Percentage of correct classification: 61.7%		• Percentage of correct classification of born global: 59.3% • Percentage of correct classification of non-born global: 69.9%
Model 4:	−2 loglikelihood: 823.689	*Chi squared: 58.523***
Percentage of correct classification: 64.3%		• Percentage of correct classification of born global: 62.5% • Percentage of correct classification of non-born global: 70.8%

***Sig. < 0.01; **Sig. < 0.05; *Sig. < 0.1

level of human capital (perceived relative export profitability by export managers), it had also three categories. In this case, the reference category is the one assuming that export sales profitability is perceived as being generally smaller versus domestic sales profitability. The other two categories (equal expected profitability or higher expected profitability of exports versus domestic sales) showed positive signs and both were statistically significant. So, when Spanish export managers expect as minimum the same profitability with exports that the one obtained with the domestic sales, then the probability of their firms being a born global as previously defined increases.

As expected, hypothesis 2 was also confirmed. Thus, the presence of a foreign trade/export department inside the firm, as an organizational resource for earlier and better conducting export activities, had a positive and significant effect on the dependent variable. Thus, the probability of being a born global firm was indeed higher when the company showed such an organizational arrangement for exporting.

However, hypothesis 3 was not confirmed, at least by using the percentage of R&D expenditure versus total sales for measuring the firm's level of technological resource intensity: those firms with a positive percentage in R&D were, interestingly, those more unlikely to be considered as born globals. Although possible explanations could be found for this unexpected result according to the past born global literature (Rialp et al., 2005), we believe that more research is needed related to the effect of technological capital on the probability of being a born global company. As a limitation, we indicate that this observed and highly significant negative influence of technological resources on the born global condition of the exporting firm would have been probably different if the analysis had been performed by means of a set of variables capturing the usually accumulative process of these technological assets (technological inputs and outputs).

Finally, hypothesis 4 was not confirmed in this first model. The coefficients of the two variables measuring relational capital (if post-sale service was performed to foreign clients, and if the firm had established cooperation agreements with other firms), showed both a negative sign and were not significant.

Models #2, #3, and #4

In spite of the analysis carried above, it could be argued that reaching a concrete level of exports could indeed depend on the specific moment in which the firm was constituted as well as on the number of years that it had been exporting. Therefore, instead of using a general percentage of export intensity in 1996 for

the total sample as the second criteria for empirically measuring the born global nature of a firm, we calculated the average export intensity of these firms in the same year after grouping them according to their different constitution period (Table 7).

Therefore, now for being considered as a born global, a firm that was started up in, for instance, 1961 should have started exporting before 1963 and being exporting at least 36.65% of its sales in 1996. Considering this refined and more exhaustive operational definition, we ran the logit analysis again, being the results presented under the column "Model 2." Basically, most of the results obtained in this second estimation as compared to the first model are maintained. However, the coefficient for the variable export sales profitability is perceived as being generally equal versus domestic sales profitability did not turn to be statistically significant as it was before. After a new variation of this second model, by making use of the Ln of revenues instead of the number of employees for capturing firm size as a control variable, the results were still the same (see "Model 3"). Those coefficients statistically significant in model 2 were also significant in model 3, and they showed the same sign. Consequently, in spite of the changes introduced in the estimation procedures, these further results seem to confirm the statistical robustness of those already obtained under the column "Model 1."

Finally, we also introduced the control variable export experience in the analysis ("Model 4") only when the second criterion for empirically defining the born global nature of a firm im-

TABLE 7. Export Intensity Ratio (% Exports-to-Total Sales)

For those firms which started up . . .	N	Mean (%)	Standard Deviation
< 1961	311	36.65	26.86
1961-1980	395	37.75	28.40
1981-1987	237	39.88	27.23
> 1987	139	49.94	32.91
Total	1,082	39.47	28.61
F test		7.852***	

***Sig. < 0.01

plied to consider the average export intensity ratio once having grouped the firms according to their establishment period. As expected, this variable had a positive and significant coefficient. This suggests that the higher the number of years a firm has been exporting, the higher the probability of being a born global as compared to those firms that were constituted in the same period.

Thus, at least according to our data, Spanish born global firms are particularly characterized by a strong combination of intangible assets but either of a human or organizational character only, and not technological neither relational-oriented capital. In particular, the existence of an export department in charge of this export activity inside the firm, the percentage of employees with higher training/studies and, finally, the managers' more positive profitability perceptions associated with exporting seem to be crucial signals of the born global condition of the Spanish industrial exporters. The importance of human capital resources found here seems to be consistent with previous results by different authors. For example, in their study of 24 INVs from at least ten countries all over the world and located in a variety of industries, McDougall et al. (1994) discovered that the founders of INVs are individuals who see opportunities from establishing ventures that operate internationally from inception. Thus, the several competencies (knowledge, networks, and background) that they have been able to develop from their earlier activities allow them to combine a particular set of resources across national borders rather than just on their home markets and form, in this way, a given INV/born global.

Contrarily, non born global exporters in the Spanish industrial sectors, those who started exports at least longer than 2 years after establishment and performed rather unsuccessfully in terms of export intensity in 1996 as compared to their counterparts born global firms, were also those who clearly lacked adequate organizational and human capital resources for developing such export behavior and performance. From a resource-based perspective, these other firms were poorly characterized in terms of critical intangible assets, as they tended to show the lowest percentage of employees with higher studies in the sample, and

had not even created an export department inside the organizational structure of the firm long after establishment. Moreover, their managers showed rather negative attitudes about profitability obtained from export versus domestic operations.

An interesting result was found in the relationship between one of the control variables, sector, and the probability of accomplish the empirical definition of born global being used. As can be observed in Table 6, those firms specifically belonging to the clothes, shoes and leather sectors showed a statistically significant higher probability of being considered born global firms as compared to others (construction). This result coincides with the general evidence that many Spanish exporting firms seem to operate successfully in these sectors both in the domestic and export markets, in which Spanish firms have traditionally manifested relevant competitive advantages. Thus, apparently, Spanish exporters in this particular sectors possess or control the level of intangible resources that allows them to implement more well-adapted export marketing strategies and, as a consequence, to obtain a sustained competitive advantage abroad. This result may also refer to the fact that the degree of control over export marketing practices on behalf of the firm varies according to the more or less advanced export stage where it is (Leonidou and Katsikeas, 1996), and to the higher likelihood of performing major control over marketing-mix decisions when export activities become regular, highly systematic and more formally planned by the exporters as it is the case for several exporting firms in these traditional Spanish industries.

CONCLUDING REMARKS AND IMPLICATIONS

This study has primarily shown that the level of intangible resources (whether of a human, organizational, technological or relational character) may partly affect the born-global character of an exporting firm. More concretely, according to our results, the Spanish exporters that can be considered as being born globals seem to differ in terms of their level of export capability due to an heterogeneous distribution of intangible resource endowments among firms (mostly in terms of human capital and organizational resources), apart from other issues regarding firm size and the class of product/sector in which they compete.

In our opinion, our results shed light on issues relevant to practitioners, policy-makers and export researchers. Hence, the evidence generated in this research could be useful for public policy-makers and export promotion agencies, which are generally very interested in improving a country's exports; mainly in terms of better estimating and developing the export potential of those firms according to their differences in terms of size and/or resources (including, of course, intangible ones). We believe that the efficiency of these institutions could be significantly enriched by means, for instance, of concentrating differently their efforts on firms showing distinct patterns and prospects towards exporting according to their specific resource endowments.

Moreover, since this study has also confirmed the importance of intangible resource management for developing export behavior, further implications of a more managerial nature emerge as well. First, and perhaps the most important thing, just by giving strategic priority to the continuous creation and development of this type of knowledge-based resources, exporting can become a more contributing activity for the firm. Second, it appears that certain intangible resources of an organizational and human dimension, such as employees training practices, managerial attitudes, and more effective organizational arrangements for exporting, also impact on a firm's more rapid development of export capabilities.

For academics and researchers in the area of export behavior, we have shown the potential relevance that the resource-based view of the firm and the issue of intangible resource analysis in particular could have for increasing our current level of knowledge about key determinants of born-global firms' export behavior. Thus, in our opinion, the application of RBV can indeed become very insightful for advancing future export-oriented research directions mostly among born-global firms. However, further research in this context should be still more explicit in terms of how to extract rents

from those resources with apparently more appropriate traits for becoming sources of long-lasting competitive advantage (Peng, 2001). Also, future research on the born global phenomenon should go beyond merely identifying the distinct profile that these firms usually show when compared with other type of exporters to include other more contingent factors potentially affecting export performance in terms of very rapid export orientation, product strategies, geographical markets served, export and other entry modes jointly applied, and control over marketing activities abroad.

Finally, some possible limitations of this research are acknowledged. First, since our data source was not referred to the specific moment in time in which all of these firms were founded, we could not establish the relevance of firm intangible assets management for explaining the emergence of born global firms, but only the combined effect of initiating exports almost from inception and being able to achieve a significant level of export intensity further on (in 1996). Second, the research study presented here is indeed highly country-specific and, therefore, should be taken carefully and conveniently extended into more widely defined sectors and/or countries of, perhaps, different income levels as compared to Spain.

REFERENCES

Aaby, N. E. & Slater, S. F. (1989). Management influence on export performance: A review of the empirical literature 1978-1988. *International Marketing Review*, 6 (4), 7-22.

Alonso, J. A. & Donoso, V. (1997). *Competir en el exterior. La empresa española y los mercados internacionales.* Madrid: ICEX.

Amit, R. & Schoemaker, P.J. (1993). Strategic assets and organizational rent. *Strategic Management Journal*, 14, 33-46.

Andersen, O. (1997). Internationalization and market entry mode: A review of theories and conceptual frameworks. *Management International Review*, 37 (Special Issue 2), 27-42.

Aspelund, A. & Moen, O. A. (2001). A generation perspective on small firms internationalization–from traditional exporters and flexible specialists to born globals. In C.N. Axinn & P. Matthyssens (Eds.), *Reassessing the internationalization of the firm.* Amsterdam, NL: JAI/Elsevier (pp. 197-225).

Autio, E., Sapienza, H.J. & Almeida, J.G. (2000). Effects of age at entry, knowledge intensity, and imitability on international growth. *Academy of Management Journal*, (43) 5, 909-24.

Barney, J.B. (1991). Firm resources and sustained competitive advantage. *Journal of Management*, 17 (1), 99-120.

Barney, J.B. (2001). Resource-based theories of competitive advantage: A ten-year retrospective of the resource-based view. *Journal of Management*, 27, 643-650.

Bilkey, W. J. (1982). Variables associated with export profitability. *Journal of International Business Studies*, 13 (2), 39-56.

Bloodgood, J., Sapienza, H.J. & Almeida, J.G. (1996). The internationalization of new high-potential U.S. ventures: Antecedents and outcomes. *Entrepreneurship Theory and Practice*, 20 (4), 61-76.

Bonaccorsi, A. (1992). On the relationship between firm size and export intensity. *Journal of International Business Studies*, 23 (4), 605-635.

Bond, J. & Michailidis, G. (1997). *Interactive correspondence analysis in a dynamic object-oriented environment*. Retrieved May 9, 2003 from *<URL: http://www.jstat.org/v02/i08/textstuff/jss/>*.

Calof, J. L. (1994). The relationship between firm size and export behaviour revisited. *Journal of International Business Studies*, 25 (2), 367-388.

Christensen, P.R. (1991). The small and medium-sized exporters' squeeze: Empirical evidence and model reflections. *Entrepreneurship & Regional Development*, 3, 49-65.

Conner, K.R. (1991). A historical comparison of resource-based theory and five schools of thought within industrial organization economics: Do we have a new theory of the firm?. *Journal of Management*, 17, 121-154.

Dichtl, E. et al. (1990). International orientation as a precondition for export success. *Journal of International Business Studies*, 21 (1), 32-41.

Dierickx, I. & Cool, K. (1989). Asset stock accumulation and sustainability of competitive advantage. *Management Science*, 35 (12), 1504-1511.

Fahy, J. (2000). The resource-based view of the firm: Some stumbling blocks on the road to understanding sustainable competitive advantage. *Journal of European Industrial Training*, 24, 94-104.

Fahy, J. (2002). A resource-based analysis of sustainable competitive advantage in a global environment. *International Business Review*, 11, 57-78.

Fernández, E., Montes, J.M. & Vázquez, C.J. (2000). Typology and strategic analysis of intangible resources. A resource-based approach. *Technovation*, 20, 81-92.

Grant, R.M. (1991). The resource-based theory of competitive advantage: Implications for strategy formulation. *California Management Review*, 33, 114-135.

Hall, R. (1992). The strategic analysis of intangible resources. *Strategic Management Journal*, 13, 135-144.

Johanson, J. & Mattsson, L.-G. (1988). Internationalization in industrial systems–a network approach. In N. Hood & J.-E. Vahlne (Eds.), *Strategies in global competition*. London: Croom Helm (pp. 287-314).

Johanson J. & Vahlne, J.-E. (1977). The internationalization process of the firm: A model of knowledge development and increasing foreign market commitments. *Journal of International Business Studies*, 8 (1), 23-32.

Johanson, J. & Vahlne, J.-E. (1990). The mechanism of internationalization. *International Marketing Review*, 7 (4), 11-24.

Knight, G.A. & Cavusgil, S.T. (1996). The born global firm: a challenge to traditional internationalization theory. In: S.T. Cavusgil & T.K. Madsen (eds.), *Export internationalizing research–enrichment and challenges*. NY: JAI Press Inc. (pp. 11-26).

Lefebvre, E., Lefebvre, L. & Bourgault, M. (1998). R&D-related capabilities as determinants of export performance. *Small Business Economics*, 10, 365-377.

Leonidou, L. C. & Katsikeas, C. S. (1996). The export development process: An integrative review of empirical models. *Journal of International Business Studies*, 27 (3), 517-551.

Lippman, S.A. & Rumelt, R.P. (1982). Uncertain imitability: An analysis of interfirm differences in efficiency under competition. *Bell Journal of Economics*, 13, 418-438.

Louter, P.J., Oouwerkerk, C. & Bakker, B.A. (1991). An inquiry into successful exporting. *European Journal of Marketing*, 25 (6), 7-23.

Madsen, T.K. & Servais, P. (1997). The internationalization of born globals: An evolutionary process? *International Business Review*, 6 (6), 561-583.

Madsen, T.K., Rasmussen, E.S. & Servais, P. (2000). Differences and similarities between born globals and other types of exporters. In A. Yaprak & H. Tutek (Eds.), *Globalization, the multinational firm, and emerging economies*. Amsterdam: JAI/Elsevier (pp. 247-65).

Mahoney, J.T. & Pandian, J.R. (1992). The resource-based view within the conversation of strategic management. *Strategic Management Journal*, 13, 363-380.

McDougall, P.P. & Oviatt, B.M. (1996). New venture internationalization, strategic change, and performance: A follow-up study. *Journal of Business Venturing*, 11 (1), 23-40.

McDougall, P.P., Shane, S. & Oviatt, B.M. (1994). Explaining the formation of international new ventures. *Journal of Business Venturing*, 9 (6), 469-487.

Miesenböck, K. J. (1988). Small business and exporting: A literature review. *International Small Business Journal*, 6 (2), 42-61.

Moen, O. (1999). The relationship between firm size, competitive advantages and export performance revisited. *International Small Business Journal*, 18 (1), 53-71.

Moen, O. (2000). SMEs and international marketing: Investigating the differences in export strategy between firms of different size. *Journal of Global Marketing*, 13 (4), 7-28.

Moen, O. (2002). The born globals: A new generation of small European Exporters. *International Marketing Review*, 19 (2), 156-175.

Oviatt, B.M. & McDougall, P.P. (1994). Toward a theory of international new ventures. *Journal of International Business Studies*, 25 (1), 45-64.

Oviatt, B.M. & McDougall, P.P. (1997). Challenges for internationalization process theory: The case of international new ventures. *Management International Review*, 37 (Special Issue 2), 85-99.

Peng. M. (2001). The resource-based view and international business. *Journal of Management*, 27, 803-829.

Peteraf, M. (1993). The cornerstones of competitive advantage: A resource-based view. *Strategic Management Journal*, 14 (3), 179-191.

Reed, R. & DeFillippi, R.J. (1990). Causal ambiguity, barriers to imitation, and sustainable competitive advantage. *Academy of Management Review*, 15 (1), 88-102.

Reid, S. D. (1983). Firm internationalization, transaction costs, and strategy choice. *International Marketing Review*, 1 (2), 44-56.

Rialp, A. and Rialp, J. (2001). Conceptual frameworks on SMEs' internationalization: Past, present, and future trends of research. In C.N. Axinn and P. Matthyssens (Eds.), *Reassessing the internationalization of the firm*. Amsterdam: JAI/Elsevier (pp. 49-78).

Rialp, A., Rialp, J. & Knight, G.A. (2005). The phenomenon of early internationalizing firms: What do we know after a decade (1993-2003) of scientific inquiry? *International Business Review*, 14 (2), 147-166.

Wakelin, K. (1998). Innovation and export behavior at the firm level. *Research Policy*, 26 (7-8), 829-841.

Welch, L. S. & Luostarinen, R. (1988). Internationalization: Evolution of a concept. *Journal of General Management*, 14 (2), 36-64.

Wernerfelt, B. (1984). A resource-based view of the firm. *Strategic Management Journal*, 5, 171-180.

Wernerfelt, B. (1989). From critical resources to corporate strategy. *Journal of General Management*, 14, 4-12.

doi:10.1300/J037v16n01_06

Internationalization and Performance: Evidence from Spanish Firms

Oscar Martín Martín
Nicolas Papadopoulos

SUMMARY. This research presents a model to describe the stages of the internationalization process, and its potential link to performance, based on cluster analysis of data from 200 interviews with Spanish companies. The results show four initial phases in internationalization that are similar to those found in earlier research, but also a new stage at the end of the process, "Globalization," which has not been reported before. Firm performance in relation to the stages of internationalization is analyzed using eight indicators, which yield somewhat different results for distinct measures of international versus overall performance. The data also show a non-monotonic "valleys and peaks" relationship of performance across the five stages, suggesting that firms face critical challenges at key points during their international expansion. The study concludes with an outline of implications for business and public policy as well as suggested directions for future research. doi:10.1300/J037v16n01_07 *[Article copies available for a fee from The Haworth Document Delivery Service: 1-800-HAWORTH. E-mail address: <docdelivery@haworthpress.com> Website: <http:// www.HaworthPress.com> © 2006 by The Haworth Press, Inc. All rights reserved.]*

KEYWORDS. Internationalization, international performance, export performance, international business, international marketing

INTRODUCTION

The economic globalization process that has been evolving worldwide (Levitt, 1984; Yip, 1992; Bartlett & Ghoshal, 2000) is bringing about important changes in the firm's international environment. Together with well known developments such as easier access to foreign markets and the overall increase in competitive pressures, recent research suggests that the internationalization process of the firm is itself changing. As Andersson (2002, p. 365) put it, an important issue for research today is to understand the process of firms "internationalising in a moving context of other firms internationalising," particularly

Dr. Oscar Martín Martín is Assistant Professor of Marketing, Business Administration Department, Faculty of Economics Science and Business Administration, Public University of Navarre, Campus Arrosadía s/n, 31006 Pamplona, Navarre, Spain (E-mail: oscar.martin@navarra.es). Dr. Nicolas Papadopoulos is Professor of Marketing and International Business, Eric Sprott School of Business, Carleton University, 1125 Colonel By Drive, Ottawa, Canada K1S 5B6 (E-mail: npapadop@carleton.ca).

[Haworth co-indexing entry note]: "Internationalization and Performance: Evidence from Spanish Firms." Martín, Oscar Martín and Nicolas Papadopoulos. Co-published simultaneously in *Journal of Euromarketing* (International Business Press, an imprint of The Haworth Press, Inc.) Vol. 16, No. 1/2, 2006, pp. 87-103; and: *Contemporary Euromarketing: Entry and Operational Decision Making* (ed: Jorma Larimo) International Business Press, an imprint of The Haworth Press, Inc., 2006, pp. 87-103. Single or multiple copies of this article are available for a fee from The Haworth Document Delivery Service [1-800-HAWORTH, 9:00 a.m. - 5:00 p.m. (EST). E-mail address: docdelivery@haworthpress.com].

as internationalization involves "connected and overlapping network processes." While Andersson (2002) did address this question in the context of channel intermediaries, the broader issue of whether this new environment has affected the traditional understanding of the internationalization process (Johanson & Wiedersheim-Paul, 1975) has not received attention. In fact, Axinn and Matthyssens (2002, p. 436) posit that "existing internationalization theories are inadequate to explain, let alone predict, the behavior actually observed in firms today."

Research on the internationalization process is needed and useful for at least two principal reasons. First, because of the broader benefit of leading to a better understanding of the behavior of firms. Second, because of its potentially critical link to the firm's international and overall performance, which, as Katsikeas, Leonidou, and Morgan (2000, p. 493) rightly stress, are matters of "vital interest" in public policy, business, and research. Yet in their seminal review these authors note that while export performance "is one of the most widely researched" issues, it also is "[one of the] least understood and most contentious areas of international marketing." They attribute this to such factors as the difficulties in conceptualizing and operationalizing international research as well as in measuring export performance itself.

Overall, therefore, it appears that current empirical research has not kept pace with potential changes to the traditional stage-based internationalization theory of the firm, which may have changed over time, let alone with its link to export performance. In light of the above, this study has two main objectives: to explore and describe the stages of a specific internationalization model based on a contemporary sample of Spanish firms; and to analyze the firms' performance in relation to their stage in their internationalization process.

The study aims to contribute to the literature in four main ways. First, it proposes an internationalization model that partly supports the general stage-based conceptualization that prevails to date, but also contrasts it by including firms that are parts of larger networks and do not have full control over their international strategies. While the study is based on firms

from one country, its findings may also be useful in explaining the processes followed by those from other countries that have significant foreign direct investment (FDI) inflows. Second, the study expands the "stages of internationalization" model to include a new and distinctive "globalization" stage, thus linking it to the contemporary environment. Third, in attempting to address some of the measurement issues identified by Katsikeas, Leonidou, and Morgan (2000), the study uses a larger number (eight) of performance indicators than most earlier studies, and suggests that internationalization appears to be linked more to international than overall firm performance. Lastly, the study suggests that key performance measures do not necessarily have a monotonic or curvilinear relationship with internationalization, as has been suggested in earlier studies and identified by Hsu and Boggs (2003), but may also display a "valleys and peaks" pattern, with performance improving in some stages but worsening in others that follow.

The study is presented in four sections following this introduction, including the literature review and hypotheses, description of the research methodology, presentation and discussion of the findings, and implications from the results along with suggestions for future research.

LITERATURE REVIEW AND HYPOTHESES

This paper adopts an empirical approach to internationalization and its relationship with performance. Accordingly, the review of the literature aims to contextualize the internationalization process and summarize the main theories that attempt to explain it, and to identify relevant insights from past studies which can help to provide the foundation for developing the hypotheses that will steer, and help to interpret the results of, the empirical work.

The internationalization of firms has been one of the key topics in international business and marketing research for the last three decades, with efforts focused mostly on explaining and describing the development process of firms' international activities (e.g., Johanson & Wiedersheim-Paul, 1975; Reid, 1983; Dunning, 1988; Johanson & Mattsson, 1988; Robertson & Chetty, 2000). Of the various theories that have been proposed, four stand out as having attracted the greatest amount of interest and were considered in this study, as outlined below.

First is the eclectic paradigm (Erramili & Rao, 1993; Dunning, 1988, 1995, 2000), which has made an important contribution to the international business literature (Dunning, 2001). Work in this area is based on theories of monopolistic competition, location, and transaction cost, and deals mostly with FDI rather than exporting. Since exporting is a mode of expansion that is most commonly found in the early stages of internationalization (Leonidou & Katsikeas, 1996), it is of great interest in this study and this limits the potential usefulness of the eclectic paradigm here. Nonetheless, elements from it, particularly those regarding ownership advantages of the firm, can be useful in describing the characteristics of the internationalization process and have been drawn upon in conceptualizing the present study.

Second, the network approach (Johanson & Mattsson, 1988; Welch & Welch, 1996; Andersson, 2002; Hadley & Wilson, 2003) is built on the degree of internationalization of the firm and the market and includes influences of external actors or organizations in internationalization. Models framed in this approach consider business to be interconnected and within a network (Andersson, 2002). Accordingly, the present study includes measures to assess the degree of the firm's independence or dependence in decision making for international operations, in order to examine its potential relevance to the various stages of internationalization.

Third, the contingency approach (Reid, 1983; Prescott, 1986; Welford & Prescott, 1994; Robertson & Chetty, 2000) posits that the success of internationalization depends on various factors and is the result of the selection of an expansion strategy from a set of competing options, directed by the characteristics of market opportunity, firm resources, and managerial philosophy (Reid, 1983). To capture the underlying philosophy of this approach, in this study we included a number of contingent characteristics and strategic alternatives, ranging from the firm's ability to operate in a set of foreign languages to a variety of potential expansion modes.

Notwithstanding the usefulness of the above three theories, this study is grounded mostly in the incremental internationalization model (Johanson & Vahlne, 1977) given its first objective of describing the stages of internationalization in the contemporary environment. In this model, increasing international experience and commitment result in a series of stages of international development. The majority of the proposed internationalization models assume a cumulative dynamic that has been described extensively in the literature. The Uppsala school (Johanson & Wiedersheim-Paul, 1975; Johanson & Vahlne, 1977) was the precursor to these models and posits that the accumulation of knowledge by experience, commitment, and reduced psychic distance over time play an important role in the firms' international expansion process.

The conceptualization of the "stages models" is based on different theories drawn from a variety of disciplines including international trade, management and organization theory, location theory, and the broader literature in international marketing and exporting (Leonidou & Kasikeas, 1996). Stages models have appeared in the literature throughout the past 30 years or so (e.g., Bilkey & Tesar, 1977; Wiedersheim-Paul, Olsen & Welch, 1978; Wortzel & Wortzel, 1981; Cavusgil, 1982; Czinkota, 1982; Barrett & Wilkinson, 1986; Moon & Lee, 1990; Lim, Sharkey & Kim, 1991; Rao & Naidu, 1992; Crick, 1995; Gankema, Snuif & Zwart, 2000). More recently, internationalization has been defined as the "gradual process by which business firms become involved in international business activities" (Rao & Naidou, 1992, p. 147). Even though some studies have questioned whether the "stages" notion is empirically supportable (e.g., Sullivan & Bauerschmidt, 1990; Millington & Bayliss, 1990), the majority of empirical research in the field clearly supports the process (e.g., Cavusgil, 1984; Jull & Walters, 1987; Kwon & Hu, 2001).

Though most of the existing models vary in the number and characteristics of the stages they describe, they share a common view of internationalization as a process under the full control of the firm. In particular, they describe the process as consisting of three to seven stages which focus mostly on distinguishing between firms in the earlier stages of internationalization, after which firms "mature" to the most advanced level of international operations. However, in countries with large FDI inflows, or, more generally, in the current environment where the incidence of international firm networks has increased, the process may exhibit distinctive new features that have not been considered before, particularly regarding firms that have reached a very high level of maturity overall but that have, in the process, lost part of their control over their own operations by virtue of being subsidiaries of major multinational companies or part of an international network. Such potential changes, resulting from the contemporary environment, are in line with the network approach and were taken into account in designing the present study.

Of the two main objectives of the study, the first is to examine empirically the stages of international development and their characteristics, intended to explore whether the traditional stages model can be validated and/or has changed. Therefore, the first hypothesis is formulated on the basis of the models that posit a stage-wise process with a cumulative dynamic:

> H_1: *The firm's internationalization process can be described in several different and distinct stages of international development.*

An important concern expressed by Leonidou and Katsikeas (1996, p. 528) is that most of the earlier models have used segmentation criteria "on an ex-post facto basis to determine the cut-off points between stages, and in most cases this was decided arbitrarily," thereby essentially arriving at a tautological result. To address this, the intent in putting forth this hypothesis is to test whether internationalization stages can be derived empirically rather than on the basis of preset criteria. If hypothesis H_1 is true, the underlying logic of the stages theory suggests that the firm's experience in, and commitment to, its international operations will increase from one stage to the next.

Accordingly, two further hypotheses can be established:

> H_2: *The higher the stage of internationalization, the higher the firm's international experience will be.*

> H_3: *The higher the stage of internationalization, the higher the firm's commitment to its international operations will be.*

In connection to the second main objective of the study, the relationship between internationalization and performance has also received considerable research attention starting in the past 10 years or so (e.g., Woodcock, Beamish & Makino, 1994; Ramaswamy, 1995; Riahi-Belkaoui, 1998; Gomes & Ramaswamy, 1999; Yip, Gomez Biscarri & Monti, 2000; Majocci & Zucchella, 2003; Hsu & Boggs, 2003). Studies on this relationship typically deal with the performance of different entry modes (Simmonds, 1990; Li & Guisinger, 1991; Woodcock, Beamish & Makino, 1994) and the shape of the relationship (Riahi-Belkaoui, 1998; Gomes & Ramaswamy, 1999; Hsu & Boggs, 2003). Most of the literature supports a relationship between degree of internationalization and the firm's *overall* or "global" performance, including domestic operations (Hsu & Boggs, 2003), while a relationship with the firm's *international* performance (Dhanaraj & Beamish, 2003) has also been described. Consequently, the link between internationalization and performance is hypothesized as follows:

> H_4: *The firm's degree of internationalization has a positive relationship with its performance.*

This relationship can be particularized in order to take into account the different dimensions and variables that capture the content of the overall (Bonoma & Clark, 1988) and international (Cavusgil & Zou, 1994; Styles, 1998; Diamantopoulos, 1999) performance constructs. Therefore, the following two additional hypotheses are proposed:

> H_5: *The firm's degree of internationalization has a positive relationship with its overall performance.*

H_6: *The firm's degree of internationalization has a positive relationship with its international performance.*

METHODOLOGY AND DATA ANALYSIS

The relative dearth of empirical studies on the international behavior of firms is a frequent lament of researchers (e.g., Douglas & Craig, 1992; Papadopoulos, Chen & Thomas, 2002). In particular, internationalization is a research topic that has both quantitative and qualitative aspects, thus necessitating empirical investigation via personal interviews (e.g., Cavusgil, 1985; Brewer, 2001; Rahman, 2003), which adds to the complexities of international research identified by Katsikeas, Leonidou, and Morgan (2000). For this study we used an in-person interviewing process with a sample of firms in an advanced and highly industrialized region of Spain and collected both qualitative and quantitative data.

Sampling and Research Instrument

The sampling frame was the population of 424 manufacturing firms in the region that have had some form of international operations for at least three years. Using stratified random sampling, 232 companies were selected to be approached and 204 agreed to participate. Only four firms provided incomplete responses and had to be removed from the final sample, resulting in 200 usable responses. Thus, the response rate was very satisfactory at 86% (47% of the total population), providing a sufficiently large sample for the intended analysis. The respondents were the firms' managers in charge of international operations. The sample was representative of the population by firm size with most of the firms being SMEs. The sectoral coverage resulted in a cross-section of industries offering both consumer and industrial products. The study used a structured questionnaire and personal interviews based on a discussion guide, both pretested with six experts and five firms to ensure the relevance and clarity of the content.

Data Analysis

Given the objective of identifying the stages of the firms' internationalization process, hierarchical cluster analysis was used to segment the sample into groups according to the firms' stage in the internationalization process, to identify the set of firms included in each group, and to describe the characteristics of each group. This type of analysis was chosen partly due to the nature of the data, which included both continuous and qualitative variables, but most importantly to enable the specification of stages of internationalization as these emerge from the data rather than by imposing arbitrary cut-off points between the stages. The software used for the cluster analysis was SPAD 5.0, mainly because it enables the use of *illustrative* metric and qualitative variables to describe the resulting clusters. Lastly, ANOVA (SPSS 13.0) was used to analyze the relationship between the firms' degree of internationalization and their performance.

Measures

The analysis was based on the 45 variables shown in Annex 1. Of these, three were used to *segment* the sample into the stages of the internationalization process and eight to analyze the firms' *performance*, and the complete set was used to *profile* the firms classified in each cluster.

Segmentation variables. In line with Leonidou and Katsikeas (1996) who note that the criteria most frequently used in past research include export sales intensity, length of exporting experience, and foreign market mode of entry, two constructs were selected to help identify the stages of internationalization: the firm's *degree of internationalization* and its *international experience*. The first of these does not have a generally accepted conceptualization and measurement in the existing literature (Sullivan, 1994; Ramaswamy, Kroeck & Renforth, 1996; Sullivan, 1996). For the purposes of this research it was defined as "the extent of the firm's links with foreign markets," which makes it possible to differentiate between "internationalization of *revenue*" and "internationalization of *operations*." Respectively, these were operationalized as the *ratio of international to total sales* and the *number of entry modes used by the firm*. The second variable, international experience, was operationalized as the *number of years during which the firm had been exporting on a regular basis*. As noted above, to overcome one of the limitations common to most of the earlier studies (Leonidou & Katsikeas, 1996) these three criteria were used as *active* variables in the cluster analysis to avoid setting arbitrary cut-off points between phases.

Descriptive variables. The descriptive variables were selected by drawing from the four main theories described in the literature review, resulting in the managerial and organizational characteristics and performance indicators shown in Annex 1. Using selected variables as examples, the eclectic, network, contingency, and stages approaches are reflected, respectively, in such indicators as the ISO certification, the degree of foreign ownership of the firm and its decision making autonomy, the full range of mode of entry (MOE) options included, and the number of foreign markets served plus the time lapse since the firm's first export order.

These indicators are also called *illustrative* variables (Morineau & Morin, 2000), that is, they are used *a posteriori* to profile the groups resulting from the cluster analysis but not to create them. The complete set includes 22 quantitative (continuous or scaled) and 23 qualitative (nominal) indicators. Of the former, eight were used to measure performance in terms of profitability, sales, and overall. Three of these indicators were selected to capture "global" performance, including the firm's domestic operations (total assets, return on assets, economic profitability) while the other five focused on international operations.

FINDINGS AND DISCUSSION

Internationalization Model

The optimal number of clusters that the program identified, between three and ten, was five. This enables relatively easy description and understanding of the resulting groups and is close to the number of stages customarily included in existing models. The interclass-to-total inertia rate (0.79), the low

indicators of intra-class inertia, and the dendrogram also showed that the clusters were appropriate. Accordingly, the Spanish firms' internationalization process can be described in five stages: Passive exporting (62), Active exporting (45), Export consolidation (52), International operations (20) and Globalization (21). The main characteristic that distinguishes this model from those in earlier studies is the presence of the final "Globalization" stage.

The statistical tests for identifying significant variables to profile all the clusters were initially carried out at alpha levels .01 and .05, and the results are shown in Tables 1 and 2 for the quantitative and qualitative variables, respectively. As can be seen from the tables, firms in Stage 3 exhibit the fewest significant differences from the sample mean, while the reverse is the case for Stages 1 and 5. This is a natural consequence of the position of each cluster in the five-stage solution and it conceals the presence or absence of the expected progression in terms of the firms' experience and range of operations through the process. The main characteristics of the model and each stage are highlighted below. For the fifth stage, we also tested for significant cluster characteristics at $\alpha = .10$ to enable a fuller profile of the firms in this distinctive cluster, which is elaborated upon in more detail.

Overview of the Process

The stage-wise theory of internationalization, and therefore hypothesis H_1, is clearly supported by the data. This conclusion is consistent with the findings of other studies on incremental internationalization (Cavusgil, 1984; Jull & Walters, 1987; Kwon & Hu, 2001). Focusing on the quantitative variables first (Table 1), the ANOVA results in the last column show that 17 of the 22 indicators significantly discriminate between the five clusters. As can be seen by examining the individual cells, 13 of the significant variables show progressive growth from Stage 1 to Stage 5 in virtually all cases, as expected (e.g., total assets, international experience, foreign languages used, foreign markets, international sales and contribution to total revenue, perceived success and international profitability), and one shows a progressive decline (main foreign mar-

TABLE 1. Cluster Profiles: Quantitative Variables

Variable	Stage 1 Passive exporting n = 62	sig	Stage 2 Active exporting n = 45	sig	Stage 3 Export consolidation n = 52	sig	Stage 4 International operations n = 20	sig	Stage 5 Global-ization n = 21	sig	Sample mean n = 200	ANOVA F d.f. = 4 n = 200	sig
Total assets	6.6	b	13.7	ns	24.9	ns	25.5	ns	43.0	b	18.6	3.2	b
Total no. of employees	49.7	ns	52.2	ns	127.4	ns	192.2	ns	440.0	a	126.4	4.6	a
Total sales	9.4	ns	18.7	ns	24.9	ns	27.1	ns	164.9	a	33.6	4.2	a
% of capital foreign owned	8.0	b	6.7	b	23.1	ns	26.2	ns	50.6	a	18.0	7.4	a
Years experience in sector	30.3	ns	28.4	ns	31.9	ns	38.1	ns	36.1	ns	31.7	0.8	ns
Years since first export order	9.3	a	12.3	a	22.0	a	26.1	a	31.3	a	17.5	24.5	a
Years exporting regularly	7.2	a	8.8	a	18.4	a	23.5	a	31.3	a	14.8	64.7	a
Years int. manager in place	5.7	ns	5.7	ns	12.1	a	7.6	ns	8.5	ns	7.9	3.9	a
Years of manager's total exp.	10.4	ns	9.2	ns	14.9	b	9.1	ns	14.7	ns	11.6	2.6	b
No. international employees	0.9	a	1.8	ns	2.5	ns	5.0	b	7.5	a	2.7	8.4	a
Foreign languages	1.5	a	2.0	ns	2.1	ns	2.7	a	2.4	ns	2.0	6.5	a
No. of countries	5.8	a	9.6	ns	13.4	ns	23.4	a	19.1	b	11.9	10.3	a
No. of entry modes	1.0	a	2.4	a	1.5	b	3.6	a	1.6	ns	1.8	129.3	a
% main foreign mkt/total int.	60.2	a	51.3	ns	51.6	ns	46.1	ns	43.6	ns	52.7	2.7	b
International sales	1.1	ns	1.5	ns	8.8	ns	12.2	ns	135.4	a	18.4	4.1	a
% change in int'l sales	53.5	b	45.0	ns	21.0	ns	11.7	ns	8.8	ns	34.0	2.3	ns
% international/total sales	12.7	a	15.0	a	42.2	a	44.8	b	79.9	a	31.2	91.9	a
Perceived success	5.4	a	5.8	ns	6.7	b	6.9	ns	7.5	a	6.2	9.1	a
Perceived int. profitability	2.8	ns	2.8	ns	3.1	ns	3.1	ns	3.3	b	3.0	3.2	b
Int. strategic performance	332.3	ns	316.5	ns	323.0	ns	340.8	ns	347.2	ns	329.4	0.9	ns
Economic profitability	5.5	ns	4.6	ns	6.2	ns	5.3	ns	6.2	ns	5.5	0.4	ns
Return on total assets	6.6	ns	5.9	ns	7.8	ns	6.8	ns	7.2	ns	6.7	0.3	ns

Significance: a: 99% (α = .01); b: 95% (α = .05); ns: not significant

ket contribution to total foreign sales). Several of the significant variables identified by the ANOVA analysis are in line with specific findings of earlier studies, including, for example, those linking internationalization to total employment (e.g., Bilkey, 1978; Yaprak, 1985; Rao & Naidou, 1992) and total sales volume (e.g., Bilkey & Tesar, 1977; Bilkey, 1978; Cavusgil, 1984; Yaprak, 1985; Rao & Naidou, 1992). Concerning the five non-significant variables, the similarities across clusters in four cases arise from the nature of these measures, which reflect overall rather than just international operations (years of experience in the sector and the last three measures of performance). On the other hand, two of the non-significant variables also are in the expected direction (lower international sales growth rate, higher self-assessed strategic performance).

The qualitative indicators in Table 2 also support H_1 and provide additional insight for interpreting the quantitative data. Only two of the variables do not contribute to the cluster profiles (firm's sector and international manager's education level). The expected progression from "less" to "more" across the stages is observed in the indicators for firm size, ISO certification, ability to operate in various major languages, and the proportion of firms that set international objectives. The number of firms that are subsidiaries is significantly higher in Stage 5, and much lower especially in Stages 1 and 2. Consequently, the proportion of firms indicating they have "total" strategic control of their international operations declines significantly in the Stage 5, with a concomitant increase in "no control." This is also reflected in the proportions of firms indicating they are "active" in international operations, which increases steadily between Stage 1 and Stage 4 but declines precipitously in Stage 5.

TABLE 2. Cluster Profiles: Qualitative Variables

Variable	Measure	Stage 1 Passive exporting n = 62	sig	Stage 2 Active exporting n = 45	sig	Stage 3 Export consolidation n = 52	sig	Stage 4 International operations n = 20	sig	Stage 5 Global- ization n = 21	sig	Sample mean n = 200
Firm size	Large	3.2	a	2.2	b	18.5	ns	27.3	ns	33.3	b	12.8
	Medium	30.7	ns	24.4	ns	22.2	ns	40.9	ns	47.6	ns	29.9
	Small	66.1	ns	73.3	b	59.3	ns	31.8	b	19.1	a	57.4
Sector	1	22.6	ns	31.1	ns	22.2	ns	18.2	ns	4.8	ns	22.1
	2	3.2	ns	8.9	ns	7.4	ns	13.6	ns	0.0	ns	6.4
	3	17.7	b	11.1	ns	5.6	ns	0.0	ns	4.8	ns	9.8
	4	11.3	ns	4.4	ns	3.7	ns	9.1	ns	9.5	ns	7.5
	5	24.2	ns	28.9	ns	18.5	ns	36.4	ns	9.5	ns	23.5
	6	6.5	ns	0.0	ns	7.4	ns	0.0	ns	14.3	ns	5.3
	7	4.8	ns	11.1	ns	11.1	ns	4.6	ns	23.8	ns	9.8
	8	6.5	ns	2.2	b	16.7	ns	18.2	ns	33.3	b	12.3
	9	3.2	ns	2.2	ns	7.4	ns	0.0	ns	0.0	ns	3.4
ISO 9000 approved	Yes	30.7	a	37.8	ns	51.9	ns	68.2	ns	85.7	a	47.6
ISO 14000 approved	Yes	1.6	a	4.4	ns	16.7	ns	13.6	ns	23.8	ns	9.8
International strategy control	Total	88.7	ns	95.6	b	77.8	ns	86.4	ns	57.1	a	83.8
	Partial	1.6	ns	2.2	ns	13.0	b	9.1	ns	4.8	ns	5.9
	None	9.7	ns	2.2	ns	9.3	ns	4.6	ns	38.1	a	10.3
Firm is subsidiary	Yes	11.3	ns	4.4	a	27.8	ns	27.3	ns	52.4	a	20.1
International behavior	Active	51.6	b	68.9	ns	72.2	ns	81.8	ns	61.9	ns	65.2
Export department	Yes	21.0	a	44.4	ns	35.2	ns	54.6	ns	42.9	ns	35.8
International manager	Yes	74.2	ns	82.2	ns	77.8	ns	86.4	ns	85.7	ns	79.4
International manager's education	Post-grad.	26.1	ns	40.5	ns	21.4	ns	47.4	ns	16.7	ns	29.6
	Higher	39.1	ns	29.7	ns	52.4	ns	42.1	ns	61.1	ns	43.2
	< higher	34.8	ns	29.7	ns	26.2	ns	10.5	ns	22.2	ns	27.2
Firm operates in: English	Yes	72.6	a	97.8	b	83.3	ns	95.5	ns	100.0	ns	86.3
French	Yes	51.6	b	66.7	ns	63.0	ns	86.4	b	85.7	ns	65.2
German	Yes	12.9	a	20.0	ns	31.5	ns	40.9	ns	52.4	b	26.5
Italian	Yes	3.2	ns	8.9	ns	11.1	ns	22.7	b	0.0	ns	8.3
Portuguese	Yes	8.1	ns	4.4	ns	13.0	ns	9.1	ns	0.0	ns	7.8
MOE: 1	Yes	0.0	a	24.4	ns	13.0	ns	50.0	a	14.3	ns	15.7
MOE: 2	Yes	3.2	a	62.2	a	24.1	ns	54.6	b	19.1	ns	28.9
MOE: 3	Yes	0.0	b	8.9	ns	0.0	ns	22.7	a	9.5	ns	5.4
MOE: 4	Yes	96.8	ns	100.0	ns	98.2	ns	100.0	ns	100.0	ns	98.5
MOE: 5	Yes	0.0	a	24.4	ns	13.0	ns	59.1	a	14.3	ns	16.7
MOE: 6	Yes	0.0	a	20.0	ns	3.7	b	72.7	a	0.0	ns	13.2
MOE: 7	Yes	0.0	a	26.7	ns	16.7	ns	59.1	a	14.3	ns	18.1
Int'l strategic objectives	Yes	54.8	a	71.1	ns	79.6	ns	90.9	b	95.2	b	73.5

Significance: a: 99% (α = .01); b: 95% (α = .05); ns: not significant
Modes of Entry (MOE): 1: International cooperation involving neither exporting nor physical presence; 2: Indirect exporting; 3: Joint exporting without physical presence; 4: Direct exporting without physical presence; 5: Direct exporting with physical presence; 6: Manufacturing abroad; 7: Foreign manufacturing plus direct exporting
Sectors: 1: Agrifood; 2: Textiles/Clothing/Footwear/Leather goods; 3: Wood/Furniture; 4: Chemicals; 5: Basic Metals Processing; 6: Non-metallic products; 7: Machinery; 8: Vehicles/Transport equipment; 9: Paper/Publishing/related

Table 3 focuses on the explanation of internationalization as a process of increasing experience and commitment through the stages process, and suggests that hypotheses H_2 and H_3 are also clearly supported. The firms' experience (number of years of regular exporting and since the first export) increases steadily along the five stages, with all differences from the sample mean being highly significant based on the cluster analysis ("stages" columns). The ANOVA results (last two columns) also significantly support the experience hypothesis. Similar results can be observed in support of H_3 from both the cluster and ANOVA analyses, based on the three commitment indicators. While the results for the "Active exporting" and "Export consolidation" stages are not significantly different from the sample mean in the cluster analysis, their values are in the expected direction and the ability of the indicators to discriminate across the five stages is confirmed by the ANOVA results. Therefore, the results empirically support models that assume internationalization as a process of progressive commitment, consistent with Kwon and Hu (2001).

In conclusion, the data support the first three hypotheses. Additional characteristics of the first four stages are discussed below, followed by the more focused discussion on Stage 5.

Additional Characteristics of Stages 1-4

Stage 1: Passive exporting. Considering that all firms had to have at least three years of continuous international experience to be selected for the sample, this cluster essentially represents generally small firms that do export but have a limited range of international operations. Their distinctive characteristics range from limited international experience to an overwhelming concentration on exporting as the principal entry mode (97%), low contribution of international to total sales (13% vs. 31%), and a small number of markets served (5.8, or less than half of the sample mean of 11.9). Nearby Portugal is these firms' main foreign market and accounts for 60% of total international revenues, a higher proportion than for any other cluster. Perhaps not surprisingly, given the relatively limited strategic importance that these firms appear to attribute to foreign markets, only 55% have established objectives for their international activities. On the other hand, their international sales are growing significantly faster (54% vs. 34%), likely due to their lower starting level and a consequence of expansion by firms that are not yet mature exporters but have survived several years of continuous foreign sales. Still, consistent with the cluster profile, only 52% of these firms characterize their international behavior as "active" (versus, for example, 82% of firms in Stage 4).

Stage 2: Active exporting. Second-stage firms still are significantly below the sample means on several measures, but, compared to their counterparts in Stage 1, virtually all indicators are in the expected direction as noted above (e.g., a much wider range of entry modes used and markets served, and greater experience, ownership advantages, capabilities, and com-

TABLE 3. Experience and Commitment

Variable	Stage 1	Stage 2	Stage 3	Stage 4	Stage 5	ANOVA		
	Passive exporting	Active exporting	Export consolidation	International operations	Globalization	F d.f. = 4	Prob.	Sig
Years since first export order	9.33[a] p = 0.000	12.31[a] p = 0.002	22.02[a] p = 0.002	26.09[a] p = 0.001	31.29[a] p = 0.000	24.49	0.000	a
Years exporting regularly	7.23[a] p = 0.000	8.81[a] p = 0.000	18.41[a] p = 0.002	23.50[a] p = 0.000	31.29[a] p = 0.000	64.73	0.000	a
No. international employees	0.92[a] p = 0.001	1.84 p = 0.121	2.54 p = 0.420	4.95[b] p = 0.016	7.48[a] p = 0.000	8.35	0.000	a
Foreign languages	1.50[a] p = 0.000	1.98 p = 0.480	2.06 p = 0.256	2.68[a] p = 0.001	2.38[c] p = 0.037	6.48	0.000	a
Countries entered	5.77[a] p = 0.000	9.62 p = 0.108	13.37 p = 0.170	23.38[a] p = 0.000	19.10[b] p = 0.005	10.33	0.000	a

Significance: a: 99% (α = .01); b: 95% (α = .05); c: 90% (α = .10)

mitment levels, as shown by their years in exporting, ISO certification levels, dedicated international employees, export department, foreign languages, presence of strategic objectives). Further, these firms depend less on their main target market (51%) than those in Stage 1, and control their international strategy (significantly higher than the mean, and highest of any stage). The performance indicators do not differ significantly from the sample means but again generally are in the expected direction. In summary, firms at this stage generally stand at levels below the overall sample means but clearly are more engaged in the internationalization process than those in Stage 1, with 69% (vs. 52%) indicating their international behavior as "active."

Stage 3: Export consolidation. Notwithstanding the overall smaller number of significant differences from the mean, as noted above, the nine observed significant differences in Tables 1 and 2, coupled with other measures that are in the expected direction, clearly signal this cluster as a "turning point." For example, a first indication of networking with other firms is provided by the proportion of foreign capital in their assets (23%, or almost four times as high as that for Stage 2), coupled with a significant difference for those with only "partial" control of international strategy (13%, vs. 6% for the sample). Further, these firms have more international experience and have almost six times as high international sales compared to Stage 2 firms. On the other hand, they use fewer entry modes than "Active exporters" and are less likely to have an export department, perhaps as a result of a strategy to consolidate their foreign operations and restructure their organization to rationalize international and domestic operations. Their "perceived success" of international operations is significantly different from the sample mean (6.7 vs. 6.2, $\alpha = .05$). Overall, firms at this stage appear to be consolidating their operations and 72% perceive themselves as "active," with international activity now taking on greater strategic importance as 80% of the cluster members set and pursue strategic objectives.

Stage 4: International operations. At this stage firms continue to accumulate international experience (over 23 years of regular exporting) and, as noted in the general overview of the model, the values of most indicators continue in the expected direction. The share of foreign capital has risen to 26%, and these firms operate in more markets using a wide range of entry modes, including foreign investment. The performance indicators are not significantly different from the sample mean, but their international and total sales have grown to €12.2 million and €27.1 million respectively, and their perceived success to 6.9 on the 10-point scale. In summary, Stage 4 firms have broadened their international horizons significantly and appear to have developed permanent and stronger links with their foreign markets. Their profile is similar to that of the "mature exporter" that was commonly reported in earlier studies as the final stage in the internationalization process.

The "Globalization" Stage

This is the distinctive stage of the sampled firms' internationalization process. Its features are illustrated in Tables 4 and 5, which contrast this cluster to the overall sample profile based on, respectively, the quantitative and qualitative variables for which there were significant differences from the sample mean. According to the tables, firms at this stage tend to be large, with an average of 440 workers and €43 million in assets, over 31 years of international experience, and significantly higher ISO certification levels, and are significantly more likely than others to have specific international strategic objectives. However, more than half have now become subsidiaries of other firms, the foreign-owned part of their capital is now over 50%, and 38% indicate they have no control over the design of their international strategy, which is evidently decided by their parent. Significant proportions of these firms are in the Vehicles/Transport equipment and Machinery sectors, where international networks are common, while their proportion in Agrifood is significantly lower than in the other clusters. The number of countries in which they operate is lower than in Stage 4 (19 vs. 23), likely due to the reassignment of markets by their parents.

Among the performance indicators, their perceived success internationally is significantly

TABLE 4. Profile of Globalization Cluster: Quantitative Variables

Variable	Cluster mean	Sample mean	Test value	Prob.	Sig
Total assets	42.98	18.61	2.56	0.005	b
Total no. of employees	440.00	126.37	3.79	0.000	a
Total sales	164.88	33.60	3.91	0.000	a
% of capital foreign owned	50.57	17.99	4.20	0.000	a
Years since first export order	31.29	17.45	5.00	0.000	a
Years exporting regularly	31.29	14.77	7.44	0.000	a
No. international employees	7.48	2.66	4.39	0.000	a
Foreign languages	2.38	1.97	1.79	0.037	c
No. of countries	19.10	11.85	2.56	0.005	c
% main foreign mkt/total int'l sales	43.61	52.73	−1.80	0.036	c
International sales	135.36	18.38	3.90	0.000	a
% international/total sales	79.88	31.16	8.84	0.000	a
Perceived success	7.52	6.21	3.42	0.000	a
Perceived international profitability	3.25	2.96	2.15	0.016	b

Significance: a: 99% (α = .01); b: 95% (α = .05); c: 90% (α = .10)

TABLE 5. Profile of Globalization Cluster: Qualitative Variables

Variable	Modality	Cluster/ sample (%)	Modality in cluster (%)	Modality in sample (%)	Test value	Prob.	Sig
Firm size	Small	3.42	19.05	57.35	−3.54	0.000	a
	Large	26.92	33.33	12.75	2.40	0.008	b
Sector	Vehicles/Transport	28.00	33.33	12.25	2.49	0.006	b
	Machinery	25.00	23.81	9.80	1.76	0.039	c
	Agrifood	2.22	4.76	22.06	−1.88	0.030	c
ISO 9000	Yes	18.56	85.71	47.55	3.57	0.000	a
	No	2.80	14.29	52.45	−3.57	0.000	a
ISO 14000	Yes	25.00	23.81	9.80	1.76	0.039	c
	No	8.70	76.19	90.20	−1.76	0.039	c
Control over int. strategies	None	38.10	38.10	10.29	3.45	0.000	a
Firm is subsidiary	Yes	26.83	52.38	20.10	3.30	0.000	a
	No	6.13	47.62	79.90	−3.30	0.000	a
Language: English	Yes	11.93	100.00	86.27	1.78	0.038	c
	No	0.00	0.00	13.73	−1.78	0.038	c
Language: French	Yes	13.53	85.71	65.20	1.92	0.028	c
	No	4.23	14.29	34.80	−1.92	0.028	c
Language: German	Yes	20.37	52.38	26.47	2.46	0.007	b
	No	6.67	47.62	73.53	−2.46	0.007	b
Int. strategic objectives	Yes	13.42	95.24	73.04	2.37	0.009	b
	No	1.85	4.76	26.47	−2.32	0.010	b

Significance: a: 99% (α = .01); b: 95% (α = .05); c: 90% (α = .10)
Legend:
Cluster/sample (%): Percentage of firms in Stage 5 vs. the complete sample that have the modality shown.
Modality in cluster (%): Proportion of firms in Stage 5 that have the modality shown.
Modality in sample (%): Proportion of firms in the complete sample that have the modality shown.
Test value/Prob./Sig.: Test and associated probability and significance for cluster vs. sample differences.

higher than the sample mean (7.5) and from that of firms at any other stage, as is their perceived international profitability. Foreign revenues are also superior to those at any other stage and account for almost 80% of their total turnover, and international activity is perceived as being highly profitable (3.3). The share of revenue coming from the main foreign market drops further from the previous stage (43.6%), as does the average annual growth rate of international sales.

In summary, this cluster groups firms that exhibit distinctive characteristics that have not been reported in past research, and that reflect elements of the network theory of internationalization: these are large companies that have a lot of "international savvy" and for which international markets are very important, but many have been taken over by other (and often multinational) firms and have less say in their international strategies. Stated differently, the profile of this cluster suggests that it represents, in part, the end of the initial autonomous, firm-controlled phase of the internationalization process that has been studied in earlier research.

Internationalization and Performance

Hypotheses H_4, H_5, and H_6 address the relationship between degree of internationalization and performance. The empirical results, shown in Table 6, are not consistent and do not support H_4, which does not discriminate between total and international performance. On the one hand, the t-test (cluster analysis) was significant for two international performance indicators in most stages (perceived success and perceived international profitability), and the ANOVA statistics provide additional support for these indicators as well as for international and total sales, which vary significantly across the five stages. As well, disregarding for a moment the lack of significance in some cases within some clusters, the progression of the measures for all four of these indicators is in the expected direction, from low to high, throughout the model. On the other hand, four variables are not significant in either the cluster or ANOVA analyses: change in international sales, international strategic performance, economic profitability, and return on total assets.

Of these, the measures for the first two do move in the expected direction, but those for the remaining two include domestic performance and appear stable regardless of stage. In summary, then, there is partial support for H_5, since three of the five international performance indicators discriminate across the stages based on the cluster and/or ANOVA analyses (perceived success, perceived international profitability, international sales), but not for H_6, since two of the three indicators (economic profitability and return on assets) do not support the relationship.

When compared to those for other stages, the results for Stage 2, "Active exporting," give rise to some interesting observations: the measures for the profitability indicators (perceived profitability, economic profitability, return on total assets) and for international strategic performance are lower than in the first stage. A possible explanation is that Stage 2 firms need to increase their resource commitment to sustain their international expansion, while the returns are not yet high enough to yield a higher level of profitability. In fact, considering sales volume as an antecedent of profitability, export sales only increase from €1.1 million in Stage 1 to €1.5 million in Stage 2, while they register significant increases during the next three stages. The same potential explanation can also be applied to Stage 4 (International operations), where economic profitability and return on total assets also fall as the firm again needs to increase its international commitment by establishing, for the first time, commercial subsidiaries and production abroad (Table 1). Coupled with our identification of Stage 3 as a "turning point" in the preceding outline of individual stage characteristics, it appears that the transition of firms between Stages 2, 3, and 4 differs materially, and is more challenging, than the transition from Stage 1 to 2 and from 4 to 5.

Lastly, a point of discussion arising from the data concerns the *form* of the relationship between degree of internationalization and performance. While the literature has mostly presented monotonic (linear) and curvilinear relationships between internationalization and overall financial performance (Hsu & Boggs, 2003), the data in this study suggest a different shape. This is shown in Figures 1 and 2, which

TABLE 6. Stages of Internationalization and Performance

Variable	Stage 1	Stage 2	Stage 3	Stage 4	Stage 5	ANOVA		
	Passive exporting	Active exporting	Export consolidation	International operations	Global-ization	F d.f. = 4	Prob.	Sig
International sales	1.12 p = 0.130	1.45 p = 0.187	8.76 p = 0.290	12.20 p = 0.421	135.36[a] p = 0.000	4.07	0.003	a
% change in int'l sales	53.50[b] p = 0.012	44.97 p = 0.165	21.04 p = 0.091	11.74 p = 0.099	8.76 p = 0.067	2.33	0.58	ns
Perceived success	5.39[a] p = 0.000	5.81 p = 0.052	6.70[b] p = 0.011	6.90[c] p = 0.035	7.52[a] p = 0.000	9.13	0.000	a
Perceived int. profitability	2.83[c] p = 0.031	2.79[c] p = 0.028	3.07 p = 0.080	3.12 p = 0.113	3.25[b] p = 0.016	3.16	0.015	b
International strategic performance	332.31 p = 0.383	316.50 p = 0.106	322.99 p = 0.225	340.82 p = 0.201	347.21 p = 0.096	0.943	0.441	ns
Total sales	9.38 p = 0.079	18.65 p = 0.242	24.90 p = 0.327	27.06 p = 0.425	164.88[a] p = 0.000	4.15	0.003	a
Economic profitability	5.48 p = 0.495	4.57 p = 0.155	6.21 p = 0.256	5.34 p = 0.462	6.22 p = 0.272	0.351	0.843	ns
Return on total assets	6.56 p = 0.434	5.87 p = 0.219	7.80 p = 0.220	6.78 p = 0.488	7.18 p = 0.383	0.247	0.911	ns

Significance: a: 99% (α = .01); b: 95% (α = .05); c: 90% (α = .10); ns: not significant

display a non-significant "valleys and peaks" link to the stages of internationalization using the two overall profitability indicators. This buttresses, but also adds further texture and a potentially different perspective to, the points made in the previous paragraph about stages that potentially represent "turning points." Specifically, the two figures suggest that firms in Stages 2 and 4 may be susceptible to a drop in their profitability, as a result of important changes in the level of commitment necessary for sustaining their operations during critical transition periods. Coupled with the discussion in the previous paragraph, this suggests that Stages 2, 3, and 4 may indeed be key turning points–but also that the middle stage (3) may represent a significant base for growth, while the other two are significantly more challenging.

IMPLICATIONS, LIMITATIONS, AND FUTURE RESEARCH DIRECTIONS

Although the data for this study come from a single geographical region, the close match between the first four stages of the model derived in this study and those reported in earlier research suggests a cautious interpretation that the findings reflect a reasonable summary of firm behavior that may be applicable in other environments. A key limitation of this study is, of course, that it uses cross-sectional data to discuss a "process." This problem is common in all studies of this type, and one that Leonidou and Katsikeas (1996) correctly attribute to the difficulty in carrying out longitudinal research that would require "years of organized effort and substantial financial support." Nevertheless, the average years of experience of the sampled firms, which increase significantly and systematically across the various stages in this study (as in others before it) do suggest a temporal dimension that adds to the intuitive validity of the approach used.

There are three main management and public policy implications from this study. First, the stages model points to the potential rewards from international activity for firms that survive the process, and to the value of experience and commitment, suggesting that support programs by governments and efforts by management for launching and sustaining international operations will be well placed. Second, the identification of discrete stages of internationalization in which firms can be classified, and the distinctive profiles of firms in each cluster, makes it easier for public institutions to target programs to the different needs that

FIGURE 1. Stage of Internationalization and Economic Profitability

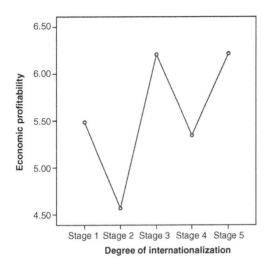

Degree of internationalization

FIGURE 2. Stage of Internationalization and Return on Total Assets

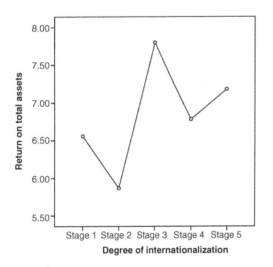

Degree of internationalization

prevail in each stage, and for managers to identify critical points that can endanger (Stages 2 and 4) further progress or can be used as a launchpad for ensuring it (Stage 3). Third, examination of the findings for each cluster can be used to point to attributes and strategies that may help firms in earlier stages to accelerate their expansion and take steps to increase their chances of success (e.g., experienced firms use a wider range of entry modes and are more likely to have specific international objectives).

The findings also suggest several potential future directions for new research in this area. Needless to say, the model needs to be retested in other environments. While the basic findings (first four stages) confirm earlier research, the fifth stage has not appeared before and deriving it may well be a function of the type of indicators used in this study. In other words, this study produced a richer portrayal of the full process, arriving at the contemporary "globalized" firm that has not been identified before simply because earlier studies had not included the relevant measures. Studies especially in countries with important flows of foreign investment could be particularly useful. Research with larger samples, which would result in including more firms especially in the last two stages, would also help (not to mention that longitudinal research also would). Generally, further validation of (or adjustments to) the model would enhance its generalizability and could make an appreciable contribution to the literature. Discriminant analysis can help to further confirm the value of the model and to assess its predictive power.

Lastly, the relationship between degree of internationalization and performance should be revisited. While this study used more (and more varied) performance indicators than others before it, there is no question that other variables, or the same ones applied differently and/or in different contexts, can help to confirm the findings or point to alternative explanations than those offered here. In particular, the distinction between international and overall performance is important especially because of the difficulty in measuring the latter in relation to internationalization. Research that is able to distinguish between the "noise" caused by domestic operations in overall performance data and the true effect of international operations on overall performance would be particularly useful. Future investigations may be able to capitalize on newer developments in performance measurement (e.g., balanced scorecard, resource-based view of the firm) and analyze the relationship using composite performance measures. Clearly, while this study has hopefully advanced our understanding of the internationalization process and its link to performance, a wide field for further improvements in the future lies ahead.

REFERENCES

Andersson, P. (2002). Connected internationalization processes: The case of internationalizing channel intermediaries. *International Business Review*, 11 (3), 365-383.

Axinn, C. N., & Matthyssens, P. (2002). Limits of internationalization theories in an unlimited world. *International Marketing Review*, 19 (5), 436-449.

Barrett, N. I., & Wilkinson, I. F. (1986). Internationalization behavior: Management characteristics of Australian manufacturing firms by level of international development. In P. W. Turnbull & S. J. Paliwoda (Eds.), *Research in international marketing* (pp. 213-233). London: Croom Helm.

Bartlett, C., & Ghoshal, S. (2000). *Transnational Management: Text, Cases and Readings in Cross-border Management*. Boston: Irwin/McGraw-Hill.

Bilkey, W. J., & Tesar, G. (1977). The Export Behavior of Smaller-Sized Wisconsin Manufacturing Firms. *Journal of International Business Studies*, 8 (1), 93-98.

Bonoma, T. V., & Clark, B. H. (1988). *Marketing Performance Assessment*. Boston: Harvard Business School Press.

Brewer, P. (2001). International Market Selection: Developing a Model from Australian Case Studies. *International Business Review*, 10 (2), 155-174.

Cavusgil, S. T. (1982). Some observations on the relevance of critical variables for internationalization stages. In M. R. Czinkota & G. Tesar (Eds.), *Export management: An international context* (pp. 276-285). New York: Praeger.

Cavusgil, S. T. (1984). Differences Among Exporting Finns Based on Their Degree of Internationalization. *Journal of Business Research*, 12 (2), 195-209.

Cavusgil, S. T. (1985). Guidelines for Export Market Research. *Business Horizons*, 28 (November-December), 27-33.

Cavusgil, S. T., & Zou, S. (1994). Marketing Strategy-Performance Relationship: An Investigation of the Empirical Link in Export Market Ventures. *Journal of Marketing*, 58, 1-21.

Crick, D. (1995). An Investigation into the Targeting of UK Export Assistance. *European Journal of Marketing*, 29 (8), 76-94.

Czinkota, M. R. (1982). *Export development strategies: U.S. promotion policy*. New York: Praeger.

Dhanaraj, C., & Beamish, P. W. (2003). A Resource-Based Approach to the Study of Export Performance. *Journal of Small Business Management*, 41 (3), 242-262.

Diamantopoulos, A. (1999). Viewpoint Export performance measurement: Reflective versus formative indicators. *International Marketing Review*, 16 (6), 444-457.

Douglas, S. P., & Craig, C. S. (1992). Advances in International Marketing. *International Journal of Research in Marketing*, 9 (December), 291-318.

Dunning, J. H. (1988). The Eclectic Paradigm of International Production: A Restatement and Some Possible Extensions. *Journal of International Business Studies*, 19, 1-31.

Dunning, J. H. (1995). Reappraising The Eclectic Paradigm in the Age of Alliance Capitalism. *Journal of International Business Studies*, 26 (3), 461-493.

Dunning, J. H. (2000). The Eclectic Paradigm as an Envelope for Economic and Business Theories of MNE Activity. *International Business Review*, 9 (1), 163-190.

Dunning, J. H. (2001). The Eclectic (OLI) Paradigm of International Production: Past, Present and Future. *International Journal of the Economics of Business*, 8 (2), 173-191.

Erramili, M. K., & Rao, C. P. (1993). Service firms' international entry-mode choice: A modified transaction-cost analysis approach. *Journal of Marketing*, 57 (3), 19-39.

Gankema, H. G. J., Snuif, H. R., & Zwart, P. S. (2000). The Internationalization Process of Small and Medium-sized Enterprises: An Evaluation of Stage Theory. *Journal of Small Business Management*, 38 (4), 15-27.

Gomes, L., & Ramaswamy, K. (1999). An Empirical Examination of the Form of the Relationship Between Multinationality and Performance. *Journal of International Business Studies*, 30 (1), 173-198.

Hadley, R., & Wilson, H. (2003). The network model of internationalisation and experiential knowledge. *International Business Review*, 12 (6), 697-717.

Hsu, C. C., & Boggs, D. J. (2003). Internationalization and Performance: Traditional Measures and Their Decomposition. *Multinational Business Review*, 11 (3), 23-50.

Johanson, J., & Mattson, L. (1988). Internationalisation in Industrial Systems–A Network Approach. *Strategies in Global Competition*, edited by N. Hood and J. E. Vahlne, Croom Helm: London, England.

Johanson, J., & Vahlne, J. E. (1977). The Internationalization Process of the Firm–A Model of Knowledge Development and Increasing Foreign Market Commitment. *Journal of International Business Studies*, 8, 23-32.

Johanson, J., & Wiedersheim-Paul, F. (1975). The Internationalisation of the Firm–Four Swedish Case Studies. *Journal of Management Studies*, 12 (3), 305-322.

Jull, M., & Walters, P. (1987). The Internationalization of Norwegian Firms–A Study of U.K. Experience. *Management International Review*, 1, 58-66.

Katsikeas, C. S., Leonidou, L. C., & Morgan, N. A. (2000). Firm-level Export Performance Assessment: Review, Evaluation, and Development. *Journal of the Academy of Marketing Science*, 28 (4), 493-511.

Kwon, Y. C., & Hu, M.Y. (2001). Internationalization and International Marketing Commitment: The Case of Small/Medium Korean Companies. *Journal of Global Marketing*, 15 (1), 57-67.

Leonidou L. C., & Katsikeas, C. S. (1996). The export development process: An integrative review of empirical models. *Journal of International Business Studies*, 27 (3), 517-551.

Levitt, T. (1984). The globalization of markets. *McKinsey Quarterly*, 3, 2-21.

Li, J., & Guisinger, S. (1991). Comparative business failures of foreign-controlled firms in the United States. *Journal of International Business Studies*, 22 (2), 209-225.

Lim, J. S., Sharkey, T. W., & Kim, K. I. (1991). An empirical test of an export adoption model. *Management International Review*, 31 (1), 51-62.

Majocci, A., & Zucchella, A. (2003). Internationalization and Performance. *International Small Business Journal*, 21 (3), 249-267.

Millington, A. I., & Bayliss, B. T. (1990). The Process of Internationalisation: UK Companies in the EC. *Management International Review*, 30 (2), 151-162.

Moon, J., & Lee, H. (1990). On the internal correlates of export stage development: An empirical investigation in the Korean electronics industry. *International Marketing Review*, 7 (5), 16-26.

Morineau, A., & Morin, S. (2000). *Pratique du traitement des enquêtes*. Montreuil: Cisia Ceresta.

Papadopoulos, N., Chen, H., & Thomas, D. R. (2002). Toward a Tradeoff Model for International Market Selection. *International Business Review*, 11, April, 165-192.

Prescott, J. E. (1986). Environments as Moderators of the Relationship Between Strategy and Performance. *Academy of Management Journal*, 29 (2), 329-347.

Rahman, S. H. (2003). Modelling of international market selection process: A qualitative study of successful Australian international businesses. *Qualitative Market Research: An International Journal*, 6 (2), 119-32.

Ramaswamy, K. (1995). Multinationality, configuration and performance: A study of MNEs in the U.S. drugs and pharmaceutical industry. *Journal of International Management*, 1, 231-253.

Ramaswamy, K., Kroeck, K. G., & Renforth, W. (1996). Measuring the degree of internationalization of a firm: A comment. *Journal of International Business Studies*, 27, 167-177.

Rao, T., & Naidu, G. (1992). Are the Stages of the Internationalisation Empirically Supportable? *Journal of Global Marketing*, 6 (1/2), 147-170.

Reid, S. D. (1983). Firm internationalization, transaction costs and strategic choice. *International Marketing Review*, 2, 44-56.

Riahi-Belkaoui, A. (1998). The Effects of the Degree of Internationalization on Firm Performance. *International Business Review*, 7, 315-321.

Robertson, C., & Chetty, S. K. (2000). A Contingency-Based Approach to Understanding Export Performance. *International Business Review*, 9 (2), 211-235.

Simmonds, P. G. (1990). The Combined Diversification Breadth and Mode Dimensions and the Performance of Large Diversified Firms. *Strategic Management Journal*, 11 (5), 399-411.

Styles, C. (1998). Export Performance Measures in Australia and the United Kingdom. *Journal of International Marketing*, 6 (3), 12-36.

Sullivan, D. (1994). Measuring the Degree of Internationalization of a Firm. *Journal of International Business Studies*, 25 (2), 325-342.

Sullivan, D. (1996). Measuring the Degree of Internationalization of a Firm: A Reply. *Journal of International Business Studies*, 27 (1), 179-192.

Sullivan, D., & Bauerschmidt, A. (1990). Incremental Internationalization: A Test of Johanson and Vahlne's Thesis. *Management International Review*, 30 (1), 48-64.

Welch, D. E., & Welch, L. S. (1996). The Internationalization Process and Networks: A Strategic Management Perspective. *Journal of International Marketing*, 4 (3), 11-28.

Welford, R., & Prescott, K. (1994). *European Business: An issue-based approach*. London: Pitman.

Wiedersheim-Paul, F., Olsen, S. C., & Welch, L. S. (1978). Pre-export Activity–The First Step in Internationalisation. *Journal of International Business Studies*, 9 (1), 47-58.

Woodcock, C., Beamish, P., & Makino, S. (1994). Ownership-based entry mode strategies and international performance. *Journal of International Business Studies*, 2, 253-273.

Wortzel, L. H., & Wortzel, H. V. (1981). Export marketing strategies for NIC and LDC-based firms. *Columbia Journal of World Business*, Spring, 51-60.

Yaprak, A. (1985). An Empirical Study of the Differences Between Small Exporting and Non-Exporting U.S. Firms. *International Marketing Review*, 2 (2), 72-83.

Yip, G. S. (1992). *Total global strategy: Managing for worldwide competitive advantage*. New Jersey: Prentice Hall.

Yip, G. S., Gomez Biscarri, J., & Monti, J. A. (2000). The Role of the Internationalization Process in the Performance of Newly Nationalizing Firms. *Journal of International Marketing*, 8 (3), 10-35.

doi:10.1300/J037v16n01_07

ANNEX 1. Operationalization of the Descriptive Variables

Variable	Measure
Descriptive/illustrative variables: qualitative	
Firm size	Small/Medium/Large
Sector	nine sectors (see Table 1)
ISO 9000 (Quality Assurance) approved	Yes/No
ISO 14000 (Environmental Management) approved	Yes/No
Degree of control over international strategies	Total/Partial/None
Subsidiary of foreign parent company	Yes/No
Firm's international behavior	Active/Passive
Firm has export department	Yes/No
Firm has international manager	Yes/No
Education of international manager	Post-graduate/Higher/Below higher
Firm can operate in English/French/German/Italian/Portuguese	Yes/No (5 separate measures)
Entry mode 1: Int'l cooperation, no exports or phys pres	Yes/No
Entry mode 2: Indirect exporting	Yes/No
Entry mode 3: Joint exporting, no physical presence	Yes/No
Entry mode 4: Direct exporting, no physical presence	Yes/No
Entry mode 5: Direct exporting with physical presence	Yes/No
Entry mode 6: Manufacturing abroad	Yes/No
Entry mode 7: Foreign manufacturing plus direct exporting	Yes/No
Establishes/pursues international strategic objectives	Yes/No
Descriptive/illustrative variables: quantitative	
Total assets	amount (million Euro/€)
Total workforce	number of employees
Percent of capital owned by foreign firms	percent
Experience within the firm's sector	number of years
Time since first export order	number of years
Time during which the firm has been exporting regularly*	number of years
Time manager has been in charge of firm's international activity	number of years
Total time of manager's international management experience	number of years
Staff dedicated to international activities (>half of workday)	number of employees
Foreign languages in which firm has capability	number of languages
Geographic scope of firm's international operations	number of countries
Diversity of methods used in international operations*	number of entry modes
Sales in main foreign market vs. total international sales	percent
Total sales (avg. last three years)**	amount (million Euro/€)
International sales (avg. last three years)**	amount (million Euro/€)
Change in international sales (avg. last three years)**	percent
Contribution of international to total sales (avg. last three years)*	percent international/total
Perceived success of int. activities (avg. last three years)**	scale 1(low)-10(high)
Perceived international profitability (avg. last three years)**	scale 1(low)-4(high)
International strategic performance**	(note a)
Economic profitability (avg. last three years)**	percent (note b)
Return on total assets (avg. last three years)**	percent (note b)

*Segmentation variables used for the cluster analysis.
**Variables used as performance indicators.
(a) Sum of respondent's perceived level of achievement of each of 10 international strategic objectives, weighed by their perceived importance on a 1-5 scale (sum ranges from min. 100 to max. 500).
(b) Data from SABI (System of Analysis of Iberic Balance Sheets), which provides information for over 700,000 Spanish and Portuguese firms.

International Entrepreneurship and Sourcing: International Value Chain of Small Firms

Per Servais
Antonella Zucchella
Giada Palamara

SUMMARY. This contribution focuses on international sourcing as an entrepreneurial act and aims at demonstrating that it is actually at the core of internationalization processes of small firms, both established and international new ventures. Another issue of this research is to understand how these firms, characterized typically by scarce financial and managerial resources, can engage in managing international value chains and not only being the passive agent of subcontracting agreements. The breadth of internationals sourcing activities and the nature of the ties established under these agreements is investigated through an empirical survey on 150 Italian SMEs, comparing early with late internationalizing ones. doi:10.1300/J037v16n01_08 *[Article copies available for a fee from The Haworth Document Delivery Service: 1-800-HAWORTH. E-mail address: <docdelivery@ haworthpress.com> Website: <http://www.HaworthPress.com> © 2006 by The Haworth Press, Inc. All rights reserved.]*

KEYWORDS. Small- and medium-sized firms, inward internationalization, international sourcing

INTRODUCTION

The entrepreneur has been identified according to his/her capacity to detect and exploit opportunities, pool and leverage on needed resources, and assume risks. From the pioneering work of Schumpeter (1934) up to the recent surge of studies on entrepreneurship, one of the expressions of entrepreneurship was recognized in the decision of foreign market entry. In particular, "the conquest of a new source of supply" (Ibid., p. 32) was included in the novel combinations Schumpeter identified as expressions of innovation, i.e., entrepreneurship.

The basic proposition of this contribution is that small firm international sourcing decision may be an entrepreneurial act, drawing a parallel consideration on the side of import compared to what Lee and Brasch (1978) wrote about export decisions. This is also based on

Per Servais is Associate Professor, Department of Marketing, University of Southern Denmark, Campusvej 55, DK-5230 Odense M (E-mail: per@sam.sdu.dk). Antonella Zucchella is Full Professor, Dipartimento di Ricerche Aziendali, Università degli studi di Pavia, via s. Felice 7, 27100, Pavia, Italy (E-mail: azucchel@eco.unipv.it). Giada Palamara is a Doctoral Student, Dipartimento di Ricerche Aziendali, Università degli studi di Pavia, via s. Felice 7, 27100, Pavia, Italy (E-mail: gpalamara@eco.unipv.it).

[Haworth co-indexing entry note]: "International Entrepreneurship and Sourcing: International Value Chain of Small Firms." Servais, Per, Antonella Zucchella, and Giada Palamara. Co-published simultaneously in *Journal of Euromarketing* (International Business Press, an imprint of The Haworth Press, Inc.) Vol. 16, No. 1/2, 2006, pp. 105-117; and: *Contemporary Euromarketing: Entry and Operational Decision Making* (ed: Jorma Larimo) International Business Press, an imprint of The Haworth Press, Inc., 2006, pp. 105-117. Single or multiple copies of this article are available for a fee from The Haworth Document Delivery Service [1-800-HAWORTH, 9:00 a.m. - 5:00 p.m. (EST). E-mail address: docdelivery@haworthpress.com].

the fact that decisions in SMEs are often concentrated in the hands of one or a few persons, and the entrepreneur has a unique and crucial role in the organization (Bloodgood et al., 1996; Westhead et al., 2001).

Exporting traditionally represented the predominant international activity of small firms (Tesar & Moini, 1998; Westhead et al., 2001; Audretsch, 2002; Kundu & Katz, 2003). Mainstream literature is now challenged by market globalization which represents not only a wider set of selling opportunities but also of sourcing opportunities. This is true also for small firms, which aim at maintaining/improving/creating their international competitive advantage, tapping knowledge wherever located and establishing new systems of ties. Moreover, the challenge to the mainstream literature comes from the need to adopt not only the perspective of sellers but also the one of buyers as well, which always existed, but has never been studied with a parallel intensity in international business studies (Servais & Jensen, 2001).

This contribution interprets international sourcing as an entrepreneurial act and aims at demonstrating that it is actually at the core of internationalization processes of small firms, both established and international new ventures. In the latter case, the international entrepreneurship perspective is further enforced by the kind of firms investigated, i.e., international new ventures and early internationalizing firms, which are *per se* the object of an important stream of entrepreneurship literature.

Another issue of this research is to understand how these firms, characterized typically by scarce financial and managerial resources, can engage in managing international value chains and not only being the passive agent of subcontracting agreements. Much has been written about the international selling side of both late and early international firms, but comparisons from the sourcing perspective between the two alternative internationalization processes are still missing.

Our work is composed by two sections: the first one proposes a literature review and a theoretical frame working, in order to identify eventual research gaps in literature and to outline some research propositions to investigate

about. In the second section, we develop the analysis on a sample of 150 Italian SMEs.

DEFINING THE SUBJECT OF INVESTIGATION: EARLY AND LATE INTERNATIONALIZING SMEs

Small enterprises are one of the key areas of research in international business and in international entrepreneurship. Together with established SMEs, new and young international ventures have recently grown in the attention of academicians and practitioners, representing an emerging and growing field of international entrepreneurship.

In a seminal article Cavusgil (1998) highlights perspectives on some fundamental questions in the field of international business and some promising research avenues. Among the mentioned avenues especially one area has called upon special research interest that is the Internationalization process of "Born Global" companies. The phenomenon of firms internationalizing right from the foundation could be found all over the world during the last decade or more. Studies from Australia on Born Globals (Cavusgil, 1994; Rennie, 1993) and USA (Knight, 2000) show the legacy of the phenomenon. The overview article by Rialp, Rialp and Knight (2005) has clearly shown the existence of these firms, whether they are called Born Globals, International New Ventures or something else. From a theoretical point of view the research on Born Global firms has always been combined with research in entrepreneurship as in the seminal articles of Benjamin M. Oviatt and Patricia P. McDougall (Oviatt & McDougall, 1994).

However, much remains to be said about the features of international new ventures: this is also true for the apparently widely explored field of "traditional" international SMEs. This contribution proposes to analyze the international sourcing behaviors of both early and late internationalizing firms, in order to explore a relatively underdeveloped field of research and to compare from this point of view the traditional (i.e., incremental or late) international SMEs with the early international ones. Investigating the area of international sourcing permits the development of a better understanding about a less known side of the international activity of small firms, but it also helps to verify the hypothesis that the international expansion of small and infant firms may be supported/accompanied by a parallel development of a network of embedded ties with foreign counterparts. This latter issue is grounded on the network perspective to internationalization (Johanson & Mattsson, 1988), which proves particularly relevant for SMEs, in order to overcome their constraints to foreign expansion.

Oviatt and McDougall (1997) point out that the reason why firms are born as international new ventures as well as their role on the international market need to be researched. The birth of a new venture is not only explained by the entrepreneurs' innovative ideas, but may also be attributed to larger firms' outsourcing decisions as well as ideas conceived by existing firms. Different sources of birth may define different roles of the International New Venture, and variations of its relations to other firms, e.g., in terms of interdependence versus dependence on the actions of other firms, or perhaps mutual interdependence of a group of firms. Furthermore, the birth and growth of an International New Venture may depend on external facilitating factors, such as information and communication technologies, as well as factors that are closely related to the characteristics of the entrepreneur and other business partners (for example prior international experience). Most scholars refer to Oviatt and McDougall (1994) who define an INV as *"... a business organization that, from inception, seeks to derive significant advantage from the use of resources and the sale of outputs in multiple countries"* (p. 49). Interpretation as well as empirical operationalization of each of the involved concepts, however, differs widely between scholars. As a consequence the empirical knowledge gathered about these firms is in most instances impossible to integrate because the firms studied exhibit a great diversity ranging from high-tech firms with activities all over the globe to low-tech firms that are very much focused on neighboring countries. This is a serious limitation of previous research in the field.

Notwithstanding the broad definition proposed by Oviatt and McDougall (1994), most of the research on Born Global firms has been focused on "sales of outputs in multiple countries" and only to a very limited extent on "the use of resources from multiple countries" (Ibid., p. 238), even though sourcing/purchasing can be regarded as an entrepreneurial act (Morris & Calantone, 1991).

The same holds true for those firms that internationalize more gradually and some years after their foundation. In this contribution we call them "late international firms," and they still nowadays represent the majority of cases in most industries.

This predominant focus on the selling side is thus not exclusive to the field of international new ventures. In a review of international business literature, Liang and Parkhe (1997) reveal a striking imbalance, because one side of the coin–the exporter side–has been extensively studied, while the importer side and the associated motives have been largely neglected. This outcome is further stressed in the findings by Lye and Hamilton (2000) who found that–in over 126 works on international exchange–106 have been confined to exporters only, 14 to studies about balanced or unbalanced dyads and only six studies dealt with importers only. More attention has been devoted to sourcing strategies–especially aimed at production or other activities delocalization–carried out by large firms.

A research gap is thus found when we consider the international sourcing activity of SMEs. Moreover, comparative studies among the two categories of small firms, viz. the early versus the late internationalizing ones, are rare and almost absent when we come to their foreign sourcing activities.

DEFINING THE OBJECT OF INVESTIGATION: INTERNATIONAL SOURCING AND ITS RELEVANCE FOR INTERNATIONAL COMPETITIVENESS AND EXPORT PERFORMANCE

International sourcing is actually one of the key activities which contribute most to the firm's competitiveness (Arnold, 1989). As a consequence, it may have a relevant role on the foreign selling performance. The lack of knowledge about international purchasing is often a factor of uncertainty which leads to a narrow focus on the domestic market. This might lower the firm's competitiveness when compared to competitors who source, or consider to do so, internationally. Also the lack of knowledge about the fit into international supply chain or production networks might hinder the firms' strategic development. Overall knowledge about other firms' experiences with international sources might lead to a keener attention to the alternative opportunities in respect of the performance of the actual purchasing function, and hence contribute to a possible overall improvement of firms' competitiveness. International sourcing and exporting can be both considered essential elements of an international value chain: international sourcing, indeed, refers to activities related to buying processes, procurement and strategic issues like relationship to different suppliers (Hill & Hillier, 1977; Luthje & Servais, 2005).

International sourcing is nowadays one of the main strategies to gain and maintain competitive advantage (Moncza & Trent, 1995). Luthje and Servais (2005) argue that the lack of knowledge about international purchasing is often a factor of uncertainty, leading to a narrow focus on the domestic market. This fact limits the development of international networks, leaving the firm with a potential lower competitiveness. On the other hand, a sourcing-based international network can be the key to new export occasions (Monzca & Trent, 1992): international competition affects the whole value chain of a firm, and export is not necessarily the first approach to foreign markets. Some authors report that internationalization is not always export driven (Liange & Parke, 1997), even for SMEs (Servais & Jensen, 2001). This involves that the perspective of international entrepreneurship must be enlarged to the sourcing activity of firms.

International purchasing emerged initially as a reaction designed to secure the availability of materials and to reduce production costs (Birou & Fawcett, 1993). Today international purchasing strategies are increasingly targeted

at gaining and maintaining competitive advantage (Monczka & Trent, 1991). In order to manufacture and deliver globally world-class products at low price and high quality firms must, regardless of their size, have access to world-class technological expertise and ability for scanning the best suppliers throughout the world (Monczka & Trent, 1992).

The driving forces for a firm to engage into international purchasing are of course of pivotal interest when studying the field of international sourcing. The specific reasons and major criteria for a domestic buyer to purchase foreign manufactured products may of course vary across industries and over time. Several studies indicate (Monczka and Trent, 1991) that importing firms expect an improvement in four critical areas by foreign purchases: Cost reduction, Quality improvement, Increased exposure to worldwide technology, and Delivery and reliability improvements.

Cost reduction. Traditionally, lower prices or cost advantage has been the main motive for international purchasing (Birou & Fawcett, 1994). Cost advantage can arise, for example, from lower labor and material cost, scale economics, better productivity and local government subsidies. Lower prices can also be due to favorable exchange rates. Purchasing from foreign markets usually rise as the home market's currency becomes stronger, and vice versa. Most firms naturally want to acquire high quality products at a low cost. For firms selling in mature markets where there is little or no product differentiation, cost reduction provides a competitive advantage in the market (Carter & Narasimhan, 1990).

Quality. Providing quality products to customers is of paramount importance on today's competitive industrial market. In this respect some foreign suppliers, such as Japan and West Germany, have achieved great success and good reputation as high quality sources, especially in the areas of consumer electronics and automobiles (Carter & Narasimhan, 1990). Indeed, Min and Galle (1991) found that US purchasing professionals participating in their study rated these countries as the first and second sources of quality products.

Availability. Availability is also a critical factor that motivates global sourcing. Domestic buyers often rely on foreign sources simply because the desired products are not available in the home market. Monczka and Giunipero (1984) found that the main reason for global sourcing in the chemical industry is unavailability of needed products in the domestic market. Behind this motive there are two rationales: (1) that the product/service is not available on the domestic market and (2) that the foreign suppliers have competitive advantages derived from the production conditions of these firms (Dunning, 1998). The missing availability on the domestic market could lead to the fact that the buyer redefines the need in order to suit the offers by domestic suppliers. But this seems not to be the case; research shows that industrial buyers in general are well informed of offerings by foreign suppliers (Birou & Fawcet, 1993; Scully & Fawsett, 1994). The different production conditions by foreign suppliers is one explanation as to some of international purchasing, but research has shown (Servais & Jensen, 2001) that not all international exchange takes place between countries with very different production factors.

Along with cost, quality and availability there are many other motives for international purchasing. Some firms pursue international purchasing as a supply chain management strategy. They may try to find additional supply sources or increase competition among domestic suppliers and thereby leverage their own competitiveness. In some cases international purchasing operations are conducted to prepare for an entry into new sales market or support current marketing and production operations in foreign markets (Arnold, 1989; Monczka & Trent, 1992). Establishing a presence in foreign supply markets may also be due to countertrade and local content requirements.

Hallén (1982) stresses, however, that other issues may influence foreign sourcing such as the firm's attitude of buying from abroad, the ability to conduct sourcing activities internationally and the actual market conditions, e.g., when there are no alternatives on the home market.

However, while it seems that international purchasing was initially used as a reactive response to global competitive pressures, that is,

for the cost reasons or as means to gain access to materials and components, international sourcing is now increasingly used as a proactive strategy to gain competitive advantage (Monczka & Giunipero, 1984): in this perspective, foreign sourcing is an expression of international entrepreneurship.

According to Monczka and Trent (1991), once firms gain international purchasing experience, the motivation is no longer survival but rather to secure cost, quality, technological, and other advantages. *"International sourcing had become a strategy to be actively pursued in a globally competitive environment"* (Ibid., p. 3). Since international sourcing stems from competitive pressures and can provide critical inputs for sustainable competitive advantage in global markets, also small firms tend to develop these practices. Moreover, the phenomenon of born global firms, as the above mentioned literature suggests, is not confined to foreign sales but extends to foreign purchases, because the two tend to be connected and the competitiveness of the former is frequently linked to the availability, cost and quality of the latter.

From the literature review proposed in this section some research avenues can be identified and expressed as research propositions, as follows:

1. Small firms engage in international sourcing, and not only in exporting. Among SMEs, infant firms show precocity not just in their foreign sales but also in their foreign sourcing.
2. Small firms have diversified sourcing approaches, involving differentiated contents for their international purchases (raw materials, components, finished goods, technologies and services), coherently with the evolving nature of international sourcing motivations.

RELATIONSHIPS WITHIN INTERNATIONAL SOURCING: COMPLEXITY, IMPORTANCE AND CONTROL

If the content of transactions between domestic and foreign firms moves from prevailing traditional import of raw materials to international sourcing of components, finished goods and services and technologies, it is likely to happen that the degree of involvement of actors increases, due to a higher level of underlying assets specificity and to their more extended contribution to the purchasing firm competitiveness. This does not necessarily imply a corresponding growth in the degree of control on foreign sources, because the actual global competitive strategy rests on a delicate balancing of involvement and flexibility in relationships. As a consequence, non equity and low equity agreements could be a viable option, especially in the case of small and infant firms where resources constraints are more severe, thus supporting effectively inter-firm sourcing.

The ties between firms can be also classified along two dimensions in international sourcing situations (Servais, 2001): perceived importance and perceived complexity. The latter also includes the issue of uncertainty, which does have a large impact on the perception of different situations. When complexity and importance are high there is much need of trust-based relationships, while in the opposite case arm's length ties can work well. This means that we can analyze foreign sourcing contracts adopting the perspective of the nature of the ties.

In the case of international purchasing we are dealing with situations which can include both arms' length relations to the supplier as well as "closer" relationships. The latter take place, for example, in international subcontracting, where a part of the suppliers' production enters in the manufacturing of the buyer own products, e.g., designed components. Typically these relations would include some reciprocal collaboration, since the supplier often would have to make some adaptation and the buyer would have to control the quality of the components. The buyer could also choose, right from the beginning to obtain the needed components from a supplier who is producing under contract from the supplier. When the quality level is agreed the buyer and seller have to work closely on supply chain management and above all production scheduling which means that the buyer must be much involved right from the beginning (van Veele, 2002). In the case of joint venture manufacturing, the buyer will set up a production facility together

with the supplier; and since the project will be dependent of incorporation of knowledge from both parties, both have to invest in physical plants and relationships. At the same time they will have to supervise intensively the performance of the joint venture facility.

Bensaou (1999) stresses that not only products, customers or suppliers should be the content in portfolios, but portfolio should extend to encompass buyer-seller relationships as well. Furthermore, Bensaou (1999) focuses on the relation between (and not on a single buyer or seller) buyer and seller establishing four different contextual profiles (market exchange, captive supplier, captive buyer, and strategic partnership). Unfortunately, this is not done in an international context. In the following, we will further elaborate on portfolios of buyer-seller relationships in an international context, since only a few studies have included both an international marketing and purchasing perspective and the studies done have focused on already established relationships (Håkansson, 1982).

In international sourcing, firms deal with situations which can involve both arm's length relations with suppliers as well as more embedded ties. Embeddedness represents a unique logic of exchange (Uzzi, 1997). Inter-organizational relationships are said to be embedded if a social dimension exists influencing the economic behavior of partners (Granovetter, 1985). Embedded ties are characterized by stronger trust, rich information exchange and joint problem solving (Powell, 1990; Uzzi, 1997; Gulati & Gargiulo, 1999). In international markets, networks of specialized producers exist and represent an intermediate form between market and hierarchy where assets specificity is found, together with flexibility and responsiveness to partners' needs, joint problem solving, and mutual trust.

Establishing a system of embedded ties, from the local to the international scale, enables small and infant firms to overcome the financial and managerial constraint to multinational growth and gives them access to a worldwide set of sourcing opportunities in order to preserve/enhance their international competitiveness. Moreover, since embedded ties are rich in bilateral information exchange, they constitute an optimal arrangement when perceived complexity and importance in transaction rise, as it is the case in actual dynamic global markets (Zucchella, 2006). The search of small and infant firms for embedded ties on a global scale leads look for partners which can be similar in terms of structure, culture and management processes, i.e., small firms.

This perspective fits with a network-based theory of internationalization, which has been proposed by the Nordic School. Johanson and Mattsson (1988)–instead of considering the internationalization as an interaction only between the firm and the market–underlined the existence of networks among independent firms. The basic assumption of the model is that enterprises need an accessible knowledge of one another in order to do business.

In this case internationalization depends on network relationships rather than on a firm-specific advantage or the psychic distance of the target market. With these relationships in place, externalization of transactions is more likely to happen than internalization. Companies can then internationalize with the help of partners who offer contacts and help to develop new partners. Thus, internationalization decisions are influenced by the various members of the firm's network. "Having a network orientation and, consequently, identifying the roles and the strengths of the actors within it gives the firm an understanding of possible constraints and opportunities for its operations" (Johanson &Vahlne, 1992, p. 12).

According to Johanson and Mattson (1988), the degree of internationalization of the network affects the internationalization process of a particular firm in the network which means that firms cannot be analyzed separately but must be understood in an interdependency context.

From the literature review proposed on this section, a third research proposition can be formulated:

3. The nature of ties established by small and infant firms is mainly embedded, coherently with: (a) the network theory of internationalization, (b) the nature of ties they privilege also locally, and (c) the growing complexity and relative importance of international sourcing for the firm competitiveness.

METHODOLOGY AND SAMPLE

The empirical survey is an exploratory one, because it moves from a literature review which identified important research gaps in the study of SMEs' foreign sourcing activities. Three main research avenues have been identified where the major gaps existed and they have been expressed in terms of research propositions. From the descriptive statistical analysis we expect to have inputs for a better definition of these propositions and for the formulation of definitive research hypotheses.

Our propositions have been tested on a sample of 150 Italian small- and medium-sized firms, defined according to the European Union parameters. According to the latter, we define small firm as an organization with a number of employees ranging between 10 and 49, and revenues less than € 10 million; we define medium-sized firm as an organization with a number of employees ranging between 50 and 249, and sales volume less than € 50 million. All the firms in the sample have in fact less than 250 employees, total revenues and assets below the ceiling according to the EU standards, and are independent (not belonging to national/multinational groups).

The original database is represented by respondents to a questionnaire survey on international activities which involved 600 SMEs (return rate 24%). The sample was extracted from a list of SMEs headquartered in North-West of Italy–an area where 60% of Italian exporters and 80% of firms involved in FDIs and international agreements are concentrated–reported by the Chambers of Commerce information systems for declaring export activity. The selection was made according to the criteria of representativeness of the population of Italian international SMEs, according to ICE (Italian Trade Commission) surveys.

All the firms are reported as manufacturing businesses and operate in different industries. The firms were first informed about the research by mail, and later on contacted by phone to obtain their support in the research. All the questionnaires have been filled through direct interviews, lasting around one hour each, with the entrepreneur and the person in charge of international activities, when they do not coincide.

The questionnaire is constituted by five different sections regarding business activities and governance; strategic positioning; ownership and relations with other firms; international activities; and entrepreneurship. Each section is constituted by direct questions with multiple choice answers.

The questionnaire was constructed through a review of the literature on international business and entrepreneurship, and through discussions and focus groups of practitioners, researchers and entrepreneurs. The result was an interview that had been previously tested with 5 entrepreneurs, who were asked to inform about problems in interpretation and to provide a feedback about the questionnaire.

This empirical survey aims at a better understanding of the above mentioned research propositions about the international sourcing behavior of small and medium firms, in order to explore a relatively underdeveloped field of research and to compare from this point of view the traditional (i.e., incremental or late) international SMEs with the early international ones. In order to operationalize these two categories, the surveyed firms have been divided into late and early internationals according to the inception of their international operations (notably export, import, or both). Firms which started exporting/importing in their first three years of life have been considered early internationals, while we labelled the remaining ones as late internationals. For a survey about the alternative spans of time proposed in literature to identify born global firms, see Rialp, Rialp and Knight (2005).

FINDINGS

Table 1 shows the distribution of the 150 SMEs according to the extent of internationalization in their value chain and to the precocity of international activities carried out. The table outcomes support our first research proposition, because effectively:

1. Small firms engage extensively in both foreign selling and foreign purchasing (more than 60% of overall sample); the model of the pure exporting firm, with local sourcing, refers actually to a minority of firms, while the majority couples import with export activity.
2. A relevant percentage of SMEs (almost 50%) starts international operations early, notably in their first three years. Starting international activity from importing seems relatively more common in early than in late international SMEs. This may support the idea that a part of the born global phenomenon could be explained by early import arrangements which open opportunities for early exporting as well.
3. The majority of early international firms from their inception have to face the challenge of internationalizing both sales and purchases, in order to strengthen quickly their competitive positioning.

Table 2 highlights the overall system of buying relationships for the surveyed firms: foreign buyers represents around one third of the total, confirming from a different perspective the first research proposition. More than two thirds of suppliers are SMEs like the respondents, providing some arguments to support the third research proposition, where we hypothesized that small firms tend to establish ties with similar firms, because this is one of the pre-requisites for long term embedded relationships. The differences between late and early international firms do not appear significant in terms of composition of suppliers both in terms of size and of location. We can only observe a relatively higher preference of early internationals for small firms.

Table 3 focuses on import only and shows the composition of import flows for the overall sample of importers and for the two groups, i.e., early and late internationals having import activity. Raw materials are still important but the remaining categories together prevail. The variety of purchases underlies a parallel variety of motives for importing. The second research proposition seems, thus, to be confirmed by these figures. Also, in this case, the

TABLE 1. The Internationalization of the Value Chain in Early and Late International SMEs

Early Internationals	Born Importer 8%	Born Exporter 16,6%	Extended Early International 25,2%
Late Internationals	Late Importer 1,3%	Late Exporter 14,0%	Late International 35,2%
	Sourcing	Selling	Both

Coordination of International Value Chain Activities

TABLE 2. Size and Location of Suppliers in International SMEs

	SMEs	Large
The Overall Sample		
International	115 (23,6%)	38 (8,7%)
National	228 (52,1%) Local: 91 (20,7%)	57 (13,0%) Local: 18 (4,1%)
Late Internationals		
International	55 (25,5%)	20 (9.2%)
National	109 (50,5%) Local: 44 (20,4%)	32 (14,8%) Local: 10 (4,6%)
Early Internationals		
International	60 (28,6%)	18 (8,6%)
National	119 (56,6%) Local: 47 (22,4%)	13 (6,2%) Local: 8 (3,8%)

differences between early and late internationals are not striking, but it is very interesting to notice that early internationals appear relatively more oriented to be part of international value chains, importing more components, semi-finished and finished goods than late internationals, where–on the other hand–the import of raw materials is more pronounced. Trying to interpret this outcome in terms of our research propositions we could argue that probably early internationals are pushed strongly by the need of quick development of international competitive positioning, and shop globally for either low cost and/or specialized suppliers. The fact that a relevant percentage of imports is due to goods different than raw materials, could lead to develop stronger relationships with suppliers because the degree of assets specificity may be higher.

Table 4 supports our third research proposition because the nature of the ties with suppliers is at a first glance similar in different sub

samples of SMEs and confirms that long term ties largely prevail over short term ones. Long term ties among small firms are grounded on personal knowledge, reciprocal trust and understanding. In a significant percentage of cases these long term relationships are not even formalized in some contractual agreement, which is symptomatic of very high trust between parties. Early international firms appear even more committed in the direction of establishing long term ties with their counterparts. This could be an indirect confirmation of personal networks which explain and support the international growth of infant international firms.

On the other hand formal relations are more developed in early internationals: this is not easy to explain with the basic information contained in our data set, but may be connected with higher levels of assets specificity, exchange of technology and know-how. Another reason could be that such firms are usually younger (their average age is 22 years, compared with 38 years of average age of late internationals) and especially the youngest ones may be required by suppliers to establish formal agreements, for the higher risks involved in the liability of newness and foreignness, jointly.

Finally, Figure 1 proposes a classification of the 143 relationships declared by the importing firms with foreign suppliers, according to the above mentioned taxonomy proposed by Servais (2001). According to this approach the two dimensions considered–perceived importance and perceived complexity–are correspondingly determined by economic importance, end-product importance, production importance, importance for the firm-specific advantage, as well as into functional complexity, usage complexity, specification complexity, commercial complexity.

It should, however, be noted that the dimensions are relative and the perception of the buying situation will change over time. A purchase that is perceived by the buying firm at a given time to be very complex may, due to learning, later on be perceived as rather simple. Another purchase may be perceived as very important to the firm, but could over time lose its importance, e.g., due to the technological development. Each person involved in the purchasing process may have different per-

TABLE 3. What Do Importers Buy?

	Raw materials	Components and not finished goods	Finished goods	Services	Patents and technologies
On importers	78 (68,4%)	36 (31,6%)	27 (23,7%)	6 (5,3%)	7 (6,1%)
On late internationals	39 (54,9%)	14 (19,7%)	12 (16,9%)	3 (4,2%)	3 (4,2%)
On early internationals	39 (47,6%)	21 (25,6%)	15 (18,3%)	3 (3,7%)	4 (4,9%)

TABLE 4. The Relationships with Suppliers

	Occasional	Long term
The Importers sample (143 relations)		
Formalized relations	28 (19,6%)	72 (50,3%)
Not formalized relations	13 (9,1%)	30 (21,0%)
On Late Internationals (94 relations)		
Formalized relations	22 (23,4%)	46 (48,9%)
Not formalized relations	9 (9,6%)	17 (18,8%)
On Early Internationals (86 relations)		
Formalized relations	13 (15,1%)	50 (58,1%)
Not formalized relations	6 (7,0%)	17 (19,7%)

ceptions of purchases and the supplier portfolio. Despite the conceivable disagreements it is, however, possible to set up some expectation as to the general behavior in different buying situations.

The classification is based on the interviews with firms, where entrepreneurs/top managers were asked to position, in Figure 1, their foreign supply relationships. In order to verify their correct positioning, the questionnaire contained questions relative to the various issues illustrated inside the boxes in Figure 1. In almost 10% of cases there was no exact correspondence between a firm positioning of its foreign relationships and the control answers. Figure 1 can be considered an approximate picture of the relationships portfolios of the interviewed firms, due to the difficulties in positioning exactly some ties, but its main results appear interesting, viz.: most ties are positioned in the upper right box, where both high complexity and high importance are found. The supplier management approach is predominant, as opposed to the traditional purchasing management, which involves the minority of foreign supply relationships and corresponds to many suppliers of standardized goods and arm's length independent relationships. The supplier management approach corresponds to a few suppliers of strategic items, frequent focus on joint R&D and/or integrated production and the kind of relationships established are partnerships based on interdependent relationships.

Early international firms are even more affected by this trend. It is likely to assume that supplier management is one of the approaches on which precocious (born international) and fast internationalization is grounded, as well as global competitive positioning of early internationals.

CONCLUSION

The evolution of international business from the 1980s has been characterized by a growth and diversification of international activities in firms, notably small and infant ones. The growth in their international activities refers to the amount of foreign sales realized by such firms, notwithstanding their limited size. Also infant firms have known a surge in their international activities, giving rise to the phenomenon of born global firms. The diversification of the international activities refers to the gradual shift from the traditional international business model of small firms, based on ex-

FIGURE 1. The Foreign Supply Relationships Portfolios of Early and Late International Firms

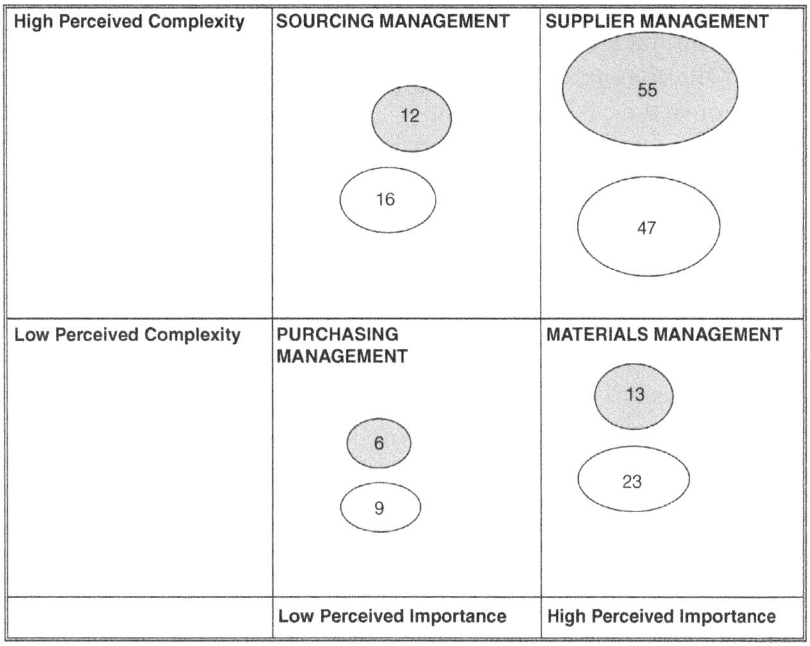

The gray ovals express approximately the number of foreign sourcing relationships established by early international firms. The white ovals refer to the same variable for late internationals.

port of home produced goods, to a new one. The latter is characterized by an increasing internationalization of their value chain and on the establishment of a system of embedded ties, as opposed to arm's length ones.

This contribution aims at verifying this evolution and at exploring further the system and nature of ties established between small- and medium-sized firms–split into early and late international ones–and their foreign suppliers. Much has been written on the topics like born global firms and the like, but some fields are still relatively unexplored. This is true not only for early international firms but also for the traditional late international ones. In particular, the side of international sourcing has not been investigated sufficiently, especially when compared to the much more explored field of international selling. Moreover, international sourcing has been rarely considered an expression of international entrepreneurship.

This contribution profiles the sourcing activity of small firms, according to the following issues: the size and location of suppliers, the kind of assets being traded internationally and the kind of relationships established with foreign buyers. In profiling the international sourcing activity of small firms the objectives were twofold: the first one is a better understanding of this relatively obscure side of international SMEs and its links with their overall international competitiveness and export activity. The second aim is a comparison between early (i.e., emergent) and late (i.e., traditional) international SMEs, in order to verify if any differences exist in terms of sourcing strategy, which could contribute to understanding of this side of the born global phenomenon.

The research propositions find adequate support in the empirical survey. Small firms–both late and early international ones–appear widely involved in international sourcing activity. The predominant model of international SMEs is actually the one of a firm which contemporarily imports and exports goods and services. Their sourcing activity is diversified in terms of assets exchanged, with early international firms relatively more prone to purchase goods characterized by higher assets specificity and complexity. The kind of ties established reveal two interesting phenomena: SMEs prefer relationships with similar firms (i.e., small- and medium-sized) and maintain them over the long term. This outcome is even stronger in the case of early international firms, where a relatively higher degree of formalization in relationships is coupled with higher percentages of long term ties and of supplying relationships with small firms.

The main limitation of this study is that it refers to a sample of 150 SMEs and actually only an explorative research has been conducted. This research permitted to refine research hypotheses for a more complete empirical test.

The managerial and policy implication of this contribution are relevant. From a managerial point of view, first we call for attention on the issue of international sourcing, because most firms are involved in this activity but they are not always well aware of the impact it may have on the overall competitiveness and in opening new export markets as well.

The second managerial implication involves the international business planning process, which–both for new ventures and for existing firms–should take into deeper consideration the core issues related to international sourcing, notably the "*where, who, what, why, how, how much, how long*" contractual issues, instead of focusing primarily on the foreign selling estimates, which depend heavily on the former.

The third managerial implication of this contribution calls for the adoption of a portfolio view of sourcing contracts where domestic and foreign agreements are mapped and monitored according to their importance and complexity.

From a policy point of view, this contribution highlights that export supporting programs are frequently characterized by a partial perspective in pursuing the competitiveness of domestic firms and should take into account the co-existence and mutual impact of foreign selling and sourcing.

REFERENCES

Arnold, U. (1989). Global sourcing–An indispensable element in worldwide competition. *International Management Review, 29*(4), 14-28.

Audretsch, D. (2002). *Entrepreneurship: A survey of the literature.* European Commission, Enterprise Directorate General: London.

Bensaou, M. (1999). Portfolios of buyer-supplier relationships, *Sloan Management Review*, (Summer), 35-44.

Birou, L. & Fawcett, S. (1993). International purchasing: Benefits, requirements and challenges. *International Journal of Purchasing and Materials Management*, (*Spring*), 28-37.

Bloodgood, J., Sapienza, H. & Almeida, J. (1996). The internationalization of new high-potential US Ventures: Antecedents and outcomes. *Entrepreneurship Theory and Practise,* (*Summer*), 61-76.

Carter, J. & Narasimhan, R. (1990). Purchasing in the international marketplace: Implication for operations. *Journal of Purchasing and Materials Management*, (*Summer*), 2-11.

Cavusgil, S.T. (1994). Born Globals: A Quiet Revolution Among Australian Exporters. *Journal of International Marketing, Editorial, 2*(3).

Cavusgil, S.T. (1998). Perspectives: Knowledge development in international marketing. *Journal of International Marketing, 6*(2), 103-12.

Dunning, J. (1998). Location and the multinational enterprise: A neglected factor*? Journal of International Business Studies, 29*, 45-66.

Granovetter, M. (1985). Economic action and social structure: The problem of embeddedness. *American Journal of Sociology, 91*, 481-510.

Gulati, R. & Gargiulo, M. (1999). Where do interorganizational networks come from*? American Journal of Sociology, 104*(5), 1439-1493.

Håkansson, H. (ed.) (1982). *International industrial marketing and purchasing of industrial goods; an interaction approach.* John Wiley & Sons, Chichester.

Hallén, L. (1982). International purchasing in a small country. *Journal of International Business Studies*, (*Winter*), 99-112.

Hill, R. & Hillier, T. (1977). *Organisational buying behavior.* London, MacMillan.

Johanson, J. & Mattsson, L. (1988). Internationalization in industrial system–A Network approach. In Hood, N. & Vahlne, J-E. (eds.), *Strategies in Global competition*, (pp. 287-314) Croom Helm, New York.

Johanson J. & Vahlne, J. (1992). Management of Foreign Market Entry. *Scandinavian International Business Review, 1*(3), 9-27.

Knight, G. (2000). Entrepreneurial orientation in the international success of small and medium scale firms. *Working paper presented at the Second Biennial McGill Conference on International Entrepreneurship: Researching Frontiers*, September 23-25.

Kundu, S. & Katz, J. (2003). Born-international SMEs: Bi-level impacts of resources and intentions. *Small Business Economics, 20*(1), 25-47.

Lee, W. & Brasch, J. (1978). The adoption of export as an innovation. *Journal of International Business Studies, (Spring-Summer)*, 85-93.

Liang, N. & Parkhe, A. (1997). Importer behaviour: The neglected counterpart of international exchange. *Journal of International Business Studies, (Fall)*, 495-529.

Lüthje, T. & Servais, P. (2005). Firms' International Sourcing and Intra-Industry Trade. *Quaderno di ricerca* n. 2–gennaio 2005, Università di Pavia.

Lye, A. & Hamilton, R. (2000). Search and performance in international exchange. *European Journal of Marketing, 34*(1), 176-189.

Min, H. & Galle, W. (1991). International purchasing strategies of multinational U.S. firms. *International Journal of Purchasing and Materials Management, (Summer)*, 9-18.

Monczka, R. & Giunipero, L. (1984). International purchasing; characteristics and implementation. *Journal of Purchasing and Materials Management, (Fall)*: 2-9.

Monczka, R. & Trent, R. (1991). Global sourcing: A development approach, *International Journal of Purchasing and Materials Management, 27*(2), 2-8.

Monczka, R. & Trent, R. (1992). Worldwide outsourcing: Assessment and execution. *International Journal of Purchasing and Materials Management, 28*(4), 9-18.

Monczka, R. & Trent, R. (1995). *Purchasing and Sourcing Strategy: Trends and Implications.* Center for Advanced Purchasing Studies. (CAPS report).

Morris, M. & Calantone, R. (1991). Redefining the purchasing function; an entrepreneurial perspective. *International Journal of Purchasing and Material Management, (Fall)*: 1-9.

Oviatt, B. & McDougall, P. (1994). Toward a theory of international new ventures. *Journal of International Business Studies, 2*, 545-64.

Oviatt, B. & McDougall, P. (1997). Challenges for internationalization process theory: The case of international new ventures. *Management International Review, 37*(2), 85-99.

Powell, W. (1990). Neither market nor hierarchy: Network forms of organization. *Research in Organizational Behavior, 12*, 295-337.

Rennie, M. (1993). Global competitiveness: Born Global. *McKinsey Quarterly, 4*, 45-52.

Rialp, A., Rialp, J., & Knight, G. (2005). The phenomenon of early internationalizing firms: What do we know after a decade (1993-2003) of scientific inquiry? *International Business Review, 14*, 147-166.

Schumpeter, J. (1934). *The theory of economic development.* Cambridge: Harvard University Press.

Scully, J. & Fawcett, S. (1994). International procurement strategies: Challenges and opportunities for the small firm. *Production and Inventory Management Journal*, Second Quarter: 39-46.

Servais, P. (2001). International sourcing: Entering and exiting different industrial networks, In C.P. Rao (Eds.), *Globalization and Its Managerial Implications*, (pp. 108-119), Quorum Books, Westport, CT.

Servais, P. & Jensen, J. (2001). The internationalization of industrial purchasing; the example of small Danish manufactures. *Advances in International Marketing, 11*, 227-254.

Tesar, G. & Moini, A. (1998). Longitudinal study of exporters and non exporters: A focus on smaller manufacturing enterprises. *International Business Review, 7*(3), 291-313.

Uzzi, B. (1997). Social structure and competition in interfirm networks: The paradox of embeddedness. *Administrative Science Quarterly, 42*(1), 37-70.

Van Wheele, A. (2002). *Purchasing and Supply Chain Management–Analysis, Planning and Practice.* 3 ed., Thomson, London.

Westhead, P., Wright, M. & Ucbasaran, D. (2001). The internationalization of new and small firms: A resource-based view. *Journal of Business Venturing, 16*, 333-358.

Zucchella, A. (2006). Local cluster dynamics: Trajectories of mature industrial districts between decline and multiple embeddedness. *Journal of Institutional Economics*, vol. 2, nr.1, April, 21-44.

doi:10.1300/J037v16n01_08

Partner Selection in International Joint Ventures

Jorma Larimo
Sami Rumpunen

SUMMARY. Although the importance of partner selection with regard to any type of cooperation has generally been agreed on, the amount of research analyzing the relationship between partner selection and IJV performance in more detail has so far been surprisingly limited. The goal of this paper is to analyze the influence of various foreign partner-specific, IJV location-specific and investment-specific variables on the relative importance of task- and partner-related selection criteria. Furthermore, the study analyzes the relationship between IJV performance and the relative importance of the selection criteria. The empirical part of the study is based on a sample of 60 IJVs established by Finnish companies in various foreign countries during the 1990s. The results indicated that IJV location-specific and investment-specific variables had influenced the relative importance of the partner selection criteria used by the Finnish companies, while foreign partner-specific variables had a much more limited influence. The influence of contextual variables in general was seen to be stronger on task-related criteria. Finally, the results indicated clear differences in the relative importance of the selection criteria between better and poorly performing IJVs. doi:10.1300/J037v16n01_09 *[Article copies available for a fee from The Haworth Document Delivery Service: 1-800-HAWORTH. E-mail address: <docdelivery@haworthpress.com> Website: <http://www.HaworthPress.com> © 2006 by The Haworth Press, Inc. All rights reserved.]*

KEYWORDS. International joint venture, partner selection, selection criteria

INTRODUCTION

The formation of international joint ventures (IJVs) and other types of alliances has increased markedly during the last twenty years for several reasons (see, e.g., Contractor & Lorange, 1988). In the planning and formation of IJVs the selection of a partner is one of the most important issues. Selection of the right partner should lead to planned/superior performance whereas selecting a non-suitable partner may lead to great problems in management and decision-making and may even lead to leakage of tacit knowledge and/or to other problems, for example, with the image of the foreign partner. Results in several studies have indicated that 20 to even 70 percent of the IJVs are failures, are unstable and/or do not meet the goals set for them. In several cases the problems are linked to the partner. Thus, part-

Jorma Larimo is Professor of International Marketing, Department of Marketing, University of Vaasa, P.O. Box 700, FIN-65101 Vaasa, Finland (E-mail: jorma.larimo@uwasa.fi). Sami Rumpunen is a Researcher, Department of Marketing, University of Vaasa, P.O. Box 700, FIN-65101 Vaasa, Finland (E-mail: saru@uwasa.fi).

[Haworth co-indexing entry note]: "Partner Selection in International Joint Ventures." Larimo, Jorma, and Sami Rumpunen. Co-published simultaneously in *Journal of Euromarketing* (International Business Press, an imprint of The Haworth Press, Inc.) Vol. 16, No. 1/2, 2006, pp. 119-137; and: *Contemporary Euromarketing: Entry and Operational Decision Making* (ed: Jorma Larimo) International Business Press, an imprint of The Haworth Press, Inc., 2006, pp. 119-137. Single or multiple copies of this article are available for a fee from The Haworth Document Delivery Service [1-800-HAWORTH, 9:00 a.m. - 5:00 p.m. (EST). E-mail address: docdelivery@ haworthpress.com].

Available online at http://jem.haworthpress.com
© 2006 by The Haworth Press, Inc. All rights reserved.
doi:10.1300/J037v16n01_09

ner selection is a key issue in the IJV decision-making process. Therefore it is somewhat surprising that partner selection–at least a more detailed analysis of the selection–has received rather limited attention (see, e.g., Glaister & Buckley, 1997; Robson, 2002; Nielsen, 2003; Reus & Ritchie 2004).

The goals of this paper are to analyze the relative importance of partner selection criteria in IJVs and to analyze the links between the selection criteria and IJV performance, in order to examine whether there are clear differences in the relative importance given to certain criteria when a partner is selected for a successful or a poorly performing IJV. More specifically, the goal is to analyze the role of partner- and task-related selection criteria introduced by Geringer (1988). In addition, the goal is to analyze how the relative importance of partner selection criteria is influenced by foreign partner specific, IJV location specific and investment-specific variables. The analysis is conducted from the point of view of the foreign partner in the IJV.

Several of the analyzed relationships in this paper, especially the relation between the relative importance of the selection criteria and IJV performance, have so far been analyzed very limitedly. Thus, the paper offers clear contribution to the present stock of knowledge on IJV partner selection.

The structure of the paper is as follows: In the second section a general review of the existing literature will be made. In the third section hypotheses for the empirical part are developed. The fourth section consists of discussion on the main methodological issues and the key issues of the sample. The results of the study are presented in the fifth section. Finally, the sixth section summarizes the results and includes the main conclusions based on the earlier findings and results of this study.

LITERATURE OVERVIEW

The influence of selecting the right partner on the success of the IJV has been suggested by a number of authors (e.g., Harrigan, 1985; Glaister and Buckley, 1997). In fact, the majority of the literature focusing on IJVs includes at least some references to partner se-

lection. However, the amount of literature focusing on IJV partner selection in more detail is surprisingly limited.

The study by Tomlinson (1970) can be regarded as the first study focusing on IJV partner selection in more detail. In his study, Tomlinson analyzed the IJV behavior and performance of UK-based companies in 71 IJVs in India and Pakistan. Some years later he conducted a joint study with Thompson (1977) focusing on IJVs established by Canadian companies in Mexico.

However, the study by Geringer (1988; 1991) can be regarded as the groundbreaking work focusing on IJV partner selection. Geringer suggested that despite the almost unlimited range of alternative criteria that might exist, it is possible to provide a simple two-fold typology of categories of selection criteria, thus dividing the selection criteria into task- and partner-related selection criteria. Task-related selection criteria concern the skills and resources a firm would look for in its prospective partner, in response to consideration of the nature of its own potential contributions along with what the new business would require to be successful. Partner-related selection criteria are those referring to the ability of the partner to work with the focal firm efficiently and effectively (e.g., compatibility of top management teams). In contrast to task-related criteria, which focus on relative partner contributions to making a business prosper, partner-related criteria are not contingent on the IJV context. Another main contribution by Geringer was the identification and estimation of the correlations of the key variables which affect the relative importance of some of the selection criteria (Glaister & Buckley, 1997).

Geringer identified in total 27 different selection criteria, categorized into task- and partner-related criteria. From the later studies the task- and partner-related selection criteria categorization has been applied with minor modifications by Glaister (1996), Glaister and Buckley (1997), Tatoglu and Glaister (2002), and Nielsen (2003). Furthermore, Robson (2002) focused only on the partner-related criteria. The study by Tatoglu and Glaister (2000) differs from the others by analyzing the views of both the foreign and the local partner, whereas in the other studies the focus has been on the selection criteria used by the foreign partner. In order to have better comparability with the results in earlier studies, Geringer's classification was also adopted in this study with minor additions.

Additional interesting studies focusing on IJV partner selection are those by Arino, Abramov, Skorobogatykh, Rykounina and Vila (1997), Al-Khalifa and Peterson (1999), Awadzi (1987), Daniels (1971) and Hitt, Dacin, Levitas, Edhec and Borza (2000). Although these five studies provide valuable insight in partner selection, they are used only as secondary reference material in this study, due to the amount of differences in the study frameworks compared to the studies presented in Table 1.

DEVELOPMENT OF HYPOTHESES

Foreign partner-specific variables. There are several foreign partner-specific variables that might condition the relative importance of the selection criteria. Here we shall focus on the size, FDI experience, IJV experience, and target country specific experience of the foreign partner.

Size of the firm is likely to be related to the underlying motives for the IJV. Smaller firms may, for example, have more problems with limited management and financial resources and be more motivated to reach economies of scale with the IJV, whereas larger firms may be more motivated to diversify their operations (i.e., form unrelated types of IJVs) or to block competition especially in saturated industries. Furthermore, if the company does not have any earlier FDI, IJV and/or target country specific experience it may be expected that the company sets more importance on the fact that the local partner has this kind of experience, and that it is able to trust its partner. More experienced firms can more easily compensate the missing experience of the local partner based on their own experience from earlier FDIs, IJVs and/or target country and the IJV may more easily be only a temporary solution.

The only finding concerning the influence of foreign partner specific variables on the selection criteria was made by Nielsen (2003) in his study concerning IJVs and alliances of Danish companies. It was found against expectations that international experience did not have any influence on the relative importance of partner-related selection criteria, but the degree of experience had some importance on the relative importance of task-related selection criteria. Thus, the earlier studies give very limited empirical evidence of the role of foreign partner specific variables on the relative importance of various selection criteria. Therefore, for the empirical part of the study is expected that:

> H1: The relative importance of partner selection criteria will vary with the foreign partner specific variables.

IJV location-specific variables. The location of the IJV, along geographic location, cultural and geographic distance between home and host countries of the IJV partners, and economic development level of the target country of the unit may also be expected to have an influence on the relative importance of the partner selection criteria. The lower the distance–economic, cultural, geographic–the more similar the home and host countries usually are and the lower the amount of expected problems between partners depending on the distance. Greater distance has been linked to higher level of IJV problems and conflict (Lane & Beamish, 1990), misunderstandings (Lyles & Salk, 1996), collaborative problems (Morewy et al., 1996), and knowledge transfer problems (Hamel, 1991).

In the study by Glaister and Buckley (1997) the location of the IJV was found to influence the relative importance of the partner selection criteria, but only concerning the partner-related criteria. Access to knowledge of local culture, access to regulatory permits, and reputation of the partner were much more weighed as the selection criteria in IJVs located in Japan than in the USA or Europe, whereas the role of the international experience of the partner was clearly lower in the former than in the latter IJVs. Nielsen (2003) found that although trust between top management, access to market knowledge, and relatedness of partner business were highly ranked in all of the four reviewed areas (Western Europe, USA, Asia, the rest of the world), the importance of sev-

TABLE 1. Summary of the Key Issues in the Main IJV Partner Selection Studies

	Geringer (1988)	Glaister (1996)	Glaister & Buckley (1997)	Tatoglu & Glaister (2000)	Nielsen (2003)
Origin of foreign partners	USA	The UK	The UK	OECD	Denmark
Location of IJVs/ partners	USA, other industrialized market economy	Western Europe	UK, abroad	Turkey	OECD, non-OECD (61% in WE)
Number of IJVs	90	37 (EJVs)	53	39	120
Response rate	82,60%	N/A*	N/A*	39,50%	33%
Number of partners	2	N/A	2	N/A	N/A
Time period	N/A	Established mainly in 1985-1992	Mean age of JVs 4,64 yrs	Established mainly in 1987-94	1985-2001
Other features		Equity (n = 37) & Non-equity IJVs (n = 13)	Equity & Non-equity IJVs		48 equity JVs, 72 non-equity JVs
Industry focus	N/A	Manufacturing/ Tertiary	Manufacturing/ Tertiary	Manufacturing/ Service	Manufacturing/ Service
Data collection	Survey, interviews	Survey	Survey	Survey	Survey
Methods of analysis	Crosstabulations (bivariate correlations), partial correlations, factor analysis	Factor analysis, Spearman rank-order correlations, multiple regression	T-test, ANOVA, factor analysis	T-Test, regression and factor analysis	T-test, ANOVA, multiple regression, factor analysis

* 46,3% in the whole project

eral of the task- and partner-related selection criteria differed strongly among various regional areas.

Hitt et al. (2000) found that developed market firms tried to leverage their resources to gain competitive advantages by searching for partners with unique competencies and local market knowledge and access, whereas firms from emerging markets were looking for partners with financial capabilities. Furthermore, Glaister and Wang (1993) found that in IJVs established by UK-based companies in China the ability to negotiate with host government, relatedness of business, trust between top management, and financial status/resources of partner were the most weighed criteria.

Thus, one would expect that for example product and/or production process related knowledge, brands and distribution systems are more weighed in OECD countries whereas such criteria as relationships with local government, access to labor, management, local markets and customs, etc., are more weighed in non-OECD countries/culturally and economically more distant countries. Furthermore, relations with local government seem to be much more important in non-OECD than in

OECD-countries. Therefore for the empirical part it is expected that:

H2: The relative importance of the partner selection criteria will vary with the IJV location specific variables.

Investment-specific variables. There is a large amount of issues that are specific only for a certain investment, with potential to effect IJV partner selection. In this study the investment-specific variables refer to the form of establishment, relatedness of the operation, relative partner size and the initiation for the IJV (i.e., which one of the partners initiated the IJV partnership). It seems that the analysis of IJVs in several studies includes only units established in the form of a greenfield investment (i.e., a separate new unit is established). However, an IJV can also be established by acquisition, i.e., one partner makes a partial acquisition of the other partner. There are some key differences between the two forms of establishment. Greenfield investment refers to everything being built from scratch whereas acquisition, here partial acquisition, refers to buying a share in an already existing company. Furthermore, greenfield investment always means expansion to the existing total capacity, whereas a partial acquisition does not mean increase in the existing total capacity. Finally, in a green-field investment the first revenues come after a possibly long time period, whereas in a partial acquisition there are revenues straight after buying a share in the unit. Because of these differences it could also be expected that there exists differences in the relative importance given to various partner selection criteria depending on the form of establishment.

What concerns the field of investment, an IJV can be either related or unrelated to the business of the present operation of the foreign partner. In a related IJV the foreign partner has earlier knowledge and experience from the field, and the goal for the unit is usually expanding into a new geographical area, increasing power and/or blocking competition. In an unrelated type of IJV the foreign partner does not have earlier knowledge or experience from the field, but the company wants to diversify in order to expand the product portfolio and risks. Although the foreign company does not have product-specific experience, the management may rely that it can transfer the managerial, marketing, etc., knowledge gained from one field to another field. However, because of these differences between related and unrelated types of IJVs, it may be expected that there will also exist differences in the relative importance given to various partner selection criteria depending on the type of the IJV.

Concerning the relative size of the IJV partner, the smaller the local IJV partner in relation to the foreign firm, the more likely it is that the relative importance of some special product- and/or production-related knowledge, access to a valuable brand(s) is higher than in cases where the relative size of the local partner is larger. In the latter case, such criteria as, for example, access to capital/financial resources or relations with local government may be expected to be given more importance than in the former cases. Against expectations, Glaister and Buckley (1997) found merely a non-significant relationship between the relative importance of the selection criteria and the relative partner size in their UK-based sample. The authors assume that the non-significant differences may be dependent on the sample of their study and of the classification

of sample firms only to two categories: the UK partner was bigger vs. the other partner was bigger.

As stated by Glaister and Buckley (1997: 203), to the extent partners are either proactive or reactive with respect to the initiative for the IJV and thus either making the initial proposal or they are reacting to the other partner's approach, differences in the importance of particular selection criteria are likely to exist between initiating and non-initiating partner firms. Their empirical results, however, indicated that the relative importance of the selection criteria was virtually independent of which partner initiated the IJV partnership. The criterion of the degree of favorable past association between partners was more important in those IJVs which were initated by the UK partner than in those initiated by the other partner or third-party intermediaries. This indicated that the UK firms which were proactive in seeking to establish an IJV solicit partners from those foreign firms that were known to them. Confining the pool of potential partners to those foreign firms which were already known clearly reduced the searching costs of finding a suitable partner. Firms which were approached with the request to form an IJV were less able to control partner choice and so gave less prominence to previous relationships. The criteria of financial status/financial resources of the partner and the reputation of the partner firm were more important selection criteria for those UK partners which did not initiate the IJV.

In summary, the influence of investment-specific variables on partner selection has been analyzed very limitedly so far. For the empirical part of the study we expect that:

> H3: The relative importance of partner selection criteria will vary with the investment-specific variables.

Selection criteria and IJV performance. The research on IJV performance has received much more attention than the more detailed analysis of the relative importance of various partner selection criteria. However, there are only a couple of studies taking a look at the relationship between performance and partner selection criteria.

Concerning the main reference studies, Nielsen (2003) analyzed the IJV performance but not its relationship with the selection criteria. Also, Tatoglu and Glaister (2000) focused only on the measurement of IJV performance and on the analysis of the influence of the agreement between partners on the performance along various performance measures.

In somewhat more detail, the relationship between the selection criteria and IJV performance has been studied by Tomlinson (1970), Beamish (1988), and Maurer (1996). Only Maurer could not find any relationship between selection criteria and IJV performance. Instead, Tomlinson found that companies which had given greatest weight to the favorable earlier relationship had experienced the best performance, while in cases where the status of the local partner and especially in cases where the partner selection was a forced choice, the level of performance had been clearly poorer. In the study by Beamish the best performance was found among companies where a high preference in partner selection was given to partner's ability to arrange capable managers to the IJV, and where the partner provided access/knowledge to the local economy and customs. The poorest performance was found among cases where high preference was given to partner's ability to satisfy requirements set by the host government concerning the share of local ownership. It is noteworthy that all of these three studies were focused on IJVs established in non-OECD countries. However, combined with the earlier discussion they give basis to assume that:

H4: The relative importance of the partner selection criteria will vary with IJV performance.

METHODOLOGY OF THE STUDY AND SAMPLE

The empirical part of the study is based on survey data related to the IJV partner selection and IJV performance in manufacturing IJVs established by Finnish-based firms in OECD and non-OECD countries mainly between 1988-2001. Based on different sources (data collected during a period of over ten years from published news about new IJVs, annual reports and www-sites of the 200 largest companies, earlier survey information by the first author) more than 130 companies having made at least one manufacturing IJV were identified. In total the companies had established somewhat more than 500 IJVs of which approximately 120 were divested before 1999. In those cases where the companies had established several IJVs, the preference was given to greenfield form of IJVs and/or on IJVs where the ownership share of the Finnish partner was 25-75% and which had been at least two years in operation. The companies were first contacted by telephone or email in order to confirm the interest of the company to participate the study and to identify the right person to answer to the questionnaire planned for the study. As discussed by Geringer (1991), in some studies a key weakness is that the respondents have not been involved in the partner selection process. Thus, during the contact it was tried to confirm that the person really had knowledge of these issues (the relationship with the IJV was also asked separately at the end of the questionnaire). The four-page questionnaire also included other issues than only questions relating to partner selection, for example, questions with regard to the later development, evaluation of the performance, and performance of the unit along various measures.

Managers from a total of 47 firms participated in the study. The total amount of IJVs covered by the survey was 69. However, in nine cases the managers did not fully answer to the section covering partner selection or performance. Thus the final sample size in this study is 60 IJVs (for more details see Table 2).

As in several earlier studies, the relative importance of the task- and partner-related selection criteria was considered first by ranking of mean responses. Then, factor analysis was employed to derive a parsimonious set of selection criteria. The hypotheses were tested by considering differences in means of the importance of the selection criteria. Based on an assumption that the sample was close to normal distribution, it was considered legitimate to use parametric tests of the hypotheses. Each of the H1 to H4 was therefore tested by conduct-

TABLE 2. Characteristics of the Sample

		n	%
Number		60	100
Number of partners	1	42	70
	> 1	18	30
Year of investment	1995 or earlier	30	50
	1996 or later	30	50
Form of investment	Greenfield	37	61,7
	Acquisition	23	38,3
Size of the foreign partner (turnover 2001)	< 500 MEUR	31	51,7
	500-1000 MEUR	7	11,7
	> 1000 MEUR	22	36,7
Location of the IJV	Western Europe	20	33,3
	Eastern/Central Eastern Europe	22	36,7
	Asia	15	25
	Other	3	5
Share of ownership of the foreign partner	> 50%	22	36,7
	50-50%	9	15
	< 50%	29	48,3
Industry of the IJV	Metal industry	23	38,3
	Forest industry	12	20
	Other (chemical, plastic, foodstuff)	25	41,7
Initial approach to the IJV	Finnish partner	43	71,7
	Local partner or other	15	25
Relative partner size	Foreign partner > 50% larger	42	70
	Other	18	30
Joint venture survival	Still operating as an IJV	45	75
(Point of view of the Finnish partner)	Changed into a wholly owned subsidiary	11	18,3
	Divested/no Finnish ownership in 2000/2001	4	6,7

ing two sample t-tests or ANOVA as appropriate. Because of the nature of the data these parametric tests were compared to equivalent non-parametric tests (Mann-Whitney U and the Kruskal-Wallis Test) as a check on their interpretation following Glaister and Buckley (1997) and Nielsen (2003).

RESULTS OF THE STUDY

Overall Results

The results of the relative importance of various task- and partner-related selection criteria are presented in Table 3. Since the five-point Likert type scale was used, the midpoint of the scale (3) can be used as the comparison. The results indicate that from the 21 task-related selection criteria the midpoint was exceeded

only by two criteria: the criteria of knowledge of the target market's economy and customs (3.18) and the criteria of ability to permit faster entry into the target market (3.05). In addition, seven criteria received values between 2.80 and 2.98. Among the eight partner-related selection criteria, three criteria–our trust in the partner (3.48), strong commitment to the venture (3.41), and trust between partners (3.39)– exceeded the midpoint. Furthermore, two criteria received values between 2.75-2.83, and two criteria values below 2. Noteworthy is that among the 29 various alternatives one of the partner-related selection criteria–partner is similar in size–received clearly the lowest value (1.50).

As discussed earlier, the comparison of results in various studies is difficult because of somewhat different selection criteria used. The results by Geringer (1988) indicated that the

TABLE 3. The Relative Importance of the Partner Selection Criteria

PARTNER SELECTION CRITERIA	Variable	Mean	Std. Dev.	Rank
Task-related criteria				
(T) Has knowledge of target market's economy and customs	T-LOCKNOW	3,18	1,38	4
(T) Permits faster entry into the target market	T-FASTENTRY	3,05	1,53	5
(T) Will enable the venture to produce at lowest cost	T-LOWCOST	2,98	1,42	6
(T) Controls favorable location for production	T-FAVLOCA	2,97	1,41	7
(T) Possesses needed manufacturing or R&D facilities	T-FACILITY	2,93	1,44	8
(T) Has a valuable reputation	T-REPUTAT	2,92	1,25	9
(T) Can supply technically skilled personnel	T-TECHSKILL	2,92	1,20	9
(T) Helps comply with government requirements/pressure	T-GOVNEGO	2,85	1,51	11
(T) Has access to marketing or distribution systems	T-MARKDIST	2,83	1,63	12
(T) Can provide better access for your company's products	T-ACCESS	2,75	1,37	14
(T) Enhances perceived local or national identity	T-LOCIDENT	2,70	1,31	16
(T) Can provide low cost labor to the venture	T-LABCHEAP	2,67	1,53	17
(T) Has access to raw materials or components	T-RAWMAT	2,62	1,46	18
(T) Can supply general managers to the venture	T-GENMANAG	2,62	1,24	18
(T) Has access to post-sales service network	T-POSTSALE	2,43	1,42	20
(T) Can enhance the venture's export opportunities	T-EXPOPPORT	2,36	1,28	21
(T) Has a valuable trademark	T-TRADEMRK	2,23	1,45	22
(T) Will provide financing/capital to venture	T-CAPITAL	2,22	1,15	23
(T) Possesses needed licenses, patents, know-how, etc.	T-LICPATENT	2,08	1,37	24
(T) Enhances venture's ability to make sales to gov./public companies	T-PUBLSECTR	1,85	1,19	27
(T) Enables venture to qualify for subsidies or credits	T-CREDIT	1,85	1,19	27
Partner-related criteria				
(P) Our trust in the partner	P-TRUST	3,48	1,14	1
(P) Seems to have a strong commitment to the venture	P-COMMIT	3,41	1,25	2
(P) Trust between partners	P-MUTRUST	3,39	1,29	3
(P) Top management of both firms are compatible	P-MANCOMPAT	2,83	1,26	12
(P) Has related products	P-RELPROD	2,75	1,34	14
(P) Prior positive cooperation	P-PRIORREL	2,07	1,26	25
(P) Has similar national or corporate culture	P-SIMCULT	1,95	1,06	26
(P) Is similar in size or corporate structure	P-SIMSIZE	1,50	0,89	29

three most important single criteria were: strong commitment to the IJV, compatible management teams, and permits faster entry into the market. Geringer did not include trust in his selection criteria whereas the others have not included strong commitment among selection criteria in their studies. The other studies have indicated the great importance of such criteria as trust between management teams, relatedness of partner's business, reputation, knowledge of local market, financial status/financial resources, access to distribution channels, and access to links with major supplier/buyers. Contrary to all other studies, including this study, Tomlinson (1970) and later on also Tatoglu

and Glaister (2000) found that earlier relationship was an important if not even the most important criteria, but according to Tatoglu and Glaister only from the local partner's point of view, not from the foreign partner's point of view.

Factor Analysis of Selection Criteria

The twenty-nine selection criteria represent a number of overlapping perspectives. Because of the potential conceptual and statistical overlap an attempt was made to identify a smaller number of distinct, non-overlapping selection criteria for the sample data by means of exploratory factor analysis. The factor analysis produced eight underlying factors (with eigenvalues over one) which explained a total of 75.15% of the observed variance. Four of the factors (see Table 4 for factor compositions) are composed of both task- and partner-related selection criteria indicating conceptual overlap between these concepts. All of the remaining four factors are composed of only task-related selection criteria and thus no factor is composed of only partner-related selection criteria. As discussed earlier, in the previous studies seven to nine factors have been identified, explaining 70.9% (Glaister & Buckley, 1997) to 78.6% (Tatoglu & Glaister, 2000) of the observed variance. Usually three or four factors have been mixed. Thus, in these respects the results of this study are very similar to the findings in earlier studies.

Five individual selection criteria are included in two different factors: REPUTAT in factors one and two, PRIORREL in factors one and seven, GENMANAG and TECHSKILL in factors one and eight, and EXPOPPORT in factors two and seven. All those variables received loadings exceeding 0.45 on both factors, and especially in the case of PRIORREL, the difference in the loadings was extremely low between the two factors. Also in the study by Geringer (1988), several selection criteria were included in two or even more factors.

Selection Criteria and Foreign Partner-Specific Variables

In H1 it was expected that the relative importance of selection criteria will vary with the foreign partner-specific variables. The size and earlier FDI, IJV and target country specific experience of the foreign partner were selected as the foreign partner-specific variables. Results in Table 5 indicate that there were in total only two cases where the factors had means which were significantly different: factor one based on IJV experience and factor three based on target country specific experience. Thus, based on the size of the foreign partner and FDI experience, no factor indicated statistically significant difference in mean values. Based on individual selection criteria results, in total 15 cases indicated statistically significant differences. Seven of those cases were related to the extent of IJV-specific and five to

the extent of target country specific experience. Thus, it may be concluded that H1 receives weak support in the cases of IJV and target country specific experience, but no support based on the size and FDI experience of the foreign partner.

Of the single mean values noteworthy are the very high mean values of the criteria of mutual trust and trust on the partner among those cases in which the Finnish firms had no earlier FDI and IJV experience (the only cases where a mean value of four was reached or exceeded). Also the earlier results by Nielsen (2003) indicated the high importance of trust especially in cases where the reviewed companies did not have earlier alliance experience. Other important selection criteria independent of level of alliance experience were partner reputation and relatedness of partner business. Furthermore, the results by Nielsen indicated that firms having earlier experience laid more weight on the financial status and size of the partner than firms having no earlier experience, whereas the latter firms laid more weight on favorable past association than the formers. In this study the criteria of financial status, firm size and prior relationship were not significant selection criteria among any of the subgroups. Instead, partner's reputation was highly appreciated by firms without any earlier IJV experience.

Selection Criteria and IJV Location

In H2 it was expected that the relative importance of selection criteria will vary with the location of the IJV. The results (see Table 6) indicate that there existed in total eight cases where the factors had significantly different mean values. Especially in relation to factor three, all four measures of location indicated statistically significant differences. In addition, statistically significant influences of location-specific variables were found on factor two and factor eight, in both cases based on the region of the IJV and level of economic development of the target country. Between individual selection criteria statistically significant differences were found in 41 cases. Thus, the results give support to the view that the relative importance of the selection criteria really tend to vary with the location of the IJV. How

TABLE 4. Factor Analysis of the Selection Criteria

FACTOR	Load	Alpha	Eigen-value (total)	% of variance	Cumulative %
Factor 1: Trust, top management and commitment		0,8895	7,406	25,538	25,5
(P) Trust between partners	0,8720				
(P) Our trust in the partner	0,8525				
(P) Top management of both firms are compatible	0,8500				
(P) Seems to have a strong commitment to the venture	0,8483				
(T) Has a valuable reputation	0,5873				
(T) Can supply general managers to the venture	0,5446				
(T) Can supply technically skilled personnel	0,4733				
(P) Prior positive cooperation	0,4641				
Factor 2: Post sale, marketing systems and trademark		0,8377	3,778	13,028	38,6
(T) Has access to post-sales service network	0,8514				
(T) Has access to marketing or distribution systems	0,8353				
(T) Has a valuable trademark	0,7005				
(T) Has a valuable reputation	0,5422				
(T) Can enhance the venture's export opportunities	0,4672				
Factor 3: Low labor and production costs		0,7529	2,754	9,497	48,1
(T) Can provide low cost labor to the venture	0,8112				
(T) Will enable the venture to produce at lowest cost	0,7502				
(T) Controls favorable location for production	0,6461				
(T) Helps comply with government requirements/pressure	0,6408				
(T) Has access to raw materials or components	0,5972				
Factor 4: Fast entry and local knowledge		0,8301	2,486	8,572	56,6
(T) Permits faster entry into the target market	0,8994				
(T) Has knowledge of target market's economy and customs	0,7288				
(T) Can provide better access for your company's products	0,6580				
Factor 5: Capital and credit		0,5654	1,649	5,687	62,3
(T) Will provide financing/capital to venture	0,7282				
(T) Enables venture to qualify for subsidies or credits	0,6423				
(P) Has related products	−0,5010				
(T) Possesses needed manufacturing or R&D facilities	−0,6924				
Factor 6: Relations to public sector and partner similarity		0,5984	1,435	4,949	67,3
(T) Enhances venture's ability to make sales to gov./public companies	0,7970				
(P) Is similar in size or corporate structure	0,7080				
(P) Has similar national or corporate culture	0,7028				
Factor 7: Industrial/Intellectual property rights and export opportunities		0,4726	1,194	4,119	71,4
(T) Possesses needed licenses, patents, know-how, etc.	0,7441				
(T) Can enhance the venture's export opportunities	0,5506				
(P) Prior positive cooperation	0,4546				
Factor 8: Technical personnel and management		0,6150	1,092	3,767	75,2
(T) Can supply technically skilled personnel	0,6599				
(T) Can supply general managers to the venture	0,4534				
(T) Enhances perceived local or national identity	−0,4631				

(T) = Task-related.   (P) = Partner-related.
Principal component analysis. Rotation method: Varimax with Kaiser normalization.
K-M-O measure of sampling adequacy = 0,518.   Bartlett test of sphericity = 1109,418; p < 0,000.

TABLE 5. Selection Criteria and Foreign Partner-Specific Variables

Factor/Criteria	Size of the Finnish partner (turnover 2001)		FDI experience		IJV experience		Target country experience	
	> 500 MEURO (n = 29)	≤ 500 MEURO (n = 31)	Yes (n = 52)	None (n = 8)	Yes (n = 48)	None (n = 12)	Yes (n = 45)	None (n = 15)
Factor 1	−0,17	0,16	−0,05	0,31	−0,12	**0,44***	−0,03	0,15
P-MUTRUST	3,07	**3,68***	3,27	**4,13***	3,19	**4,17****	3,36	3,47
P-TRUST	3,24	3,72	3,40	4,00	3,35	**4,00***	3,43	3,64
P-MANCOMPAT	2,55	**3,10***	2,79	3,13	2,71	3,33	2,84	2,80
T-REPUTAT	2,79	3,03	2,87	3,25	2,75	**3,58****	2,93	2,87
P-PRIORREL	1,86	2,26	2,12	1,75	2,08	2,00	**2,24***	1,53
Factor 2	0,08	−0,07	−0,01	0,05	0,01	−0,34	0,03	−0,03
T-EXPOPPORT	2,17	2,53	2,25	3,00	2,19	**3,00***	2,45	2,07
Factor 3	−0,12	0,12	−0,03	0,16	0,04	−0,16	−0,15	**0,44***
T-LABCHEAP	2,34	2,97	2,60	3,13	2,75	2,65	2,38	**3,53*****
T-LOWCOST	2,62	**3,32***	2,94	3,25	3,04	2,75	2,76	**3,67****
T-GOVNEGO	2,96	2,74	2,88	2,63	2,85	2,83	2,64	**3,47***
Factor 4	0,15	−0,15	0,05	−0,28	0,05	−0,17	−0,01	0,02
Factor 5	0,11	−0,11	0,04	−0,23	−0,09	0,32	0,03	−0,04
T-CREDIT	2,07	1,67	**1,98****	1,00	1,85	1,83	1,86	1,80
Factor 6	0,10	−0,10	−0,01	0,06	−0,03	0,09	−0,05	0,19
Factor 7	−0,16	0,15	0,03	−0,15	0,03	−0,10	0,12	−0,39
T-EXPOPPORT	2,17	2,53	2,25	3,00	2,19	**3,00***	2,45	2,07
P-PRIORREL	1,86	2,26	2,12	1,75	2,08	2,00	**2,24***	1,53
Factor 8	0,08	−0,08	−0,04	0,26	−0,05	0,18	0,06	−0,11

* p ≤ 0,1   ** p ≤ 0,05   *** p ≤ 0,01   **** p ≤ 0,001

much do they vary, depends on the measure of location. There were clearly more differences based on the region of the unit and level of economic development of the target country than based on cultural distance and especially on physical distance. However, in general it can be concluded that the H2 is supported.

Glaister and Buckley (1997) found only very limited support for the assumption that the relative importance of the selection criteria tend to vary with the nationality of the partner, whereas Nielsen (2003) found strong support to the respective assumption. One explanation for the differences in the results may be that a part of the IJVs analyzed in the first study were located in the UK, not abroad, whereas all IJVs in the latter study were located in foreign countries as was the case also in this study. Unfortunately, neither Glaister and Buckley nor Nielsen measured the influence of the partner nationality/location with other measures than regional distribution.

The results of this study indicate that in IJVs established in Western Europe (WE) all individual means in factor two received clearly higher values than in other areas. Noteworthy is especially the high mean value for the importance of marketing and distribution systems. Tight competition in the WE markets demands strong marketing and distribution arrangements. There is also some support to the assumption that firms without any earlier IJV experience lay more weight on the export opportunities, and therefore the marketing and distribution systems of the partner not only in the target country but also in the neighboring countries were of importance. Also, reputation of the partner and relatedness of the operation were much more highly rated in WE IJVs than in IJVs located elsewhere. Technical skills and general management were clearly more important in IJVs located in CEE and EE than elsewhere, whereas low costs and ability to negotiate with government were appreciated

TABLE 6. Selection Criteria and IJV Location-Specific Variables

Factor/Criteria	Region			Cultural distance		Physical distance		Level of development	
	WE (n = 20)	EE/CEE (n = 22)	Asia (n = 15)	> 1,50 (n = 30)	≤ 1,50 (n = 30)	> 2000 km (n = 22)	≤ 2000 km (n = 38)	NON-OECD (n = 32)	OECD (n = 28)
Factor 1	−0,16	0,18	−0,09	−0,23	0,21	−0,09	0,05	0,19	−0,23
P-MANCOMPAT	2,80	2,95	2,60	2,53	**3,13***	2,68	2,92	2,94	2,71
T-REPUTAT	**3,40***	2,77	2,47	2,60	**3,23****	2,59	3,11	2,69	3,18
T-GENMANAG	2,25	**3,09***	2,33	2,47	2,77	2,45	2,71	2,81	2,39
T-TECHSKILL	2,40	**3,41****	3,20	2,83	3,00	2,77	3,00	**3,25****	2,54
P-PRIORREL	1,75	2,14	2,53	2,03	2,10	2,18	2,00	**2,44****	1,64
Factor 2	**0,55*****	−0,31	−0,45	−0,21	0,19	−0,15	0,08	−0,30	**0,36****
T-POSTSALE	**3,15****	2,14	1,93	2,17	2,70	2,27	2,53	2,03	**2,89****
T-MARKDIST	**3,70*****	2,32	2,33	2,43	**3,23***	2,86	2,82	2,41	3,32
T-TRADEMRK	**3,15*****	1,91	1,60	2,00	2,47	1,77	**2,50***	1,69	**2,86******
T-REPUTAT	**3,40***	2,77	2,47	2,60	**3,23****	2,59	3,11	2,69	3,18
T-EXPOPPORT	**2,85***	2,33	1,87	2,10	2,62	2,09	2,51	2,19	2,56
Factor 3	−0,55	0,17	**0,56*****	**0,33****	−0,29	**0,48*****	−0,28	**0,43******	−0,51
T-LABCHEAP	1,50	3,18	**3,33******	**3,17*****	2,17	**3,32****	2,29	**3,34******	1,89
T-LOWCOST	2,30	3,18	**3,67****	**3,40****	2,57	**3,50****	2,68	**3,53******	2,36
T-FAVLOCA	2,80	2,77	3,47	3,13	2,80	**3,45****	2,68	3,19	2,71
T-GOVNEGO	1,95	3,09	**3,64*****	**3,24****	2,47	**3,52*****	2,47	**3,35*****	2,29
T-RAWMAT	2,30	2,73	3,00	2,47	2,77	2,73	2,55	**3,06*****	2,11
Factor 4	0,08	−0,17	0,00	0,05	−0,04	0,26	−0,15	−0,17	0,21
T-FASTENTRY	3,40	2,82	2,93	2,97	3,13	3,14	3,00	2,72	**3,43***
T-ACCESS	3,00	2,59	2,60	2,77	2,73	2,86	2,68	2,41	**3,14****
Factor 5	−0,22	0,17	0,00	−0,01	0,01	0,06	−0,03	0,11	−0,13
P-RELPROD	**3,40****	2,50	2,27	2,33	**3,17****	2,59	2,84	2,59	2,93
Factor 6	−0,08	0,07	−0,03	0,05	−0,05	−0,08	0,04	0,04	−0,05
P-SIMCULT	1,95	2,09	1,73	1,67	**2,23****	1,77	2,05	2,06	1,82
Factor 7	0,31	−0,12	0,06	0,01	−0,01	−0,14	0,08	−0,14	0,17
T-EXPOPPORT	**2,85***	2,33	1,87	2,10	2,62	2,09	2,51	2,19	2,56
P-PRIORREL	1,75	2,14	2,53	2,03	2,10	2,18	2,00	**2,44****	1,64
Factor 8	−0,34	**0,41***	0,11	0,04	−0,04	−0,09	0,05	**0,21***	−0,25
T-TECHSKILL	2,40	**3,41****	3,20	2,83	3,00	2,77	3,00	**3,25****	2,54
T-GENMANAG	2,25	**3,09***	2,33	2,47	2,77	2,45	2,71	2,81	2,39

$* \ p \leq 0,1 \quad ** \ p \leq 0,05 \quad *** \ p \leq 0,01 \quad **** \ p \leq 0,001$

especially in IJVs located in Asian countries. Only one of the criteria in which a statistically significant difference occurred between IJVs in different regions was partner-related, all of the rest were task-related. Also, the differences between physically near and distant IJVs concerned only task-related criteria. A strong inter-correlation between the IJV location specific variables of cultural and physical distance and the level of economic development was noticed–most non-OECD countries were culturally and physically in the more distant group. Almost all individual means related to

factor three were clearly more highly rated in the non-OECD, culturally and physically more distant group. Especially cheap labor, production costs, and relations to the government/ public institutions received clearly higher means in these subgroups whereas in OECD countries fast entry and providing better access to the company's products were clearly more important than in non-OECD countries. Both results coincide with the earlier results.

Both Glaister and Buckley (1997) and Nielsen (2003) found that the selection criteria of access to knowledge of local culture and access to regulatory permits/market and regulatory knowledge were much more important in Asia than in other areas. Furthermore, as in this study, the results by Nielsen indicated that the criteria of partner's ability to negotiate with the government was clearly more important in Asia than elsewhere, whereas the results by Glaister and Buckley did not indicate support for these findings. Furthermore, no statistically significant difference was found in the role of trust between different geographic areas in neither of the two studies. Thus in this respect the results were similar to the findings in this study. In the study by Glaister and Buckley the criteria of partner's reputation was found to be more important in Japan than elsewhere, whereas the results by Nielsen as well as the results in this study indicated the highest importance of reputation in WE. Thus the results in this study coincide rather well especially with the earlier findings by Nielsen.

Selection Criteria and Investment-Specific Variables

In Hypothesis 3 it was expected that the relative importance of selection criteria will vary with the investment-specific variables. The results (see Table 7) indicate that there existed in total eight cases where the selection criteria factors were significantly influenced by an investment-specific variable: three factors were influenced by the form of investment, two by the type of investment and relative partner size, and one by the initial approach to the IJV. Related to factors six and seven, no statistically significant relationships were found along any of the four investment-specific variables. Thus, the diversification of differences along factors was greater than in the cases of foreign partner and IJV location-specific variables. Based on individual selection criteria statistically significant differences were found in 43 cases: six were based on the initial approach to the IJV, eight on the relative partner size, ten on the type of investment and 19 were based on the form of investment. Thus, in summary it can be concluded that the results give strong support for H3 along the form of investment, moderate support along the type of investment and the relative partner size, and limited support based on the initial to the IJV.

The individual means of various selection criteria in factors one, three and eight received clearly higher means in IJVs established in the form of greenfield investment than in partial acquisitions (reputation as the only exception). The opposite situation was found related to selection criteria in factor two. Noteworthy are the exceptionally high mean values of management commitment and trust among greenfield IJVs, and also the clearly greater importance of technical skills, general management, cheap labor, and access to capital (mean values over 3.00 in the first three cases) compared to the IJVs formed via acquisition.

What concerns the type of investment in cases of statistically significant differences, the higher mean values of the importance of each criteria were always in the group of partly or totally unrelated IJVs and the differences were mainly focused on the selection criteria in factors one and eight. Of interest are the high mean values laid on trust in unrelated types of IJVs, but the great differences in the importance of the selection criteria of technical skills, general management, and raw materials between unrelated and related types of IJVs should also be noticed. The first two differences are easier to understand but the difference in the third case needs further analysis in future.

Based on the relative size of the partner, noteworthy is that all the mean values are below 3.55–thus no very high mean values on any criteria among neither of the subgroups–and that the differences are focused on selection criteria in task-related criteria in factors four and five. In the cases in which the Finnish partner was clearly larger the companies had laid more importance on local knowledge, facilities and on the relatedness of the operation, whereas especially capital was clearly more important in cases in which the size of the partners was more equal. Also in the study by Glaister and Buckley (1997) it was found that access to capital was important when the non-UK partner was larger than the UK partner.

As discussed above, the fact of who had made the initial approach to the IJV had a smaller influence than the other three investment-specific variables on the relative weights of various selection criteria. Statistically significant differences were found in six cases

TABLE 7. Selection Criteria and Investment-Specific Variables

Factor/Criteria	Form of investment		Type of investment		Relative partner size		Initial approach	
	Greenfield (n = 37)	Acquisition (n = 23)	Totally related (n = 39)	Partly/ totally unrelated (n = 19)	Finn. partner > 50% larger (n = 43)	Other (n = 18)	Finnish partner (n = 43)	Other (n = 15)
Factor 1	**0,30*****	−0,45	−0,06	0,21	0,01	−0,03	−0,10	0,28
P-MUTRUST	**3,69****	2,91	3,21	**3,84***	3,41	3,33	3,26	**3,93***
P-TRUST	**3,75****	3,05	3,35	**3,95***	3,53	3,39	3,34	**4,00***
P-MANCOMPAT	**3,14****	2,35	2,74	3,11	2,71	3,11	2,74	3,20
P-COMMIT	**3,81*****	2,78	3,42	3,53	3,36	3,53	3,17	**4,13*****
T-REPUTAT	2,84	3,04	2,74	**3,32***	2,88	3,00	2,88	3,17
T-GENMANAG	**3,03******	1,96	2,38	**3,21****	2,60	2,67	2,60	2,87
T-TECHSKILL	**3,30******	2,30	2,64	**3,58*****	2,93	2,89	2,91	3,07
P-PRIORREL	**2,32****	1,65	2,08	2,16	1,95	2,33	1,93	2,53
Factor 2	−0,23	**0,35****	−0,07	0,16	−0,02	0,05	0,03	−0,09
T-POSTSALE	2,08	**3,00****	2,38	2,63	2,45	2,39	2,40	2,53
T-MARKDIST	2,51	**3,35***	2,92	2,79	2,83	2,83	2,72	3,13
T-TRADEMRK	1,89	**2,78****	2,08	2,53	2,33	2,00	2,28	2,13
T-REPUTAT	2,84	3,04	2,74	**3,32***	2,88	3,00	2,88	3,13
Factor 3	**0,37******	−0,56	−0,09	0,30	0,03	−0,08	−0,18	**0,49****
T-LABCHEAP	**3,19******	1,83	2,56	3,05	2,83	2,28	2,42	**3,27***
T-LOWCOST	**3,30****	2,48	2,90	3,32	3,02	2,89	2,60	**3,87*****
T-FAVLOCA	3,16	2,65	2,82	3,42	3,02	2,83	2,72	**3,67****
T-GOVNEGO	**3,31*****	2,13	2,89	2,95	2,93	2,65	2,64	3,20
T-RAWMAT	**3,03*****	1,96	2,41	**3,21****	2,40	**3,11***	2,51	2,87
Factor 4	−0,05	0,08	**0,22****	−0,36	**0,19****	−0,47	−0,08	0,21
T-FASTENTRY	2,86	3,35	3,28	2,63	**3,29***	2,50	2,93	3,13
T-LOCKNOW	3,22	3,13	3,23	3,21	**3,45****	2,56	3,05	3,47
T-ACCESS	2,51	**3,13***	2,87	2,58	2,86	2,50	2,70	2,73
Factor 5	0,17	−0,26	0,05	−0,04	−0,28	**0,69******	0,04	−0,10
T-CAPITAL	**2,59******	1,61	2,21	2,37	1,90	**2,94******	2,14	2,47
T-CREDIT	1,89	1,78	1,92	1,79	1,67	**2,29***	1,76	1,80
P-RELPROD	2,57	3,04	2,69	2,89	**3,05*****	2,06	2,67	2,87
T-FACILITY	2,95	2,91	2,79	3,26	**3,31******	2,06	2,79	3,27
Factor 6	0,00	−0,01	−0,14	0,29	0,01	−0,01	0,01	−0,02
P-SIMCULT	2,03	1,83	1,79	**2,37***	1,95	1,94	1,91	2,20
Factor 7	−0,17	0,25	−0,11	0,17	−0,03	0,07	−0,05	0,14
P-PRIORREL	**2,32****	1,65	2,08	2,16	1,95	2,33	1,93	2,53
Factor 8	0,14	−0,22	−0,28	**0,52*****	−0,08	0,19	0,12	−0,32
T-TECHSKILL	**3,30******	2,30	2,64	**3,58*****	2,93	2,89	2,91	3,07
T-GENMANAG	**3,03******	1,96	2,38	**3,21****	2,60	2,67	2,60	2,87
T-LOCIDENT	2,81	2,52	2,90	2,32	**2,93****	2,17	2,56	3,07

* p ≤ 0,1   ** p ≤ 0,05   *** p ≤ 0,01   **** p ≤ 0,001

which were all related to factors one and three. In all of those six cases the higher mean values were among the projects initiated by the other partner. Noteworthy are firstly the very high mean and difference related to the criteria of commitment and trust, which were clearly higher among the IJVs which were initiated by the other partner than in those initiated by the Finnish partner. The exceptionally high importance of commitment and trust in cases in which the other partner is the initiator is rather easy to understand. Instead the clearly higher importance of the three other selection criteria–low cost production, favorable location, and cheap labor–is not necessarily as clear. Glaister and Buckley (1997) found only little support for the influence of initial approach to partner selection. They found that financial status and reputation were more weighed in the cases in which the initial approach was made by the foreign partner and the criteria of favorable past association was more important in the cases in which the UK partner initiated the IJV. Thus what concerns the general influence of the initiator on partner selection, the results in this study and in the study by Glaister and Buckley are rather similar, but the selection criteria in which the differences were found are very different.

Selection Criteria and Performance

In H4 it was expected that there exists differences in the relative importance of selection criteria in cases of well and medium-to-low performing IJVs. The performance of the reviewed IJVs was measured along five point Likert-scale based on the foreign partner's view on three measures of performance: the overall performance of the IJV, the financial performance of the IJV, and performance of the IJV compared to the main competitors in 2000-2001. The selection of these three criteria was based on the survey made. The survey included a question about the relative importance (scale 1 to 5) of ten different alternative criteria in the evaluation of the IJV performance. The mean values of the three criteria of performance used in this study were: overall performance 3.49, financial performance 3.51, and performance compared to the main competitors 3.98. Thus, based on the third measure the managers were somewhat more satisfied with the results than based on the two first measures. The overall performance correlated rather highly with financial performance (0.741) and performance compared to competitors (0.693), but the correlation between the two other performance measures was clearly lower (0.458). In general, the results indicate that the Finnish firms were rather satisfied with their IJVs. However, they were not as satisfied as in the companies which were analyzed in the studies

by Nielsen (2003) and Tatoglu and Glaister (2000).

The results (see Table 8) indicate statistically significant differences related to the mean values of two factors (factors one and six) in four cases. Two of those cases were based on overall performance, one case based on financial performance and one on performance compared to competitors. Based on individual selection criterion the results indicated statistically significant differences in 16 cases. In all those cases greater relative importance was given by the well performing IJVs subgroup. Results based on overall performance and financial performance indicate differences in the relative importance of selection criteria in several factors, but based on performance compared to competitors only in the relative importance of selection criteria in factor six. Based on overall and financial performance the criteria of mutual trust, management fit and similar culture received clearly higher mean values in the better than in the poorly performing IJVs. Furthermore, based on overall performance, in the well-performing cases the management had laid more importance on the criteria of commitment to the IJV, credit, and similarity in size than in poorly performing cases. In all but one of the cases the differences related to both performance measures concerned the weights given to partner-related criteria, as could have also been expected. It can be concluded that the results give at least weak support for the finding that relative importance given to various selection criteria in better performing IJVs have been different from those in poorly performing IJVs.

CONCLUSIONS

The goals of this paper were to analyze the relative importance of partner selection criteria in IJVs and to analyze the links between the selection criteria and IJV performance, in order to examine whether there are clear differences in the relative importance given to certain criteria when a partner is selected for a successful or a poorly performing IJV. In addition, the goal is to analyze how the relative importance of partner selection criteria is influenced by foreign partner-specific,

TABLE 8. Selection Criteria and Performance of the IJV

Factor/Criteria	Overall performance		Financial performance		Performance compared to main competitors	
	Very/mostly unsatisfied/neutral (n = 27)	Very/mostly satisfied (n = 30)	Very/mostly unsatisfied/neutral (n = 25)	Very/mostly satisfied (n = 28)	Very/mostly unsatisfied/neutral (n = 15)	Very/mostly satisfied (n = 38)
Factor 1	−0,21	**0,28***	−0,26	**0,35***	0,02	0,13
P-MUTRUST	3,04	**3,83***	3,17	**3,82***	3,36	3,58
P-MANCOMPAT	2,44	**3,30***	2,56	**3,32***	2,67	3,08
P-COMMIT	3,15	**3,83***	3,29	3,75	3,43	3,58
P-PRIORREL	1,96	2,20	1,80	**2,50***	2,00	2,24
Factor 2	−0,03	0,01	0,08	0,01	0,33	−0,07
Factor 3	0,04	−0,05	−0,06	0,00	0,22	−0,11
T-LOCATION	2,96	2,93	2,60	**3,25***	3,00	2,92
Factor 4	−0,17	0,20	−0,11	0,09	−0,13	0,06
Factor 5	−0,16	0,10	0,04	0,03	−0,04	0,06
T-CREDIT	1,44	**2,10***	1,63	2,04	1,43	2,00
P-RELPROD	2,59	2,93	2,36	**3,11***	2,73	2,76
Factor 6	−0,30	**0,15***	−0,10	−0,01	−0,56	**0,14***
T-PUBLSECTR	1,70	1,93	1,92	1,82	1,33	**2,08***
P-SIMCULT	1,59	**2,23***	1,48	**2,36***	1,53	**2,11***
P-SIMSIZE	1,22	**1,70***	1,52	1,50	1,13	**1,66***
Factor 7	0,09	−0,06	0,16	−0,07	0,01	0,02
P-PRIORREL	1,96	2,20	1,80	**2,50***	2,00	2,24
Factor 8	0,19	−0,15	0,13	−0,10	0,12	−0,06

* p ≤ 0,1   ** p ≤ 0,05   *** p ≤ 0,01   **** p ≤ 0,001

IJV location-specific and investment-specific variables.

Based on the earlier literature five hypotheses were developed for testing. The sample of the study was based on 60 manufacturing IJVs established by 47 Finnish companies established mainly during the 1990s in OECD and non-OECD countries. In the analysis of results similar methods were used as in earlier studies (mean values, ANOVA, Independent sample t-tests).

The five most important selection criteria used by the Finnish companies from the 29 criteria were: our trust in the partner, strong commitment to the venture, trust between partners, knowledge of the target market's economy and customs and ability to permit faster entry into the target market. The three most important criteria of those five–the three mentioned first–are partner-related and the two others task-related. The results of this study match very well with the findings in earlier studies (Geringer, 1988; Glaister, 1996;

Glaister and Buckley, 1997; Tatoglu and Glaister, 2000; Nielsen, 2003).

The reviewed 29 selection criteria represent a number of overlapping perspectives which were partly confirmed by the correlation matrix of selection criteria which displayed a number of low to moderate inter-correlations between selection criteria categories. In order to identify a smaller number of distinct, non-overlapping selection criteria, exploratory factor analysis was used. The factor analysis produced eight underlying factors which explained a total of 75.15% of the observed variance. In general the results were rather similar to earlier studies, but the factor compositions were in several respects rather different from the findings in earlier studies.

Concerning hypotheses one to three, the results indicated that the IJV location-specific variables (especially the geographic area) and the investment-specific variables (especially the form of establishment) had a significant influence on the relative importance of the selection criteria. Instead, the foreign partner-specific variables had a very limited influence on the importance of the selection criteria used. The more detailed results indicate that across the characteristics of the sample the relative importance of selection criteria differed most in connection to Factor 3 (low labor and production costs) where in eight cases a statistically significant difference between reviewed groups was found.

The greatest differences between well and poorly performing IJVs were found on factors one and six. Concerning factor one, the managers of the well-performing units had laid much more importance on the criteria concerning mutual trust, management fit and management commitment. Concerning factor six, the greatest difference related to the importance of the selection criteria of similar culture and similarity in size which had been much more important as the selection criteria in better than in poorly performing units. However, the mean values of these criteria were much lower than the mean values of the criteria in factor one even in well performing units. Thus, in total also hypothesis four received moderate support. The results of the study are summarized in Table 9.

Contrary to the results in this study, Glaister and Buckley (1997) found moderate support only for the role of location of the IJV (in the UK vs. abroad), but not for the influence of other reviewed variables (nationality of the partner, industry, purpose, initial approach, relative partner size). Furthermore, results by Nielsen (2003) indicated strong support for the influence of partner nationality on the relative importance given to various selection criteria. His results also indicated that prior alliance experience had influenced the relative importance given to task-related selection criteria, but not as much the weights given to partner-related criteria. Thus, the results of this study coincide rather well with the earlier findings by Nielsen.

From the management point of view the results indicate that partner-related selection criteria–especially the criteria of trust in the partner and between partners and management commitment–have been the most important selection criteria. Furthermore, differences in the relative weights of selection criteria between well and medium-to-low performing IJVs are noteworthy. An additional interesting finding was that all of the eight companies which were extremely satisfied with the IJV performance stated that the most important selection criteria was a task-related selection criteria. Thus, as may be expected, trust and commitment alone do not guarantee a successful future for the IJV–there has to exist, for example, enough strategic fit between the partners in order to enhance the resource base and competitiveness of the foreign (and local) partner.

The contribution of the study is based on the rather limited amount of research of these issues, especially focusing on the relationship between the relative importance of the selection criteria and IJV performance. Some earlier studies and also the results in this study indicate the potential conceptual overlap between task-related and partner-related selection criteria. Therefore we can fully agree with Glaister and Buckley (1997) that a more fundamental approach to the identification of the core differences between the two types of criteria is definitely needed. Furthermore, the results indicate that differences seem to exist in the relative importance of various selection criteria depending on the foreign partner-specific, location-specific and other investment-specific variables as well as motives for the IJV formation. The results also indicate variation in the relative importance of selection criteria between well and medium-to-low performing IJVs.

However, there are many limitations in the study. The sample was based only on IJVs where the foreign partner was a Finnish firm. Furthermore, although the size of the sample was about the same as in most other studies, the size of the sample was rather limited. Thus, in future possible avenues for further research would be expansion of the sample to include more Finnish IJVs, but also, for example, IJVs established by other Nordic firms. This would give a basis to evaluate the existence of differences in the partner selection behavior of Finnish vs. other foreign companies and/or to evaluate whether the differences are more related, for example, to the location of the IJVs. Also, the influence of strategic motives for the IJV on the relative weights given to various selection criteria is an aspect that should be ex-

TABLE 9. Summary of the Results of the Study

H1: Foreign partner-specific variables	Firm size	FDI experience	IJV experience	Target country exp.
	Not supported	Not supported	Weak support	Weak support
H2: IJV location-specific variables	Region	Cultural distance	Physical distance	Level of developm.
	Strong support	Weak support	Weak support	Strong support
H3: Investment-specific variables	Form of inv.	Type of inv.	Relative partner size	Initial approach
	Strong support	Moderate support	Moderate support	Weak support
H4: Performance	Overall perf.	Financial perf.	Perf. compared to main competitors	
	Weak support	Weak support	Weak support	

amined, following the lead of Glaister (1996), Tatoglu and Glaister (2000) and Nielsen (2003). What is clear is that there is a definite need for further research of the partner selection criteria and relationships between IJV performance and the selection criteria. Furthermore, this study included only the view of the foreign partner regarding the relative importance of various selection criteria, not the view of the local partner. Thus, one possible avenue to continue would be to follow Tatoglu and Glaister (2000) by also including the view of the local partner concerning the motives and the selection criteria. Also, more emphasis should be placed on issues related to strategic fit and resource fit in IJV partner selection research, beyond looking at the similarity of the partners' objectives.

REFERENCES

Al-Khalifa, A. K. & Peterson, E. (1999). The partner selection process in international joint ventures. *European Journal of Marketing*, 33 (11/12), 1064-1081.

Arino, A., Abramov, M., Skorobogatykh, I. & Vila, J. (1997). Partner selection and trust building in West European–Russian joint ventures. *International Studies of Management and Organization*, 27 (1), 19-37.

Awadzi, W. (1987). *Determinants of joint venture performance: A study of international joint ventures in the United States*. Ann Arbor, MI: UMI Press.

Beamish, P. (1988). *Multinational joint ventures in developing countries*. London, England: Routledge.

Contractor, F. & Lorange, P. (1988). Why should firms co-operate? The strategic and economic basis for co-operative ventures. In F. Contractor, and P. Lorange (Eds.), *Co-operative Strategies in International Business* (pp. 3-28). Lexington, MA: Lexington Books.

Daniels, J. (1971). *Recent foreign direct manufacturing investment in the United States*. Ann Arbor, MI: UMI Press.

Demirbag, M., Mirza, H. & Weir, D. (1995). The dynamics of manufacturing joint ventures in Turkey and the role of industrial groups. *Management International Review*, 35 (special issue), 35-51.

Dunning, J. (1993). *Multinational enterprises and the global economy*. Wokingham, England: Addison-Wesley Publishing Company.

Geringer, J. M. (1988). *Joint venture partner selection: Strategies for developed countries*. Westport, CT: Quorum Books.

Geringer, J. M. (1991). Strategic determinants of partner selection criteria in international joint ventures. *Journal of International Business Studies*, 22 (1), 41-54.

Glaister, K. (1996). UK-Western European strategic alliances: Motives and selection criteria. *Journal of Euromarketing*, 54 (4), 5-35.

Glaister, K. & Buckley, P.J. (1997). Task-related and partner-related selection criteria in UK international joint ventures. *British Journal of Management*, 8 (3), 199-222.

Glaister, K. & Wang, Y. (1993). UK joint ventures in China: Motivation and partner selection. *Marketing Intelligence & Planning*, 11 (2), 9-15.

Hamel, G. (1991). Competition for competence and inter-partner learning within international strategic alliances. *Strategic Management Journal*, (Summer Special Issues), 83-103.

Harrigan, K. (1985). *Strategies for joint ventures*. Lexington, MA: Lexington Books.

Hitt, M., Dacin, T., Levitas, E., Arregle, J.L. & Borza, A. (2000). Partner selection in emerging and developed market contexts: Resource-based and organizational learning perspectives. *Academy of Management Journal*, 43 (3), 449-467.

Hofstede, G. (1980). *Culture's consequences*. Beverly Hills, CA: Sage Publishers.

Hofstede, G. (2001). *Culture's consequences*, 2nd edition. Beverly Hills, CA: Sage Publishers.

Lane, H. & Beamish, P. (1990). Cross-cultural cooperative behavior in joint ventures in LDCs. *Management International Review*, 30 (special issue), 87-102.

Lyles, M. & Salk, J. (1996). Knowledge acquisition from foreign parents in international joint ventures: An empirical examination in the Hungarian context. *Journal of International Business Studies*, 27 (5), 877-903.

Maurer, N. (1996). *Joint venture partner selection by American manufacturing firms in southern China.* Ann Arbor, MI: UMI Press.

Morewy, D., Oxley, J. & Silverman, B. (1996). Strategic alliances and interfirm knowledge transfer. *Strategic Management Journal* 17 (Winter Special Issue): 77-91.

Nielsen, B. (2003). Managing knowledge in international strategic alliances: Theory and practice. *Ph.D–serie 2.2003.* Copenhagen, Denmark: Copenhagen Business School Press.

Porter, M.E. & Fuller, M.B. (1986). Coalitions and global strategy. In M.E. Porter (Ed.) *Competition in global industries* (pp. 315-344). Cambridge, MA: Harvard University Press.

Reus, T.H. & Ritchie, W. J. III (2004). Interpartner, parent, and environmental factors influencing the operation of international joint ventures: 15 years of research. *Management International Review*, 44 (4), 369-395.

Robson, M. (2002). Partner selection in successful international strategic alliances: The role of co-operation. *Journal of General Management*, 28 (1), 1-15.

Robson, M., Leonidou, L. & Katsikeas, C. (2002). Factors influencing international joint venture performance: Theoretical perspectives, assessment, and future directions. *Management International Review*, 42 (4), 385-418.

Tatoglu, E. & Glaister, K. (2000). *Dimensions of Western foreign direct investment in Turkey.* Westport, Connecticut: Quorum Books.

Tomlinson, J. (1970). *The joint venture process in international business: India and Pakistan.* Cambridge, MA: MIT Press.

Tomlinson, J. & Thompson, M. (1977). A study of Canadian joint ventures in Mexico. *Working paper.* Vancouver, Canada: University of British Columbia.

doi:10.1300/J037v16n01_09

Advertising in Czech and French Magazines

Christian Dianoux

Jana Kettnerová

Zdeněk Linhart

SUMMARY. The aim of this research is to determine the main features in which the Czech and French advertisements are similar and in which they differ. The study concerns the content analysis of 577 printed advertisements published in the 10 most representative magazines in the Czech Republic and France. The five largest categories of magazines in terms of their focus are represented as follows: women, men, businesses, seniors and juniors. The results show some noticeable divergences in the basic structure and content of advertising, such as the size, the presence of children or elderly people, the number of product features and the indication of prices. Some convergences appear as well, such as the human presence, the use of testimonies and/or celebrities and the mention of the brand only. These results open up new possibilities for future research in order to verify the key factors, which advertisers could standardize or adapt for their advertising campaigns. doi:10.1300/J037v16n01_10 *[Article copies available for a fee from The Haworth Document Delivery Service: 1-800-HAWORTH. E-mail address: <docdelivery@haworthpress.com> Website: <http://www.HaworthPress.com> © 2006 by The Haworth Press, Inc. All rights reserved.]*

KEYWORDS. Print advertising, cross-cultural studies, content analysis, cultural values, observation grid, Central and Western Europe, Czech Republic, France

INTRODUCTION

Recently, Al-Olayan and Karande (2000) noted that the largest number of studies exploring the cross-cultural differences between advertisements concentrated mostly on just a few countries: USA (the first rank with 40 out of 59 studies in the meta analysis of Abernathy and Franke, 1996), the Western European countries (France, Sweden, Great Britain, etc.), and the leading countries in Asia (Japan–the second range–and Korea).

On the other hand, countries such as those from the former Soviet block have had very

Christian Dianoux is Senior Lecturer and a member of the research team of the Universities of Metz and Nancy (GREFIGE-CEREMO), IUT de Metz, Ile du Saulcy, 57070 Metz, France (E-mail: Christian.dianoux@univ-metz.fr). Jana Kettnerová is a PhD student, Faculty of Economics and Management, Czech University of Agriculture, Prague, U kruhovky (Kamýcká) 942 / 2, 165 21, Praha 6, Suchdol, Czech Republic (E-mail: kettnerova@pef.czu.cz). Zdeněk Linhart is Associate Professor, Faculty of Economics and Management, Czech University of Agriculture, Prague, Kamycka 129, 16500 Prague 6, Czech Republic (E-mail: linhart@pef.czu.cz), and is Chairman of the Agentura Agropro Company.

[Haworth co-indexing entry note]: "Advertising in Czech and French Magazines." Dianoux, Christian, Jana Kettnerová, and Zdeněk Linhart. Co-published simultaneously in *Journal of Euromarketing* (International Business Press, an imprint of The Haworth Press, Inc.) Vol. 16, No. 1/2, 2006, pp. 139-152; and: *Contemporary Euromarketing: Entry and Operational Decision Making* (ed: Jorma Larimo) International Business Press, an imprint of The Haworth Press, Inc., 2006, pp. 139-152. Single or multiple copies of this article are available for a fee from The Haworth Document Delivery Service [1-800-HAWORTH, 9:00 a.m. - 5:00 p.m. (EST). E-mail address: docdelivery@ haworthpress.com].

few studies despite their increased economical importance and their integration into the European Union.[1] In fact, the introduction of eight of these countries (Czech Republic, Estonia, Hungary, Latvia, Lithuania, Poland, Slovakia, and Slovenia) into the EU in May 2004, now allows advertisers to develop communication strategies with the same EU regulations (notably those dealing with misleading advertising and comparative advertising), which will enable them to benefit from homogenous constraints. But on the other hand, "although there is evidence of converging economic systems in Europe, there is no evidence of converging value systems. Indeed, there is evidence that consumer behaviour is diverging in Europe as reflected in the consumption, ownership, and usage of many products and services" and if "international marketers would like us to believe that in the *new Europe* with a single currency, consumers will become more similar, will increasingly eat the same food, wear jeans and cross-trainers, and watch the same television programs. Reality is likely to be different" (De Mooij & Hofstede, 2002, p. 62).

The objective of this paper is based on the current research trend, which aims at better understanding of the advertisers' communication policies in a Central European country (the Czech Republic) and to compare them with those of a Western European country (France),[2] which is the second largest investor in that country (after Germany). It also aims at responding to questions posed by Whitelock and Chung (1989): "Which approach is adopted by practitioners is, however, still a matter for some speculation, since the writers have confined themselves to giving only anecdotal examples in support of their arguments." The analysis presented here is concentrated on the analysis of the contents of printed advertisings in the Czech Republic and in France. It expresses itself in the following manner: the focus of literature on the comparative research at the international level and on what we know about the two countries, this review will help us to formulate our working hypothesis. Then we will present the methodology used, and the obtained results. Finally, we will conclude by revealing the principal tendencies observed, the managerial recommendations that emerge,

and will indicate the limits of this work from which several research perspectives arise.

REVIEW OF THE LITERATURE AND THE HYPOTHESIS

The Global Communication Debate

The debate on the standardization of the policies of multinational enterprise communication was born several decades ago with the research, notably, of Elinder (1965) and Fatt (1967), who alleged that the evolution of societies brings about a bigger convergence level between countries and has a tendency to eliminate cultural barriers in permitting the emergence of standardized international communication. Roostals (1963), several years previously, noted that even if standardization of advertising developed logically (more naturally for airline companies or automotive companies, than for soap or cigarettes, however), there will always remain some differences, not because of the diversity of the languages in Western Europe or the media and the laws, but because of the specific demands of the nationality of the consumers. Other authors have also shown that the general debate on the standardization was futile because this question was notably dependent on the existence of homogeneous international segments and that in this case it justified itself but not in the other (Baalbaki & Malhotra, 1993).

Adding to the debate, numerous studies which have been led to analyse the practices of enterprises, have shown that the practice of total standardisation was rare, with most cases having a tendency to adapt their communication. However, this adaptation trend must not be considered as uniform. According to Harris (1994), after a study on the practice of multinational American and European companies in the European Union, there exists, in reality, a very large spectrum of practices from the total adaptation to the total standardisation. This spectrum can be considered as a sort of continuum in which all the states were represented:

- no adaptation, limited, moderate or high adaptation;
- a visual, a text or only a slogan adaptation;

• an adaptation that varied according to the markets.

Finally, if the total adaptation is the exception, so is the pure standardisation, even if there has been a strong tendency during the last 40 years to move towards standardisation, because even though it is not always effective, it permits to envisage significant economy of scale and to diffuse the same image position around the world (Agrawal, 1995).

In such context, the study of differences between countries based on the analysis of the contents of the advertisements is most interesting. This is so because, besides the consumer study and what the enterprises claim to practise, the analysis of the contents permits one to give objective indications on the actual practices of the advertisers. Even though this approach is not moving in the sense that was recommended by Taylor (2002) who stated that the academic research on international advertising produced too many content analyses and not enough experiments: "what we need is experimental research in which the impact of specific executional variables is isolated," it is not far from the end. For us, the analysis of the contents is not an end in itself but a first step permitting an orientation towards future investigation of the elements of execution of experimental testing. Before looking at the comparison of the efficiency of this or that element of execution between two or more countries, it seems more important to us that we should, firstly, define the limits of the advertisers' practices and, secondly, provide orientation for future research.

This approach is also useful for advertisers who wish to enhance the standardisation of their ads. Indeed, as shown by Solberg (2002), the level of standardisation is significantly affected by the level of market knowledge. According to the author, the more a firm knows the local markets the more it can locate the similarities between such markets, and the more it can standardize the advertisements. It is worth noting that sometimes another resistance to standardization comes from the local executive staff because of their desire to be in control. For instance, Toshiba France had refused to use the slogan "In touch with Tomorrow" because the French consumers would not

have accepted it, and the Philips Company had a slogan with the same idea. Toshiba Headquarters requested a survey which showed that there was no problem. Since then the slogan has been used in France and has been a success. This indicates that if the headquarters had known the local market well beforehand, it would have been easier for them to have argued their case.

Differences Between the Czech Republic and France

If, as already stated, the majority of the comparative studies were based on the advertising styles, they concerned essentially the comparisons between the Americans and Asians, or the Americans and Europeans. The comparisons concerning European countries are fewer (Walliser & Moreau, 2000), and those concerning the comparisons of Eastern and Western Europe are fewer still. However, the small number of studies on this subject does allow us to point out the following:

• In France, amusing advertisements are preferred to the informative ones (Mandel, 1991). They tend to orientate the creation towards messages mostly centred on a global image of a product rather than on the explanation of facts (Hall & Hall, 1990; Walliser & Moreau, 2000). The greatest proportion of the ads is emotional (Zandpour, Chang & Catalano, 1992) and built with rich messages where subtle hints and non verbal expressions (Fleury, 1990) are dominant. In Poland, advertising uses humorous symbols or the historic and literary past of the country with word plays and linguistic expressions with double meanings that are only understood by the Poles (Dianoux, Domanski, & Herrmann, 2000; Domanski, Dianoux & Herrmann, 2003).

• By contrast, Vida and Fairhurst (1999) did not find a strong ethnocentricity in Poland, the Czech Republic, Hungary and Estonia, in comparison with the western European countries.

• The study of Kaynac and Kara (2001), even though dealing mostly with Asia, shows that the creative strategies emphasizing family values were more obvious in the countries where there was a strong family image.

- According to Grapard (1997), even if the solid communal bases between the European countries on the geographic and social-political plans leave us to assume that there are many similarities, many differences actually subsist, notably between the East and the West. This is because of the tendencies of the consumers situated in clarified levels, affinities and diverse cultural influences, distinct expressions in their languages, rapid and brusque reforms, and economic performances which have not yet converged.

Parallel to these studies, which were focused on the consumer behaviour, are numerous differences mentioned in management manuals that can equally be pointed out. With the Czechs it is, for example, preferable to avoid the seriousness and aloofness that characterize the French in business relations; the Czechs tend to weave personal relationships into their business relationships with their partners. Misunderstandings with the Czechs are possible. The Czechs happen to be between the cultures with a high context communication like the Russians for example, and a culture with a low context communication like the Germans. The first is based on implicit communication, the second on explicit communication (see Hall, 1976). For the Russians, posture, tone, facial expressions, silences and gestures are just as important bearers for the sense of things as words, while the Germans express themselves essentially by the spoken word.

In the same line of thinking, general studies emphasize thoughts like those of Todd (1990, quoted by Demorgon, 1996): "The family community, which is not very large and strong in Western Europe, affirms in East Europe as an absolute, divine authority and salvation for everyone."

The observation of Hofstede's values shows significant differences between Czech Republic and France (Table 1) concerning two dimensions (distance between power and masculinity), suggesting the idea that the Czechs would be more inclined than the French to accept the

TABLE 1. Hofstede's Country Scores (Adapted from Hofstede, 1991)

	Power distance	Individualism	Masculinity	Uncertainty avoidance
France (1)	68	71	43	86
Czech Republic (2)	78	68	81	81
Germany (1)	35	67	66	65
Poland (2)	62	55	85	87
Russia (1)	95	47	40	75

Adapted from: (1) http://www.centreurope.org/france/france-in-figures/hofstede-analysis-france.htm (in December 2006) and (2) Kolman et al. (2002) calibrated positions of the countries.

differences between the status and the dependence on a leader. For Kolman et al. (2002) the Czech respondents came out of their survey on the Czech Republic, Hungary, Poland and Slovakia as having the second highest score on power distance after Slovakia. On the other hand, although the Czech Republic had, in this case, a far higher score than France on masculinity, it had the lowest score in their survey.

Bearing in mind the numerous marked differences between the Czech and French consumers, and despite the tendencies noted in standardized multinational communication (Laroche, Kirpalani, & Darmon, 1999), it seemed probable that the advertisers, voluntarily or not, had a natural inclination to adapt their communications to the two countries. Furthermore, De Mooij and Hofstede (2002) noticed that a trend toward more adaptation can be observed in some multinational firms. For example, they quoted Coca-Cola in 2000 which decided to get closer to local markets and the CEO who said "we kept standardizing our practices, while local sensitivity had become absolutely essential to success." We must, therefore, find this tendency in the contents of the advertisements in the two countries. So the following hypothesis must be demonstrated:

> Hypothesis 1: The Czech ads differ substantially in their content, their form, and their discourse from the French ads.

METHODOLOGY

In order to record the contents of the ads in the two respective countries, an observation pattern had to be created first (see Appendix 1). This was established after the principal elements of the differences were identified and listed on the basis of the literature review. At the same time, the research criteria had to be limited to a reasonable number so as not to complicate the task of the observers, nor to multiply the risk of error or oversight. We divided them according to the three headings held by Okazaki (2004):

- the type and amount of information;
- the creative strategy used;
- the cultural values reflected by the message.

For a survey of the type and the amount of information required, outside the classic information permitting a description of the general context (color or black and white; photo or design; presence of a product, an animal or people in the ad; type of person, number of people), and the text (brand name, slogan, length of the text), we had reserved several items intended for approximate evaluation of the informative character of the advertising. To determine the informational dimension of the advertisement (informational cues), numerous studies use the criteria proposed by Resnik and Stern (1977). Instead of this approach, which is very detailed and not useful for our purposes (for example, the authors use the following items: quality, performance, availability, warranty, special offer, etc.), we preferred to opt for a quicker solution which permitted us to simply identify the presence or the absence of information relative to the functional characteristics or the technicalities of the product, its price (or similar information, such as the bank credit interest) or, finally, the environment or ecological characteristics of the product (an aspect which is not taken into account in the pattern proposed by Resnik and Stern).

Concerning the determination of the creative strategies in the different criteria reserved by Okazaki (2004) notably after the work of Leong et al. (1998), Gudykunst and Ting Toomey (1998), we kept the four following ones: information is symbolic; the product is compared with the others (quotation of a competitor); the advertisement proposes a promo-

tional offer; the presence of at least one celebrity (star, sports champion, etc.). To these criteria, we have added eroticism on the assumption that France is a country very open to this form of expression. To measure it, we took into account the resort to nudity, sharing the principle that among the different forms that can cover eroticism (or sex appeal), nudity is the most used expression (Reichert, 2003). The other characteristics suggested by Okazaki (2004) were not used because they seemed too ambiguous to evaluate such as, for example, "logical reasoning," or "curiosity arousal."

Finally, to record the different cultural values conveyed by the ads, we focused on the significant relations put into place by Albers-Miller and Gelb (1996) between the advertising appeals of Pollay and the four dimensions of Hofstede. Only the susceptible points of extreme divergence between the two countries have been used. In a parallel direction, we added four other appeals (marked by *) used in literature to complete the measures:[3]

- for the reaching effects of power: this ad shows the importance of social status (+), it shows that the product is a good deal (−), the presence of a personality (*), this ad is non-conforming (*);
- for intolerance of uncertainty: this ad incites adventure (−), it is very concentrated on security (*);
- for masculinity: this ad is based on the efficiency of the product (+), it evokes the values of tenderness (*);
- for individualism/collectivism: this ad evokes family values (+).

The sample of ads was constituted according to the following criteria:

- we used the 5 most important categories of magazines (managers, men, seniors, teenagers and women);
- for each of the 5 categories of magazines, the 2 most distributed in part of the Czech Republic and the other part in France were chosen except when there was the same review in the two countries and it corresponded with one of the 10 most distributed reviews in each of the two countries (see the list of utilised reviews in Appendix 2). This last point permits a

minimum basis of identical reviews in the two countries (Elle and Maximal), this would have been impossible in the first case because there is no corresponding review having a high circulation between the two countries;

- all the ads have been looked at whatever their format (only the minor ads such as sales of houses, personal objects, job offers, etc., have been excluded);
- after a detailed briefing, the Czech and French student teams in the second and third cycles in marketing, were given the task of examining all the ads that they found in different reviews. To ensure certain homogeneity of judgements, each ad was given to three different persons. The only criteria that were kept were those that had the minimum of two convergent opinions. For the criterion which had a dispersion of less than three points between extremes on a 10 point scale, an average was calculated.

Finally, 577 different ads were used in the evaluation which represents an average of nearly 29 ads per magazine, 309 of which were Czech and 268 were French (the difference coming from the larger number of losses on the French side). Other information presented was collected from the following sources:

- for the diffusion: from the data 2004 of the Institute ABCCR for the Czech Republic and from the OJD for France;
- the prices of the ads come from the data indicated on the the Internet sites of the different magazines in 2005, the standard basis used was the normal page in four colours;
- the prices in the Czech and French currencies were calculated on the basis of 30 crowns = 1 Euro.

RESULTS

The Comparison of the Structure of the Advertisements

Of all of the product categories used, the most significant differences occurred in the categories of computers, automobiles and books (see Table 2). We observed that in the other categories there was no difference between the Czech and French reviews. The advertisements concern similar categories of products.

As for the fact that we found brands which were more or less known in the two countries, no difference was observed (Chi^2 = 0,42; p.c. = 0,52), with 32% of the brands being the object of an ad in a Czech magazine were sold in France, against 30% for the opposite cases.

Concerning the location of the brand name (at the top, the bottom or the middle of the ad), there was no difference, except the fact that in France the brand is repeated in different places in the ad, which was not the case in the Czech Republic. If such a difference appears odd, it is sufficient to study the dimensions of the ads for a better understanding, since the fundamental difference rests, without doubt, on this point: the format of Czech ads is clearly inferior to those observed in France (Table 3). So it is easier for the French advertisers to repeat the brand name than for the Czech advertisers. Equally important, even if the percentage stays

TABLE 2. Repartition of the Advertisements in the 20 Magazines

Product Category	Czech Reviews base: 309 ads	French Reviews base: 268 ads	Total base: 577 ads
Food and Cleaning Products	5.2%	6.0%	5.5%
Cosmetics, Health and Hygiene	19.7%	23.9%	21.7%
Clothing-Textiles	10.7%	12.3%	11.4%
Computers, Hifi-sound-image, Telephones	10%	1.5%	6.1%
Automobile, Motorcycles	3.9%	8.2%	5.9%
Books, Magazines, DVDs	10.4%	5.2%	8.0%
Other products	6.8%	12.0%	9.2%
Banks and Insurance	4.2%	6.7%	5.4%
Telecommunications	4.5%	6.3%	5.4%
Tourism and Transport	3.2%	4.9%	4.0%
Entertainment	9.1%	4.9%	7.1%
Other services	12.3%	8.3%	10.4%
	100%	100%	100%

Note: These figures do not take into account the size of the ads.

TABLE 3. Advertising Dimensions

(N = 577)	Less than one page	One page or more	Total
Czech Republic	53.7%	46.3%	100%
France	15.3%	84.7%	100%
	35.9%	64.1%	100%

The dependence is very significant. $Chi^2 = 92.11$, ddl = 1, p < .001

TABLE 4. Comparison of Contents of French and Czech Ads

(N = 577)	USA[1]	UK[1]	France[1]	France	Czech
Black and white	6%	11%	13%	2%	5%*
Comparison	10%	5%	1%	2%	4%*
Minority race	7%	5%	7%	7%	7%
Elderly person	3%	2%	1%	11%	3%*
Children	16%	4%	6%	16%	9%*
Photograph	72-82%[2]	74-68%[2]	48-60%[2]	80%	85%
Product shown	57-41%[2]	60-49%[2]	49-37%[2]	77%	75%
Price shown	16-6%[2]	24-8%[2]	16-15%[2]	21%	31%*
Description	68-43%[2]	67-42%[2]	72-39%[2]	52%	55%
Symbolic	10-6%[2]	16-23%[2]	37-20%[2]	36%	44%*

[1]The data in the first three columns come from the study of Cutler, Javalgi, and Erramilli (1992), and are given an illustrated title.
[2]The first number corresponds to the durable product category, the second to the non durable.
*Significantly different at p < .05 (Chi[2] test)

low, the Czech ads were more often produced in black and white (5.7%) than the French ads (1.1%), probably for economical reasons.

This search for savings with the cutting of the ad size is easy to understand when we look at the tariffs used by the Czech media. In fact, if the average tariffs used in France for the magazines we have surveyed (see Appendix 2) are largely greater (6.860 euros in the Czech Republic per normal page in four colours vs. 26.721 euros in France), the average of the Cost Per Thousand (CPT) is significantly higher in the Czech Republic with 135 euros vs. 58 euros in France because of the low distribution of magazines. This is a problem inherent in countries with a low population even if the numbers of the Czech readers are proportionally greater in relation to the total population of the country (the number of French readers per review is on average 4 times greater, even though the French population is 6 times greater than Czech population).

The Comparison of the Factual Ad Content

In respect to the differences according to the contents of the Czech and French ads, we can similarly observe significant differences outlined in Table 4.

Apart from the racial minority characteristics, the use of the photography, the presentation and the description of the products, the ads presented in the Czech reviews had, in a significant way, a tendency to differ from those presented in the French reviews. Taking into account only the international brands (known and sold in both the Czech Republic and France) did not change the results, except for the teenager magazines (no significant difference between the two countries). It seems that, in general, the advertisers adapt the content of their communications to the local context.

We have equally indicated the results obtained by Cutler, Javalgi, and Erramilli (1992) within the framework of a comparative study between the USA, Great Britain and France (note that the study also concerns India and Korea, which are not discussed here). The important differences which appear in the Table 4 between our study and this study about France illustrate one of the principal problems encountered with the content analysis: the selection of the magazines and ads. In their study, Cutler, Javalgi, and Erramilli (1992) only used three magazine categories (women, business, general interest) and these magazines were scrutinised as closely as possible in all of the studied countries. Moreover, they excluded ads concerning fashion clothing and all ads which did not have a one page format.[4] On our part, we believe that the selection carried out by the authors leads to a poor appreciation of the advertising tendencies in a given country because the exclusions lead to an "imperialist" analysis, accentuating the tendencies of the native country of the researchers. As an example, if we had used only one-page or more ads in this study, we would have rejected the majority of the Czech ads and would have had partially false results.

For other criteria used in our study, Table 5 shows very few differences between the two countries, except for the environment used in

TABLE 5. Comparison of the Content of French and Czech Advertisements in Other Items

(N = 577, except for (1) N = 361)	France	Czech
Indoor Environment	77%	88%*
Photo or drawing of at least one animal	6.4%	6.2%
Photo or drawing of at least one person (1)	66%	63%
Female Presence (1)	78%	75%
Use of a celebrity (1)	16%	19%
Use of Nudity (1)	3.4%	2.9%
Text of at least four lines	55%	59%
Only the brand name	12%	11%
Testimony of one person	6.2%	6.8%
Promotional offer	15%	18%
Information with at least 6 characteristics	13%	27%*

*Significantly different at $p < .05$ (Chi^2 test)

TABLE 6. Comparison of the Values Used by the Ads of International Brands

	France	Czech	t-test
Evoking Family Values	4.26	3.24	n.s.
Non conformer	4.71	4.56	n.s.
Appeal to Adventure	5.05	4.52	n.s.
Based on the efficiency of product	6.24	5.78	n.s.
Focus on security	5.42	4.70	n.s.
Social Status	5.48	4.34	F = 4.42*
Gentleness	4.38	2.71	F = 6.44*
Bargains	5.93	4.36	F = 7.20**
Erotic	3.00	3.35	n.s.
Full of Humour	4.82	2.83	n.s.

Significantly different at *$p < .05$, **$p < .01$

the images (the Czech ads having a greater tendency than the French to use the interior environments), and the number of characteristics presented (the Czech ads use a number of characteristics very significantly elevated to show the merits of the product).

Comparison of the Values Used by the Advertisements

Taking into account the values used by the ads shows the results fundamentally different when we consider only the brands known in the two countries (qualified here by international brands, see Table 6) or the brands known only in one country (qualified here by the "locals," see Table 7).

The results show a certain degree of homogeneity between the two countries in the different values measured, the homogeneity is probably aligned with the research of a uniform international positioning. In fact, as highlighted by Moriarty and Duncan (1990) the positioning is often standardised when the relative execution decisions are made locally. Also, according to the work of Laroche, Kirpalani, and Darmon (1999), this degree of standardisation can be reinforced by the degree of control by the headquarters of the subsidiary. The headquarters give priority to the control of the strategic decisions and the objectives of the campaign, the subsidiary having the most influence on the decisions linked

TABLE 7. Comparison of Values Used in Ads for Local Brands

	France	Czech	t-test
Based on the Product Efficiency	6.46	4.75	F = 23.65***
Bargains	6.01	4.30	F = 18.36***
Evoking Family Values	5.38	3.97	F = 7.33**
Focus on Security	5.35	3.79	F = 9.49**
Gentleness	5.16	2.55	F = 49.62***
Appeal to Adventure	5.06	3.49	F = 11.73***
Social Status	4.94	3.50	F = 10.92**
Full of Humour	4.60	2.84	F = 7.50**
Erotic	4.39	2.83	F = 7.25**
Anticonformist	3.74	3.08	n.s.

Significantly different at *$p < .05$, **$p < .01$, ***$p < .001$

to the environmental choices, notably the media plan.

On the other hand, if Table 6 shows that the values used by the ads of international brands are close enough between the two countries, we cannot say the same for those concerning the local brands. In fact, other than the "non conformist" item, the ads for "local brands" are generally different between France and the Czech Republic in a manner which is often very significant (Table 7).

So we could advance that the values in the advertisements for international brands are more or less similar (except for three items) while, on the other hand, the values in the advertisements for local brands are very different between the two countries.

CONCLUSION

We strongly ascertain that there is a large number of differences between France and the Czech Republic in the area of creative advertising, whatever the structural plan (formats are smaller in the Czech Republic), or in terms of contents (in the Czech Republic the price is more often mentioned, the number of characteristics is bigger, and children and older persons are used less). Our hypothesis *that the Czech ads differ substantially in their content and their form, from the French ads*, is therefore largely supported by the collected data and we can conclude that the advertisers have the tendency to adapt the contents of their communication in conjunction with the Czech or French context.

Concerning the cultural values, we have also found important differences between the two countries. In fact, the overall examination of the results (Tables 6 and 7) shows a strong tendency towards the French marks being higher in whatever the items are (the only exception for all the scores–2 × 10 items–concerns the item of eroticism for international brand ads).[5] Faced with such a result, one has the right to ask if the given marks are not also influenced by a dissimilar assessment approach between the Czech and French observers. Remember that when each ad was analysed by three evaluators, they stayed with the magazines of their own country, the French analysed the French ads and the Czechs analysed the Czech ads. Nevertheless, the "objective" observations such as, for example, the size of the advertisement or the presence of individuals, should not vary because of the nationality of the evaluator. On the other hand, anything that is associated with interpretation is susceptible to its being influenced by nationality (e.g., an advertisement with family values).

Research into this issue should be undertaken because if this cultural methodological problem was confirmed, the best solution to remedy it would be to disperse the evaluators (50% of the Czechs to evaluate the French advertisements and *vice versa*) and thus obtain a homogeneous opinion. But there would be two problems again. Firstly, when something is judged non conformist in one country, can it also be judged as non-conformist in another?

Indeed, there are many values which vary by culture as De Mooij (1998, 2005) pointed out in her explanations about value paradoxes to advertising appeal. She takes "Freedom," for example, and explains that freedom can be the bipolar opposite of dependence in France, of Harmony in Japan, of belonging in the Netherlands, and of order in Germany. How can a nonnative speaker codify the ads? Secondly, it would be difficult to find evaluators who would be fluent in two, or more different languages. But according to Lerman and Callow (2003) it would not be a good way because their study shows that monolingual narrative coding is preferable to bilingual narrative coding since the non native speakers cannot perceive the implicit context as well as the native speakers. We can also add that consumers from high-context communication systems are more apt than those from low-context to derive implicit meaning from visual images in printed ads (Callow & Schiffman, 2002).

From the methodological point of view, this study also shows the importance of taking into account a statistically sufficient (large) advertising sample from each country, in order to avoid the methodological choices proposed by Cutler, Javalgi, and Erramilli (1992) mentioned earlier. In this sense, it is important to pay attention to the following issues:

- to use a large category of magazines covering different segments of the population and then post information such as "X % of the persons in the ads are older persons" (Cutler, Javalgi, & Erramilli, 1992) logically would not make great sense when the selected magazines are not targeting the senior segment;
- selecting identical magazines in different countries is interesting because it permits a homogenous target but it also generates a greater problem of concentrating on groups which could be marginal in the studied countries. If we wish to have a representative sample, it seems preferable to keep magazines in separate categories in relation to their respective level;
- similarly, to exclude certain advertisings can generate important biases (except, of course, those which can be qualified as

short ads and not advertisements, communicating on single product, offer or request for employment, real estate sales, etc.). Also, being limited to one page formats risks, according to the country, a creation of important distortions such as has been the case between the Czech Republic and France. This confirms the comments of Avery and Franke (1996) within the framework of their meta-analysis.

From the managerial point of view, the principal differences between the Czech and French ads, whatever the product category, brand, or magazine are: the Czech ads are smaller, more often in black and white, with fewer or without children and elderly people, with a bigger number of characteristics and, notably, more prices and comparisons, than the French ads. For a French advertiser who wants to do publicity in the Czech Republic, or vice-versa, it would be worthwhile to pay attention to these tendencies. But, at the same time, it would be appropriate to try to answer the following question: Are these differences between the two countries relevant? Hoeken et al. (2003), for example, have found no difference in the capacity to persuade in the ads that appeal to adventure and/or in the ads that appeal to security between countries such as the Netherlands and France, even though differences of attitudes to the consideration of these values do exist between the two countries.

This first tour of the horizon of the universe of the Czech and French advertising has permitted us to have an overall view of the practices of the advertisers in the two countries. However, knowing that the idea of "what is practiced is what is effective" (Taylor, 2002), does not always reveal the truth, it will be interesting to follow the suggestion of Harris and Attour (2003). The authors propose that instead of looking for the winning tools of a complete adaptation or a total standardization (which is, without doubt, a fantasy), it would be better to try to understand the benefits taken from the standardized forms that are applied. In this way, one can imagine that there are basic characteristics which permit advertising to be as efficient in France as in the Czech Republic, notably those in which we have observed the most differences between the two

countries, such as the communication on the number of functional attributes and the price. For the size of the ads, it will be also interesting to test if the savings that the advertisers think they make with half the size advertisements really exist, or if it will be more efficient to use a full size for the ads, notably for the increase of arousal and memorization.

NOTES

1. Note that before 1989, the socialist economies were more concentrated on the offer rather than on the demand, the behaviour of the consumer wasn't useful (Nasierowski, 1996), this could contribute to the tardiness noticed at present.
2. The main economic features of:
    France: $ 1,600 billion GDP (Gross Domestic Product); 58.5 million people
    Czech Republic: $ 161 billion (GDP); 10.2 million people
3. For the items taken from the Albers-Miller and Gelb article (1996), the sign "+" signifies that the authors have found the relation between the measure and the dimension of Hofstede vary positively, the sign "−" signifies the inverse.
4. Note that they also excluded adverts for employment or for real estate. We have also excluded them because they cannot be considered as real ads proposing permanent products.
5. It is interesting to note that this tendency is inverse for local brands. This might be because the French observers are used to seeing this kind of ad?

REFERENCES

Abernethy, A. M., & Franke, G. R. (1996). The Information Content of Advertising A Meta-Analysis. *Journal of Advertising*, 25 (2), 1-17.

Agrawal, M. (1995). Review of a 40-year Debate in International Advertising, *International Marketing Review*. 12 (1), 26-48.

Albers-Miller, N., & Gelb, B. (1996). Business Advertising Appeals as a Mirror of Cultural Dimensions: A Study of Eleven Countries. *Journal of Advertising*, 25 (4), 57-70.

Al-Olayan, F., & Karande, K. (2000). A Content Analysis of Magazine Advertisements from the United States and the Arab World. *Journal of Advertising*, 29 (3), 69-82.

Baalbaki, I. B., & Malhotra, N. K. (1993). Marketing Management Bases for International Marketing Segmentation: An Alternative Look at the Standardization/Customization Debate. *International Marketing Review*, 10 (1), 19-44.

Bollinger, D., & Hofstede, G. (1987). *Les différences culturelles dans le management. Comment chaque pays gère-t-il ses hommes?* Paris: Les Editions d'Organisation, 268 p.

Buzzel, R. D. (1968). Can You Standardize International Marketing? *Harvard Business Review*, 46, 103-113.

Callow, M., & Schiffman, L. (2002). Implicit meaning in visual print advertisements: A cross-cultural examination of the contextual communication effect. *International Journal of Advertising*, 21, 259-277.

Cutler, B., & Javalgi, R. (1992). A Cross-Cultural Analysis of the Visual Components of Print Advertising; The United States and the European Community. *Journal of Advertising Research*, 32 (1), 71-80.

Cutler, B., & Javalgi, R., & Erramilli, K. (1992). The Visual Components of Print Advertising: A Five-country Cross-Cultural Analysis. *European Journal of Marketing*, 26 (4), 7-20

De Mooij, M. K. (1998-2005). *Global Marketing and Advertising, Understanding Cultural Paradoxes* (2nd ed.). Sage Publications.

De Mooij, M., & Hofstede, G. (2002). Convergence and divergence in Consumer Behavior: Implications for International Retailing. *Journal of Retailing*, 78, 61-69.

Demorgon, J. (1996). *Complexité des cultures et de l'interculturel.* Paris: Anthropos.

Dianoux, C., Domanski, T., & Herrmann, J.-L. (2000). Comparative advertising in central and Eastern Europe: The case of Poland. *Proceedings of the 8th Annual Conference on Marketing Strategies for Central and Eastern Europe*, Vienna, Austria, december, Edited by P. Chadraba et R. Springer, 59-71.

Domański, T., Dianoux, C., & Herrmann, J.-L. (2003). Reklama porównawcza w œwietle prawa. *Marketing y Rynek*, 2, 2-6.

Domański, T., Dianoux C., & Herrmann J.-L. (2003). Wpływ reklamy porównawczej na zachowania konsumentów. *Marketing y Rynek*, 3, 2-6.

Elinder, Erik (1965). How International Can European Advertising Be? *Journal of Marketing*, 29 (2), 7-11.

Fatt, A. C. (1967). The Danger of Local International Advertising. *Journal of Marketing*, 31 (1), 60-62.

Fleury, P. (1990). Au-delà des particularismes. Quels fonds universels? *Intercultures*, 8, 119-130.

Grapard, U. (1997). Theoretical Issues of Gender in the Transition from Socialist Regimes. *Journal of Economic Issues*, 31 (3), 665-685.

Gudykunst, W. B., & Ting-Toomey, S. (1998). *Culture and Interpersonal Communication.* Sage Editions.

Hall, E. T. (1961). *The Silent Language.* New York: Anchor Press.

Hall, E. T. (1976). *Beyond Culture.* New York: Anchor Press/Doubleday.

Hall, E. T., & Hall, M. R. (1990). *Guide du comportement dans les affaires internationales.* Paris: Ed. du Seuil.

Harris, G. (1994). International Advertising Standardization: What Do the Multinationals Actually Standardize? *Journal of International Marketing*, 2 (4), 13-30.

Harris, G., & Attour, S. (2003). The International Advertising Practices of Multinational Companies: A Content Analysis Study. *European Journal of Marketing*, 37 (1/2), 154-169.

Hoeken, H., Van Den Brandt, C., Crijns, R., Dominguez, N., Hendriks, B., & Planken, B. Starren, M. (2003). International Advertising in Western Europe: Should Differences in Uncertainty Avoidance Be Considered When Advertising in Belgium, France, The Netherlands and Spain? *The Journal of Business Communication*, 40 (3), 195-218.

Hofstede, G. (1991). *Cultures and Organisations, Software of the Mind, Intercultural Cooperation and Its Importance for Survival.* New York: McGraw-Hill.

Kaynac, E., & Kara, A. (2001). An Examination of the Relationship Among Consumer Lifestyles, Ethnocentrism, Knowledge Structures, Attitudes and Behavioural Tendencies: A Comparative Study in Two CIS States. *International Journal of Advertising*, 20 (4), 455-482.

Kolman, L., Noorderhaven, N. G., Hofstede, G., & Dienes, E. (2002). Cross-Cultural Differences in Central Europe. *Journal of Managerial Psychology*, 18 (1), 76-88.

Laroche, M., Kirpalani, V. H., & Darmon, R. (1999). Determinants of the Control of International Advertising by Headquarters of Multinational Corporations. *Canadian Journal of Administrative Sciences*, 16 (4), 273-290.

Leong, E. K. F., & Huang, X. (1998). Comparing the Effectiveness of the Web Site with Traditional Media. *Journal of Advertising Research*, 38 (5), 44-51.

Lerman, D., & Callow, M. (2003). The Consumer versus the Judge: An Empirical Comparison of Approaches to Content Analysis in Cross-Cultural Advertising Research. *Advances Consumer Research*, 30 (1), 230-231.

Levitt, T. (1983). The Globalizations of Markets. *Harvard Business Review*, 61, 92-102.

Linton, R. (1945). *The cultural background of personality*, traduit en français par Andrée Lyotard, *Le fondement culturel de la personnalité.* Paris: Dunod, 1965.

Manrai, L., Lascu, D. N., Manrai, A., & Babb, H. (2001). A Cross-Cultural Comparison of Style in Eastern European Emerging Markets. *International Marketing Review*, 18 (3), 270-286.

Marcoux, J.-S. (1995). L'influence de l'origine de fabrication de produits sur les préférences des consommateurs polonais. *11ème Congrès de l'Association Française de Marketing*, Reims, ESC, 73-95.

McCullough, L. (1993). Leisure Themes in International Advertising: A Content Analysis. *Journal of Leisure Research*, 25 (4), 380-388.

Mendel, D. (1991). Comparaison des cultures allemande et française et implications marketing. *Recherche et Applications en Marketing*, 6 (3), 31-75.

Moriarty, S., & Duncan, T. (1990). Global Advertising: Issues and Practices. *Current Issues and Research in Advertising*, 13 (2), 313-341.

Nasierowski, W. (1996). Emerging Patterns of Reformations in Central Europe: The Czech Republic, Hungary, and Poland. *Journal of East-West Business*, 1, 143-171.

Okazaki, S. (2004). Does Culture Matter? Identifying Cross-national Dimensions in Japanese Multinationals' Product-based Websites. *Electronic Markets*, 14 (1), 58-69.

Raju, P. S. (1995). Consumer Behavior in Global Markets: The ABCD Paradigm and Its Application to Eastern Europe and the Third World. *Journal of Consumer Marketing*, 12 (5), 37-56.

Resnik, A., & Stern, B. L. (1977). An Analysis of Information Content in Television Advertising. *Journal of Marketing*, 41 (1), 50-53.

Roostals, I. (1963). Standardization of Advertising for Western Europe. *Journal of Marketing*, 27 (4), 15-20.

Solberg, C. A. (2002). The Perennial Issue of Adaptation or Standardization of International Marketing Communication: Organizational Contingencies and Performance. *Journal of International Marketing*, 10 (3), 1-21.

Taylor, C. R. (2002). What Is Wrong with International Advertising Research? *Journal of Advertising Research*, 42 (6), 48-54.

Vida, I., & Fairhurst, A. (1999). Factors Underlying the Phenomenon of Consumer Ethnocentricity: Evidence from Four Central European Countries. *International Review of Retail, Distribution and Consumer Research*, 9 (4), 321-337.

Walliser, B., & Moreau, F. (2000). Comparaison du style français et allemand de la publicité télévisée. *Décisions Marketing*, 19, 75-84.

Whitelock, J., & Chung, D. (1989). Cross-Cultural Advertising: An Empirical Study. *International Journal of Advertising*, 8, 291-310.

Wind, Y., & Douglas, S. P. (1986). The Myth of Globalization. *Journal of Consumer Marketing*, 3, 23-26.

Zandpour, F., Chang, C., & Catalano, J. (1992). Stories, Symbols, and Straight Talk: A Comparative Analysis of French, Taiwanese, and U.S. TV Commercials. *Journal of Advertising Research*, 32 (1), 25-38.

Zandpour, F., & Harich, K. (1996). Think and Feel Country Clusters: A New Approach to International Advertising Standardization. *International Journal of Advertising*, 15 (4), 325-345.

doi:10.1300/J037v16n01_10

APPENDIX 1. Observation Grid

A- General Information (you can tick two or more cases if necessary)

1- Category of product ☐₁ GOODS ⇨ ☐₂ SERVICE ⇨	☐₁ Cosmetic, perfume, health, hygiene ☐₄ Hi-Fi/sound/image ☐₇ Food & liquid ☐₂ Wearing, shoes, bags, jewellery,… ☐₅ Automotive, motorbikes ☐₈ Cleaning ☐₃ Computer, phone, office automation ☐₆ Household appliance ☐₉ Book, magazine, music ☐₁₀ Other goods ☐₁₁ Bank and Insurance ☐₁₃ Tourism & transport ☐₁₅ Institutional ☐₁₂ Telecommunications ☐₁₄ Distribution ☐₁₆ Entertainment ☐₁₇ Other service
2- Name of the brand if any	*Write in capital letters:*
3- Position of the brand name if it is there	☐₁ Middle of the ad ☐₂ Top of the ad ☐₃ Bottom of the ad
4- Size of the advertising	☐₁ Less than ¼ page ☐₂ ¼ page ☐₃ ½ page ☐₄ 1 page ☐₅ 2 pages or more
5- Colour	☐₁ Colour ☐₂ Black and white

B- Image (you can tick two or more cases if necessary)

1- Type of image	☐₁ Photo ☐₂ Drawing
2- The product advertised is	☐₁ Showed in the ad ☐₂ Not showed in the ad **2b- If yes, the product is showed on:** ☐₁ At least a quarter of the advertisement ☐₂ Less than a quarter
3- The environment is	☐₁ Mountain ☐₂ Urban ☐₃ Sea ☐₄ Countryside ☐₅ Indoor ☐₆ Other ☐₇ Indeterminate environment
4- In the image is there animal(s)?	☐₁ Yes ☐₂ No
5- Are there people in the image?	☐₁ None ☐₂ One ☐₃ Two or Three ☐₄ Four or Five ☐₅ Six and more
	If there is one or more people, answer to the following questions, if not, go directly to grid C **5b- Sex of people:** ☐₁ Male(s) ☐₂ Female(s) ☐₃ Indeterminate **5c- Age of people** ☐₁ Child ☐₂ Adult ☐₃ Elderly person ☐₄ Indeterminate **5d- Race** ☐₁ White ☐₂ Black ☐₃ Yellow ☐₄ Other ☐₅ Indeterminate **5e- Type of person** ☐₁ Celebrity person ☐₂ Unknown person ☐₃ Not sure (I don't know if that's a celebrity) **5f- Nudity** ☐₁ Naked person (breast or back visible) ☐₂ No naked person

C- Information (you can tick two or more cases if necessary)

1- Appearance of text in the ad (tick as many options as you have found)	☐₁ Name of the brand ☐₂ Slogan ☐₃ Explanatory comments up to 3 lines ☐₄ Explanatory comments four lines and more
2- The argumentation is based on (tick as many options as you have found)	☐₁ There is not a written argumentation (only the name of the brand) ☐₂ Symbolic information ☐₃ Description or use of the product ☐₄ Comparison (talk about a named competitor or implicit named competitor) ☐₅ Testimonial ☐₆ Promotional offer (special price, 2 in 1, game, …) ☐₇ Other type of argumentation
3- Type of information (tick as many options as you have found)	☐₁ Functional or technical features (focused on the utilisation of the product or its characteristics) ☐₂ Price or value or similar information (e.g., interest rate for a bank) ☐₃ Environmental features (focused on ecological information) ☐₄ Nothing of these information
4- Number of characteristics	If there is information about functional or technical features, the number of distinctive characteristics are: ☐₁ One or two ☐₂ Three or four ☐₃ Five or six ☐₄ More than six
5- If you have to judge this advertisement, you will say *Tick 0 if absolutely not* *Tick 5 if neither yes nor no* *Tick 10 if absolutely yes*	a- This ad evokes family values ☐₀ ☐₁ ☐₂ ☐₃ ☐₄ ☐₅ ☐₆ ☐₇ ☐₈ ☐₉ ☐₁₀ b- This ad is nonconformist ☐₀ ☐₁ ☐₂ ☐₃ ☐₄ ☐₅ ☐₆ ☐₇ ☐₈ ☐₉ ☐₁₀ c- This ad incites to the adventure ☐₀ ☐₁ ☐₂ ☐₃ ☐₄ ☐₅ ☐₆ ☐₇ ☐₈ ☐₉ ☐₁₀ d- This ad is based on the efficiency of the product ☐₀ ☐₁ ☐₂ ☐₃ ☐₄ ☐₅ ☐₆ ☐₇ ☐₈ ☐₉ ☐₁₀ e- This ad is focused on the importance of safety ☐₀ ☐₁ ☐₂ ☐₃ ☐₄ ☐₅ ☐₆ ☐₇ ☐₈ ☐₉ ☐₁₀ f- This ad shows the importance of the social status ☐₀ ☐₁ ☐₂ ☐₃ ☐₄ ☐₅ ☐₆ ☐₇ ☐₈ ☐₉ ☐₁₀ g- This ad evokes tenderness values ☐₀ ☐₁ ☐₂ ☐₃ ☐₄ ☐₅ ☐₆ ☐₇ ☐₈ ☐₉ ☐₁₀ h- This ad is focused on the bargain you could do ☐₀ ☐₁ ☐₂ ☐₃ ☐₄ ☐₅ ☐₆ ☐₇ ☐₈ ☐₉ ☐₁₀ i- This ad is erotic ☐₀ ☐₁ ☐₂ ☐₃ ☐₄ ☐₅ ☐₆ ☐₇ ☐₈ ☐₉ ☐₁₀ j- This ad is humorous ☐₀ ☐₁ ☐₂ ☐₃ ☐₄ ☐₅ ☐₆ ☐₇ ☐₈ ☐₉ ☐₁₀

APPENDIX 2. List of Magazines

Type of magazine	Title	Periodicity	Date	Price (Euro)	Total number of pages	Total number of ads	Circula-tion	Ad rates for 1p 2005	Cost per Thousand (Euro)
List of French magazines									
Managers	Capital	Monthlies	March 05	2.5	148	31	361 000	37 500	104
Managers	Challenges	Semi-month.	March 05	2.5	148	23	234 000	16 400	70
Men	Entrevue	Monthlies	March 05	3	124	27	590 000	28 900	49
Men	Maximal	Monthlies	March 05	3	124	19	147 000	13 900	95
Seniors	Notre Temps	Monthlies	March 05	3.1	174	76	1 029 000	31 500	31
Seniors	Pleine Vie	Monthlies	March 05	3	168	48	1 042 000	26 400	25
Teenagers	Fan 2	Bimonthlies	March 05	3.5	92	15	298 000	-	-
Teenagers	Star Club	Monthlies	March 05	2.7	104	24	305 000	16 300	53
Women	Elle	Weeklies	March 05	2.3	158	53	351 000	26 000	74
Women	F. Actuelle	Weeklies	March 05	1.2	104	34	1 346 000	37 650	28
List of Czech magazines									
Managers	Ekonom	Weeklies	Feb 05	1.17	66	29	23 171	5 933	256
Managers	Euro + E8	Weeklies	Feb 05	1.17	124	24	24 414	5 633	231
Men	Maxim	Monthlies	Feb 05	1.63	99	21	36 342	5 833	161
Men	Playboy	Monthlies	Feb 05	3.3	119	16	9 097	5 167	568
Seniors	Nedělní Blesk	Weeklies	March 05	0.4	47	34	342 685	9 467	28
Seniors	TV magazín	Weeklies	March 05	0.27	47	25	584 301	11 667	20
Teenagers	Bravo	Fortnightlies	Feb 05	0.65	47	9	90 362	8 667	96
Teenagers	Top dívky	Monthlies	Feb 05	1.3	83	23	60 573	3 833	63
Women	Elle	Monthlies	Feb 05	2.83	179	99	43 776	7 000	160
Women	Svět ženy	Monthlies	Feb 05	0.4	74	38	296 201	5 833	20

An Investigation of the Effect of Provocative Imagery on Norwegian and Thai Consumers' Attitudes Toward Products: A Cross-Cultural Study

Sunita Prugsamatz
Lars Ofstad
Michael Allen

SUMMARY. Despite growing interest and research in cross-cultural advertising, little has been done to address the influence of provocation on consumers' attitudes. This research investigates the effect of provocative imagery on Norwegian and Thai consumers' attitudes toward products. This study focuses on cross-cultural advertising using a nested experiment designed to investigate the impact of the provocative contents of a print advertisement on the two different cultural groups. One hundred adult subjects per culture were asked to rate two different products (Walkman and chocolate). For each culture, an experiment group (Group A) and a control group (Group B) was established. Significant differences in product ratings and attitudes were found between the groups for each culture. Norwegian respondents' attitudes were on average more negative than Thai respondents' attitudes when exposed to the provocative imagery. The findings suggest the need for advertisers to consider the impact of such provocative material in these cultures. doi:10.1300/J037v16n01_11 *[Article copies available for a fee from The Haworth Document Delivery Service: 1-800-HAWORTH. E-mail address: <docdelivery@haworthpress.com> Website: <http://www. HaworthPress.com> © 2006 by The Haworth Press, Inc. All rights reserved.]*

KEYWORDS. Provocative imagery, cross-cultural advertising, Thais, Norwegians, product ratings

INTRODUCTION

Past international marketing literature contains numerous studies concerning behavioral differences in consumers across nations (e.g., Brass 1991; McCarty and Hattwick 1991; Hafstrom, Chae et al. 1992; Lynn, Zinkhan et al. 1993; Nakata and Sivakumar 1996: Chu,

Sunita Prugsamatz is Associate Lecturer, Griffith Business School, Department of Marketing, Logan Campus (L08_1.25), Griffith University, University Drive, Meadowbrook, Queensland 4131, Australia (E-mail: s.prugsamatz@griffith.edu.au). Lars Ofstad is a PhD Candidate, Discipline of Marketing, Economics and Business Building (H69), The University of Sydney, New South Wales 2006, Australia (E-mail: l.ofstad@griffith.edu.au). Dr. Michael Allen is a Senior Lecturer in Marketing, Discipline of Marketing, Economics and Business Building (H69), The University of Sydney, New South Wales 2006, Australia (E-mail: m.allen@econ.usyd.edu.au).

[Haworth co-indexing entry note]: "An Investigation of the Effect of Provocative Imagery on Norwegian and Thai Consumers' Attitudes Toward Products: A Cross-Cultural Study." Prugsamatz, Sunita, Lars Ofstad, and Michael Allen. Co-published simultaneously in *Journal of Euromarketing* (International Business Press, an imprint of The Haworth Press, Inc.) Vol. 16, No. 1/2, 2006, pp. 153-164; and: *Contemporary Euromarketing: Entry and Operational Decision Making* (ed: Jorma Larimo) International Business Press, an imprint of The Haworth Press, Inc., 2006, pp. 153-164. Single or multiple copies of this article are available for a fee from The Haworth Document Delivery Service [1-800-HAWORTH, 9:00 a.m. - 5:00 p.m. (EST). E-mail address: docdelivery@haworthpress.com].

Available online at http://jem.haworthpress.com
© 2006 by The Haworth Press, Inc. All rights reserved.
doi:10.1300/J037v16n01_11

Spires et al. 1999; Steenkamp, Hofstede et al. 1999; Husted 2000). Social psychology suggests that cultural variation has significant impact on the way people view the world and that these views ultimately affect behavior (Manstead 1997). Seemingly, there is agreement in the marketing literature that culture greatly influences the way consumers perceive and behave (Hall 1976; McCracken 1988).

A number of past studies have made valuable contributions to the understanding of the differences among cultures in terms of informational and emotional contents in advertisements as well as use of humor, comparative cues, and sex role portrayal. These studies examining cross-cultural differences in advertising expressions can be grouped into two broad categories: the first category of studies has examined advertising expression across cultures (e.g., Japan and USA) that clearly have very dissimilar value systems (Belk and Bryce 1986; Gilly 1988; Hong, Muderrisoglu, and Zinkhan 1987; Mueller 1991; Tansey, Hyman, and Zinkhan 1990); and the other category has analyzed advertising expressions in countries (e.g., USA and Great Britain) that have less obvious cultural differences (Dowling 1980; Weinberger and Spotts 1989).

This paper extends the research in cross-cultural advertising by investigating the differences in two cultures' (Norway and Thailand) attitudes and product ratings when exposed to provocative imagery. Little or nothing has been done to examine the differences between these two cultural groups' perception of a provocative print ad despite the significant differences between the two cultures. Porter and Samovar's (1982) scale of social-cultural differences determined that Western and Eastern cultures exhibit maximum difference. Previous research studies have shown that most Asian cultures (e.g., Japanese, Chinese, and Thai) fall at the high-context culture end of the continuum, which means that consumers in these cultures tend to take very little interest in the coded, explicit part of the information message (Gudykunst and Nishida 1986). Additionally, this difference in the quantity of information and consumer-message interaction between Western (e.g., Norway) and Eastern (e.g., Thailand) marketing messages can be ex-

plained by Hall's (1976) cultural context theory. According to Hall's theory, the expression of message, especially the informativeness of the message, varies in different cultures (Wells, Burnett, and Moriarty 1995). In other words, consumers from low-context cultures (i.e., Western) may tend to draw substantially more information from the explicit content presented in communications by interacting with various messages (e.g., searching, editing, and manipulating provided contents) than do those from high-context cultures (i.e., Eastern).

Thailand and Norway seemed to be a logical pair of countries for this study for two reasons: (1) the sharp contrast in the use of provocative advertising in Thailand and Norway, and (2) the significant cultural differences between the two countries. Hofstede (1991) reported that Thailand is a high-context culture with a low individualism rank. In contrast, Norway is low-context culture with high individualism rank (low collectivist score).

Provocative appeals can reflect several aspects such as sex, nudity, violence, drugs, political and racial appeals (Vezina and Paul 1997). Sex appeal in advertising can be executed in a number of ways; some examples include double entendre, sexual attractiveness, nudity, and suggestiveness (Belch et al. 1982; Bello, Pitts and Etzel 1983; Rothschild 1987). Sex and nudity has over the years become more and more widely accepted by the society that appears less shocked and provoked by nudity in general. However, other forms of provocative appeals remain a controversial issue (Simpson, Horton and Brown 1996). Examples can be found in the area of social marketing where the understanding of the use of these controversial appeals is still at the stages of evolving research. Emotional and political appeals, as suggested by Vezina and Paul (1997), can be distinguished from sexual and other provocative appeals with the execution of strategies that apply the use of guilt, shock and compassion. This study considers an emotional and political appeal by portraying an image of an undernourished (apparently starving) child from a third-world country to respondents. This study then attempts to investigate the impact of such an image on Norwegian and Thai consumers and their attitudes towards the product and their subsequent rating of the products.

This paper will first present an overview of provocative advertising and emotional appeals, followed by the hypotheses developed for this study. The methodology has then been outlined with details of the experimental design and data analysis techniques. The final section of this paper includes reporting of the findings, discussion and implications of the results and limitations and directions for future research.

Provocative Advertising

Provocative advertising can be defined as a "deliberate appeal" (Vezina and Paul 1997) to capture audience attention. This form of advertising is founded upon three basic elements: its distinctiveness, its ambiguity and its transgression of norms and taboos (De Pelsmacker and Van Den Bergh 1996). These elements can be viewed as eliciting both negative and positive responses from audiences. Negative responses are more likely to occur with audiences' feelings of guilt, remorse or shock. However, positive responses can also be elicited as research suggests that audiences' attention to the advertisement, their memory and retrieval of information is influenced by distinctive stimuli (Childers and Houston 1984).

Current studies suggest that the use of provocative appeals such as sexual content in advertisements increases the amount of interest and attention of audiences (Bello et al. 1983) and it can also be assumed that emotional and political appeals could elicit a similar degree of interest and attention especially in terms of the shock value across national and cultural boundaries (Vezina and Paul 1997). Emotional and political appeals have been used in several social marketing contexts by organizations such as World Vision and Red Cross foundations. These organizations have sought donations and awareness through their strong advertising campaigns that use images of starving children and people from third-world countries as the key images in their advertisements. Additionally, donations and charity work have seen a revolutionary increase in the world today. In the year 2002, the member countries of the European Union donated in total 668,540 million Euro to developing coun-

tries, amongst others, African countries such as Angola, Sudan, Ethiopia and Burundi (Statistics Norway 2003). The United States of America gave 11.4 billion dollars in humanitarian aid in the year 2001. This equals 0.11 percent of its gross national income (GNI) (Statistics Norway 2003). Having such an increase in donations has not decreased nonprofit organizations' quest for better campaigns and more effective cause-related advertisements.

Research related to the advertising of causes has begun to evolve with many researchers' contributing to the understanding of such advertising, for example: Bagozzi and Moore (1994), Bendapudi, Bendapudi, Singh and Bendapudi (1996), and Brunel and Nelson (2000). Despite the growing interest, there seems to be a lack of substantial research conducted in the specific area of the effects of provocative advertising. This study is an attempt at contributing to the evolving research in the area of provocative advertising by attempting to investigate the impact of emotional provocative appeals on two different cultural groups' (low vs. high context, individualistic vs. collectivist) product ratings and attitudes towards the product.

Effects of Provocation and Emotional Appeals

The implementation of emotional advertisement messages by advertisers specially designed to "shock the emotions and make the brain itch" (Moore 1989) is a widely utilized advertising strategy. Such advertising strategies are aimed at stimulating both positive emotions and negative emotions by usually employing high impact, sensually evocative appeals (e.g., several cosmetic companies' use of highly attractive models and romantic backdrops in perfume advertisements) or graphic and extreme negative emotional advertising appeals (e.g., government sponsored antismoking ads, road safety campaigns, anti-alcohol abuse campaigns, etc.). A clear example of an extreme negative emotion ad is one TV advertisement produced and sponsored by the Australian Government featuring male and female smokers and lungs that are filled with tar. The ad contains several graphic images. A healthy lung is shown followed by another lung emersed in black tar with the voice-over appeal warning consumers of the amount of tar that can collect in human lungs when smoking for a given period of time. This ad was successful in creating awareness and although it generated mixed emotional reaction from the media audiences, it has currently been exported to several European nations that are now broadcasting the same advertisement to their audiences.

An important aspect of understanding such types of advertisements is its impact on consumers' attitudes. Previous research has proven that ad-induced emotions have a direct impact on attitude formation (Batra and Ray 1986; Edell and Burke 1987; Holbrook and Batra 1987). It has been shown that attitudes toward the ad can be influenced by both negative and positive emotions brought about by exposure to an advertising appeal (Bagozzi and Moore 1994; Stayman and Aaker 1988). However, it should also be noted that each individual could possess significantly different levels of emotional intensity and therefore have different responses to an advertising stimulus (Larsen 1984). Therefore, due to the scope of differences of their affective response to emotionally provocative appeals, some individuals may experience intense emotional discomfort when exposed to negative emotional appeals while others may be only mildly affected. However, it is unclear from past research whether the presumed individual differences in consumers' emotional reactivity do influence the way they respond to high impact emotional appeals, particularly the consumer's attitude (based on cultural factors such as high/low context cultures) toward the product.

Imagery

Advertisers can communicate provocative messages in several ways through several media, contexts and contents. The content of an advertisement is perhaps the most important factor in influencing how the advertisement is perceived and interpreted by the consumer (MacInnis and Price 1987). Ad-contents become an even more crucial aspect for advertisers when dealing with provocatively emotional appeals due to the highly visual and graphic imagery that could be portrayed in such ads. In print advertisements, emotionally provocative appeals are best portrayed with the use of imagery. Although it is important to acknowledge the integrated effect of all the elements of an advertisement, this study focuses on emotional imagery as a key contributor to consumer attitudes especially in terms of product ratings. Imagery has been defined in several ways as: "a mental event involving visualization of a concept or relationship" (Lutz and Lutz 1978), and it has also been defined as ". . . a process . . . by which . . . sensory information is represented in working memory" (MacInnis and Price 1987, p. 45).

The power of imagery in advertising is indisputable. Individuals are able to process additional information and form mental impressions and imaginations that are related to the images in the advertisements without the actual stimulus being present in the ad itself. Rossiter (1982) suggests that advertisers should particularly focus in on the operation and consequences of imagery and the implication this has on consumers and the potential of it being an influential factor on consumers' decision making. Imagery has its advantages when it comes to understanding and interpreting the complex behavior of consumers. Imagery is useful in aiding individual's "high elaboration" (MacInnis and Price 1987) processes by extracting information into an individual's working memory that had been stored in their long-term memory. By aiding this high elaboration process, it is suggested that more effective communications can be achieved (MacInnis and Jaworski 1989). Additionally, the individual's own mental processes could aid in the generation of personally relevant understanding based on the individual's past experiences.

In view of the role of imagery in consumer behavior, MacInnis and Price (1987) re-examine the three elicitation approaches (instructions to imagine, concrete words, and pictures) and agree with other researchers such as Alesandrini and Sheikh (1983) and Lutz and Lutz (1978) that imagery elicitation has practical value to advertisers. This study focuses on the usage of "pictures" as it main elicitation approach and this has several implications to advertisers and their development of ads and strategies.

Research in imagery can be traced back to its cognitive psychology roots where memory was the main focus of research in this area. Since recall is a concern of advertisers, tremendous amounts of research have been conducted in this area. Studies have shown that there is better recall when consumers are exposed to imagery in advertisements (Anderson 1978; D'Agostino, O'Neill and Paivio 1977; Elliot 1973; Lippman 1974; McKelvie and Demers 1979; Paivio and Csapo 1969; Peterson and MacGee 1974; Robbins et al. 1974; Slee 1978; Wittrock and Goldberg 1975; Wortman and Sparling 1974). Research by Krosnick et al. (1992) also showed that participants attributed more positive personality characteristics to positively primed targets and judged these people as more attractive, compared with negatively primed targets. This was achieved by manipulating affective responses to target individuals by preceding them with either positive or negative subliminal images.

Hypothesis Development

An understanding of consumers' attitudes towards different products when exposed to provocative imagery is crucial for marketers in terms of understanding whether such imagery would influence their product rating and to what extent does it do so. It is believed that attitudes will differ between cultures, and that advertisement will have a lesser negative influence on Thais than Norwegians. This is assumed due to the obvious cultural differences that do exist between the two nations (Hofstede 1991). Thais are from a high context culture and therefore would rely more on the implicit content as opposed to the explicit messages of the advertisement. Furthermore, secondary research also shows that Thai newspapers, magazines and TV-channels frequently use shocking, often repulsive, imagery from various events around the world, including starved children, mutilated bodies from bomb blasts and surgical procedures to name a few. In contrast, Norway is a highly developed country enjoying the highest standard of living in the world. Having an educated and generally well-informed population, consumers should be expected to have seen, or at least be familiar with, such imagery from the news media.

Finally, it is believed that consumers' attitudes towards a product would perhaps be more negative when emotional provocative imagery (stimulus) is present, than when the image is not present. This is believed because provocative emotional appeals would perhaps trigger emotional responses from individuals that are negative such as: shock, anxiety, guilt, compassion and even fear.

The literature on the differences between Thai and Norwegian cultures, and the resulting differences in their perception of images (analysis of implicit and explicit messages), led to the following hypotheses, each of which is divided into four separate sub hypotheses, which were tested and reported separately:

- H1: When exposed to the provocative print advertisement, there will be significant differences in product ratings between Thai and Norwegian consumers.
- H2: When Thais and Norwegians are exposed to the provocative print advertisement, product ratings toward the chocolate will be significantly different from product ratings toward the walkman.
- H3: There is a significant difference in product ratings between group A (Experiment group) and group B (Control group) in Thailand.
- H4: There is a significant difference in product ratings between group A (Experiment group) and group B (Control group) in Norway.

METHODOLOGY

Measures Development

Differences in product ratings and attitudes toward the advertisement between the two nations (Thailand and Norway) are measured using a nested-factorial (or sometimes called "between subjects") experimental design (Anderson and McLean 1974; Hicks 1973). Experimental design refers to the manner in which the experiment will be set up, specifically the way the treatments were administered to subjects (Pedhazur and Schmelkin 1991). The relative advantages and disadvantages of nested designs are opposite to those of crossed designs. Firstly, carry over effects is not a problem, as individuals are measured only once. Secondly, the number of subjects needed to discover effects is greater than with crossed designs (Anderson and McLean 1974).

The design and structure of the experiment was pre-set prior to the experiment. Two groups were chosen from each nation as the sample experiment groups with one group per nation (hereafter called Group A) designated to be exposed to the provocative stimulus and the other group per nation designated as the control group (i.e., without exposure to the provocative stimulus–hereafter called Group B). The structure of the experiment was that both groups in each country were asked to rate their opinions based on the two products Walkman and chocolate (shown to them) at the start of the experiment. Questionnaires were provided for the respondents to rate their opinions on the two products. However for Group A, prior to the respondents attempting to answer the questionnaire, the experimenter interrupted the group by presenting a digital enlargement of a provocative image. This image is then exposed throughout the experiment for the respondents to view while the attempt their questionnaires. The control group, on the other hand, were not exposed at all to the provocative stimulus.

The picture used in the experiment featured a malnourished, starving (and perhaps dying) child of African origin. The child is likely to be between 3 to 6 years of age, and is shown lying down on a piece of white cloth, with a visible presence of flies. (See Figure 1.)

Selection of the picture was done with the assistance of two senior marketing academics. A search was conducted on the World Wide Web, resulting in four relatively similar pictures of starving children being found. The most suitable image for this study was then chosen on the basis of relevance and its provocative communicative ability. The picture used in this study was selected because of its highly disturbing capabilities, as well as it being similar to those images of starving children used by, e.g., Benetton and the Red Cross

FIGURE 1. Imagery Used in the Experiment

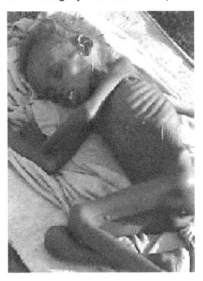

in various commercial and social advertising campaigns.

The two brands of products used in this study was a Sony Walkman (a portable CD-player), and a 300 gram box of Nestle chocolates. The specific products were chosen because they both represent typical consumer products that most people living in developed parts of the world take for granted. Products were also chosen based on the characteristics of "luxury" goods as opposed to basic survival products (such as bread and water). Additionally products are chosen based on consumers' general familiarity of such items (most consumer are familiar with chocolates and portable CD players as opposed to video game consoles or fashion items that have exclusive product lines). The products were also chosen due its convenience and accessibility in both countries. Although the pairing of the products with the image of a starving child may not be a rational one, it is believed that new advertising techniques are being introduced that cater to the media-literate audience by presenting a variety of modified and often seemingly unrelated images (Heiligmann 2003). For instance, Benetton's ads focus on race, AIDs, religion, the death penalty and other political and social issues. Benetton sells clothes and fashion items but based on the ads alone, it would be hard to tell. Advertisers are indeed competing to create the most perverse and bizarre advertisements with their main intention: to shock.

Subjects

The Thai study was conducted in a major university in the Bangkok metropolitan area. Data was collected by the first author and one senior marketing academic. The Norwegian study was conducted in a major university in the Oslo metropolitan area. The second author, assisted by one research student, undertook data collection. The respondents from both nations are chosen randomly from the population of undergraduate business students. There were a total of 50 respondents in Group A and 50 respondents in Group B in both countries, totaling 211 participants. Eleven participants were later eliminated after manipulation checks were performed. The experiment was conducted at two different time periods due to the convenience of timing for both researcher and respondents (the first experiment was conducted on Group A and the second experiment was conducted one week later on Group B). The subjects in the Group B were asked to complete a number of semantic differential items assessing attitudes towards the brands. Two questions related to gender and age, the last one asking for the respondents' mood at that time, ensuring manipulation control as general mood could be a factor that influences the respondents' attitude. Eleven respondents found to be in a bad mood at the time of the experiment were eliminated. The products (portable CD-player and chocolates) were placed clearly visible to the subjects on a table standing in front of the classroom. The subjects in Group A were asked to complete that same number of semantic differential items assessing attitudes towards the brands. However, this time the subjects were exposed to the provocative imagery (stimulus exposed from the start of the experiment), in the form of the picture of a starving child.

A total of 100 responses were collected in each country, out of which 52 were male and 48 were female in Thailand. The Norwegian sample had 50 males and 50 females. The age of the respondents ranged from 18 to 44 years, with a mean age of 23.98 years (sd = 5.00).

Measures

In this study, a seven point semantic differential scale measuring the pleasure-related aspects of a consumer's attitude toward some specific product was used. The development and testing of this scale have first been reported in a paper by Stayman and Batra (1991). The pleasure related aspects used were bad/good, unfavourable/favourable, negative/positive, dislike/like, unpleasant/pleasant, disagreeable/agreeable, low quality/high quality, bad reputation/good reputation, irresponsible/responsible and not trustworthy/trustworthy. In total, ten scales measuring attitude towards the products were used. Higher scores on the scale indicate a more positive attitude to the product. Stayman and Batra (1991) reported alphas of .85 and .96 on the four- and six-item versions of the scale. The scale used in this study is the six-item scale (developed from the format of Stayman and Batra's (1991) scale) and proved to be a reliable scale with an alpha of 0.932 obtained after reliability tests were conducted for this study.

RESULTS

The hypotheses for this research were tested and the data analyzed using techniques such as Independent Samples t-tests, two-way ANOVA and descriptive statistics. Hypothesis 1, 2, 3 and 4 were tested using Two-way ANOVA and Independent Samples T-tests, with the dependent variable for this hypothesis being the product ratings. Grouping variables were the group types, which the respondents belonged in (Group A = Experiment group; Group B = Control Group). Independent sample t-tests were used to compare the means of the two independently sampled groups (Group A and Group B) for the two countries. Two-way ANOVA technique was chosen for this study to help investigate how respondents (from the two cultures rated products when shown the provocative imagery with the advertisement). This technique was deemed appropriate as two-way ANOVAs are used when one interval dependent in terms of the categories (groups) are formed by two independents, one of which may be conceived as a control variable (Tabachnick and Fidell 1996). For this study, the dependent variable is the product ratings (Walkman and chocolate) and the independent variables being group type (Group A/Group B) and country. Finally, Two-way ANOVA is less sensitive than one-way ANOVA to moderate violations of the assumption of homogeneity of variances across the groups (Pedhazur and Schmelkin 1991).

Hypothesis 1 and 2: A two-way ANOVA was conducted to test for any significant differences between Thai and Norwegian respondents, as well as differences in product ratings. Results indicate that Thai consumers rated the products similarly (i.e., both the Walkman and chocolate are similar), indicating that they were less influenced by the provocative image. On the other hand the Norwegians were more influenced by the provocative image. Therefore it could be said that there are significant differences between how Thais and Norwegians rated the products. Additionally viewing the mean scores, Norwegians had a lower score, which means that they rated the products more negatively than the Thais. Hypothesis 1 is supported. The interaction effect of nationality and product rating resulted in a significance level of 0.004 for the Walkman and 0.006 for the chocolate. This indicates that there is a difference between how each product is rated and the provocative imagery had a greater impact on the product ratings of the chocolate. Therefore, Hypothesis 2 is also supported. The independent variable product rating gave a significance level of 0.000 for the Walkman and 0.009 for the chocolate. (See Table 1.)

Hypothesis 3 and 4: Initial independent samples T-tests conducted for the product Walkman, resulted in a significance level of 0.002 for Thailand and 0.005 for Norway (this probability level is lesser than the 0.05 level). The t-values were similar, with 7.954 and 7.877, and 7.894 and 7.822, respectively. The significance level for the Walkman was 0.000. However, using chocolate as the test variable and group type as the testing variable, this also resulted in a significance level of p < 0.05. The two-tail significance level indicates that p < 0.05 which is significant.

Independent samples T-tests for both products (Walkman and chocolate) gave a significant result for both countries (0.000), thereby indicating that Thais and Norwegians will dis-

play a less favourable attitude toward the products in the presence of a provocative image than a similar individual will display to the same products in the absence of such an image. The result of the T-tests for the Walkman product can be found in Table 2.

For the product chocolate, the results were rather similar (still significant results were obtained), and can be found in Table 3.

Independent samples T-test between groups (Walkman and chocolate) gave significant results when it comes to whether or not there is a difference between group A and group B in each country. It was found that Norwegian consumers' attitudes differed the most, indicating a stronger impact of the provocative image. The ANOVAs further support the T-tests with a significant result for differences between groups (0.000). This indicates that when exposed to the provocative imagery both cultures rated the products slightly lower than when not exposed to such imagery. However, the impact of the provocative imagery is slightly greater on Norwegians than on Thais. Therefore Hypothesis 3 and 4 are supported.

DISCUSSION

This study attempts to understand how respondents from two different cultures perceive provocative imagery in print advertisement. Results indicate that the advertisement had a more negative influence on the Norwegian respondents' attitudes towards the products and their subsequent product ratings than it did on Thai respondents. Additionally, Norwegian respondents' attitudes towards the chocolate and Walkman were significantly different (less favorable) when the image was present than when it was not present. Reasons for why this result is obtained for both the chocolate and Walkman needs further research. However, one could assume the results to be attributed to several factors. Firstly, Thais are from a high context culture and have a tendency to be more collectivistic than Norwegians (Hofstede 1991)–this suggests the provocative imagery is seen as an "explicit" message and therefore would not have a very high impact (Gudykunst and Nishida 1986). As for Norwegians, the chocolates paired with a

TABLE 1. Two-Way ANOVA Results: Test of Between-Subjects Effects

Tests of Between-Subjects Effects Dependent variable: Product ratings			Tests of Between-Subjects Effects Dependent variable: Product ratings		
	Sig.	Mean		Sig.	Mean
Group type (Thai)	.004	4.811	Group type (Norwegian)	.003	4.445
Product rating	.000	5.895	Product rating	.000	5.019
Group (Thai)*Product rating	.016		Group (Nor)*Product rating	.002	
Dependent variable: Product rating Walkman				Sig.	Mean
Group type (Thai/Norwegian)				.003	4.445
Product rating Walkman				.000	5.879
Group (Thai/Norwegian)*Product rating				.004	
Dependent variable: Product rating Chocolate					
Group type (Thai/Norwegian)				.002	4.698
Product rating chocolate				.009	5.112
Group (Thai/Norwegian)*Product rating				.006	

starving child could have been the results of the explicit message triggering feelings of guilt and compassion. Compassion and guilt can be attributed as the major elicited emotions due to the reasoning that chocolate is a luxury product that in most western countries can be considered as standard consumer goods. This was further confirmed during pre-tests and focus group interviews (done in the exploratory stages). Furthermore, when pairing the products and the image of a starving child, the respondents might have experienced guilt as they could have processes that the starving child did not have access to either what we consider essential nutrients, and certainly not chocolate and a Walkman. Second, the fact that the image has a shocking and disturbing capability can have transferred the negative attitude of the subjects to the product. Third, the fact that chocolate is something one can consume, can cause the respondents to create a strong emotional link between the product and the image of a starving child. Further research is needed to better understand the influence of these factors.

Interestingly, Thais respondents' attitudes towards the chocolate and Walkman were neutral (no significant difference) even when the provocative image was present. This result indicates that Thai respondents were less "shocked" by the provocative imagery than

the Norwegian respondents. This could be attributed to the differences between the two cultures (high versus low context cultures). Additionally it could be that Thais may have more exposure to provocative and typically shocking imagery (i.e., poverty, etc.) than Norwegians. Evidence from media releases (such as local newspapers: The Bangkok Post, Tharn Seartakit, etc.) clearly indicates the common use of explicit and provocative imagery (for instance, clear imagery on the actual remains of the person who has been hit by a car without any censorship is placed next to a Mercedes Benz ad). This could help explain the reason why Thai respondents' attitudes were not as influenced by the provocative advertisement as their Norwegian counterparts. Finally, it can be concluded that most people who are exposed to such a provocative stimulus will ultimately rate the products more negatively than when not exposed to such a stimulus. Additionally, it can be generalized that if the provocative imagery (stimulus) has some link to the product (such as the picture of the starving child used in this experiment and chocolate) it would have a higher impact on consumer's product ratings than a product that is non-related to the stimulus.

This study compliments the previous findings by Batra and Ray (1986), Edell and Burke (1987) and Holbrook and Batra (1987) that proves ad-induced emotions have a direct impact on

TABLE 2. Independent Samples Test–Product Walkman

	Sig.	T	Sig. (2-tailed)	Mean
Product: Walkman Country: Thailand	0.002	7.954	0.000	6.667
Product: Walkman Country: Norway	0.005	7.877	0.000	5.428

TABLE 3. Independent Samples Test–Product Chocolate

	Sig.	T	Sig. (2-tailed)	Mean
Product: Chocolate Country: Thailand	0.009	7.876	0.000	6.117
Product: Chocolate Country: Norway	0.024	7.924	0.000	4.798

attitude formation. On the basis of the findings of this study, it is suggested that a provocative image with an emotional appeal has an impact on attitudes toward products. The findings in this study are therefore of importance to marketers, as they can contribute in forming certain guidelines on where to place advertisements for consumer goods. It also provides an understanding of the impact of such provocative stimuli on Norwegian and Thai consumers' attitudes. Managers should be aware of the possible differences between the two consumer groups, and use caution when placing advertisements in print media in Norway. Also it can be predicted that a similar TV-ad could have the same effect as the image in this study. If this is the case, provocative ads on TV may affect consumers' attitudes toward the other programs scheduled, and their advertising content.

Limitations and Areas for Future Research

There are several limitations to this study. The main limitation being forced exposures were used when gathering data, rather than a longer repeated study. That would have required the use of imagery from real advertisements in order to avoid the experimental setting. Since this study investigates the effects of provocative imagery on attitudes toward products for the first time, it was deemed the most viable

alternative. Only two basic experiment groups were used (Group A and Group B) per culture and this could be a limiting factor as multiple experiment groups would have increased the confirmation of the findings of this study and perhaps provided a more in-depth view of results. However with using two products instead of one, the researchers attempted to increase the internal validity of the experiment. Future research should investigate the impact of the exposure of other provocative stimuli such as nudity, racism, etc., on consumers' attitudes toward different brands, loyalty, and other variables. Additionally, future research can be undertaken to see the impact of such provocative imagery (stimuli) on other variables other than product ratings such as consumers' loyalty, brand equity, corporate reputation, and other variables. Future research in this area could investigate if the placement of an advertisement between TV shows that are provocative in nature (such as shocking documentaries, horror films and erotic programs/films) would have a significant impact on consumers' (who were exposed to such a stimuli) attitudes of the product/brand being advertised. This would prove highly useful for marketers and advertisers both in the development of advertising strategies and campaigns and in the overall understanding of consumer behaviour.

REFERENCES

Alesandrini, K. L., & Sheikh, A. A. (1989). Research on Imagery: Implications for Advertising. *Imagery: Current Theory, Research and Application*, Annes A. Sheikh, ed., New York: John Wiley, 535-556.

Anderson, J. R. (1978). Arguments Concerning Representations for Mental Imagery. *Psychological Review, 85*, 249-277.

Anderson, V. L., & McLean, R. A. (1974). *Design of Experiments: A Realistic Approach*. Marcel Dekker Inc., New York.

Bagozzi, R. P., & Moore, D. J. (1994). Public Service Advertisements: Emotions and Empathy Guide Prosocial Behavior. *Journal of Marketing, 58* (January), 56-70.

Batra, R., & Ray, M. J. (1986). Affective Responses Mediating Acceptance of Advertising, *Journal of Consumer Research, 13*, (September), 234-249.

Belch, M. A., Holgersan, B. E., Belch, G. E. & Koppman, J. (1982). Psychophysiological and Cognitive Responses to Sex in Advertising, in *Advances in Consumer Research*, (9), Andrew Mitchell (ed.), Ann Arbor, MI: Association for Consumer Research, 424-427.

Bello, D. C., Pitts, R. E., & Etzel, M. J. (1983). The communication effects of controversial sexual contents in television programs and commercials. *Journal of Advertising, 12*, (3) 32-42.

Bendapudi, N., Singh, S. N., & Bendapudi, V. (1996). Enhancing helping behavior: An Integrative framework for promotion planning. *Journal of Marketing, 60* (3), 33-49.

Brass, P. R. (1991). Ethnicity and Nationalism: Theory and Comparison. *Newbury Park*: Sage Publications.

Brunel, F. F., & Nelson, M. R. (2000). Explaining gendered responses to 'help-self' and 'help-others' charity and ad appeals: The mediating role of world views. *Journal of Advertising, 29* (3), 15-28.

Childers, T. L., & Houston, M. J. (1984). Conditions for a picture-superiority effect on consumer memory. *Journal of Consumer Research, 11* (September), 643-654.

D'Agostino, P. R., O'Neill, V. J. & Paivio, A. (1977). Memory for Pictures and Words as a Function of Level of Processing: Depth or Dual Coding? *Memory and Cognition, 5* (2), 252-256.

De Pelsmacker, P., & Van Den Bergh, J. (1996). The communication of effects of provocation in print advertising. *International Journal of Advertising, 15* (3), 203-222.

Edell, J. A., & Burke, M. C. (1987). The Power of Feelings in Understanding Advertising Effects. *Journal of Consumer Research, 14*, (December), 421-433.

Elliott, L. (1973). Imagery Versus Encoding in Short- and Long-Term Memory. *Journal of Experimental Psychology, 100 (2)*, 270-276.

Gudykunst, W. B., & Nishida, T. (1986). Attributional Confidence in Low- and High-Context Cultures. *Human Communication Research, 12 (Summer)*, 525-549.

Hall, E. T. (1976). *Beyond Culture*. New York: Anchor Press. Doubleday.

Heiligmann, R. W. (2003). *How elemental codes of representation work to create meaning in contemporary print advertisements: A semiotic content analysis of advertisements appearing in the top circulated magazines of 2000*. Bowling Green State University.

Hicks, C. R. (1973). *Fundamental Concepts in the Design of Experiments* (2nd ed.). Holt, Rinehart and Winston, New York.

Hofstede, G. (1991). *Cultures and Organizations: Software of the Mind*. London: McGraw-Hill.

Holbrook, M. B., & Batra, R. (1987). Assessing the Role of Emotions as Mediators of Consumer Responses to Advertising. *Journal of Consumer Research, 14*, *(December)*, 404-420.

Hyman, M. R., Tansey, R. & Zinkhan, R. (1990). The Ethics of Psychoactive Ads. *Journal of Business Ethics, 9 (February)*, 105-114.

Krosnick, J. A., Betz, A. L., Jussim, L. J., & Lynn, A. R. (1992). Subliminal conditioning of attitudes. *Personality and Social Psychology Bulletin, 18*, 152-162.

Larsen, R. J. (1984). Theory and Measurement of Affect Intensity as an Individual Difference Characteristic. *Dissertation Abstracts International, 85*, 2297B (University Microfilms No. 84-22112).

Lippman, M. (1974). Enactive Imagery in Paired-Associate Learning. *Memory and Cognition, 2 (2)*, 385-390.

Lutz, K. A., & Lutz, R. J. (1978). Imagery-eliciting Strategies: Review and Implications of Research. In *Advances in Consumer Research, Vol. 5*, ed. H. Keith Hunt, Ann Arbor, MI: Association for Consumer Research, 611-620.

MacInnis, D. J., & Jaworski, B. J. (1989). Information Processing from Advertisements: Toward an Integrative Framework. *Journal of Marketing, 53 (October)*, 1-23.

MacInnis, D. J., & Price, L. L. (1987). The Role of Imagery in Information Processing: Review and Extensions. *Journal of Consumer Research, 13 (March)*, 473-491.

McCracken, G. D. (1988). *Culture and consumption: New approaches to the symbolic character of consumer goods and activities*. Bloomington, IN: Indiana University.

McKelvie, S. J., & Demers, E. G. (1979). Individual Differences in Ported Visual Imagery and Memory Performance. *British Journal of Psychology, 70, Part 1, (February)*, 51-57.

Moore, D. J. (1989). Advertising That Makes the Brain Itch. *MBA Update, Bureau of Business Practice*, Old Lyme, CT: Simon & Schuster Inc.

Paivio, A., & Csapo, K. (1969). Concrete Images and Verbal Memory Codes. *Journal of Experimental Psychology, 80 (2)*, 279-285.

Pedhazur, E. J., & Schmelkin, L. P. (1991). *Measurement, Design, and Analysis: An Integrated Approach*. Hillsdale, New York: Lawrence Erlbaum and Associates.

Peterson, M. J., & McGee, S. H. (1974). Effects of Imagery Instructions, Imagery Ratings, and Number of Dictionary Meanings Upon Recognition and Recall. *Journal of Experimental Psychology, 68 (3)*, 355-359.

Porter, R. E., & Samovar, L. A. (1982). *Approaching Intercultural Communication*. In *Intercultural Communication*, Larry A. Samovar and Richard E. Porter, eds., Belmont, CA: Wadsworth.

Robbins, D., Bray, J. F., Irvin, J. R., & Wise, P. S. (1974). Memorial Strategy and Imagery: An Interaction Between Instructions and Rated Imagery. *Journal of Experimental Psychology, 102 (4)*, 706-709.

Rossiter, J. R. (1982). Visual Imagery: Applications to Advertising. *Advances in Consumer Research, (9)*, ed. Andrew A. Mitchell, Ann Arbor, MI: Association for Consumer Research, 101-106.

Rothschild, M. L. (1987). *Marketing Communications*, Lexington, MA: D.C. Heath and Company.

Simpson, P., Horton, S., & Brown, G. (1996). Male Nudity in advertisements: A modified replication and extension of gender and product effects. *Journal of the Academy of Marketing Science, 24 (3)*, 257-262.

Slee, J. (1978). The Consistency of Different Manipulations of Visual Imagery: A Methodological Study. *Australian Journal of Psychology, 30 (1)*, 7-20.

Statistics Norway (2003). *Expenditures on development aid in the OECD countries.* Retrieved 28th May, 2003 from http://www.ssb.no/english/subjects/12/01/10/uhjelpoecd_en/

Stayman, D. M., & Aaker, D. A. (1988). Are All the Effects of Ad-induced Feelings Mediated by a Subliminal Ad? *Journal of Consumer Research, 15, (December)*, 368-373.

Stayman, D. M., & Batra, R. (1991). Encoding and Retrieval of Ad Affect in Memory. *Journal of Marketing Research, 28 (2)*.

Tabachnick, B. G., & Fidel, L. S. (1996). *Using Multivariate Statistics.* California State University, Northbridge: HarperCollins.

Vezina, R., & Paul, O. (1997). Provocation in Advertising: A Conceptualization and an Empirical Assessment. *International Journal of Research in Marketing, 14 (2)*, 177-192.

Wells, W., Burnett, J., & Moriarty, S. (1995). *Advertising Principles and Practice.* Englewood Cliffs, NJ: Prentice Hall.

Wittrock M. C., & Goldberg, S. I. (1975). Imagery and Meaningfulness in Free Recall: Word Attributes and Instructional Sets. *The Journal of General Psychology, 92*, 137-151.

Wortman, P. M., & Sparling, P. B. (1974). Acquisition and Retention of Mnemonic Information in Long-term Memory. *Journal of Experimental Psychology, 102 (1)*, 22-26.

doi:10.1300/J037v16n01_11

International Counterfeiting in the European Union: A Host Country Approach

J. Freitas Santos

J. Cadima Ribeiro

SUMMARY. This paper adopts a host country approach to empirically test the factors that attract international counterfeiting to the European Union. Our empirical tests show that countries' attractiveness to international counterfeiters is closely linked to corruption. Another finding is that economic development (measured by GDP per capita) is inversely associated with international counterfeiting. Therefore, counterfeiting must be seen as a public policy issue that affects society as a whole and that needs intervention from both nation-states and international authorities. Other key partners are brand owners, who need to have their own intellectual property protection in place and develop anti-counterfeiting tactics to prevent or reduce trademark counterfeiting. Global mutual cooperation between international companies is also important to lobby governments and politicians in general to ensure more effective enforcement of IPR (Intellectual Property Rights) laws and alert users and consumers about fakes. doi:10.1300/J037v16n01_12 *[Article copies available for a fee from The Haworth Document Delivery Service: 1-800-HAWORTH. E-mail address: <docdelivery@ haworthpress.com> Website: <http://www.HaworthPress.com> © 2006 by The Haworth Press, Inc. All rights reserved.]*

KEYWORDS. Counterfeiting, European Union, corruption, economic development

INTRODUCTION

In the last two decades counterfeiting and piracy have grown to a point where they have now become a widespread phenomenon with a global impact. It has fed on the steady growth of the information society and international trade, on the internationalisation of the economy, on the expansion of communication infrastructures and on the emergence of modern, sophisticated technologies that are easy to use for the purpose of copying products (Commission of the European Communities, 1998). Also, new, highly active markets for the production and consumption of counterfeit and pirated goods have sprung up in central and eastern Europe, in the former Soviet Union and in Asia (particularly China).

According to the Counterfeiting Intelligence Bureau (CIB), set up by the International

J. Freitas Santos is Professor of International Business, Institute of Accountancy and Administration, Polytechnic of Porto, Rua Jaime Lopes de Amorim, 4465 S. Mamede de Infesta, Portugal (E-mail: jfsantos@iscap.ipp.pt). J. Cadima Ribeiro is Professor of Economics, School of Economics and Management, University of Minho, Campus de Gualtar, 4710-057 Braga, Portugal (E-mail: jcadima@eeg.uminho.pt).

[Haworth co-indexing entry note]: "International Counterfeiting in the European Union: A Host Country Approach." Santos, J. Freitas, and J. Cadima Ribeiro. Co-published simultaneously in *Journal of Euromarketing* (International Business Press, an imprint of The Haworth Press, Inc.) Vol. 16, No. 1/2, 2006, pp. 165-176; and: *Contemporary Euromarketing: Entry and Operational Decision Making* (ed: Jorma Larimo) International Business Press, an imprint of The Haworth Press, Inc., 2006, pp. 165-176. Single or multiple copies of this article are available for a fee from The Haworth Document Delivery Service [1-800-HAWORTH, 9:00 a.m. - 5:00 p.m. (EST). E-mail address: docdelivery@ haworthpress.com].

Chamber of Commerce (ICC), the increase of the value of counterfeiting as a percentage of world trade rose massively from about 3.6% in 1990 to 5.6% in 1995. European companies have lost between 400 and 800 million Euros within the Union, but up to 2000 million Euros outside it (Commission of the European Communities, 1999). Both the extent of the losses and the geographic spread of the phenomenon have become a focal point of international discussion (World Trade Organisation–WTO, European Union–EU), government action (USA) and corporate responses (Green & Smith, 2002). Due to its scale, counterfeiting and piracy have a damaging effect not only on businesses, national economies and consumers, but also on society as a whole. Counterfeiting is much more than a blight on the economic and social order, as it also affects public health and public security.

Scholars in international business have dealt with counterfeiting by investigating anti-counterfeiting strategies (Chaudhry & Walsh, 1996; Green & Smith, 2002), examining common counterfeiting methods (Harvey & Ronkainen, 1985) and evaluating the economic consequences of international product counterfeiting (Globerman, 1988). However, studies which focus primarily on the causes or factors that promote counterfeiting are relatively scarce and are mostly related with intellectual property rights protection (Fink & Primo Braga, 1999; Javorcik, 2002; Ronkainen & Guerrero-Cusumano, 2001; Aryanto, 2003).

There are two empirical facts that motivate this paper. First, the increased seizures of counterfeit goods at the external borders of the EU, and the concomitant growing international concern about the problem. Second, the volatility of the seizures by EU member states, suggesting that some host countries are more vulnerable to counterfeiters than others.

This paper adopts a dual approach in assessing the impact of counterfeiting on the EU. First, some data on seizures in the EU countries are analysed in order to approach the size and evolution of the phenomenon. Then, we search for counterfeiting related variables in order to understand why some countries are more vulnerable than others.

The definition and legal framework of counterfeiting are presented in the next sec-

tion. The following section defines the nature and extent of the counterfeiting phenomenon in the EU member states. The next section presents a literature review of the linkages between counterfeiting and corruption, trade (imports), economic development (GDP per capita) and economic freedom. The remainder of the paper is dedicated to analysing the methodology used and the results of the econometric work. We conclude by discussing managerial and policy implications.

COUNTERFEITING INDUSTRY: LEGAL FRAMEWORK AND DEFINITION

The work of the World Intellectual Property Organisation (WIPO) and the Agreement on Trade-Related Aspects of Intellectual Property Rights (TRIPS) of the World Trade Organisation (WTO) provide the legal framework for the enforcement of intellectual property rights and the limiting of trade of counterfeit goods. According to the TRIPS agreement, the owner of a registered trademark has the exclusive right to prevent all third parties from using an identical or similar mark without the owner's consent, if this use would create a likelihood of confusion (article 15).

In the European Union, Regulation (EC) nr 3295/94 states that counterfeit goods are those bearing a trademark that is identical to, or indistinguishable from, a trademark registered to another party and that infringes the rights of the holder of the trademark. Pirated goods are copies that were made without the consent of the holder of the copyright or related rights.

According to the Green Paper (Commission of the European Communities, 1998), the concepts of counterfeiting and piracy cover all products, processes and services that are the subject-matter or result of an infringement of an intellectual property right (trade mark or trade name, industrial design or model, patent, utility model and geographical indication), of a copyright or neighbouring right (the rights of performing artists, the rights of producers of sound recordings, the rights of the producers of the first fixations of films, the rights of broadcasting organisations), or of the *sui generis* right of the maker of a data base. This broad definition covers not only the case of products that are copied fraudulently (fakes), but also the case of products that are identical to the original ones but are made without the rightholder's consent. Piracy in the services sphere covers mainly broadcast services and services linked to the development of the information society.

The definition does not cover look-alike products (duplication of the original product and bearing different names, but not a private label of a branded industrial product), reproductions that are not exact copies or unconvincing imitations.

The absence of a uniform international definition of counterfeiting and piracy raises problems in circumscribing the boundaries of legal and illegal pratices. On the side of intellectual property right-holders, the incentive is to extend the boundaries in order to include practices that some observers would deem legitimate manifestations of competition. The international organisations' (WTO, EU) role is to maintain the legal infrastructure surrounding intellectual property, but it should not create incentives for anti-competitive or other rent-seeking behaviours beyond those already inherent to the acquisition of an exclusive property right (Globerman, 1988; Organisation for Economic Co-operation and Development, 1998).

As there is no generally agreed clear demarcation between piracy and counterfeiting, this paper will refer to all cases as counterfeiting, as collected by the services of the European Commission (Taxation and Customs Union Directorate-General, 2005).

PATTERNS OF COUNTERFEITING AT THE EXTERNAL BORDER OF THE EUROPEAN UNION (2000/2004)

The European Commission surveyed seizures of counterfeit products between 2000 and 2004 (Taxation and Customs Union Directorate-General, 2005). During this period, 50,904 cases were reported by the Customs Authorities of the 15 European Union countries. The largest numbers came from Germany (16,220 cases), the United Kingdom (7,490 cases) and France (7,237 cases).

Smaller countries like Portugal, Greece and Luxembourg reported also the smallest number of cases (Table 1).

The total number of seizures between 2000 and 2004 improved in all countries, with significant increases in the last three years in Italy (+658%), Austria (+756%), the Netherlands (+230%), France (+200%) and Spain (+190%). One of the reasons for this continuing growth in fakes is due to sophisticated technologies that criminals use to produce goods on an industrial scale.

As displayed in Table 2, the type of products confiscated by customs officials between 2000/2004, included clothing and accessories (57.6% of cases), media (15.2%) and watches and jewellery (10.1%). Most fakes imitate well-known brands of clothing, accessories and watches (luxury goods) of high quality, making identification difficult to consumers. Media products (CDs, DVDs and software) continued to be popular choices for counterfeiters, ranking second in the number of cases seized by customs. The counterfeiting of toys and games, which could damage health and safety of European children, grew during this period and these were the fifth most counterfeited products found at the external border of the EU.

Table 3 lists the three most counterfeited brands, by product, for the 2000/2004 period. A brand is a very valuable, intangible asset, the result of consumer goodwill built up over years. A global brand not only symbolises the sum of attributes that make up the brand, but also creates an image in the minds of consumers. The image of counterfeit merchandise at the external border of the EU tended to centre on *Armani*, *Chanel* and *Boss* perfumes, *Nike* and *Adidas* sportswear, *Ralph Lauren* polo shirts, *Vuitton* bags, *Nokia* cellular phones, *Rolex* watches and *Nintendo* games. Well-known global brands such as *Sony*, *Epson*, *Intel* and *HP* (*Hewlett Packard*) were ranked first during this period on items related with computer equipment. Both the IFPI (The International Federation of the Phonographic Industry), who represents the majority of record producers worldwide, and the MPA (the Motion Picture Association, a similar organisation to the movie industry), reported an increased number of pirated CDs and DVDs.

TABLE 1. Ranking of the Most Counterfeiter Host Countries, by Number of Cases Registered in the External Border of EU15 (2000/2004)

Countries	2000/2004		Ranking
	N	%	
Germany	16,220	31.9	1
United Kingdom	7,490	14.7	2
France	7,237	14.2	3
Netherlands	4,374	8.6	4
Spain	2,996	5.9	5
Belgium	2,721	5.3	6
Austria	2,272	4.5	7
Italy	2,090	4.1	8
Denmark	1,506	3.0	9
Ireland	1,345	2.7	10
Sweden	1,293	2.5	11
Finland	653	1.3	12
Luxembourg	359	0.7	13
Portugal	213	0.4	14
Greece	135	0.2	15
Total	50,904	100.0	

Source: Taxation and Customs Union Directorate-General, 2005.

TABLE 2. Ranking of the Most Counterfeited Products, by Number of Cases Registered in the External Border of EU15 (2000/2004)

Product type	2000/2004 (a)		Ranking
	N	%	
Clothing and accessories	29,862	57.6	1
CD (audio, software, etc.), DVD	7,861	15.2	2
Watches and jewellery	5,210	10.1	3
Other goods	4,245	8.1	4
Toys and games	1,868	3.6	5
Electrical equipment	1,546	3.0	6
Perfumes and cosmetics	479	0.9	7
Cigarettes	446 (b)	0.8	8
Computer equipment	255	0.5	9
Foodstuffs, alcoholic and other drinks	111	0.2	10
Total	51,883	100.0	

Source: Taxation and Customs Union Directorate-General, 2005.
Notes: (a) EU25 for 2004; (b) registered after 2003.

As displayed in Table 4, the vast majority of counterfeited products originated in China. In 2004 in particular, China was ranked first in seven of the nine product categories seized by the customs authorities at the external border of the EU. Thailand (clothing and accessories), Hong Kong (computer equipment) and Turkey (perfumes and cosmetics) were very common sources too. Statistics of the Member States seem to show that European countries such as Belgium, Greece, Spain and Portugal were also involved in the production of counterfeit goods.

DEVELOPMENT OF HYPOTHESES AND MEASURES

The European Commission collects data on all counterfeit goods confiscated at the external border of the EU (Taxation and Customs Union Directorate-General, 2005). For every case, the EU customs services record the country of origin, type of product and brand, among other characteristics of the seizure. Given the illegal nature of counterfeiting, these cases represent only a fraction of fraudulent goods entering the EU marketplace each year. Therefore, the number of cases detected may say more about the efficiency and competency of the EU customs authorities than about the level of counterfeiting. However, ambiguity arises when there is no agreement about the factors that should be taken into account when calculating the scale of counterfeiting (Green & Smith, 2002). As this specific issue is rather debatable and beyond the scope of this paper, we will use the data from the European Commission in order to achieve a measure for counterfeiting, that is, the average seizure of counterfeit goods detected at the external borders of the EU countries.

As there is a lack of prior empirical evidence on the linkage between counterfeiting and other variables, we propose that the presence of counterfeiting in a host country would be the result of the presence of corruption, economic freedom, level of economic development and trade (imports).

Counterfeiting and Corruption

There is no consensus among researchers regarding the measurement of corruption. Objective measures are hardly available because of the obvious secrecy that surrounds corrupt dealings. Subjective measures relying on ques-

TABLE 3. Three Most Counterfeited Brands (Number of Cases), by Product Type (2000/2004)

Product type	Years	1°	2°	3°
Foodstuffs, alcoholic and other drinks	2000	Nintendo	Disney	Moskovskaya
	2001	Nintendo	Disney	Guiness
	2002	Charles	Disney	Grant's
	2003	Disney	Aust. Apples	Konar Lebe
	2004	Lipton	Spirits P. Inter.	Coca-Cola
Perfumes and cosmetics	2000	Armani	Calvin Klein	Dior
	2001	Chanel	Armani	Dior
	2002	Boss	Calvin Klein	Gucci
	2003	Boss	Armani	Vuitton
	2004	Beiersdorf	P&G	L'Oreal
Clothing and accessories	2000	Nike	Adidas	Ralph Lauren
	2001	Nike	Adidas	Vuitton
	2002	Nike	Adidas	Ralph Lauren
	2003	Vuitton	Nike	Burberrys
	2004	Vuitton	Nike	Adidas
Electrical equipment	2000	Nokia	Motorola	Ericsson
	2001	Nokia	Disney	Ericsson
	2002	Nokia	Philips	Panasonic
	2003	Nokia	Philips	Sony
	2004	Philips	Nokia	Osram
Computer equipment	2000	Sony	Intel	Nintendo
	2001	Epson	Sony	Nintendo
	2002	Sony	Epson	Philips
	2003	Intel	Philips	Epson
	2004	HP	Samsung	Sisvel
CD (audio, software, etc.), DVD	2000	Sony	IFPI	FDV GVU
	2001	IFPI	Philips	Disney
	2002	MPA	IFPI	Nintendo
	2003	MPA	IFPI	Philips
	2004	Philips	FACT	Philip Morris
Watches and jewellery	2000	Rolex	Breitling	Cartier
	2001	Rolex	Breitling	Gucci
	2002	Rolex	Breitling	Gucci
	2003	Rolex	Breitling	Cartier
	2004	Rolex	Adidas	Gucci
Toys and games	2000	Nintendo	Disney	Sony
	2001	Nintendo	Disney	Warner
	2002	Taiwan Moto	Nintendo	Disney
	2003	Nintendo	Hasbro	Disney
	2004	Konami	Upper Desck	Disney
Other goods	2000	Pfizer	Nintendo	Disney
	2001	Nokia	Nintendo	Disney
	2002	Nokia	Pfizer	Disney
	2003	Nokia	Pfizer	Disney
	2004	Duracell	Bic	Pfizer

Source: Taxation and Customs Union Directorate-General, 2005.

tionnaire-based surveys represent an acceptable alternative as they measure the perception of corruption rather than corruption per se (Husted, 1999; Habib & Zurawicki, 2002; Zhao, Kim & Du, 2003; Robertson & Watson, 2004). Various corruption indices have been developed by several institutions and have been used by various researchers (Tanzi, 1998). In this study, the Transparency International Corruption Perceptions Index is used.

Transparency International (2005) defines corruption as the misuse of public power for private benefit. The index is based on ten international surveys of the perceptions of business people and country experts regarding corruption in over 50 countries around the world. The index was calculated by taking the simple average of the normalized results of the individual surveys. The corruption index is a continuous scale from 0 to 10, where 10 repre-

TABLE 4. Three Most Counterfeiter Countries (Number of Cases), by Product Type (2000/2004)

Product type	Years	1°	2°	3°
Foodstuffs, alcoholic and other drinks	2000	Turkey	Poland	Czech Rep.
	2001	Turkey	China	Portugal
	2002	Thailand	China	Turkey
	2003	Turkey	Poland	Chile
	2004	Russia	Ukraine	Dom. Rep.
Perfumes and cosmetics	2000	Greece	Turkey	South Korea
	2001	Turkey	UAE	USA
	2002	Turkey	Spain	China
	2003	UAE	Turkey	Thailand
	2004	UAE	Turkey	USA
Clothing and accessories	2000	Thailand	Czech Rep.	Turkey
	2001	Thailand	China	Turkey
	2002	Thailand	Turkey	China
	2003	Thailand	China	Turkey
	2004	China	Thailand	Turkey
Electrical equipment	2000	Taiwan	Hong Kong	China
	2001	Hong Kong	China	Taiwan
	2002	China	Hong Kong	Turkey
	2003	China	Hong Kong	Taiwan
	2004	China	Hong Kong	UAE
Computer equipment	2000	Hong Kong	China	Taiwan
	2001	Hong Kong	China	Japan
	2002	Hong Kong	Taiwan	China
	2003	China	Hong Kong	UAE
	2004	China	Hong Kong	Russia
CD (audio, software, etc.), DVD	2000	Thailand	Malaysia	Singapore
	2001	Thailand	Belgium	Taiwan
	2002	Thailand	Malaysia	Belgium
	2003	Thailand	Malaysia	Pakistan
	2004	China	Thailand	Malaysia
Watches and jewellery	2000	USA	Thailand	Hong Kong
	2001	Thailand	USA	Hong Kong
	2002	Thailand	Hong Kong	China
	2003	Thailand	China	Hong Kong
	2004	China	Hong Kong	Thailand
Toys and games	2000	China	USA	Hong Kong
	2001	China	USA	Hong Kong
	2002	China	Thailand	Hong Kong
	2003	China	Thailand	Hong Kong
	2004	China	India	Hong Kong
Other goods	2000	USA	China	Poland
	2001	China	Hong Kong	Taiwan
	2002	China	USA	Hong Kong
	2003	China	Hong Kong	India
	2004	China	India	Hong Kong

Source: Taxation and Customs Union Directorate-General, 2005.
Notes: UAE–United Arab Emirates; USA–United States of America.

sents a completely clean country and 0 represents an absolutely corrupt one. This index was transformed by subtracting it from 10 in order to obtain an increasing scale of corruption (Husted, 1999; Sanyal & Samanta, 2004).

To counterfeiters, a high presence of corruption may foreshadow a potential market in which the regulatory regime perceives counterfeiting as a minor problem and is less aware of enforcement of intellectual property rights and of the need to implement anti-counterfeit-ing policies. Thus, the following relationship is hypothesized:

H1: The higher the level of perceived corruption, the higher the incidence of counterfeiting.

Counterfeiting and Economic Freedom

Economic freedom is defined as the absence of government coercion or constraint on the production, distribution or consumption of goods and services beyond the extent necessary for citizens to protect and maintain liberty itself (Beach & Miles, 2002).

To measure economic freedom, we used the Economic Freedom Index (EFI) that has been developed by an American think tank (Heritage Foundation, 2006). This composite index incorporates 50 independent economic variables that fall into 10 broad categories of economic freedom. Countries are rated from 1 to 5, where a score of 1 reflects maximum economic freedom and five the least. The ten categories of economic variables used to develop the summary index are: trade policy, fiscal government burden, government intervention in the economy, monetary policy, capital flows and foreign investment, banking and finance rules, wages and prices, property rights, regulation and black market activity. As with other overall measures, we can argue about the relative importance of the different variables. However, the EFI can be used as a basis for comparing countries (Sanyal & Samanta, 2004).

In some countries where EFI is high, there is a prevailing belief that counterfeiting constitutes no wrongdoing. On the contrary, intellectual property is generally considered a common good of mankind and a precious tool for economic development. Therefore, relevant laws on intellectual property should allow free access rather than place restrictions on its use. Concomitantly, many foreign governments are unable or unwilling to enforce anti-counterfeiting laws because of expected economic and political repercussions (Nill & Shultz, 1996). Currently, the government of China does not advocate intellectual property theft and counterfeiting; yet, it does have as one of its primary economic policies the acquisition of free technology through its government controlled companies. Some developing countries accepted TRIPS (Trade-Related Aspects of Intellectual Property Rights) not necessarily because the adoption of intellectual property was high on their list of priorities, but partly because they seemed to endorse the view that the overall package offered numerous benefits, including the reduction of trade protectionism in developed countries

(Aryanto, 2003). Thus, the following relationship is hypothesized:

H2: The lower the level of economic freedom (higher values in the index), the higher the incidence of counterfeiting.

Counterfeiting and Economic Development

Economic development is a multifaceted concept that conveys improvements in the quality of life and life opportunities (Rephann, 1999). A surrogate indicator to measure economic development is gross domestic product (GDP) per capita. Purchasing power parity estimates of GDP per capita were used, since these estimates reflect differences in the cost of living from country to country (United Nations Development Programme, 2004).

Some studies have examined the economic impact of international counterfeiting (Nill & Shultz, 1996; Organisation for Economic Co-operation and Development, 1998). In general, they tend to conclude that foreign counterfeiting has ambiguous overall welfare effects for the host economy, per se. The most obvious benefit to domestic consumers is an increase in consumer surplus associated with lower priced imports that are acceptable substitutes for authentic goods. However, potential costs to domestic consumers have been found due to losses in status and low quality or related damages of counterfeit goods. Also, domestic producers have to face competition from imported counterfeits or incur costs to prevent and surveil counterfeiting. Therefore, the net welfare effect is likely to vary across countries depending upon, among other things, the country's stage of development and the sophistication of its consumers (Globerman, 1988). In rich countries where consumers are more sophisticated we expect less interest in counterfeited goods. This leads to the following relationship:

H3: The higher the level of GDP, the lower the incidence of counterfeiting.

Counterfeiting and Trade (Imports)

We measured trade as the percentage of imported goods from extra member states, at market prices, in the gross domestic product, since seizures of counterfeited goods are detected at the external border of the EU. Trade data were gathered from the Statistical Office of the European Communities (European Commission, 2004).

This hypothesis attempts to examine the extent to which counterfeiting is trade-related (Fink & Primo Braga, 1999), specifically imports, as we can argue that seizures are dependent on the total volume of imports. The greater the volume of host country imports, the bigger the probability of counterfeited goods being caught at the external borders of EU member states. According to this rationale, we expected the following relationship:

> H4: The higher the level of imports, the higher the incidence of counterfeiting.

METHODOLOGY

To empirically test the hypotheses outlined above, we have collected data from the 15 countries of EU in the years 2000, 2001 and 2002. The result is a database with 45 observations. As the detection of counterfeited goods at the external borders of the EU by customs authorities is random, we may consider this a random sample.

We have modelled counterfeiting seizures using a simplified form approach. The mathematical expression of our model is specified as follows:

$$LCTF_{it} = \alpha_i + \beta_1\, ECDV_{it} + \beta_2\, ECFR_{it} + \beta_3\, CORR_{it} + \beta_4\, IMP_{it} + \varepsilon_{it}$$

$$\varepsilon_{it} = \mu_i + \nu_{it}$$

where i denotes different countries, t denotes different years, L indicates the natural logarithm and CTF (Counterfeiting) is the number of articles seized, divided by the number of cases as reported to the European Commission by the customs authorities of the member states (Taxation and Customs Union Directorate-General, 2005). $ECDV$ (Economic Development) is measured by the natural logarithm of the per capita gross domestic product (United Nations Development Programme, 2004). $ECFR$ (Economic Freedom) is the index of

economic freedom reported by the Heritage Foundation (2006). $CORR$ (Corruption) is the index published by Transparency International (2005). IMP (Imports) is extra EU imports of goods measured as a percentage of gross domestic product at market prices (European Commission, 2004). α_i denotes the unobserved individual effects.

The residual term, ε_{it}, includes two components: the unobservable host country specific effects, μ_i, and the remaining disturbance, ν_{it}. Here, we explicitly assume that there are some unobservable country individual effects, μ_i, such as cultural factors, which cannot be explained by the included explanatory variables. This assumption poses the problem of omitted variable bias, which means that the impact of the factors not included in the model are captured partly by other factors. However, the extension of the model, in view of the scarce number of observations, would most likely be counter-productive, as degrees of freedom would be reduced.

Another problem is endogeneity, which means that it may be difficult to separate the impact of different exogenous variables. In our model, although some variables are expected to be correlated, we have some confidence that their coefficients will not necessarilly be capturing effects of other explanatory variables.

Since the objective of this study was to explain international counterfeiting to EU host countries and not estimate the individual contributions of the exogenous variables, we can surpass these problems.

RESULTS

To determine the validity of the hypotheses (H1-H4) concerning the variables that attract counterfeiting to EU countries, we used an OLS (Ordinary Least Squares) regression analysis. Prior to running multiple regression, tests were conducted using Pearson correlations to test the relationship between the variables.

Table 5 reports the means, standard deviations, and correlations of all variables included in the study. We have tested the presence of

TABLE 5. Descriptive Statistics and Pearson Correlation Matrix

	Mean	SD	LCTF	ECDV	ECFR	CORR	IMP
LCTF00	9.07	1.82	1				
LCTF01	8.86	1.62	1				
LCTF02	8.36	2.08	1				
LCTFtot	8.76	1.83	1				
ECDV00	10.12	0.25	−0.286	1			
ECDV01	10.14	0.26	−0.32	1			
ECDV02	10.22	0.28	−0.491	1			
ECDVtot	10.16	0.26	−0.393*	1			
ECFR00	2.17	0.25	0.556**	−0.713**	1		
ECFR01	2.13	0.29	0.481	−0.735*	1		
ECFR02	2.12	0.31	0.539**	−0.536**	1		
ECFRtot	7.71	8.48	0.141	−0.106	1		
CORR00	2.42	1.67	0.374	−0.426	0.485	1	
CORR01	2.45	1.55	0.412	−0.51	0.61**	1	
CORR02	2.44	1.64	0.521**	−0.40	0.801*	1	
CORRtot	2.44	1.58	0.433*	−0.462*	0.136	1	
IMP00	14.09	5.97	0.169	0.58**	−0.578**	−0.095	1
IMP01	13.58	5.39	−0.008	−0.245	−0.671*	−0.188	1
IMP02	12.61	4.88	−0.368	0.627**	−0.503	−0.217	1
IMPtot	13.43	5.34	−0.045	0.58*	−0.02	−0.16	1

Note: N = 45; *Correlation is significant at the 0.01 level (2-tailed); **Correlation at the 0.05 level (2-tailed).

multicollinearity in the model. The correlations between exogenous variables are not so high as to prevent us from a precise analysis of their individual effects, e.g., the variable-inflation factor (VIF) is less than 5.3, a threshold value that indicates the presence of multicollinearity (Hair, Anderson, Tatham & Black, 1995).

The results indicate a moderate positive relationship ($r^2 = 0.43$) between high average seizures of counterfeiting (LCTF) and high corruption (CORR). Also, counterfeiting is positively correlated with economic freedom (ECFR), suggesting a higher incidence of counterfeiting in markets where the degree of economic freedom is lower. Economic development (ECDV) and the level of counterfeiting are inversely associated ($r^2 = -0.393$), suggesting that the higher the level of GDP per capita, the lower the incidence of counterfeiting.

We also noted moderate correlations between the variables ECDV, ECFR, CORR and IMP when the three years period was considered.

Analyzing each of the four regression equations, we observe some instability in the independent variables, as the seizures of counterfeited goods are random, varying greatly during different periods across the

different countries. The adjusted coefficient of determination ranged from 0.57 to 0.10 across the four regressions. The 2000/2002 regression was used to accommodate the variability of the data and test the hypotheses.

The results are reported in Table 6 and provided support for two of our hypotheses. First, the corruption hypothesis (H1) was supported, as countries that have perceived higher levels of corruption tended to have higher levels of incidence of counterfeiting. From the counterfeiter perspective, a corrupted country means less enforcement of property rights protection and easier access to its market and business transactions. Otherwise, to the host country corruption represents lost tax revenues, since the counterfeiters are normally sold through clandestine channels. From the producers' point of view, the existence of corruption means direct losses in sales and consumer goodwill, unfair competition and more costs in protecting and enforcing intellectual property rights (IPR).

Secondly, the economic development hypothesis was supported (H3). Countries characterized by higher levels of GDP per capita tended to have lower incidence of counterfeiting. In poor countries most consumers are not willing to pay a considerably higher price for the authentic good if the counterfeit item of-

TABLE 6. Results of OLS Regression (Dependent Variable LCTF)

	2000/2002	2000	2001	2002
Constant	34.158** (2.64)	−7.524 (−0.35)	4.301 (0.166)	22.031 (0.756)
ECDV	−0.388** (−2.079)	−0.032 (−0.121)	−0.124 (−0.325)	−0.204 (−0.551)
ECFR	0.483 (0.483)	1.018** (3.63)	0.836** (1.825)	0.095 (0.184)
CORR	0.281*** (1.82)	−0.285 (−0.285)	−0.045 (−0.131)	0.322 (0.704)
IMP	0.226 (1.35)	0.771** (3.26)	0.624 (1.661)	−0.121 (−0.334)
N	45	15	15	15
R^2 Adj	0.27	0.571	0.186	0.109
F statistic	3.758**	5.656**	1.801	1.429

Note: Standardization coefficients with T statistics in parentheses.
*$p = < 0.01$; **$p = < 0.05$; ***$p = < 0.10$.

fers similar qualities. Consumers who purchase these goods subject themselves to social risk because the goods are of high symbolic value and social visibility. However, as long as the counterfeit good is not readily discernible as fake, it fulfills its function as well as the authentic item (Nill & Shultz, 1996).

We found no support for the economic freedom hypothesis (H2), and the trade related one (H4). Therefore, lower economic freedom, although positively correlated with counterfeiting, does not appear to be statistically significant in explaining the attraction of counterfeited goods to the external border of the EU. The variable IMP shows no significant relationship with the measure of counterfeiting.

CONCLUSION: POLICY AND MANAGERIAL IMPLICATIONS

What policy and managerial implications do these results have for the study and control of counterfeiting? Since counterfeiting activities are intrinsically related with corruption and lack of economic development, then governments, international agencies and organisations have strong reasons to be worried about counterfeiting. Corruption is an obstacle to investment and business efficiency and when associated with counterfeiting has severe

consequences on employment creation, tax revenue, innovation, and economic growth. Therefore, counterfeiting must be seen as a public policy issue that affects society as a whole and so needs intervention from both nation-states and international authorities.

At European Union level, an action plan to halt the increase in counterfeiting has already been implemented. This plan focuses on enforcement of existing IPR laws, supported by the creation of public-private partnerships, giving priority to the most problematic third countries where enforcement actions are concentrated. To attain this goal, stress is laid on technical cooperation and assistance and some initiatives to raise user and consumer awareness. In the case of systematic violations of IPR, sanction mechanisms (bilateral and multilateral) could be activated against any country (European Union, 2004).

Beyond the EU, various international and regional agreements have been enacted to assist in protecting IPR. The North American Free Trade Agreement (NAFTA) provides guidance for the protection of IPRs in Canada, the United States and Mexico. In South America, the Southern Cone Common Market (MERCOSUR) implemented a regional protection plan that includes provisions to combat counterfeiting. The Andean Community adopted a Common Intellectual Property regime to harmonize its members' IPR laws in accordance with TRIPS Agreement. The Association of Southeast Asian Nations (ASEAN) also has a general framework in place to improve IPR enforcement, administration, legislation and public awareness (International Trademark Association, 2004, p. 5). Other international agencies are helping to prevent illegal practices of counterfeiting, such as the World Intellectual Property Organisation (WIPO), a specialised agency of the United Nations, the World Customs Organisation (WCO), and the World Health Organisation (WHO) (Council of Europe, 2004).

Other key partners in the fight against counterfeiting are property owners who see consumer goodwill and their brands' prestige erode and their competitive advantage disappear. Many counterfeiters boast highly-skilled workforces, high-tech distribution networks and sophisticated manufacturing facilities, allowing them to compete head-on with legitimate companies. Therefore, the role played by international firms should be analysed at two different levels. First, brand owners need to have their own intellectual property protection in place. After that, developing anti-counterfeiting tactics can be an effective way of preventing or reducing trademark counterfeiting. This often includes using key features on the genuine article that are difficult to copy, such as official seals or distinctive detailing. Many brand owners also use the addition of forensic features to products or packaging as a means of authentication. This includes overt features such as holograms, or covert features such as invisible fluorescent inks, taggants, digital water marking, bar coding or tracking (International Trademark Association, 2004, p. 6).

Secondly, international firms must be enrolled in global mutual cooperation associations such as the International Trademark Association (INTA), the International Anti-Counterfeiting Coalition (IACC) and the Global Business Leaders' Alliance Against Counterfeiting (GBLAAC), as well as industry specific groups, including the International Federation of the Phonographic Industry (IFPI) and the Business Software Alliance (BSA), to lobby governments and politicians in general to ensure better enforcement of IPR laws and alert users and consumers about fakes. Thus, the fight against international counterfeiting is a complex phenomenon that must be pursued on many fronts. The greatest mistake that can be made is to rely on a strategy that depends excessively on actions at a single level (intergovernmental agencies, national governments, nonprofit organizations, coalitions of firms, firms). Any realistic strategy must start with an explicit recognition that there are those who supply counterfeit goods, but there are also consumers willing to pay for them. This suggests the need for sustained improvements in education, employment, and income, as well as for social and economic policies that favour law enforcement.

The results of this exploratory study are encouraging, but should be evaluated in the context of the following limitations, some of which also provide directions for future research. First, valuable insights into the relationship between counterfeiting and culture can be gained from future studies that examine culture implications for host and source countries. These may include Hofstede (1991) four cultural dimensions: large versus small power distance, individualism versus colectivism, masculinity versus femininity, and strong versus weak uncertainty avoidance. Second, new measures of counterfeiting should be investigated in order to compare the results associated with each and enrich the analysis. Finally, future research using a longer period of time, more explanatory variables, and different methodologies might also be able to shed more light on counterfeiting from the empirical side.

REFERENCES

Aryanto, V. D. W. (2003). Intellectual property rights theft in far east countries. *Journal of Business Administration*, 2 (2), article 1, Retrieved March 1, 2005, from http://jbao.atu.edu/articl1.html

Beach, W. W., & Miles, M. A. (2002). Explaining the factors of the index of economic freedom. Retrieved February 13, 2006, from http://www.heritage.org/research/features/index/chapters/pdfs/Index2006_chap5.pdf

Commission of the European Communities (1998). Green paper: Combating counterfeiting and piracy in the single market. Office for Official Publications of the European Communities, Luxembourg.

Commission of the European Communities (1999). Final report on responses to the European Commission green paper on counterfeiting and piracy. Office for Official Publications of the European Communities, Luxembourg.

Chaudhry, P. E., & Walsh, M. G. (1996). An assessment of the impact of counterfeiting in international markets. *Columbia Journal of World Business*, XXXI (3), 34-48.

Council of Europe (2004). Counterfeiting: Problems and solutions. Retrieved March 5, 2005, from http://assembly.coe.int/Documents/WorkingDocs/doc04/EDOC10069.htm

European Commission (2004). Statistical Annex. *European Economy*, n. 6, Office for Official Publications of the European Communities, Luxembourg.

European Union (2004). EU strengthens fight against piracy and counterfeiting beyond its borders. Retrieved November 10, 2004, from http://www.eurunion.org/News/press/2004/200400160.htm

Fink, C., & Primo Braga, C. A. (1999). How stronger protection of intellectual property rights affects international trade flows. *World Bank*, Working Paper, 2051.

Globerman, S. (1988). Adressing international product piracy. *Journal of International Business Studies*, 19 (3), 497-504.

Green, R., & Smith, T. (2002). Executive insights: Countering brand counterfeiteirs. *Journal of International Marketing*, 10 (4), 89-106.

Habib, M., & Zurawicki, L. (2002). Corruption and Foreign Direct Investment. *Journal of International Business Studies*, 33 (2), 291-307.

Hair, J. F., Anderson, R. E., Tatham, R. L., & Black, W. C. (1995). Multivariate data analysis. Fourth Edition, Prentice Hall, New Jersey.

Harvey, M. G., & Ronkainen, I. A. (1985). International counterfeiters: Marketing success without the cost and the risk. *Columbia Journal of World Business*, XX (3), 37-45.

Heritage Foundation (2006). The index of economic freedom. Retrieved 13 February, 2006, from http://www.heritage.org/research/features/index/scores.cfm

Hofstede, G. (1991). Cultures and Organizations: Software of the mind. McGraw-Hill, London.

Husted, B. W. (1999). Wealth, culture and corruption. *Journal of International Business Studies*, 30 (2), 339-360.

International Trademark Association (2004). Counterfeiting Special Report 2004. Retrieved December 6, 2005, from http://www.inta.org/membersonly/bulletin/special/pdf

Javorcik, B. S. (2002). The composition of foreign direct investment and protection of intellectual property rights: Evidence from transition economies. *European Economic Review*, 48, 39-62.

Nill, A., & Shultz, C. J. (1996). The scourge of global counterfeiting. *Business Horizons*, November/December, 37-42.

Organisation for Economic Co-operation and Development (1998). The economic impact of counterfeiting. Retrieved February 13, 2004, from www.oecd.org/dataoecd/11/11/2090589.pdf

Rephann, T. J. (1999). Links between rural development and crime. *Papers in Regional Science*, 78 (4), 365-386.

Robertson, C. J., & Watson, A. (2004). Corruption and change: The impact of foreign direct investment. *Strategic Management Journal*, 25, 385-396.

Ronkainen, I., & Guerrero-Cusumano, J. (2001). Correlates of intellectual property violations. *Multinational Business Review*, 9 (1), 59-65.

Sanyal, R. N., & Samanta, S. K. (2004). Determinants of bribery in international business. *Thunderbird International Business Review*, 46 (2), 133-148.

Tanzi, V. (1998). Corruption around the world: Causes, consequences, scope and cures. *IMF Working Paper*, WP/98/63.

Taxation and Customs Union Directorate-General (2005). 2000, 2001, 2002, 2003, 2004 Statistics of Counterfeiting. Retrieved November 5, 2005, from http://europa.eu.int/comm/taxation_customs/customs/customs_controls/counterfeit_piracy/statistics/index_en.htm

Transparency International (2005). 2000, 2001, 2002 Annual Report. Retrieved September 3, 2004, from http://www.transparency.org/publications/annual_report

United Nations Development Programme (2004). Human Development Report 2004. Oxford University Press, London.

Zhao, J. H., Kim, S. H., & Du, J. (2003). The impact of corruption and transparency on foreign direct investment: An empirical analysis. *Management International Review*, 43 (1), 41-62.

doi:10.1300/J037v16n01_12

Index

Active exporting, 95-96
Advertising, 1. *See also* Provocative advertising
   cross-cultural differences in, 5-6,153-155
   in Czech Republic, xviii-xix, 141-142
   in France, xviii-xix, 141-142
   imagery and, 156-157
   literature review of, 140-141
   in Norway, 154
   overview of, 139-140
   research study of
      conclusions for, 147-148
      methodology for, 142-144
      results for, 144-146
   in Thailand, 154
Äijö, Toivo, 1
Allen, Michael, 5
Andean Community, intellectual property rights and, 174
Association of Southeast Asian Nations (ASEAN), intellectual property rights, 174-175

Born global pathway, to growth and internationalization, 9,12-13
Born globals (BGs). *See also* International new ventures (INVs)
   characteristics of, 61
   hypotheses for, 75
   literature review of, 72-73
   overview of, 37-38
   research on, 107
   research study of
      discussion for, 83
      implications of, 83-84
      methodology for, 75-80
      results for, 80-83
   resourced-based model on, 73-75
Business Software Alliance (BSA), 175

Capital
   human, 74,77-78
   intellectual, 74
   organizational, 74,76-77
   relational, 74,77
   technological, 74,75-76

Collaborative pathway, to growth and internationalization, 9,13-14
Commitment
   to co-operation, xiv, 27-28
   in export circles, 29-30
   to internationalization, 26-27
Contingency approach, to internationalization, 93
Continuity, co-operation and, 28
Co-operation, commitment to, 27-28. *See also* Export co-operation
Corruption
   counterfeiting and, 168-170
   defined, 169-170
Counterfeiting. *See* International counterfeiting; Piracy
Czech Republic, advertising in, xviii-xix, 141-142

Dianoux, Christian, 5-6

Early management, INVs and, 41-42
Eclectic paradigm, of internationalization, 89
Economic development, counterfeiting and, 171-172
Economic freedom, counterfeiting and, 170-171
Economic Freedom Index (EFI), 171
Emotional appeals, 155-156. *See also* Provocative advertising
Enterprise resource planning (ERP), 16
Entrepreneurs
   born globals and, 61
   exporting and, 105-106
   INVs and, 41-42
Entry modes, for INVs, 42
ERP. *See* Enterprise resource planning (ERP)
European Union
   patterns of counterfeiting, 167-168
Export assistance, governments and, 23-24
Export circles, role of commitment in, 29-30
Export co-operation, 2
   findings and conclusions for, 31-33
   findings for, 29-31
   measurement development for, 26-29
   overview of, 24-25
   research design, 25-26
   success of, 28-29
Export/import start-ups, 40
Exporting
   active, 95-96

BOOK ORDER FORM!

Order a copy of this book with this form or online at:
http://www.HaworthPress.com/store/product.asp?sku= 6000

Contemporary Euromarketing
Entry and Operational Decision Making

___ in softbound at $60.00 ISBN-13: 978-0-7890-3540-0 / ISBN-10: 0-7890-3540-5.

COST OF BOOKS _____

POSTAGE & HANDLING _____
US: $4.00 for first book & $1.50
for each additional book
Outside US: $5.00 for first book
& $2.00 for each additional book.

SUBTOTAL _____

In Canada: add 6% GST. _____

STATE TAX _____
CA, IL, IN, MN, NJ, NY, OH, PA & SD residents
please add appropriate local sales tax.

FINAL TOTAL _____

If paying in Canadian funds, convert
using the current exchange rate,
UNESCO coupons welcome.

❑ **BILL ME LATER:**
Bill-me option is good on US/Canada/
Mexico orders only; not good to jobbers,
wholesalers, or subscription agencies.

❑ **Signature** _____

❑ **Payment Enclosed: $**_____

❑ **PLEASE CHARGE TO MY CREDIT CARD:**

❑ Visa ❑ MasterCard ❑ AmEx ❑ Discover
❑ Diner's Club ❑ Eurocard ❑ JCB

Account #_____

Exp Date_____

Signature_____
(Prices in US dollars and subject to change without notice.)

PLEASE PRINT ALL INFORMATION OR ATTACH YOUR BUSINESS CARD

Name _____

Address _____

City _____ State/Province _____ Zip/Postal Code _____

Country _____

Tel _____ Fax _____

E-Mail _____

May we use your e-mail address for confirmations and other types of information? ❑ Yes ❑ No We appreciate receiving
your e-mail address. Haworth would like to e-mail special discount offers to you, as a preferred customer.
We will never share, rent, or exchange your e-mail address. We regard such actions as an invasion of your privacy.

Order from your **local bookstore** or directly from
The Haworth Press, Inc. 10 Alice Street, Binghamton, New York 13904-1580 • USA
Call our toll-free number (1-800-429-6784) / Outside US/Canada: (607) 722-5857
Fax: 1-800-895-0582 / Outside US/Canada: (607) 771-0012
E-mail your order to us: orders@HaworthPress.com

For orders outside US and Canada, you may wish to order through your local
sales representative, distributor, or bookseller.
For information, see http://HaworthPress.com/distributors

(Discounts are available for individual orders in US and Canada only, not booksellers/distributors.)

Please photocopy this form for your personal use.
www.HaworthPress.com
BOF07

For Product Safety Concerns and Information please contact our EU
representative GPSR@taylorandfrancis.com Taylor & Francis Verlag GmbH,
Kaufingerstraße 24, 80331 München, Germany

Printed and bound by CPI Group (UK) Ltd, Croydon, CR0 4YY

08/05/2025

01864537-0001